READER'S DIGEST

CONDENSED BOOKS

FIRST EDITION

THE READER'S DIGEST ASSOCIATION LIMITED
25 Berkeley Square, London W1X 6AB

THE READER'S DIGEST ASSOCIATION
SOUTH AFRICA (PTY) LTD
Nedbank Centre, Strand Street, Cape Town

Printed in Great Britain by Petty & Sons Ltd, Leeds

Original cover design by Jeffery Matthews F.S.I.A.D.

ISBN 0 340 25791 1

Reader's Digest
CONDENSED BOOKS

THE TIGRIS EXPEDITION
Thor Heyerdahl

THE KEY TO REBECCA
Ken Follett

HOROWITZ AND
MRS. WASHINGTON
Henry Denker

BULLET TRAIN
Joseph Rance and Arei Kato

THE LAST ENEMY
Richard Hillary

COLLECTOR'S LIBRARY
EDITION

In this Volume:

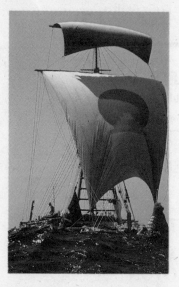

The TIGRIS Expedition

by Thor Heyerdahl (p. 9)

Could a fragile reed sailing boat survive in the open sea? Thor Heyerdahl believed it could, just as he believed that ships like *Tigris* had crossed vast oceans before the dawn of Biblical history. With eleven fellow-adventurers he set sail from the site of the Garden of Eden on a voyage back through time. He soon found, however, that the hazards created by modern man could be quite as deadly as those that had faced Noah.

The KEY to REBECCA

by Ken Follett (p. 79)

In the summer of 1942 Rommel's army was advancing confidently across the desert towards Cairo. Major William Vandam felt impotent, useless, sitting in his Cairo office trying to catch spies while out in the desert his country was losing the war.

But perhaps there *was* a role for him to play in defeating the enemy. What was a popular English novel doing in a captured German wireless post? Was it part of a code? Could it lead him to the brilliant enemy agent who seemed to know the Allies' most secret plans? Somehow, somewhere, he must find the key to *Rebecca* . . . .

by Henry Denker (p. 233)

Horowitz and Mrs. Washington

Sam Horowitz was insufferable. He found fault with everyone. Then he had a stroke and a nurse was called in. One look at her and he almost had another stroke. For Mrs. Washington was black. Sam Horowitz had nothing against blacks—he just didn't like them. But getting rid of a woman as determined as Mrs. Washington wasn't going to be easy.

Bullet Train

by Joseph Rance and Arei Kato (p. 345)

Oblivion within a hair's breadth. The motorman watches his red needle flicker on the speedometer dial before him. If it dips below fifty miles per hour his express supertrain will disintegrate in a blinding flash and its fifteen hundred passengers will be blown to eternity. The bomb on board it must be found and deactivated.

The Last Enemy

by Richard Hillary (p. 449)

In the Battle of Britain, as in all battles, the enemy finally to be faced was fear: the fear of death itself. Men faced it for many complex and important reasons. In this classic and powerful autobiography, written two years afterwards, fighter pilot Richard Hillary recalled his own exploits, and his own reasons.

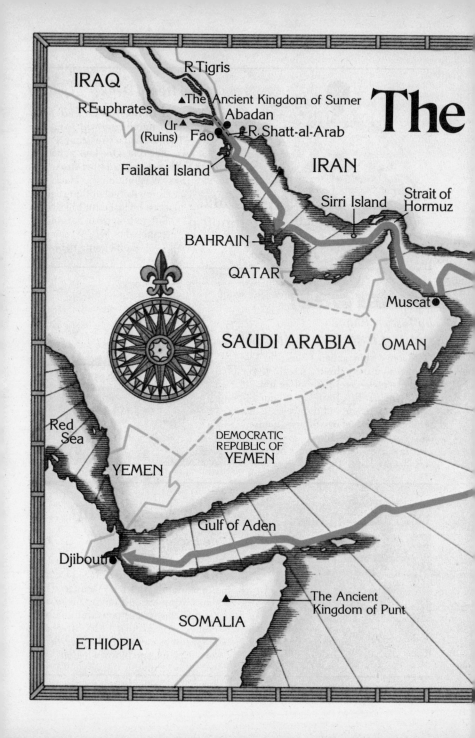

IRAQ

R.Tigris

R.Euphrates

▲The Ancient Kingdom of Sumer

Abadan

Ur ▲
(Ruins) Fao   R.Shatt-al-Arab

Failakai Island

IRAN

Sirri Island

Strait of
Hormuz

BAHRAIN

QATAR

Muscat ●

SAUDI ARABIA

OMAN

Red
Sea

DEMOCRATIC
REPUBLIC OF
YEMEN

YEMEN

Gulf of Aden

Djibouti

The Ancient
Kingdom of Punt

SOMALIA

ETHIOPIA

The

TIGRIS
Expedition

A CONDENSATION OF THE BOOK BY
Thor Heyerdahl

TITLE PAGE BY RAY HELLIER
PUBLISHED BY ALLEN AND UNWIN

PAKISTAN

Indus Valley

Karachi

INDIA

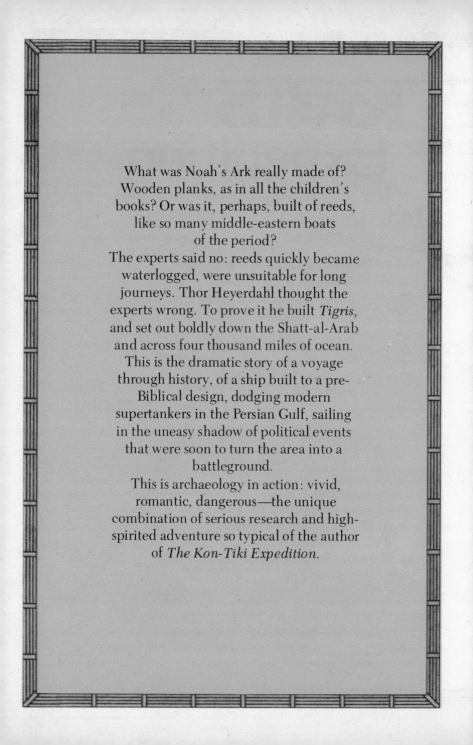

What was Noah's Ark really made of?
Wooden planks, as in all the children's
books? Or was it, perhaps, built of reeds,
like so many middle-eastern boats
of the period?
The experts said no: reeds quickly became
waterlogged, were unsuitable for long
journeys. Thor Heyerdahl thought the
experts wrong. To prove it he built *Tigris*,
and set out boldly down the Shatt-al-Arab
and across four thousand miles of ocean.
This is the dramatic story of a voyage
through history, of a ship built to a pre-
Biblical design, dodging modern
supertankers in the Persian Gulf, sailing
in the uneasy shadow of political events
that were soon to turn the area into a
battleground.
This is archaeology in action: vivid,
romantic, dangerous—the unique
combination of serious research and high-
spirited adventure so typical of the author
of *The Kon-Tiki Expedition*.

1

The beginning. The real beginning.

This was the place.

This was where written history began. This was where mythology began. This was the source of three of the mightiest religions in human history. Two billion Christians, Jews and Moslems all over the world are taught by their sacred books that this was the spot chosen by God to give life to mankind.

Here two large rivers, the Euphrates and the Tigris, drift slowly together, yet the narrow point of green land where they meet is not a spectacular scene. Silent as the rivers are the narrow rows of date palms lining the banks, while sun and moon, passing over the barren dessert, are reflected day and night on the calm waters. A canoe glides by, with men casting nets.

Yet this, much of mankind believes, was the cradle of civilization: paradise lost.

Today, between the rivers, at the very point of the land, a little resthouse faces the sunrise over the River Tigris, a modest building that bears, in big letters above the door, an impressive name: THE GARDEN OF EDEN RESTHOUSE.

Hardly a stone's throw from the resthouse are a couple of inconspicuous green trees leaning over the Tigris. Between them lies the thick, short stump of an aged tree, solemnly fenced in as a very simple sanctuary and venerated by modest candles. The long-lost branches of this tree certainly had never carried apples, but a

9

placard tells the rare passer-by that this was the abode of Adam and Eve. Abraham, it says, came here to pray. Indeed, according to scripture, Abraham was born at Ur, only a few miles away.

I moved with my luggage into this resthouse one evening early in 1977. I was there to disentangle a controversy, and as I leaned over the terrace fence to watch the rings made by fish as they broke the surface, there was adventure in the air.

Upstream the Tigris had its source at the foot of the soaring cone of Mount Ararat, where Hebrews recorded that Noah grounded his ark. Downstream the waters merged into a single river, the Shatt-al-Arab, and drifted past Sindbad Island, named after the great yarn-spinning sailor. For here was the homeland of the *Thousand and One Nights* also, of Aladdin's Lamp, and Ali Baba and the Forty Thieves.

Today this land is known as the Arab Republic of Iraq. Temple-pyramids, minarets and oil drills stand side by side, and the oil flows through pipelines across sterile deserts which were once productive pastures and irrigated fields. But men of antiquity had known this place under many different names. First among these names was Sumer; later names were Babylonia, Assyria, and Mesopotamia. For this is the cemetery of entire civilizations, among them the oldest ancestor to our own.

In tombs and temples here, archaeologists have come across incredible art treasures of gold and silver. Bright dunes of arid sand have rolled over colossal stepped pyramids erected to forgotten gods, and covered abandoned cities ruled by kings, witness to a level of civilization so outstanding that simpler minds of our own day suspect that these long-vanished people came from outer space. Intellectuals may shrug their shoulders, but such entertaining books and films have spread like wildfire in recent decades.

They satisfy modern man's desire for an answer to a question science has only slowly begun to disentangle: How did it all begin?

What could the first Sumerians have told us? Among the excavated palaces and dwellings scientists have uncovered tens of thousands of baked clay tablets incised with the earliest script known. These tablets record how they came and where they came from. It was not by spacecraft. They came by ship from a place they called Dilmun to the coast of this twin river valley where they founded the civilization which was to affect in one way or another

10

every corner of our world. But where was this eastern land of Dilmun from which the seafaring Sumerians said they came?

Most scholars believe that it was the island of Bahrain, where recent archaeological work has uncovered extensive towns, tombs and temples which in part even antedate Sumerian times. And if we are to believe the Sumerians, their merchant mariners returned to Dilmun many times. In their own time, at least, their ancestral land was within reach of Sumerian ships from Sumerian ports. But one little piece missing from the big puzzle was that nobody knew the range of the Sumerian ships. Their seagoing qualities were forgotten with the men who built them.

One thing is clear however: the early Sumerians were great ship-builders and mariners. Their civilization was based on the import of copper, timber and other raw materials. And since they had no access to copper and little chance of trade locally, it seemed obvious that their sailors must have gone very far indeed. Just how seaworthy were their vessels?

No motif is more common on Mesopotamian seals than the reed boats used by legendary heroes of Sumerian times. These boats are similar to those shown on Egyptian seals—sickle shaped, with crosswise lashings around the vessel and reeds spreading at bow and stern. Yet there was one fundamental difference. The Egyptian reed boat builders had access to papyrus which grew along the banks of the Nile, and after my experiments with an Egyptian style vessel I knew that a papyrus ship could cross an ocean: we had sailed one all the way from Africa to America.

But the Sumerians had no papyrus; instead, the marshes of Mesopotamia offered another tall reed, locally known as *berdi*. And berdi differs markedly from papyrus both in form and in substance. It was generally believed that it quickly absorbs water, and that Sumerian reed ships, accordingly, could have served only over short distances, as river boats.

How could this verdict be reconciled with the ancient texts and illustrations? This was the question that had led me to move into The Garden of Eden Resthouse. I wanted to build a berdi ship, to see how long it would float, and I wanted to retrace some of the obscure itineraries recorded in the old tablets, with their references to the ancient civilization of Dilmun—and to two other long-forgotten lands, Makan and Meluhha.

11

I had ended up beside Adam's tree by happy accident. I had been granted permission by the Iraqi government to assemble my expedition in Iraq. Representatives of the Ministry of Information showed me the plot by the side of Adam's tree for the building of my ship, and generously offered me the resthouse as an assembly site.

From here we could sail straight down the river to the open sea. Even with the help of Aladdin's Lamp I could not have been offered a better solution. Also endless berdi reed marshes began a few minutes from the door, for here in the flooded area where the twin rivers converge are vast stretches of green marshes full of birds and fishes; here too a unique culture has survived since Bible times, hidden in a world of canes and reeds that grow tall and dense as a jungle. Probably more Sumerian blood runs in the veins of these marsh dwellers, or Madans, than in any other Arab tribe. They alone of the ancient peoples seem to have been blessed with eternal life, while the great kingdoms around them have collapsed.

Five years before I had visited the marshes, and it had been clear to me then from their reed houses that the Madans could teach me lessons about the uses of reed not found in any scholarly books. But reed boats belonged to the past. Today marsh Arab boats, or *mashhufs*, are pegged together from imported wood and covered with a smooth coating of natural black asphalt. Therefore I had needed to talk to some really old men. And thus I had been sent on my last visit to a village out among the marshes, where a man lived who was said to be a hundred years old.

As I reached the first water channel with my interpreter, two tall marshmen in flowing Arab gowns were waiting for us, each with a long punt-pole of cane. One held back his long, flat bottomed mashhuf with his big bare foot as they welcomed us aboard.

I stepped into the unsteady vessel and sat down on a pillow. The two slim Madans standing erect at either end, punted with long, slow strokes. The water was crystal clear; plants grew on the bottom. We slid silently in between high walls of canes and bulrushes, these tall water plants closing in about us.

The water in the marshes is too deep for wheeled traffic and too shallow for normal boats. Only the Madans know the hidden labyrinths of narrow and shallow passages through the six thousand square miles of bulrush jungle, and for this reason have been left to lead their own lives.

A few columns of smoke far apart revealed to us that people were living in the marshes. Not a roof disclosed the whereabouts of the villages. Geese and ducks and other waterfowl of all colours and sizes abounded and brilliantly coloured birds sat and swayed everywhere in the reeds. Huge water buffalo waded lazily, their broad black bodies shining like wet sealskin in the sun. They stopped to watch us with friendly bovine eyes as we passed, flicking their slim tails to shake off flies as they patiently chewed the green sedge hanging from their jaws.

Suddenly the village was before us. A revelation in its harmony with nature! The vaulted reed houses were as much at one with the environment as were the birds' nests that hung among the canes. Some houses were small, scarcely more than shelters, but most were big and roomy, previously hidden from us simply because we had travelled behind high and unbroken screens of greenery. In their elegant perfection, the structures were astonishingly beautiful, each dwelling recalling a little temple outlined against a cloudless sky.

Madan villages are built on artificial islands formed by untold generations of rotting reeds and buffalo dung. Quite often these islands are actually afloat and rest on the bottom only in the dry season, the Madan families bobbing up and down on swaying reed carpets with their ducks, hens, and water buffaloes. New top layers have to be added annually as the bottom layers disintegrate. To prevent the islands from being washed away, they are fenced in with tight palisades of canes stuck into the bog bottom, while the canals between them permit the passage of the slender Madan boats and make up a village complex in the pattern of Venice.

A marsh Arab can rarely walk more than a couple of steps before he has to enter his boat. Some of the islands are so small that with a big house or buffalo stable on top they look like some sort of Noah's ark, and the buffaloes have to dive in with the ducks and swim for the reed fields every morning when their owners unfasten the mat barriers of their vaulted reed stables.

I had not expected much memory from a man one hundred years old, and when I saw old chief Hagi Suelem in his white gown and with a long white beard, sitting in the opening of his own large reed house, like an image of Methuselah, I was no more optimistic. But when old Hagi had risen to meet me and wish me peace I looked into a pair of alert and friendly eyes. He was obviously greatly respected by the men who assembled around us and sat on the clean oriental mats on the floor inside the house, facing each other in two rows. We listened to old Hagi's wisdom and humour with interest. A tea tray was soon beside the flickering fire, and some big, broad fish, split open like giant butterflies, were balanced close to the flames. Crisply toasted, but white and juicy inside, the fish was delicious.

Hagi was aware that we in the cities would not survive without automobiles and electricity. But he was not at all sure that his people would be made happier by projects to bring electricity cables into the marshes and bricks for building houses. When people are happy they smile, he said. Nobody had smiled at him when he had visited the streets of Baghdad.

Looking at Hagi, I found myself thinking of Abraham. I had lived with so-called primitive peoples in Polynesia, America and Africa, but this marshman was not primitive in any sense of the word. He was civilized, but differently from us. His culture had been proved viable by persisting while the Assyrian, Greek and Roman civilizations had collapsed. In this stability is reflected something the rest of us lack: respect for our progenitors and confidence in the future.

Hagi did remember reed boats. There were three types when he was young. Two were small and hollow like canoes, asphalt-coated inside and out. Then he pointed to the huge bundles of reed that arched high above us in the lofty ceiling of his house. Beginning as columns thicker than a man on either side and gradually narrowing towards the apex of the roof, they were all of one piece from base to base. The third kind of reed vessel he said, was built of bundles like these, except that the bundles got narrower towards either end instead of in the middle. In that way many lashed together would create a compact watercraft raised and pointed at either end. Berdi had been used for the bundles and *kassab*, or cane, for the shelter on top. To make the berdi boat float for a long time, Hagi added, each bundle should be pressed as tight as two men could pull a rope round it; it should be as hard as a log. Above all, the berdi has to be cut in August; if cut in any other month the reeds would absorb water and lose buoyancy. In reply to my direct question, Hagi answered that he had never known of asphalt or other impregnation used on this kind of bundle boat.

As Hagi sat there and described the building principle of this great reed boat, it sounded like a famous vessel described in the Old Testament. Mention Noah's Ark and people will smile with happy childhood memories of the Hebrew story of a houseboat packed with pairs of elephants, camels, giraffes, monkeys, lions, tigers and other beasts and birds, herded by a friendly old man with a long beard. But the Assyrians, too, were familiar with the story of a flood that had destroyed the majority of mankind, while the Sumerians, although they do not say that the survivors of the flood landed on a mountain top, record that after such a flood mankind first settled in Dilmun, somewhere across the sea towards the sunrise. Only later, in this version, did the gods lead them to their present abode at the mouth of the rivers.

The essence of all three versions is their reference to big ships, and to the existence of cities and kingdoms before the flood. Five thousand years ago scribes put on record what today is the oldest known attempt at written history. It begins with families and live-stock, after some catastrophic event, landing somewhere with a big ship. The ship or "ark" described was surely a Sumerian watercraft.

For the Sumerians, then, the landing was at a place called Dilmun and from there, they sailed to Ur, close to where I now was. Beneath the ruins of Ur, the royal city of the Sumerians in Mesopotamia, a layer of homogeneous mud, ten to thirteen feet thick, has been found. Under this again lie the ruins of the first city which was there when some gigantic flood buried all lower Mesopotamia under twenty-five feet of water. To the few survivors, this would have seemed to be the destruction of the world.

When, after an interval of five years, I went back to Hagi's village, I missed the old reincarnation of Abraham. He was in hospital in Basra. But his sons were there and gave me a royal reception. Sha-lan, the eldest son, got excited when I told him I had come back to find people in the marshes who could help harvest berdi and build a bundle boat like the ones old Hagi had described to us five years earlier. I needed twenty men. Sha-lan assured me that this was no problem. Gatae, a master reed house builder, was thought to be the best man to lead the work.

15

Gatae proved to be a fine elderly marshman with a humorous twinkle in his eyes. Tall and slim, he stood in the canoe as straight as a mast. We met as if we had been friends for a lifetime. We agreed that twenty men under Gatae's leadership should come to Adam's tree and begin the building in September, but I should first return in August and see that the reeds were cut and properly dried by Madans in another village, closer to the building site.

August came, and I was back in the marshes again. The thermometer wavered between 40° and 50°C (105° and 120°F) in the shade, but there was no shade in the open swampland where we cut the reeds. The marsh Arabs advanced with curved machetes into the reed thickets like a band of warriors and the stalks fell like slaughtered troops. I lost all count of the number of mashhufs towering with green berdi which were punted through the channels to be left on the banks to dry. It looked as if I was planning to build a ship every bit as big as Noah's.

In the meantime I had to return to Europe for a few weeks to organize the expedition, planned to start in November, before the winter rains. I chose Hamburg, because I had good friends there. In three days I had purchased everything required, including two specially-carved twenty-five-foot rudder oars and a dozen rowing oars. A conscientious sailmaker handsewed two sails from Egyptian cotton canvas; they tapered from top to bottom as in pre-European times. One was bigger and thinner than the other and was intended for good weather only. We needed flags and signal lights, paraffin lamps for illumination, primus stoves, and pots and pans for the kitchen. Also fishing gear. And a tiny inflatable rubber dinghy with a 6-hp outboard motor.

From Hamburg I flew to London to meet representatives of an international consortium of TV companies, improvised for the occasion by the BBC. A contract was signed, obliging television organizations in Great Britain, France, Germany, Japan, Sweden and the USA to finance the expedition. America's National Geographical Society and their television producers, insisted on sending with us their own cameraman. I agreed.

I also went to the University of Southampton, where a plastic model of the reed ship, built according to my own drawings, was being tested. It was beautiful to see the six-foot model bobbing in the waves while the nautical experts from the university pressed buttons that made the rudder oars twist and the little vessel turn and roll sideways to the waves.

The lesson of the experiment was that the bigger the sail and the oar blades, the better the ship tacked into the wind. The final result from the wind-tunnel studies would be mailed to me in Iraq.

Just outside Southampton was the beautiful Broadlands estate, the home of Admiral of the Fleet, Earl Louis Mountbatten of Burma, where I was expected for lunch. Common interests in the sea had made us friends in recent years; the old Sea Lord was a very active president of the United World Colleges, of which he had made me honorary vice-president. The United World Colleges brought together bright boys and girls from all nations, and put a good deal of stress on marine life-saving and on boating.

Years before I had promised Lord Mountbatten to bear in mind some of the graduate students if I ever had plans for further maritime experiments. Now I was fulfilling my promise, for I wanted a truly multi-national crew on my planned voyage from Iraq. The late secretary general of the United Nations, U-Thant, had granted me the right to sail *Ra I* and *Ra II* under the UN flag, and his successor, Kurt Waldheim, had kindly repeated the permission for my forthcoming expedition. I wanted to give priority to any of the crew of my previous reed boat experiments who cared to come along again, but I would be delighted to draw reserves from the United World Colleges.

It was great to be back at Broadlands and enjoy a meal in the bright dining room facing the park and its old giant trees.

"Thor, would you believe that you have got me into international trouble?" Lord Mountbatten looked at me sternly as we took our seats at table and were served melon by a butler in naval uniform. "You have brought the anger of the Shah upon me."

"Of course I believe that," I replied, laughing to show that of course I did not believe it.

Lord Mountbatten stopped eating and looked at me: "What can I do to make you realize that I am not joking?" He showed me a letter from the Imperial Court in Teheran. It was a long and sharp protest against the wording of the circular from the United World Colleges which quoted me as planning to sail down the river Shatt-al-Arab into the "Arabian Gulf". How could an international college institution use such a fictitious geographical term? Was this the result of the growing tendency to flatter the Arabs? The true and only name for this body of water was the "Persian Gulf".

I was sorry. This was an unforeseen problem. I explained to Lord Mountbatten that I had originally used the name "Persian Gulf", which I had learned in school. But officials in Baghdad had corrected me and made it abundantly clear that if I wanted to sail anywhere from Iraq it had to be into the "Arabian Gulf". This was a forewarning that the twentieth century, with all its radar and lighthouses, was not the easiest one for avoiding hidden reefs. Lord Mountbatten saw my problem. His solution was that the place should not be referred to at all.

A Norwegian medical student headed the list of candidates from the United World Colleges. As a former sergeant in the Engineers, he had the advantage of being specialized in rope work and bridge building. I telephoned the young applicant, and Hans Peter Böhn, who insisted on being called HP, joined me in Rome with a rucksack and camera, and together we flew to Baghdad.

After seven hours by car we reached The Garden of Eden Resthouse. There was plenty of work ahead to prepare the building site for the arrival of all the groups of helpers and the expedition members. The three bedrooms would not suffice, but two rooms could be made serviceable upstairs under the roof, and mattresses and camp beds could be put up everywhere.

With HP I began to prepare the ground for the combined jig and building scaffold for the ship. My idea was to dig two deep, broad trenches side by side in the garden, so that the boat builders could walk under the vessel when the thick ropes had to be wound around the two final bundles. Half a dozen Arab workmen from Qurna came with picks and shovels and began digging. On the third day a committee of solemn Arab gentlemen in European dress came and to my surprise began to measure our trench. Soon afterwards one of them spoke in Arabic to my interpreter, who sat with me in the pleasant shade of a date palm. "They say we should dig two metres closer to the road," said my interpreter.

"No," I protested. "We must be close to the river."

The digging was resumed, but as I saw gesticulations around the trench I went over to clear up the misunderstanding. A little man with a prominent nose, who spoke English well, introduced himself as a Mr. Ramsey, then showed me in a very friendly way where he wanted the trench to go.

"It makes little difference," I admitted, "but the closer to the banks the easier will be the launching of the ship."

"Launching? Ship?" He looked at me as if I had escaped from an asylum. "You make fun of me, sir. I have my orders to add twenty-five bedrooms to the resthouse just here, from the Ministry of Information!"

"That is the ministry that granted me the right to build here."

Obviously we had dealt with two different offices at the ministry. "If you build your house now," I went on, "I cannot build my ship here afterwards. But if I build my ship now we will sail away and you can build your rooms two months from now."

The little engineer looked at me in despair. Then he pointed upwards. "Do you see that date palm? You will find me hanging with a rope around my neck just up there if I go back before I do my job!"

As Mr. Ramsey had come with all his luggage I suggested that he stay in the resthouse until both jobs were completed. So he capitulated, and an engineer I had not asked for joined the project as a local consultant. We were to discover we really needed him.

About this time another extremely friendly, middle-aged man turned up: Mr. Shaker al Turkey, appointed by the museum authorities to be my local guide and liaison officer. Unfortunately, both my interpreter and Shaker were in Basra when an army of Arabic-speaking truck drivers knocked at my door next morning. The road outside was lined with lorries laden sky high with dry golden berdi. Here they all were, waiting for me to explain what to do. I ran and opened the iron gate to The Garden of Eden. Soon I had lorries all around me inside the fence, trying to get rid of their loads, all blocking the passage for each other, and in the struggle to get in and out, driving over the brittle stalks unloaded by others. I ran between the drivers, who shouted angrily to each other in Arabic and smiled happily at me, ignoring the orders I gave in various European languages that were all Greek to them! At sunset I finally found myself alone with the silent river, the whole garden a dense chaos of reed piles, leaving no place to build a ship or even place a foot.

Next morning Gatae and his chosen men showed up as if by magic. And when Shaker came back we set everybody to work for two days assembling the berdi in piles within convenient reach of the building site. All the broken stalks were thrown on the banks and those that were not carried away by old women for kitchen fires were turned by jubilant children into a flotilla of reed rafts.

For a wooden jig, a temporary cradle for the ship, HP succeeded in raising a sturdy crisscross framework of barkless poles and sticks. We could now turn our attention to the actual making of reed bundles.

One difficulty was that, although the Madans were masters in reed work, ship building from reed bundles was to them a lost art. The intricate construction system still survived, however, in the region around the ruins of South America's spectacular prehistoric civilization, Tiahuanaco. There, on Lake Titicaca, high in the Andes, Indians still build watercraft identical to those of ancient Egypt and Mesopotamia. So Aymara Indians from South America would soon be coming to Iraq to turn the bundles made by the Arabs into a boat. I had taken four Aymara Indians with their interpreter from Lake Titicaca to build the papyrus ship *Ra II*, and that reed ship had crossed the Atlantic Ocean without a reed lost. Since nobody else could do the job like them, I would get them across the Atlantic again, this time to Iraq.

Although The Garden of Eden Resthouse was virtually bursting with reporters and photographers, the key people had not yet arrived. In addition to the Aymara Indians, we expected the rest of the expedition members and three Asiatic dhow sailors from Bombay who could help us to rig the vessel and then guide us through the gulf to the Arabian Sea. In panic I got through to the ministry and learned that although Iraq had been closed to tourists and journalists since the recent revolution in the republic, they were letting anybody in who was coming to me.

Finally, in early October, a stationwagon rolled up in front of the overcrowded building and five short, broad men tumbled out and embraced me in silence, the greeting Aymaras reserve for chiefs. In spite of the heat they still wore their traditional ponchos of llama wool and woven caps with ear-flaps, and each carried a bag in which they brought a round water-worn stone and a wooden hook, all they needed for working the ropes and reeds.

They showed no surprise when they entered The Garden of Eden and saw the endless stacks of reeds. But when they picked up pieces of the berdi and tore it to bits with their hands, they calmly condemned it as no good for boat building. Gatae and our marshmen stood curiously in a circle around us and asked me to explain to the sceptical Aymaras that once the brittle reeds were wet they would be tough and as flexible as rope. This the Aymaras knew well, for their own totora reeds had that same property. But the berdi was not made of simple stalks like totora; this plant fanned into thin branches like grass, and they did not know how to handle it.

The Aymaras hurried to their room and I was afraid they wanted to go home. But as it became cooler towards evening, the Aymaras came down to take a second look. With Señor Zeballos, their Bolivian interpreter, as mediator, Gatae and I convinced them that if they would just show us how to combine the bundles into a boat, the marsh Arabs would make the bundles to any size the Aymaras ordered.

Nothing on the whole expedition was more pleasing to observe than the spontaneous friendship between the Indians and the marsh Arabs as they began handling the reeds together. The conversation began with the Indians speaking to Señor Zeballos in Aymara which he translated to me in Spanish, and I to Mr. Shaker in English, who then told the marshmen in Arabic what the Aymaras wanted. The system was cumbersome, but it did not last long. Next morning, I found the Aymaras and the marshmen squatting around a long mat they had produced together. They were talking to each other, smiling, asking for reeds and handing each other what was wanted. I ventured closer to hear what language they had in common: the Aymaras spoke Aymara and the Arabs spoke Arabic, but these people had the reeds in common.

On the first day the Aymaras taught the marshmen how to tie together the woven mats that would be folded around each huge composite side bundle of the ship like a tight sausage skin. When several of these mats had been made in strips about sixty feet long by three feet wide, they were carefully carried into the cradle-shaped jig. The giant sausage skins were now ready to be filled with the bundles. Thirty-eight bundles two feet in diameter were needed to give the ship the desired proportions. Open spaces between them would be filled with thin bunches of reeds.

When dry, however, the berdi was brittle, so it had to be drenched on the outside to become pliant before it could be tied into mats and bundles. With Baghdad and other major cities upstream, the river Tigris was so polluted that we feared it might affect the reeds. But Mr. Ramsey solved the problem: he had two big tanks installed on the roof. They were pumped full of drinking water, and Señor Zeballos could spray the reeds all day long. But the waterpipes of the resthouse passed through the same tanks, and the busy kitchen and crowded guestrooms competed with Zeballos and his rubber hose. Not infrequently some soap-covered television man would roar angrily under a shower that had run dry.

Gradually the ship took shape under a burning sun. Bundle after bundle was hoisted on the men's shoulders, carried up onto the feeble scaffolding and lowered into the two huge sausage skins. The air cooled slightly. Three weeks after the Aymaras arrived the vessel was in two parallel halves. Each half was separated from the other by a wide passage where the backbone of the vessel was to go: the invisible third bundle.

At this stage, I began to feel in desperate need of the three Indian dhow sailors who were to guide us through the Gulf. The BBC had promised on my behalf to locate them through a seamen's agency in Bombay: the requirements were three men thoroughly familiar with sailing these waters and at least one with some knowledge of English.

While the Bombay agency tried to locate the dhow sailors, the expedition members started to arrive. First came a gentle, soft-spoken young Arab who spoke flawless English as he introduced himself: Rashad Nazir Salim, art student from Baghdad, recommended by the Norwegian consulate as expedition member to represent Iraq. Next Detlef Soitzek, a young captain in the German merchant navy, came to take his place as my right-hand man in the shipyard. Then came three of the crew of both *Ra I* and *Ra II*: the expedition navigator and second in command, Norman Baker from the USA; the expedition doctor, Yuri Senkevitch from the Soviet Union; and the Italian mountain climber Carlo Mauri. The rest followed a few days later: Toru Suzuki, underwater cameraman from Japan; my Mexican globetrotting friend Gherman Carrasco; Asbjörn Damhus, a young Dane from the United World Colleges; and Norris Brock, the American film photographer sent to us by the National Geographical Society.

We were seated at a table in the big hall on 2 November eating an excellent supper when the happy news arrived that the lost Indian dhow sailors were standing in reception. We hardly gave them time to wash their hands before we dragged them into the restaurant hall. At first embarrassed and then delighted at our comradeship, they grabbed half a chicken each and poured down one beer after the other.

Next morning at sunrise I woke them up. In pyjamas they followed me up to the guesthouse roof where we had a magnificent view of the river and the garden. Our crescent-shaped vessel looked marvellous in the half-light; it was as if a golden new moon had landed on the banks of the river Tigris. In recent days the Aymaras had filled the open space between the two half-vessels with the slim bundle serving as a sort of backbone, and had managed to pull the two big halves together at each end to form one complete ship. The backbone was tied to each of the side bundles by a rope, hundreds of yards long, wound in a continuous spiral from bow to stern. When these two ropes were pulled tight, the backbone was literally squeezed into the two main sections. The result was a sort of compact catamaran with no gap between the twin hulls.

From the roof I let the three sleepy dhow sailors look down upon the beautiful vessel. For a while they seemed to admire it in silence. Then one of them said: "And where is the engine?"

"Engine?" I said. "There will be no engine!"

"But how will it move?"

"By sail, of course. Aren't you dhow sailors?"

"We are dhow sailors. But our dhows go with engines."

None of them knew how to sail! I was horrified. But at least they could serve us as pilots through the gulf. The gulf? None of them had seen the gulf. I gave up. We had to send them back to Bombay and plan to do without them. They were visibly relieved at this decision and showed clear signs of horror when they took their last look at the reed ship.

Now winter was approaching and I wanted to launch before the rains began. The report from Southampton University had arrived and Norman, my second-in-command, was so impressed by it that he insisted on a bigger sail and bigger blades on the rudder oars. So we found a couple of sailmakers locally, and Norman split our best sail along the central seams for them to add extra canvas in the middle and thus leave intact the strong outer edges with their rope reinforcements and cringles. The sailmakers struggled with the work for half a day and then declared themselves unable to add the new pieces because they did not have the proper tools. Too bad, I said, then you'll have to put the sail back as it was.

But in spite of all their attempts, they were unable to put the sail together again. There was no time to send the pieces back to Hamburg, so we had to start our voyage with nothing but a thin downwind sail. Fortunately there would be a north wind blowing from Iraq down the gulf. We would therefore have a following wind all the way to the island of Bahrain, where everybody assured us we could find sailmakers to fix our sail.

Norman had more luck when he wanted to enlarge the blades of the rudder oars: we got help from a truly professional carpenter. With a master's hand he helped Norman to peg and glue lateral boards to the blades of the rudder oars until they were so huge that thicker shafts were needed. By fitting extra wood even the shafts became colossal, and were oval in cross-section instead of round.

We had to concentrate now on getting our ship into the water. The wooden jig would remain ashore; the vessel, which weighed about thirty-three tons, rested on an iron sledge that would be pulled into the river and then sink free when the ship began to float.

The road to the river was clear. The river ran into the long gulf that opened into the Indian Ocean. A gateway to unknown adventures stood wide open in The Garden of Eden, and Noah's Ark lay ready to float as more rain clouds gathered on the horizon.

Zero hour. All flags up
   "Are we ready?"
   "Ready!"
   "OK! Let go!"
The Garden was packed with curious spectators. The atmosphere

was that of a big theatre when the rumbling of countless voices became suddenly silent as we set to work to pull the heavy vessel into the river.

The silence was broken by the roar of thousands of jubilant voices as the reed colossus began to move and then to slide slowly along the metal rails towards the flowing river below.

The spectators pressed forward for a better look, and the Iraqi police were in difficulties to protect visiting dignitaries from being pushed beneath the advancing Sumerian curiosity. Even the river was full of mashhufs, police boats and motor launches.

It was a great relief to see the monster moving out of its wooden jig and onto the improvised steel beams which had been welded together as rails to the water's edge. The bow of the corn-coloured vessel rose proudly like a swan's neck, covered by red human handprints from the recent Arab naming ceremony.

There had been some discussion about this ceremony. The marsh Arabs wanted six beautiful sheep sacrificed, and I was supposed to handprint their blood on the bow of the new vessel. This I refused to do. The marshmen, on the other hand, refused to let the ship enter the river unless the proper sacrifices had been performed. They were a custom adhered to since the days of Abraham. So we found a compromise. The marshmen could carry out their own rite beforehand, but the official naming ceremony at noon should be the way I wanted it.

Late in the morning of 11 November, I found Gatae by the ship with a bloodstained right palm. He was still stamping red handmarks on the bow from the sacrificed sheep, while his men sat happily devouring roast lamb—with no effort to conceal that this was to them the most important part of the ceremony.

Gatae's beautiful little granddaughter, Sekneh, was to name the vessel. At midday Gatae stepped up from the river's edge leading this tiny lady in colourful costume by the hand. Little Sekneh carried a traditional bottle-gourd full of water from the river that was to give the ship its name. With sparkling eyes she splashed it successfully on the bow, then forgot all her lessons. Her grandfather took over and declared with a loud voice in Arabic: "This ship is to enter the water with the permission of God and the blessing of the Prophet, and will be called *Dídglé Tigris*." ("Dídglé" was the local name for the Tigris.)

No sooner had these words been proclaimed than a low rumble of thunder was heard in the south. Heads were turned in surprise or awe; even those of us who were not superstitious felt a shiver down the spine at this timely comment from the weather-god.

It took an hour to pull the *Tigris* to where the slope began to run steeply down to the river. Then the giant began to slide downhill. The bow hit the water with a splash. Thousands of jubilant voices rose in triumph as the broad bow began to float in the river, high as a rubber duck, while most of the ship was still up on dry land.

What uplift, what buoyancy! But suddenly the stern which was still on the river bank stopped, just when the bow rose on the water. I heard a terrible crash and saw the steel beams of the sledge twist like spaghetti under the broad body of the ship. The applause died as the vessel slowly settled on the solid ground like a rebellious hippopotamus refusing to enter water.

An army of volunteers ran to try to help push the vessel down into the river. In vain. Only a few could get their shoulders to the curving stern and those who tried to push along the sides sank into loose earth and river mud. The dignitaries saluted politely and left with the police. One by one the crowd also melted away as evening approached and drizzle began to fall.

We took turns at using the few shovels available, trying to let water in under the stern. Gatae and the marsh Arabs commented that six sheep was not enough for such a big vessel; we should have sacrificed a bull.

These pessimistic observations were hardly uttered before the rumble and strong headlights of a huge Russian truck made us drop the shovels. The heaven-sent visitor bumped in through the gate and two husky Russian drivers jumped out. With Doctor Yuri as interpreter, we explained that we needed a push, but that our ship was as brittle as crispbread until in contact with the water. They then helped us rig up thick reed fenders. Finally, in the dark, a most unconventional launching began. With a steady thrust from the truck the vessel slid slowly forward into the thick mud where we had dug. As mud and broken timber floated away with the current we held the ship on tight ropes and made her fast

Top right: Venice in Iraq: a marsh Arab village.
Bottom right: The marsh Arabs
made us forty-four huge reed bundles for the
building of our ship.

beside the resthouse terrace. The Russians saluted and left. We would have to wait for daylight to judge the damage.

As daylight broke we were all on the spot. Our new ship looked magnificent. She rode very high on the river, and above the turbid water there was not a scratch.

Detlef and Gherman swam under *Tigris* and seemed gone an eternity before they came up with their reports. Visibility was nil in the muddy water, but feeling their way all along the ship's bottom they were both left with the impression that every loop of the spiral lashings was still intact. The ship was undamaged.

It took two weeks to rig and load the vessel. On the resthouse lawn our Madans had prefabricated two huts of green kassab cane. These huts were tall enough for us to sit in but not to stand upright. The larger measured about four yards by three and had just enough space for eight men to sleep outstretched on the floor. The smaller was only half that size and was intended for three men and the camera equipment.

Both cabins were carried aboard, lashed across the main bundles and covered with green tarpaulins. The main cabin was set aft with an opening on either long side wall facing the sea. The little cabin was set forward, with a single door opening facing the central deck and the main cabin behind. The huts were only intended as sleeping quarters and retreats in bad weather. Our daytime living quarters were to be the open spaces between them.

There also we hoisted our sail on the double mast, its straddling legs resting one on each of the twin bundles, and set into large wooden "shoes" lashed on top of the bundles. Crossbars held the two legs together and formed a convenient ladder to the top. Between the ladder and the forward cabin we tied polished scaffold planks together with rope to form a long table with two benches. Behind the ladder the roof and walls of the main cabin were extended to form an open galley. This small shelter could hold four primus stoves and all our pots and pans.

On the last day tons of food and water were carried aboard. Clothing and personal property were stored together with vulnerable equipment in boxes set together to form a raised floor in the main cabin. This floor was our common bed.

Left: "Let go the moorings! Hoist the sail!"

Tigris was shipshape and ready to sail the moment the two huge rudder oars were lashed astern, one on either side. A wooden steering platform or "bridge", three feet wide and three feet above deck, permitted the two helmsmen to see over the roof of the main cabin. The oar shafts were rotated on their axes by crosswise tillers near the upper end to make the blade turn like a rudder.

TIGRIS was ready to sail.

"Let go the moorings! Hoist the sail!" I was filled with relief and pleasure as I shouted the orders and waved to the incredible new crowd of spectators that had gathered in The Garden of Eden. For the first time we saw unfolded the tanned Egyptian canvas on which our Iraqi art student Rashad had painted a huge, reddish sun.

Norman was in charge of the sail, and Carlo and I were on the bridge with one rudder oar each. It was grand to see the banks of The Garden move away. It had been a great place, but it was high time to get on to the ocean. To Adam's tree, farewell! Farewell Gatae and all our other Iraqi friends.

We were gaining speed. We were heading for the other bank of the Tigris. Carlo and I turned the clumsy oars over. The current already had us in its grip, and the vessel obeyed beautifully. As we passed the green point of land where the twin rivers meet and become the Shatt-al-Arab, people lined the banks shouting and waving. As we moved downstream men and boys began to follow us along the riverbanks, but we moved faster than they could run.

"Hurrah, we're sailing!" It was Norman's voice, full of joy. There were high spirits on board. We would reach the gulf in a few days. A motor-driven boat with ten Arab pilots came along to guide us. They had just disappeared around a sharp bend ahead of us when I realized that our ship was out of control. No matter how much we turned the rudder oars and adjusted sail, we were being pulled towards the green grassy bank. We turned with the river and followed the bends so close to the shore that the port side rudder oar began to dig up mud like a plough. All hands not fighting the land with our long punting poles tried to pull up the colossal rudder oar before it broke under the pressure. But the oar jammed and at any moment we expected a deafening crash from the shaft, which was as thick as a telegraph pole.

The Arabs running with us ashore tried to push us away, but

neither they nor we on board could do much to prevent what looked like disaster. Norman and his master carpenter had done an amazing job, however. The oar held; instead the whole steering bridge to which it was fastened began to creak and squeak and lose shape. Carlo and I were ready to jump the moment the rope lashings burst and the bridge, perhaps the whole stern, was torn apart. Our pilots were on their way back now, and some jumped ashore to help push. But Norman suddenly got a new angle on the twisted sail and we rushed away from the river bank like a bird.

There was barely time to draw breath before we looked to the other bank and saw a solid forest of palm trunks rushing towards us. Quick manoeuvres helped us shoot back towards the bank we had just been ploughing. The motorboat now followed us from side to side like a drunken companion, trying to serve as a fender between us and the bank. Suddenly it turned around and disappeared upstream. It was gone for two hours, looking for the men left ashore where they had been running along the banks to push.

In the meantime we had become masters of the situation. We began to know our new vessel. Soon the Shatt-al-Arab began to flow straight and even as an autostrada. Few houses. No traffic. In the late afternoon the surface around us became as motionless as a lake, and before the tide began to flow the other way we asked our pilots, newly returned, to show us a safe anchorage for the night. They recommended the west bank near Shafi village, where we furled sail and threw out our two small anchors on their ropes. Our experienced companions thrust punt poles into the muddy bottom to keep us, like the floating islands in the marshes, in one spot when the river began running the other way.

It was a great evening. Our first on board. The sun set red behind the smoking brick kilns that had functioned down this section of the river since the days of Abraham. Carlo got a primus going, and we all gathered at the deck table for his steaming spaghetti. Exquisite. *Buonissimo. Wunderbar.* Carlo received his well-deserved praise in many languages, and for the first time for many days all eleven of us had a chance to relax.

There were men seated at our table whom I knew really well and others who were completely new acquaintances. There was my old friend Norman Baker from the USA, wiry and strong. Our wakes had first crossed in Tahiti twenty years earlier. Norman was now in his late forties; commander in the US Navy Reserve, and a building contractor in private life, he had been my second-in-command on both the *Ra* expeditions. Norman alone was enough to make me feel like skipper Noah. He was as agile as a monkey, strong as a tiger, stubborn as a rhinoceros, had a canine appetite and in a storm could be heard trumpeting like an elephant.

At his side sat our robust Russian bear, Yuri Senkevitch, doctor to Soviet astronauts, forty years old, built like a wrestler, as peaceful as a bishop. He had sailed with us on both *Ra* expeditions and had later turned into a bit of a globetrotter, introducing a weekly travel programme to millions of Soviet television viewers. Yuri could hardly open his mouth without laughing or cracking a joke.

Carlo Mauri of Italy, in his late forties, had also been with us on both reed ship voyages across the Atlantic. Carlo was one of Italy's most noted mountaineers. He was to be our principal cook, and was to take the expedition's still pictures. Carlo could not live without a rope in his hand, and he was to improvise the most ingenious knots and crisscross lashings each time a mast foot, or a leg of the bridge began to wobble.

Detlef Soitzek I had not known before. Twenty-six years old, one of the youngest captains in the West German merchant marine, he was also an enthusiastic sportsman and a climbing instructor. He rarely spoke without good reason, but was a keen listener and would chuckle more than any at a good joke.

Gherman Carrasco, fifty-five, industrialist and amateur film producer from Mexico, was our entertainer. With his chubby build he seemed likely to be most at home in a wide sombrero under a cactus. But not at all. Several times a year he leaves his four rubber factories in Mexico City to fly off somewhere. A scar around his eyes testifies to the day when he fell from a jungle tree while filming orang-utangs. He had tramped with me in the burning sand of the Nubian desert, filming rock carvings of pre-dynastic ships, and we had waded together in the pouring jungle rain of the Mexican Gulf, filming Mayan pyramids.

Beside Gherman sat Toru Suzuki, a Japanese underwater photographer in his middle forties. I knew little about him yet, except that he had spent several years filming marine life at the Great Barrier Reef. Toru's English was fluent; he was a well built athlete of few words, but always ready with a smile and a helping hand.

34

In this mixed company the two Scandinavian students seemed like twins. Both were recommended by United World College headmasters. Asbjörn Damhus from Denmark, twenty-one, "HP" Böhn from Norway, twenty-two, typical descendants of the Vikings. They were always up to something, technically minded and full of resource. They were looking forward to plenty of adventure before returning to their university desks.

Youngest of all was Rashad Nazir Salim, twenty years old, the art student from Iraq. Slender but athletic, the young Rashad had a keen brain, always eager to listen and learn and yet not without his own strong opinions. He spoke flawless English, and knew Europe since the days when his father had been an Iraqi diplomat; now the diplomat had turned into a notable painter, and Rashad wanted to follow in his footsteps.

Half a head taller than all the others at the table, and wonderfully agile, was our eleventh man: Norris Brock. Professional US cameraman, forty years old. I did not know him. I had not chosen him. He was, until we met him, a clause in the contract with the television consortium. Norris used his eyes more than his mouth. He seemed to be everpresent with his baby, his waterproofed sound camera, at his chest. He would nurse it at the top of the mast and even dive with it from the cabin roof while it was working.

With his privilege of recording everything we did or said, I suspected that he might help to quell what we call "expedition fever" at its very outset: the squabbling that is sure to come when men share cramped quarters for a long time at sea.

I had told Norris that, although he was free to behave as a passenger, so as not to feel isolated I thought he ought to take the same steering watches, and other routine duties shared by us all. He could be relieved any time he wanted to film. Norris answered that he had intended to ask for this. He wanted to become one of us. And he did.

WE REMAINED three days anchored off Shafi village, repairing and strengthening our steering bridge with better lashings. We even built two outboard toilets, one on either side aft, which we screened with mats. It was winter now, and although the day temperature was 17°C (62°F), the wind was biting cold at night and we pulled the canvas down on one side of the cane wall of the sleeping cabin, which was so airy otherwise that we could see the stars between the wickerwork.

Our pilots had stayed with us. On the afternoon of the third day we hoisted sail and continued the voyage down river. We agreed that at the first place we could dock we must pull the rudder oars ashore and reduce them closer to their original size, as they threatened to destroy the bridge whenever we turned and their oval shafts jammed.

The sailing was good, with an estimated three knots, and at sunrise next day we saw a vast industrial complex. West German engineers from the settlement came and with a crane helped us to lift the two gigantic rudder oars ashore. We cut off one third of each blade, and chopped down the sides of the oval shafts so that they became much lighter and fairly round. The friendly German engineers invited us to lunch and then to dinner. They were building a modern paper mill, converting cane to paper pulp.

Next morning it was a great relief to have oar shafts that now rotated smoothly. But all that day and the next the wind died down. Completely. The river still ran. We drifted. Slowly. A beautiful, undisturbed landscape: date plantations, water buffaloes, geese, ducks and kassab canes. Small villages on the riverside with happy, dancing children. Barking dogs. We saw a couple of canoes with fishermen. Nothing else. Peace.

Next day we again reached modern civilization, as if with the wave of a magic wand. Enormous crowds awaited us as we passed Sindbad Island and entered Basra harbour. All the cargo ships blew their sirens and rang their bells. The Iraqi navy vessels had their officers and crews lined up in salute on deck. Yuri grabbed our own bronze foghorn, jumped onto the roof and trumpeted right and left while the rest of us waved and shouted from the steering bridge. It was hilarious. It was scaring. Supposing we got no farther than just down this river?

As night approached our pilots insisted on stopping. Somewhere around the next bend was Iran's large modern city of Abadan, and we would probably have to take a tow between the oil tankers and refineries. A huge bright halo surrounded the moon, which had been full two nights before.

Early next morning we saw the silhouette of Abadan against a dawn sky. Tall smoke stacks, radio towers, a whole city of lofty oil tanks. The wind turned against us and a faint current still ran against the bow, so we lowered the sail and let our pilots tow us slowly through the worst pollution we had ever seen. From a paradise our golden ship had suddenly found herself in a modern inferno. The surface between the big ships and the dock installations was a soup of black crude oil and floating refuse.

In the afternoon a town rose above the level wasteland on the Iraqi side. Fao. The last town at the river's mouth. Yet in a sense the river continued; at low tide it wound its way like a shiny sea serpent through empty tidal flats, until finally there would be no more sign of land. We were longing to get there; out where seagulls waited to escort us into the freedom of the gulf.

THERE WAS NO MORE river. No more land. Our pilots had been paid off and had left us to ourselves.

We had docked at Fao long enough to fill our vessel with tomatoes, green salad, citrus fruits, carrots and potatoes, and also a good supply of onions, garlic, raisins, local nuts, and grains that would keep at sea. From there *Tigris* had been towed to the open gulf through a long narrow channel that had been dredged through the vast tidal flats. Mud, mud, nothing but mud. We had passed lazily with the outgoing tide before sunrise. The pilot boat left us when we met the first slight swells from the gulf. We were filled with expectation.

By leaving the mouth of the channel I felt as if I were about to break a scientific taboo. According to what we had all been taught, not until the Sumerians invented wooden boats did they have access to the gulf. I knew as we hoisted sail, therefore, that this would seem to be a vote of no confidence in long accepted teachings. Perhaps it was. But it was fair play. To those who really believed in the old doctrine we should now be about to prove that they were right, and I wrong.

We were still floating incredibly high. So high that we could not bend over and wash our hands, a fact which annoyed those of us who were used to *Ra I* and *Ra II* where we had been able to have our morning wash without the use of canvas buckets.

As the heavy yardarm was hoisted to the top of the straddle mast, our sail unfolded and the red morning sun seemed reflected in the big red sun painted on our sail. Ours rose behind a painted stepped pyramid. The real one rose freely above the misty sea. We had expected a strong wind from Iraq behind us. In the open gulf there was nothing to give shelter. But the wind was just not there.

Strange. For this was the second day of December and during all the winter months a steady north wind was supposed to blow strongly down the full length of the gulf. The plan was to follow the Arabian side to the island of Bahrain, as close to shore as reefs and shallows would permit. There the streams of big ships would not interfere with our free movement.

Our two navigators carefully studied the charts to find the best route beyond the traffic and clear of oil platforms and islets. Norman suggested steering 135°. Detlef proposed 149°. But a voice from the top of the mast recommended that we first take a good look ahead. We did. In the morning haze we detected ships at anchor wherever we looked. From left to right, I counted forty and then I caught sight of a colossal and lofty oil platform with a supertanker moored at its side. I forgot to count further. There were masts everywhere out there. Some were almost invisible in the mist. This was not only a filling area for tankers; it was an anchorage for ships waiting their turn to deliver their cargoes to Iraqi and Iranian ports.

Norman and Detlef agreed that we should keep a course close to a buoy ahead, which I could barely make out in the mist as a red dot behind a cluster of ships, and then hang on to it until we got a better wind. It took us two hours to pass the ships and get within a hundred yards of the buoy. We were close. But then we noted we had been still closer a moment earlier. In fact we were drifting back the way we had come. The sail gave us absolutely no help. It was quite clear that the tide was sending us back towards the river's mouth. At this moment we saw an orange-coloured lifeboat being lowered from one of the anchored cargo ships, about a mile away. It approached us in complete silence. No motor, no sail, and no oars. Never had we seen a boat like this. It was packed with husky men, most with bare chests and with bands around their foreheads. They sat facing each other from either side in two rows, rhythmically turning one long common crank-handle, which obviously operated a propeller. Perfect teamwork. Then a head rose up in front: "Yuri! Yuri Alexandrovitch Senkevitch!"

They were Russians. They knew Yuri by his full name. Carlo

quickly threw them a long rope, which Yuri asked them to tie to the buoy which was now about 300 yards away. They immediately started their cranking operation, steering for the buoy. They could not tow us but they carried our heavy mooring rope. Carlo worked desperately to tie on more sections of rope, until there was no more, and to his dismay the last end slipped away overboard. We waved to them to come back but they only waved back in salute, cranking as fast as they could for the buoy. Dead tired, they dragged the heavy rope to it, making the.end fast. Then they signalled to us to start pulling in free rope, but we were already far from our own lost end.

The Russians at first seemed quite bewildered. But not for long. We had no time to think of them or of the great length of lost rope. We had to prepare to run aground. Fortunately there were neither reefs nor rocks awaiting us.

"Look!" Norris, on the cabin roof, pointed to the lifeboat's mother ship coming straight towards us. Minutes later we had one end of the lost rope back again, with the other end secured to the lifeboat, which in turn was towed to the buoy by the big ship.

A short, thickset sea dog led the whole operation from the lifeboat. Afterwards he asked for permission to visit our vessel. He jumped onto the reeds like a short-legged kangaroo and introduced himself with a broad smile as Captain Igor Usakowsky. Ruddy, jovial, middle-aged and dressed in shorts, our visitor was in command of the big cargo ship, the Soviet freighter *Slavsk*. He was as excited as a boy and had to stand on our steering platform, lie down on our cabin floor, and sit on our tied-together benches. And then, before we knew it, we were all sitting around two long tables in Captain Igor's own officers' mess on board *Slavsk*, eating Russian borscht. There was vodka, wine and Russian champagne. There were pork chops, meat cakes, cabbage-and-carrot salad and cheese. Captain Igor rose to speak; I did, we all did. Our host was a great humorist and big eater. His glass seemed open at both ends. He had been born in Georgia, the son of a Polish nobleman who had joined the revolution. At the beginning of the evening he called me "Captain", but later he called me "Father".

I wondered if he could really take me to be that much older than himself, until he added that he referred not to age but experience. "Then you had better call me grandson," I retorted, for

Igor was a real sea dog. He had begun at an early age, whaling in Arctic waters. Later he had mastered big ships on all seas.

Many hours later we cranked ourselves back to *Tigris* with the hand-propelled lifeboat (we had seen the regular motor-launch under repair on the freighter's deck).

We crept into our sleeping bags in ample time before sunrise. It was still dark when I awoke, feeling a chilly draught on my face through the cane wall at my side. Wind. I woke the others. Wind! Sleepily we tumbled to the sail and the rudder oars. Sleepily we discovered that this strong wind blew from the southeast. The very opposite to normal. We wanted to steer for Bahrain, but that was exactly where this wind was coming from.

Slavsk pulled us clear of the anchorage area, and we hoisted the only sail we had, the thin downwind canvas. With this big, light sail we moved with great speed away from the tanker channel. The best we could do was to take the wind straight in athwart and hold a course to the southwest in the direction of Failakai Island. If we tried to do better we quickly lost headway. This was not bad sailing and it did not yet take us totally off course. We had to get farther west anyhow in order to avoid the gulf's busy shipping lanes. The wind ought to resume its normal heading soon.

But the wind did not turn to its normal heading. The fresh southeasterly continued, digging up a choppy sea coming at us athwart and making us roll heavily. Asbjörn gave us a seasick smile and apologized as he crawled to bed in the forward cabin. The long mast legs began to jump and hammer.

With this wind there would be shelter on the north coast of Failakai. Although our navigation chart showed no harbour or anchorage in that area, marking it as unnavigable due to unbroken shallows, with our flat bottom and modest draught we could venture where others could not. Norman searched for information on that area in the *Persian Gulf Pilot*, recently published in London, and read aloud: ". . . this coast is rarely visited by Europeans, and it is probably unsafe to wander away from the towns on the mainland without an armed escort."

The wind blew stronger. Our speed westwards increased. The day passed and when the sun sank in the choppy sea ahead of us I proposed that we all get some early sleep. We were heading for troubled water and could expect a lively night. The chart showed a tall lighthouse visible at sixteen miles built on a small island to mark the southwestern end of Failakai, and a good mile to the north of it a dangerous reef was shown.

I had barely turned in at 8:00 p.m. when Norman's worried face appeared in the cabin door. We were going fast, and heading straight for the lighthouse rocks. The helmsmen were unable to press us past outside the lighthouse and the rock pile to its starboard. Too much leeway with this wind. There was no choice but to try to steer a more northerly course, into the shallows between the lighthouse and Failakai Island.

The flashes from the lighthouse in the black night came closer. Asbjörn, who was in better shape now, lay stretched out on the upcurved reed bundles forward, his head out beyond the bow, to scout for rocks. While the rest of us strained our eyes in vain from deck and mast, Carlo came crawling out of the cabin and said he heard surf. We all listened. Sure enough, a growing rumble came out of the night somewhere ahead, and to the starboard, it seemed. The dangerous side.

Land. Rocks. Very clearly. We turned even farther to the north. The rumble of water on rocks came from the port side now. Then slowly it was drowned again in the normal roar of breaking seas, and shortly afterwards we stopped rolling. We were in the shelter of the lighthouse island. This was surely the best place to anchor and wait for a favourable wind. Ahead of us were only the extensive shallows and sharp rocks of Failakai Island.

I ordered the ship turned all about and the sail down. Each man did his job perfectly, and the sail was packed up around the yardarm on deck before the anchor was thrown overboard. Perfect teamwork. It was 10.30 p.m.

Moments afterwards we heard shouts from the bow, and Detlef came fumbling out of the dark to report that the anchor rope had snapped.

"Hurry! The other one!"

Our second anchor went overboard, but it did not seem to take hold. Someone quietly suggested that perhaps we had lost that one too. Silence. Detlef tried the rope. An empty end came out of the black water. Detlef remained speechless, the short piece of rope dangling from his hand.

No matter how we turned our rudder oars, we were drifting

northwards, straight for the invisible coast of Failakai. We could clearly see the many dim lights scattered along it. They soon spanned the entire horizon where the wind was carrying us, a lee shore we could not escape, even if we hoisted our sail.

If only it had been daylight we would have seen land. We might have picked our course and steered towards the less rugged parts of the island described in the pilot book. But it was now just before midnight. We would be shipwrecked in complete darkness.

There was obviously one thing to try: slow down as much as we could. Then we might delay our crash landing until dawn. "Throw out the sea anchor!"

The sea anchor was nothing but a long conical canvas bag to be trailed in our wake. This simple device acted as a most effective brake. Never had I seen a sea anchor function so marvellously; we just hung on it as if fixed in the sea.

I sent a few SOS signals towards land with a torch. But no reply. To the left over Failakai the black night sky reflected the glow of a distant modern city: Kuwait, thirty miles away. We heard the sound of an aeroplane passing above the clouds. Norman tried to contact Kuwait coastal station with our tiny radio transmitter. There was no answer. Nobody could hear us.

We shared double watches for the remainder of the night and slept fully dressed with life jackets as pillows. Again I sent light signals to the island. No response. I crawled back to bed and left the watch to Toru and Yuri.

Shortly before 6:00 a.m. we began to detect the indistinct contours of Failakai, a long, low, treeless island. I kept on morsing. No reply. Next we began to see the outlines of three small ships at anchor. Probably dhows. One of the boats began to move, carefully, as if manoeuvring through a difficult channel. With binoculars we could see that the men on board were watching us. But they turned away in the opposite direction once they reached open water and disappeared around the island. No other living soul could be seen anywhere.

Norman had gone to sleep at last. Detlef was fiddling with the tiny radio box when he heard a faint voice calling, "*Tigris, Tigris, Tigris*" followed by babbling in an unintelligible language. Then he plainly heard the word "*Slavsk*".

"Yuri! Yuri!"

In two jumps Yuri was on the bridge. *Slavsk* was gone. Nothing. Norman came and called, "SOS *Slavsk*, SOS *Slavsk*". Suddenly a voice was there again: Captain Igor! Yuri beamed with pride and happiness as he translated. *Slavsk* was already weighing anchor. Igor wanted our position.

As daylight broke we saw a few small huts far apart along the coast. No smoke. No people. The sea around us was greyish-green, filled with sand or mud. We were deep inside the Failakai shallows, with hardly room for a flounder to swim under our ship.

It was not yet noon when we sighted *Slavsk* as a black spot on the eastern horizon. Half an hour later her motor launch came dancing towards us. The big ship prudently anchored in blue water three miles away. We recognized Captain Igor in the bow of the orange lifeboat with his crew. With a broad smile he jumped on board our reed bundles.

All was joy now. The men in the orange lifeboat began pulling up our sea anchor. It was as heavy as lead, full to the brim with greyish mud. It had saved us from shipwreck in the dark.

No sooner was the sea anchor up before we and the lifeboat began to drift off together with great speed. The lifeboat crew started their engine and began to tow. But although they had a powerful motor the wind took a strong grip on the high curves of our reed ship, with the result that *Tigris* began towing the Russians—backwards! It soon became clear that we were drifting towards the much worse shallows east of Failakai. *Slavsk* became more and more indistinct, and in the afternoon she disappeared completely. The wind increased in force to twenty-four knots.

At this moment a primitive-looking dhow with a powerful engine and shallow draught suddenly appeared from nowhere. It circled around us beyond hailing distance. The men on board were clearly afraid of getting close. No wonder. Many generations had passed since a vessel like ours had been seen in these waters.

We inflated the tiny rubber dinghy brought along for filming. Asbjörn and Rashad rowed close enough to the dhow for Rashad to shout to the fishermen in their own language. A moment later our two men came back and reported that the crew of the dhow wanted 300 Kuwaiti dinars—more than a thousand US dollars—to tow us out to *Slavsk*.

I was ready to start bargaining, but Igor refused to listen and told Rashad to row back and offer six bottles of vodka and two cases of wine. The two boys came back again with the message that the men in the dhow were Moslems and did not drink alcohol. The dhow seamen now took off with no further bargaining.

The only solution left to us was to hoist sail on *Tigris* and sail across the wind, but still towards the coast. The Russians could then try to pull our bow slightly into the wind away from the coast and out into deep water.

Captain Igor had a walkie-talkie and spoke to his officer in charge on *Slavsk*, who reported that their ship was going to follow us as close as possible along the outer edge of the shallows. And their radar showed us approaching dangerous reefs.

A second dhow appeared from the direction of Kuwait. While the crew of the first had looked like fishermen, this lot looked like real bandits. When Rashad went over and explained our trouble they doubled the price in Kuwaiti dinars. Again Igor was furious and refused to deal with bandits. His angry gesticulations left no need for translation, and, uninterested in further bargaining, the newcomers broke contact. As the dhow picked up speed Rashad heard a cynical warning: without their help we would all be doomed. We were filled with contempt and anger.

Far ahead now we saw the reefs, with the two dhows anchored near them, waiting like jackals for our disaster. The Russians could not make the lifeboat pull more strongly, and we on *Tigris* had not yet discovered how to tack into the wind. We began to realize what awaited us the next night if we ran aground.

The sun was slowly on its way down towards the horizon when a third dhow appeared. Precisely the same process was repeated, for the third time. Even the ransom was the same as the last. I began to suspect that the three dhows probably had contact with each other by radio. They were certainly no fishermen.

"Look at that man." Detlef was at my side with binoculars. He had pointed out a fat man with a big turban, who sat crosslegged on pillows and scrutinized us calculatingly. His fat hands had certainly never touched a fishing line and he looked the archetype of a hardened crook.

It was clear that these men were demanding ransom money. Igor again vigorously opposed my entering into a deal with them. It was equally clear that if we did not pay, they would just hang around with the other two gangs and harvest all we had when we were forced to jump onto some reef or the swampy shallows.

In an hour or so the sun would set. This dhow was clearly the last chance to get out into deep water before nightfall. Captain Igor was still furious at the mere idea of dealing with gangsters. But I felt the responsibility was mine. "Captain Igor," I said, "now I accept that I am your father. Then I am in command. I will consent to pay the dhow."

I could see how Igor fought to keep his mouth shut. I crawled into the cabin and rolled up my mattress to look for my dwindling supply of cash. The bandits would not yield a penny and even insisted on keeping Rashad as a hostage until we reached *Slavsk*. Without the slightest sign of fear, Rashad agreed.

They threw a tow to the Russian launch and the procession of three small vessels slowly began to work to windward. Night fell over us again, blacker than the last. Except for our own paraffin lamps there was nothing to be seen in any direction. No lights on the island. No lighthouse. No *Slavsk*. The pitching and rolling were formidable. But the rascals ahead of us in the pitch dark did a good job, and at last Norris shouted from the mast that he saw the lights of a ship ahead. It was *Slavsk*.

The pulling ceased, and the dhow suddenly appeared at our side, now with a paraffin lamp lit. We feared that as one boat rose up on a wave crest and the other sank down, their wooden gunwales would rip the reed rolls of *Tigris* to shreds. But we had to venture close to pay the ransom and get Rashad back. So I stepped onto the side roll of *Tigris* and stretched out over the water as far as I could with a thick stack of dinars in my free hand. A dark-faced sailor on the dhow stretched out to meet me. The man grabbed the cash and took it to the chief on the pillows, who counted the wad of notes one by one. Then he nodded and in a leap Rashad was with us. *Slavsk*, fully lit, was now coming to our side. The men on the dhow blew out their lamp and like Aladdin's genie they vanished into the darkness.

Slavsk was alternately pitch black and blood red as we were tossed up and down past her waterline, and we had to take great care not to be smashed against her hull. It was difficult enough for the lifeboat crew to get onto the staircase lowered from the deck of the big ship but it was worse still for Captain Igor who had to repeat this wild performance from *Tigris* to *Slavsk* by way of the riotous lifeboat. We all held our breath when he almost tumbled into the sea as the lifeboat shot skywards just when he jumped.

Soon we hung on a long rope behind the empty lifeboat, now in the tow of its Russian owners. We felt violent jerks from the bow whenever the ship, the lifeboat and *Tigris* rose and sank out of time, but Igor had refused to let us loose before we were safely out of the reach of the dhow men. He had promised to go as slow as his pistons could churn the propellers, for nothing was harder on a reed ship than to be towed at speed in open sea. Norman and I had our hands on our knives several times, ready to cut the tow-rope if we felt the bow might be ripped apart. But nothing seemed to happen, so we slept in turns.

The sea was moderately rough when I awoke at sunrise. It had been a restless, unpleasant night. When the snatches at the bow had been too brutal I had suffered as if it was I who was pulled by the hair and not *Tigris*. The strain on our ship was sometimes scaring. Terrible shrieks and cracking noises came from ropes, lashed wood, bamboo and berdi. The huge shafts of the rudder oars banged from side to side in their wooden forks so hard that they shook the ship. How I welcomed the sun as it rose above the horizon!

As we gathered at the breakfast table, however, suddenly we observed that the violent hugging and lugging came at much shorter intervals. Water cascaded in front of the bow. We were going faster. I hurried up to the cabin roof and waved desperately for *Slavsk* to slow down. But nobody on the ship ahead understood my signals. Before we could cut ourselves free of the lifeboat the towline tore away in a last violent jerk. *Slavsk* went on alone.

Asbjörn climbed over the bow and reported that he had found a huge hole ripped in it. In front of the hole the spiral ropes hung loose across a cavity as large as a dog kennel. This was a frightening discovery. We forced our fingers under the lashings on deck up front, but the spiral rope there was still as tight as if glued to the reeds. The bundles had swollen so much that they squeezed the lashings fast between them. We faced no immediate catastrophe, but we had to find a way of filling the hole should it begin to grow and cause the whole bundle boat to fall apart.

Slavsk came back in a great circle and Captain Igor appeared with a megaphone. He refused to let us remain loose and told his men to throw us a new towline. Igor shouted that the ship's engineer had raised the speed because going dead slow in these seas might be harmful to the propeller shaft. But they would not exceed two knots again. We made it clear that we wanted to continue on our own the moment the wind permitted us to set course for Bahrain.

For two more days the wind continued its southerly direction, and *Slavsk* towed us. Then, in the early afternoon of the fourth day out from the river estuary, we reached the entrance to the navigable channel through the limestone shallows surrounding the island of Bahrain. *Slavsk* received radio orders from Bahrain to stop right there. Someone would come out for *Tigris*. The Russians may have saved us from the reefs, but no Russian ship was to be admitted to the Emirate of Bahrain. *Slavsk* anchored, and we hung on.

As the sun began to set a coastguard vessel came close to our side and offered us a tow to Bahrain. We accepted with thanks and waved farewell to Captain Igor. While we were towed towards the lights of Manama City and the island's modern port, *Slavsk* weighed anchor and returned to join the ships that waited at the mouth of the distant Shatt-al-Arab.

We were heading for a tiny nation booming with modern development and seemingly limitless wealth. The great prosperity of Bahrain lies not so much in its oil supply, now rapidly dwindling, as in its geographical location as a terminal for pipelines from Saudi Arabia. In fact, its location has made it a crossroads for merchants of all epochs. Today even Concorde calls there.

We were blinded by floodlights and illuminated installations as we were towed past anchored tankers to the side of an enormous drydock. We climbed a long iron ladder to a crowd of official and unofficial spectators. First to stand out snow-white in the floodlights was the long Arab attire of a cordial dignitary, His Excellency Tariq Al-Moayyed, the Minister of Information. He welcomed us and wanted to know our verdict on the reed boat. I was able to tell him that we were all exceedingly happy with the vessel. It was still strong and sturdy and floated very high. But we

47

had failed to solve the problem of our big new sail which was still in pieces, and we hoped to find a sailmaker here in Bahrain.

The minister had introduced us to a young man dressed like himself. "Khalifa will help you with that," he said. "But what would you like to see while you are here?"

I told him we had hoped to see the remains of the earliest sea-farers that had come to Bahrain. By this remark it was as if I had rubbed Aladdin's Lamp. The familiar face of the famous British archaeologist, Geoffrey Bibby, in his picturesque turban, appeared out of the dark. As he stepped aboard, he reminded us of Captain Igor by the cheerful way he enjoyed our unusual craft.

Bibby had flown down from Denmark when he learned that we were heading for Bahrain. He wanted a personal impression of a ship built after the earliest type known in the gulf area. Bibby's interest was deeply rooted, for in his own archaeological work he had done more than anyone to demonstrate that Bahrain was the site of the ancient trading centre of Dilmun, recorded in Mesopotamian inscriptions. And he agreed to take us for a tour of his main excavations.

When Geoffrey Bibby came to fetch us the following day and we drove away from the city area, we were plunged, with space-craft velocity, back through five thousand years of human history. We quickly reached the open desert that today dominates the island. "This is Dilmun," said Bibby and pointed with his pipe towards a landscape of giant mounds which stretched like a choppy sea of wavetops to the horizon and beyond.

Prehistoric tombs. I had seen groups of burial mounds in many parts of the world, but nothing like this. There were about one hundred thousand such man-made tumuli on Bahrain. This was the largest prehistoric cemetery in the world, and these tombs had evidently belonged to people who believed in a life after death and therefore left personal treasures in the grave for the deceased to use in his afterlife. But archaeologists' first efforts had been distressingly fruitless: not one of the numerous tombs opened had been spared by ancient grave robbers. All that had been left were bones, potsherds, a couple of copper spearheads and fragments of a copper mirror.

Bibby believes that Dilmun was to the Sumerians, a land blessed by the gods after the flood. Dilmun was the place where

Man, in the Sumerian story of Ziusudra (the priest-king called Noah by the Hebrews), was given eternal life. The symbolic meaning of this is probably that Ziusudra was given eternal life through his descendants, while all other men drowned.

For ancestor-worshippers it would seem tempting to bring deceased persons of importance to Dilmun, where the "spirits" would join the ancestral gods. But it is difficult to see why the little island of Bahrain should house the world's largest ancient cemetery unless it had a special importance to people even outside the island itself.

A Sumerian poem tells how the seafaring god, Enki, had asked the supreme god of the heaven, the sun god, to bless Dilmun with fresh water. Water was a divine gift to any people in the gulf area where deserts and dry wasteland dominate coasts and islands. On Bahrain, however, fresh water rises from the ground in springs and fountains, and flows endlessly into the sea. On our way to the tombs Bibby took a sideroad to a true oasis of palms and green grass. Inside was a beautiful pond of crystal clear water. Young Arabs were diving, and one of them was sitting soaping himself in the water while three women washed clothing. But a constant overflow sent the soapsuds away down a drainage ditch, and the water remained as clear as morning dew. No wonder that its origin had been ascribed to divine intervention.

Once we had seen Enki's wells and pools and the galaxy of burial mounds, Bibby drove us to a buried city where people had once made their living by such profane activities as trade and shipping. There is something intriguing about a buried city. From the sand dunes at the foot of a sixteenth-century Portuguese fort on Bahrain's north coast we climbed down into a sunken city that had been teeming with life in Sumerian times. In the last twenty years, Bibby and his colleagues had found, hidden under a large sandy mound overlooking the sea next to this fort, a complete buried city, and under it another, and still another. The earliest city was contemporary with the mound burials and Sumerian voyages to Dilmun. We walked together down into the oldest city, and stopped at a huge wall with a gate directly facing the sea. Bibby pointed through the lofty gate.

"Here ships docked four to five thousand years ago," he said. He turned from the gate and pointed to the ground in the open square we stood on: "And here where the cargo was unloaded we found the evidence of overseas trade: scraps of unworked copper, copper fish-hooks, bits of ivory, steatite seals and a carnelian bead, all of which are foreign to Bahrain."

Bibby took all of us up on the wall to see shallow tide flats in front of the maritime gate. At high tide the water must have flowed right up to the wall of the city. "A flat-bottomed reed ship like *Tigris* could come all the way in at high tide," he commented. "With its twin body it could settle on the bottom without capsizing when the water went out. Beached at the gate it would be perfect for loading and unloading cargo."

The scraps of unworked copper that he had found had their own story to tell and filled a gap in a jigsaw puzzle. Copper was perhaps the most important of all raw materials imported to Sumeria. Dilmun was not the place where the copper ore was quarried, but clearly it was a trading centre where it was bought and sold. The weight of some of the shiploads of copper moving in the gulf in Sumerian times was considerable. Bibby figured out from written tablets found in the ruins of Bahrain that one shipment acquired in Dilmun was no less than eighteen and a half metric tons.

It would be foolish of us today to underestimate the early Sumerians just because they lived when the world at large was peopled by savages. From them we learned to write. From them we got the wheel, the art of forging metals, of building arches, of weaving cloth, of hoisting sail, of sowing our fields and baking our bread. They gave us our domesticated animals. They invented units for weight, length, area and volume. They initiated mathematics and devised a calendar system. They were well at home in geography also: how else could they know where to travel to locate copper, gold and the great many other substances in their material culture?

History too was to them a major subject. They worshipped their ancestors and their minds were focused on the events and heroes of the past. Noah is a legend to us, but Ziusudra was history to them. Dilmun may seem a castle in the air to us, but to them it was a trading centre three days' sailing time away. To navigate such seas in their reed boats they must have been far better sailors than we, and I determined there and then to improve our sailing technique.

I WAS BROUGHT back from my reverie about ancient Dilmun to modern Bahrain by the shrill sound of a horn from one of the waiting cars. Time to return. Bibby now brought us westwards along the coast to a locality known as Barbar. Here his team had made their first major discovery: a temple. And it was a very special temple. It had been a compact, solidly filled elevation with right-angled corners, rising in steps above the terrain. The facing slabs of each of the superimposed terraces were blocks of fine, close-grained limestone carefully cut to fit together without mortar. The stones on the top platform were shaped like the tapering ice-blocks of an igloo, to form a circular enclosure only six feet in diameter. As excavations revealed the staircases and ramps that led up to the summit temple, Bibby realized they had hit upon a ziggurat, a terraced mound like a Sumerian temple-pyramid.

With the Sumerian deluge story in mind it was significant that a temple had been discovered on Bahrain with Sumerian affinities. And the excavations of the temple uncovered quantities of potsherds, lapis lazuli beads, alabaster vases, a copper figure of a bird, and, the final proof of Sumerian contact, a little copper statuette of a naked man with a shaven head standing in the attitude of supplication typical of Sumeria between 2500 and 1800 BC.

It was fascinating to visit this temple mound and hear how Bibby linked it to long-range Sumerian sailing and Dilmun trade. But there were, sadly, more urgent problems to solve. We had come to Bahrain with a sail to be assembled. Also with a huge hole in our bow, which we had to repair, otherwise there was nothing to stop the loss of reeds until the whole ship came apart.

We did carry a modest quantity of spare reeds for minor repairs, but it would not be enough. What could we use? Happily Bibby now recalled having seen craft made of bundles of reeds used by fishermen of Bahrain. Together we drove across the island to the tiny fishing village of Malakiya near the southwest coast. We left our car at the road and passed through a shady palm forest till we stood in the baking sun on a long and beautiful sandy beach. Drawn up on the white sand was a small raft-boat which had just been pulled up from the water and was still wet. We caught sight of an old man about to disappear with a bundle of shiny fish. We called him back and he told us that this was his fishing boat and he had built it himself. It was his *farteh*, and was a professional job, exact in every detail. The material was not reed, but the slender mid-stem of date-palm leaves. The old man did not know if they would maintain their buoyancy as long as reeds. After use the boats were always dried ashore. He doubted they would float more than a week.

Despondently, we walked along the beach and found two more boats of the same kind pulled up among the palms. I bent down to pick up a single palm-leaf stem tossed up on the beach. The thin end was densely overgrown with a colony of chalk-coloured molluscs. It dawned on me that here was silent testimony that these palm·stalks did not in fact dissolve quickly in sea water. This one must have been months in the sea for the molluscs to have grown to such a great size, and it was still as tough as new.

We ran after the old fisherman. He promised to bring two hundred such palm stems to the dock next Friday if we sent a car for him. Friday came, and so did the two hundred stalks. Carlo worked above water and Toru and Gherman below. When the spiral loops were so full and tight that not a single further stalk would enter, a crisscross net of string was tied over for extra security. *Tigris* looked as trim as when we raced towards Failakai.

But there was still our second problem to be solved. We could not continue with our mainsail in separate pieces and it seemed after all that there was not a single soul left on Bahrain today who could sew a sail. I had a crazy plan. The Hamburg sailmaker who had made the sail could put it together again! I counted my dwindling supply of cash. Just sufficient to risk sending Detlef back to Germany with the dissected sail.

We remained more than three weeks on Bahrain waiting for Detlef to return from Hamburg. Then, a couple of days before Christmas he arrived with our original mainsail back in one piece again. So the eleven of us celebrated Christmas Day together ashore, and early next morning we reloaded our ship for departure.

We unfolded our good new sail in the historic waters of Dilmun and felt as if we had opened wings and taken off. The sail was set to catch the wind perfectly and gave us an uplift we could feel, a thrilling sensation known only to the winged species of man, gliders and sailors. Our vessel was responding marvellously to our manoeuvres with the long tillers. This was exciting. Real fun. We now had to get out of this gulf and into the freedom of the ocean. But the Strait of Hormuz, the outlet from the gulf, was a needle's eye. Even with the wind long since returned to its normal northerly course, would we be able to hit it? In addition, the Hormuz Strait was one of the busiest shipping lanes in the world, making it an extremely hazardous playground for small sailing vessels. The captain of a Norwegian supertanker told me that early one morning, upon entering this strait, his watchman had discovered a dhow sail hanging from the bow. Nobody had seen the dhow itself, nor did they ever hear a thing about its crew.

In Bahrain, Norman and I had repeatedly spoken to the owners of many motor-dhows. One of these captains, Said Abdulla from Oman, said there was a narrow passage, sheltered from the Hormuz Strait shipping lane by some rocks, which they used to avoid the fast big ships. He agreed to pilot us through if we followed in his wake.

Said had a compass but no map. He set a course for the north-western coast of Qatar which we reached just as the sun set. The moon was full, the sky was clear; it was great to be sailing on our own, at peace with the wind and the rhythm of the waves.

Next morning we barely escaped a severe collision with the dhow when two hissing seas threw both boats down into the same trough. Said had come back to inform us that the dhow now had trouble with its bilge pump and he wanted to alter course more northerly to put in at Sirri Island for repair. We located this island on our map and found to our delight that we could make it in spite of leeway, so we kept on more or less in company, the dhow sometimes disappearing far ahead of us and sometimes far behind.

Shortly after noon Norman climbed the mast ladder and a moment later we heard his triumphant yell from the masthead: Sirri was to starboard of our bow! We saw some low land with big trees, and some enormous buildings and oil installations ashore.

We agreed to sail into the harbour facing us and wait for the dhow to be repaired. Said again took the lead, speeding up ahead of us. It began to rain. A short while later he came back at full speed. This was not Sirri Island! This was a Persian island!

Complete confusion. Further map-reading on *Tigris* in the pouring rain. Spelling shouted back and forth in Arab, English and German. This was certainly Sirri Island, and it did belong to Iran. It appeared then that Captain Said had wanted to go to Sir Island, near the coast of Oman, and not Sirri.

No harm done. We were now in a more favourable position to sail straight for the Hormuz Strait. We could go in to Sirri together and have the damage to the dhow repaired there. But no thank you. The mere thought of being in Iranian national territory made Captain Said desperate. He had no documents permitting him to sail in Persian waters. He now confessed that there was something wrong with his engine too. Yet before we had a chance of reaching any kind of agreement the dhow put up full speed downwind and left us, never to come back.

We ventured into the sheltered water on the south side of the island and sailed very close along the shore. The sudden silence of the sea, and the abrupt end to the violent pitching and rolling, left us with a comfortable feeling. But the peaceful hours in the shelter of Sirri were few. The wind blew with redoubled force, and the swells rose bigger and wilder as night fell on us again.

Just before sunrise the wind went mad, with violent gusts, and the sea was chaotic. All hands came on deck in a terrible fight to keep control of our vessel. The wind threw itself upon the rigging and bamboo walls with a violence not yet experienced on this voyage. The thick sail battered with a force that would lift any man off the deck. Like savages we clung to the canvas and ropes, and in the mad fight that followed the wooden block that held the port side topping lift split asunder and the yardarm with the sail sagged to port. The flapping and slashing sail had to come down quickly before all the rigging broke. But the loops of the halyard were under such pressure that for a while none of us was able to unfasten it.

It was Carlo who eventually loosened the jammed rope while half a dozen of the men hung on the halyard to reduce its drag on the knot. The sail came down, Norman replaced the broken block, and the sail went up again at an adjusted angle, enabling the two helmsmen to turn *Tigris* onto course. Breakfast porridge was now consumed standing, as the choppy sea sent heavy spray into cups and pots left unguarded.

It was still a desperate situation; the sea was now so rough that time and again we lost steering control, and each of us had a personal lifeline tied around his waist and lashed to the superstructure. We were racing ahead at full speed when we heard Asbjörn's calm voice from the steering bridge: "Look, what is that?"

There were white cloud-banks along the entire horizon ahead. I grabbed the binoculars. For a moment I could hardly believe my eyes. Above the cloud-banks was land, solid rock.

We dug out of our boxes a land map of Oman. It showed that the Arabian peninsula, with the Hormuz Strait at its tip, rose steeply to 6,400 feet above the gulf. Instantly we tried to turn away from the coast while there still was time. We had clearly come much farther south than we ought to have done.

The mountains were soon near enough to take the form of real rocks, first rising out of the sea and then piercing right through the cloud belt. We fought our way up the coast, getting ever closer to the cliffs. A more forbidding land I had never seen: not even scrub or a green tuft of grass to brighten up the sterile ascents. The stormy weather struck these walls head on, and rebounded with full force for many miles, stirring up a chaotic turmoil of tossing and leaping waves. The rocks drew nearer. Yet if we turned further into the wind to try to clear the headland our sail would flap and we would lose all steerage way. My only hope was that these conditions would change when we came closer to land: the current would be forced to turn parallel to the coast instead of against it, and so would the wind when striking the rocks at sea level. The only opening in the compact wall was the Hormuz Strait. If nature was forced to follow such an escape route, we would be dragged along too.

We continued our course, trusting that we would be able to turn to safety closer to land. We were near enough now to see the foot of the precipices where they fell into the frothing surf. By five thirty it was pitch dark. We were rolling so desperately that nothing could be left loose on board. Inside the cabin, shirts, jackets and trousers hanging from bamboo rods on walls looked like an army of robots doing morning exercise together with clockwork precision.

I heard Norman shouting to us from the top of the swaying mast that he saw light-flashes ahead, the reflections of revolving beams from a distant lighthouse beyond the horizon. It must be the lighthouse on the other side of the entrance to the Hormuz Strait. We had to keep it to starboard to clear the invisible cape, but later we had to turn at a sharp angle and keep it on the port side as we swung into the open strait.

By now the wind had turned more westerly, fulfilling our wildest hopes. I was convinced that the flow of the sea beneath us had also been turned by the impassable rock barrier and was forced to follow the coastline in our direction. The lighthouse danced into sight in front of us. Carlo shouted in triumph that he could see it on our starboard side, which meant that we had at last turned *Tigris* away from the shore. We were winning.

We began to see ships' lights everywhere. Because there was no dhow to show us the unofficial passage between the closely packed islands of the cape, we were heading at full speed and with limited control straight into the world's busiest shipping channel.

Never on any sea had we seen so many brilliantly lit ships in motion at the same time. But when Detlef ordered a sharp turn to starboard into the main traffic lane of the Hormuz Strait, we immediately received a violent air stream straight at our back and *Tigris* raced in between the superships as if we were all of a kind.

Things went almost ridiculously well, and Carlo and I could crawl inside the cabin to steal a snooze before our next turn at the steering oars. Gone was the threat of shipwreck and collision; we were travelling as if on a double-tracked railway line.

At half-past midnight I was awakened by Detlef crawling over my legs heading for his own berth. "We've made it," he said. "We're outside."

I crawled to the starboard door opening. It was an unforgettable change of scene. The rolling had ceased and the sky was full of stars over vaguely moonlit rocks and hillocks. No roaring wind or shrieking wood. Peaceful and idyllic. Somehow even the big modern ships we had dreaded inside the gulf seemed friendlier out here. A brightly-lit luxury cruiser with coloured lamps in garlands on all decks passed us, and made us feel as if we too were on a pleasure trip. It was the last day of the year and the revellers were probably still in the bars, but we certainly envied nobody. We were safe outside the gulf. It was great to be afloat on a Sumerian reed boat.

We had decided to lay our course down along the east coast of Oman. Norris had pleaded for a chance to go close inshore along the Arabian peninsula, since the rugged peaks and fierce cliffs of Oman offered some really impressive film sequences. Norman supported this itinerary. He said it would take us down to the port of Muscat, where we could overhaul the rig and the steering system before we set off for Pakistan, the former realm of the ancient Indus Valley civilization. I too had a reason for wanting to follow this shoreline. The day before we set sail down the rivers of Iraq, a German reporter had called on me with exciting news. According to dependable sources, a stepped temple-pyramid had been found in the sand somewhere in Oman. It had seemed almost too good to be true that a Sumerian ziggurat should be discovered in a distant land facing the Indian Ocean, just as we were hoping to go that far in a Sumerian boat.

As we sailed down the coast in the direction of Muscat we soon lost sight of the wild mountains of northern Oman. The landscape was now flat, with just a few scattered tall trees. We had been told over the radio by the authorities in Muscat to keep away from the coast of Oman until we received permission to land, so we anchored for the night among the offshore islets of Suwadi. All the afternoon we had seen a beautiful white beach, fringed by scattered palms and other trees, with calm water in front and the shadows of blue mountains far beyond.

At 8:00 a.m. the next day we hoisted sail and left the islands. We followed a long low coast with the blue mountains barely visible in the background until we were close enough to Muscat to see ships at anchor and others heading for port.

Norman received a new message from Muscat: it was not yet decided whether we would be allowed ashore. "Believe it or not," he said, "they say it is because we have a Russian on board."

Shortly, countless city lights were lit on the coastal plateaus and in the valleys. Way ahead the night twinkled with navigation lights and ships in increasing numbers. Muscat clearly had a busy modern port. Finally, as night fell, we were permitted to anchor in the harbour in the midst of a most picturesque group of dhows.

The dark rock above us had barely begun to turn mustard-coloured in the first rays of the sun next day when motorboats came racing to our side. First came a helpful Swede, representing the Gulf Agency, who told us that our landing was approved. Then an extremely polite police officer arrived in a launch to pay some sort of courtesy visit. Some hours later we were boarded by a most cordial Scottish customs officer, who sat down at our table for a long good-humoured chat.

Few ports can be more picturesque than this large new harbour, named Port Qaboos after the sultan himself. From the modern docks and warehouses, dark lava rocks run up to the walls of a mediaeval Portuguese fort perched on naked cliffs and dominating the whole harbour. A sweet fragrance as from mixed incense and tropical spices wafted into the harbour from a row of tall, white-painted Arab buildings at the foot of the cliffs.

On our first evening ashore, at a dinner party given us by Barry and Kate Metcalfe, the English manager of Port Qaboos and his wife, I heard somebody say there were supposed to be small boats similar to our own near Sohar, the ancient capital of Oman. I realized that the man who had mentioned the bundle boats was the noted Italian archaeologist Paolo Costa, from Oman's Directorate of Antiquity. Costa was a most jovial person, and we were soon way back in distant millenia. Up north there were copper mines dating from prehistoric periods, he said. There were also burial mounds of the same period as those in Bahrain.

I could no longer suppress my curiosity about the rumoured ziggurat, and I asked Costa if it were true that a Sumerian temple-pyramid had been found in Oman. "Something has been found," he replied. "Whether it is Sumerian I cannot say, but it shares all its characteristics with a Sumerian ziggurat!"

We wasted no time. At sunrise we were outside the gates of the port, with Costa in his Land Cruiser as guide. Driving from the modern settlements on the outskirts of Muscat, every fifty miles seemed to take us another millennium back through the ages until we reached the mountain town of Al Hamra, about one hundred and fifty miles away. Life in this town was hardly changed since the days of the ancient Middle East civilizations. The setting was out of the Bible, or rather, out of the Koran.

From the clusters of mud-brick houses barefooted women in

colourful costumes walked like queens, with pottery vessels crowning their heads, to the old aqueducts in the shade of the date-palm plantations. Their tinkling jewellery, like the silver daggers in the belts of the men, were collectors' items. The narrow rock streets, polished to a shine by hoofs and feet, climbed steeply from the palm gardens between cool arcades, crowded with robed men sitting or standing, thinking or talking, as unconcerned about the clock as the little pack-donkeys sharing the shade with them.

Before long Costa drove sharply off the road and we bumped along camel tracks that wound ahead into a hidden world of dried-up riverbeds and small alluvial flats until we rounded a black, conical peak. On the plain before us lay what we had come for.

We were still in the Land Cruiser when some large chocolate-coloured boulders, staked to form the terraced wall of a partly buried building, met my eyes, before Costa even had time to point in that direction. It was difficult to remain calmly seated until we came to a stop at close range. This was what I had hoped for but had not dared believe. There was no longer any doubt.

Costa took us to the side where a long, narrow ramp led from the ground up to the top terrace. Huge boulders had been used to wall in a rectangular structure that rose above the plain in compact terraces, four of which were seen above ground. The stone-lined ramp led up one side as in the temple-pyramids of the sun-worshippers of Mesopotamia. There were vestiges of other walls and an elaborate system of aqueducts.

I was amazed that nobody had started digging. Costa shrugged his shoulders. There had been no time. This discovery was new; the site was stumbled upon by mining geologists four years ago when the sultan permitted a general archaeological and geological survey of Oman.

A stone's throw from the temple-mound the sun shone on some piles of prettily coloured cinders: red, brown, violet, yellow and green. This was mining slag. "Remember I told you about the prehistoric copper mines?" said Costa. "They are here!"

The parts of a long unsolved puzzle seemed to fit logically together. "Makan," I exclaimed.

Costa turned to show us the spectacular sight. "Yes," he confirmed, "this may well be Makan, the legendary Copper Mountain of the old Sumerians. There is no copper nearer to Mesopotamia."

The import of copper, so dearly required by all Bronze Age cultures, had been of paramount importance to the founders of Sumerian civilization, and ancient tablets record that the imports had come by sea from a land known to them as Makan or Magan.

Many scholars have postulated different theories as to the whereabouts of Makan. But, since a large number of Sumerian copper objects have been found to contain a slight trace of nickel, geography and geology combine to argue strongly that northern Oman was the copper country of Makan. Nickel is fairly rare in copper, but it has been found in copper coming from Oman.

It would therefore seem plausible to suspect that the seemingly misplaced mini-ziggurat discovered by the mining prospectors had been built by the sun-worshipping merchant mariners from the twin-river country, who had come here because it was the nearest site for mining and smelting copper.

7

"Port side row, starboard rest! . . . Both sides row! . . . Ready . . . row! . . . Ready . . . rooow!"

I felt like a galley slave-driver as I stood high in the stern, steering while my friends toiled rhythmically, their sweat pouring and their long oars sweeping in unison like the legs of a centipede.

It was an exciting test, and one I had never yet attempted. *Tigris* had been idle for a full week now, and we wanted to row our reed ship out of port, and, with Toru and Carlo in our rubber dinghy to film and photograph, only eight men were left to man the oars: four on either side and myself at a rudder oar.

"Ready . . . rooow! . . ." We were leaving Port Qaboos, and bound for the coast of Pakistan. The men put every ounce of their strength into propelling the heavy ship through the water. After an hour and a half we reached the gap in the final breakwater where the ocean swells rolled against the concrete blocks of the jetty. By this time the men, untrained in rowing, were really exhausted and we decided to hoist the sail. It was up at record speed. In a few moments we were out in the open sea.

Right: The ship's company. On the cabin roof, Norman, Thor, Yuri and Carlo; up the mast ladder, Norris, Toru, Detlef, Gherman, Rashad, Asbjörn and HP.

Top left: Archaeologist
Geoffrey Bibby and
the author with the
proud owner of a
brand new Bahrainian
fishing boat.

Centre left: Inside the
main cabin. The floor
is made up of the tops
of the boxes
containing our
personal possessions.

Bottom left: A village
in the Indus valley.
The cart in the
foreground is similar
to four-thousand-
year-old miniatures
found in the area.

The wind blew from the south-southeast, and there was no sign of the northeast winter monsoon we had expected in the middle of January. Our sailing speed was so slow that we found ourselves unable to tack, and had to sail north again. Long before dark we began to see a familiar sight: the masts and bridge-houses of distant ships forming an uninterrupted line along the eastern horizon. Soon we were once more in the very midst of the shipping lane, trying to cross it. On my midnight watch with Detlef we barely escaped collision as a small cargo ship came straight for us and we were both able to turn aside only at the very last moment.

The next day, before sunrise, the wind changed to the north-northwest and we turned to steer eastwards with sail filled and at good speed, wriggling our way through the shipping lane. That night we felt as if we were travelling across prairies with light from scattered homes here and there in the darkness.

On the third day after leaving Muscat, the good northerly wind eased, slowing our progress. For two days we lay in the midst of dense traffic, fighting with sail and steering oars to get out of the way of fast ocean liners and tankers as they thundered by and left us rocking so violently that the steering platform under our feet seemed ready to tear loose from the reeds.

Towards evening on the fifth day the weather changed. Heavy clouds rolled up over the horizon and we heard distant thunder. I crawled into the main cabin to get some sleep before my own night watch. My ears registered the rhythmic drumming of distant engines that slowly grew in strength and then died away as ships came and passed us. Then a terrified yell came from the steering platform, followed by the sound of a ship's pistons. I barely had my head out of the portside door opening when I saw our sails brightly lit by something big and noisy on the opposite side of the cabin. As I rose to my feet, everything seemed in chaotic movement and I was almost blinded by the many lights from a tall black wall. A fully lit cargo ship rose out of the dark so close that for a few seconds all seemed part of one unit: the two bamboo cabins and the black wall. Then, it was torn away again before we had a clear idea of what we had seen, just time enough to hang on as our bundle boat was tossed aside by foaming cascades.

Left: Farewell, Tigris! *A sad but noble end: a flaming torch, a symbol carrying a message of peace for the whole world.*

We had barely time to exchange exclamations of horror and relief, when a new yell came from Yuri on the bridge aft:

"Crazy! Another one!" Yuri's voice was drowned by the thunder of a second ship racing into vision right alongside *Tigris*, sending us sidelong with its wake, ploughing us casually out of its way.

"That was a container ship," commented Detlef dryly. "They often make thirty knots."

We all remained on deck for a while, commenting on the poor visibility. The weather did not look promising. It began to drizzle. Then, incredibly, a strong following wind sprang up. We had had enough. The giant tankers were left racing in their own track off the coast of Oman as we made use of the fresh southeast wind to sail farther out and away towards the northeast. Out in the unfrequented part of the sea we were no longer Lilliputians in a world of robots without flesh and blood; we were human beings once again, in an environment shared with fish and birds.

FOR DAYS we sailed northeast across the Arabian Sea with no other company than patrolling sharks, a faithful escort of dolphins, and brief visits from playful porpoises and curious whales. Colourful tropical birds landed on our deck to rest, and, attracted by the broad shadow beneath our bundles, multi-coloured fish swam with us like domesticated animals in vast quantities. Every day HP, Asbjörn and Carlo extended our provisions by fishing and spearing two of the most savoury species: the gold-mackerel, which shone in colours of green, rust and bright gold when patrolling in its own kingdom, but was flat and faded when brought on deck, and the streamlined rainbow-runner with its slim torpedo shape which merited its name in or out of the water.

This was when Carlo insisted he heard a grasshopper during his night watch. We refused to believe him, but then I found one in my own bed, yellow-green and as long as a finger. Soon we saw grasshoppers everywhere, crawling and jumping about on reeds and bamboo, and even taking wing on short circuits over the sea, but always coming back to our marine haystack. They seemed to be happiest among the bushy ends of the reed bundles at the top of the high bow and stern. Obviously they'd embarked as silent stowaways in Oman, never having seen such a wealth of vegetation in any part of the barren Arabian land from which they came.

On Tuesday 31 January we woke up to find ourselves in the calm waters of Ormara Bay, in Pakistan. The sky was clear and for once all eleven men could crowd around the deck table at the same time. Gherman served porridge and fresh eggs, which he had preserved by painting each one with oil before departure. Norman and Rashad were left on watch while the rest of us took shore leave. The dinghy ferried us two at a time into shallow water and we waded onto a broad and beautiful beach. Miles of white sand and not a human soul but ourselves, stepping on shells and sponges and scaring little crabs into their wet holes as we trampled barefoot to the dry sand.

I had had strong reasons to steer for Pakistan and visit this part of Asia. I wanted to see Meluhha. So far Meluhha had been for me nothing but an unidentifiable name common on Sumerian tablets. Dilmun and Makan were always being named together, often with a third land, that of Meluhha. We had been to both Dilmun and Makan. Where was Meluhha? Convinced that Dilmun and Makan had been properly identified, it seemed to me that Meluhha, by a process of elimination, had to be the Indus Valley region. There was no other important coastal civilization nearer to ancient Mesopotamia, and there was a wealth of evidence to prove contact between Mesopotamia and the Indus Valley.

We started walking across the sandy isthmus and the houses we passed on our way were so similar to the reed dwellings of the marsh Arabs that it was difficult to see how they could build homes so similar without a common heritage. We finally reached a charming little village, with three tiny mosques and a market-place straight out of the *Thousand and One Nights*. We pushed past camels, donkeys, dogs, cats and chickens and, with a horde of children at our heels, reached a shopping street, with about half a dozen small alcoves raised a yard above the sand on poles. Each had an open front wall where the staff of one sat cross-legged, with the humble merchandise before his legs. I took the inventory of the smallest shop: seven carrots and five potatoes. Most had saucers or small bowls with grains or seeds in front of them, but one had biscuits, Arab cigarettes and bits of crude soap and candy. Not a single woman could be seen in this exotic crowd, except beautiful girls below the age of six or seven and old crones with green stones dangling from nose-rings.

THE COLOURFUL LIFE of that timeless village was still vivid in our memories a week later when we entered the prehistoric city of Mohenjo-Daro, deep within the Indus Valley. We had left *Tigris* in the busy modern port of Karachi, where the Pakistani authorities had given us a hearty welcome. A young guide from the National Museum took us by mini-bus through various Pakistani towns to the ruins of Mohenjo-Daro, 350 miles from Karachi.

Mohenjo-Daro means simply "Mound of the Dead". No one knows what the city was called during its thousand years of life, from about 2500 to 1500 BC. The broad Indus river, which once flowed past the city has long since withdrawn. What is left now is the empty shell of a city planned by expert architects within a rigidly organized society and ruled by a priest-king, regarded as a demi-god. These streets, carefully orientated to the sun, had seen his wise men walking about among the common crowd. The elite of this society created an empire that left its ruins and monuments throughout the plains of the Indus Valley. We find, furthermore, that the Indus civilization was not only strikingly similar to those of Sumer and Egypt, but also contemporary. The founders of the Egyptian and Sumerian dynasties began to leave their traces on their riverbanks—and to illustrate their large reed ships—just when the Indus Valley was settled by a third civilization. All three established themselves in the three major river valleys centring upon the Arabian peninsula.

To me there was no longer any doubt. I agreed with those who identified the Indus region with Meluhha. Dilmun, Makan and Meluhha belonged together. Now we had visited all three.

Departure from Asia. A cold wind from the north blew through the fissures in the cane wall as I woke up at early dawn. This wind was good, for we were bound for Africa. The men were back from the last shore leave, probably for a long time.

During the night all lights from ships and land sank behind us. Huge swells indicated interference from a strong current, and on the second day at sea the northerly wind increased in strength. By the third day the wind had risen to half a gale, and we lashed on two rowing oars beside the rudder oars to help steady our course. Sharks began to join us.

Tigris had been afloat for three months. The cigar-shaped twin bundles still floated higher than *Ra II* did after three weeks. The buoyancy of our reed ship had more than stood up to the requirements of any long-distance voyage. Now, around the deck table we began to discuss our future course. We had so far voyaged between the legendary Dilmun, Makan and Meluhha of the Sumerians. Across the Indian Ocean lay the Horn of Africa, Somalia, considered to be the legendary Punt of the Egyptian voyagers. If we could reach that coast also, then we would have tied all the three great civilizations of the Old World together with the kind of ship all three had in common.

Our discussions were interrupted as distant lightning flashes suddenly leaped across the sky, splitting the black clouds above the mast with a violent clatter. Our little boat was tossed about like a toy over mountainous waves, and in the faint light of our swinging paraffin lamps, colliding wave crests rose around us like small volcanoes smoking with foam and spray. By now we were certain that the twin-bundle ship was too broad to turn bottom up and too buoyant to be forced down under water; capsizing was no threat. It was a comfort to know we were on a compact bundle boat and not inside a fragile plank hull.

The storm raged all night. The wind howled and whistled in the empty rigging and the cabins. Like Noah we waited inside cover for the weather to abate. No worry about the vessel springing a leak; no need for bailing. Even with breaking seas tumbling on board by the tens of tons, by the next moment all the frothing water whirling around the cabins was gone, dropping straight down through the sieve-like bottom. And the boat rose from the sea like a surfacing submarine, glitteringly wet in the lamp-light, and sparkling with the phosphorescent plankton trapped on board.

By morning the storm abated. Sporadic rain-squalls continued, and the sharks that had taken to our sides in the rough weather showed no sign of leaving. The side-on rolling to the sea was terrific. It was hard to keep balance around the table, and the food that spilled during meals was not easily swept up from the berdi stalks beneath us. But stowaway crabs helped keep the ship clean, operating like toothpicks between the reeds.

Thunderclouds and lightning continued to circle around the horizon for a couple of days, but as we entered the second half of February all storm clouds disappeared. We sailed into a blue world, all sky and water, a planet where all land was hidden deep below the sea. No ships, no planes. For days and weeks we were the only human beings, but not the only life.

We never tired of hanging with our heads over the side bundles or trailing on a rope outside, watching the changing world on the yellow reeds. By now the white goose-barnacles, small when we left Oman, were as big as flat pigeon eggs. It was Detlef who discovered that by boiling a pot-full of the biggest barnacles with garlic, spices and some dried vegetables, he had invented the best variety of fish soup we had ever tasted, particularly when some bits of flying fish were thrown in.

Flying fish are a blessing to any reed ship voyager in warm waters. As a delicacy they are second only to breakfast herring, and as bait they are superior to the most expensive artificial tackle. A single one put on a hook would straightaway catch a golden mackerel three feet long, which sufficed as dinner for everyone. And when the secret of how to lure flying fish on board was demonstrated we had no trouble attracting all we needed. Asbjörn simply lit all our paraffin lamps and placed them outside the cabin walls at night. Flying fish began raining on board like projectiles. Several times we were awakened by the cold fish landing in our beds.

Then, three weeks after we left Pakistan, we were torn away from the world of fish. Norman established good radio contact with a man called Frank at Bahrain Radio, who sent messages with depressing regularity. *Tigris* was suddenly on a collision course with political events.

We had hoped to sail from Meluhha to Punt. But requesting permission to land there we learned that Somalia was at war. Yachts trespassing Somalian waters had been seized and their crews imprisoned. This meant that fifteen hundred miles of African coast from the Gulf of Aden southwards was closed to us.

Then came a warning from London that the Arabian side of the Gulf of Aden was also forbidden territory, for South Yemen with its Communist government had closed its borders to capitalist visitors. South Yemen filled the entire thousand mile stretch of the Arabian peninsula between Oman and North Yemen.

We now had to navigate with caution and try to follow the mid-line of the Gulf of Aden, without touching the forbidden lands on either side. Our intentions caused anxiety for our security among our consortium contacts in London; but we were sure we could navigate this course. We aimed for the narrow strait leading into the Red Sea from the far end of the Gulf of Aden.

Suddenly a political breakthrough came. Djibouti, a tiny new African republic in the innermost corner of the Gulf of Aden, just at the entrance to the Red Sea, gave permission for our landing. That little nation, not much more than a good port surrounded by a small piece of desert, was neutral.

ON A REED SHIP sailing between the continents there is plenty of time to meditate. With man's pedigree recently pushed back to over two million years, we have much to learn from future excavations. But the greatest discovery of recent years is how incredibly little we yet know of our past, of the beginning.

What we do know from radio-carbon analysis is this: in approximately 3000 BC, allowing for the usual radio-carbon margin of error of about a century plus or minus, a major geological catastrophe in the Atlantic formed a lasting split in the ocean floor and right across the green countryside of Iceland. We also know that all the great civilisations of antiquity known to us today appeared one by one in the centuries immediately after 3000 BC.

There was the sudden booming of civilisation at the mouth of the Mesopotamian rivers and on the banks of the Nile and the Indus. But not only there. 3000 BC marked also new cultural eras in Crete and Cyprus and Malta, while on the other side of the Atlantic we find that the amazingly accurate Mayan calendar began with the zero year of 3113 BC.

Tigris had brought us to Makan, Meluhha and now to Punt. It had also brought us to Dilmun, where the Sumerians say their forefathers settled after a world catastrophe when most of mankind drowned. We in our own "ark" had thus traced the beginning of history, back to the days of Noah and the flood.

On 28 March we heard the growing drone of an aeroplane. "By gosh, he's coming straight for us!" Detlef shouted from the bridge. We all rushed out into the burning sun of the Gulf of Aden just as a twin-engined military plane dived down over our mast top, so low that the sails flapped back with the wind pressure. The plane turned and, very low, came straight back at us. "Here they come again!" I yelled as I saw it turning.

"Hurrah, they are American marines!" cheered Norman.

A moment later the droning came back louder than ever and of a different kind. We looked up and two helicopters appeared, one on either horizon, coming towards us from different directions. They met above us and we were safe, for one was American and the other French. Friendly pilots photographed us from the air. We had reached the inner end of the gulf. On our port side was Somalia, at war with Ethiopia. On our starboard was South Yemen and the old port of Aden, also closed for political reasons.

We saw the blue mountains of Africa that evening and we steered by the lights from the shore. Long before daybreak we passed the lighthouses outside Djibouti harbour, and dropped anchor. As day broke we found ourselves riding with a huge battleship of some sort as our nearest neighbour. The sun rose and a small yacht came out of port and guided us in, past the flagship and other units of the French Indian Ocean fleet. This little republic had just been granted its independence from France.

Bruce Norman and Roy Davies from the BBC were there to collect our films. They brought with them the news that Massawa, where I had hoped to end the *Tigris* voyage after an estimated five more days of sailing, was in a state of siege. The city and the port were in the hands of the Ethiopians, supported by Russians, but the surrounding coasts were held by Eritrean liberation forces.

There was suddenly nowhere to sail in any direction. It did not matter a bit that we were not allowed to add another five days to an experiment that had gone on for five months. But what hurt all of us was that we had come back to our own world, and met again the results of twenty centuries of progress since the time of Christ.

We had to abandon ship and end the expedition here, that was certain. I took a hard decision. Instead of being left to rot, *Tigris* should have a proud end, as a protest, a torch that would call to men of reason to resume the cause of peace in a corner of the world where civilization first took hold. We should set the reed bundles ablaze as a fiery gesture against the accelerating arms race and the fighting in Africa and Asia.

The others were informed of my decision as they gathered around the breakfast table next morning. They were shocked at first, but everybody gave wholehearted support to the plan.

Tigris was towed out of the harbour and anchored, sails up, off a small coral isle outside Djibouti. Before we lowered the United Nations flag I wrote a telegram to the man who had granted *Tigris* the right to sail symbolically under this flag. The message was passed to everyone on board for approval:

Secretary General Kurt Waldheim,
United Nations.

As the multinational crew of the experimental reed ship *Tigris* brings the test voyage to its conclusion today we are grateful to the secretary general for the permission to sail under United Nations flag and we are proud to report that the double objectives of the expedition have been achieved to our complete satisfaction.

Ours has been a voyage into the past to study the qualities of a prehistoric type of vessel built after ancient Sumerian principles. But it has also been a voyage into the future to demonstrate that no space is too restricted for peaceful coexistence of men who work for common survival. We are eleven men from countries governed by different political systems. And we have sailed together on a small raft-ship of tender reeds and rope a distance of over six thousand kilometres. In spite of different political views we have lived and struggled together in perfect understanding and friendship in cramped quarters, always according to the ideals of the United Nations: cooperation for joint survival.

When we embarked last November on our reed ship *Tigris* we knew we would sink or survive together, and this knowledge united us in friendship. When we now, in April, disperse to our respective homelands we sincerely respect and feel sympathy for each other's nation, and our joint message is not directed to any one country but to modern man everywhere. . . . Today we burn our proud ship to protest against the inhuman elements in the world of 1978 to which we have come back as we reach land from the open sea. Surrounded by military aeroplanes and warships from the world's civilized and developed nations we are denied permission by friendly governments, for security reasons, to land anywhere but in the tiny and still neutral republic of Djibouti, because elsewhere around us brothers and neighbours are engaged in homicide with means made available to them by those who lead humanity on our joint road into the third millenium.

To the innocent masses in all industrialized countries we direct our appeal. We must wake up to the insane reality of our time. We are all irresponsible unless we demand from the responsible decision makers that modern armaments must no longer be available to the people whose former battle axes and swords our ancestors condemned. Our planet is bigger than the reed bundles that have carried us across the seas and yet small enough to run the same risks unless those of us still alive open our eyes and minds to the desperate need of intelligent collaboration to save ourselves and our civilization from what we are about to convert into a sinking ship.

The Republic of Djibouti, 3 April 1978.

Everybody signed. All eleven. Then we ate a last meal at the plank table between the two cabins. We had great memories from around this table: Norman remarked that we had sailed 6,800 kilometres together; 4,200 miles. This was the third of April; *Tigris* had been afloat 143 days.

Norris looked at his watch. The sun would soon set behind the blue mountains of Africa. It was zero hour for *Tigris*. Asbjörn had been in charge of our paraffin lamps and knew where to find the fuel. HP, as a demolition sergeant, knew where to pour it. I looked at the empty table as I jumped into the dinghy after the others. Nobody had troubled to clean the table tonight.

We lined up ashore and none of us could say much as the flames licked out of the cabin door. The sail caught fire in a rain of sparks, accompanied by sharp shotlike reports of splitting bamboo. Nobody else spoke, and I barely heard myself mumble:

"She was a fine ship."

Thor Heyerdahl

In Oslo today there stands a handsome modern building, the Kon-Tiki Museum, one of the most popular museums in Norway. In it are housed both the balsa raft *Kon-Tiki* and the papyrus boat *Ra II*, together with many priceless archaeological treasures. All these have derived from the work of Thor Heyerdahl, who today is a respected and world-famous archaeologist and explorer. But his reputation was not always so secure.

His whole life, in fact, has been the familiar up-hill struggle of the man with flair and vision, ceaselessly critical of accepted theories. Scorning the derision of academics he has often set out to justify his controversial ideas in the best way possible: by practical demonstration. The high points in his career have been the famous voyages of *Kon-Tiki*, *Ra II*, and now *Tigris*—each one a spectacular triumph, and each one causing learned men to scratch their heads and think again.

Thor Heyerdahl was born in 1914, in Narvik, Norway. His mother was head of the small local museum, and so fired her small son with her own enthusiasm for zoology that even while he was still in primary school a whole room was set aside in their house for his collection of zoological specimens. Soon archaeology was added to his interests, and then geography which, together with zoology, he subsequently studied at Oslo University.

Inevitably his studies were interrupted by the war, when he served in the Free Norwegian Forces, becoming a lieutenant in a parachute unit. In 1945, however, he eagerly returned to the work that was to make him world famous. As well as undertaking his many expeditions he has written numerous scientific books and articles, and has been awarded an impressive number of academic distinctions. Increasingly, also, his work has shown him the pettiness and folly of present-day international tensions, and he is now a very active vice-president of the Association of World Federalists, an organization dedicated to the breaking-down of national and racial barriers.

A few years ago he moved his home from Oslo to a small mediaeval hilltop town in Northern Italy, where he now lives with his young Norwegian wife and their three daughters.

The KEY to REBECCA

A condensation of the book by
KEN FOLLETT

Illustrated by Kevin Tweddell
Published by Hamish Hamilton

In 1942 Rommel seemed invincible. It was as if he had access to the most secret plans of the Allied generals. Was there a brilliantly successful German agent working for him in Cairo? And if so, could the man be silenced in time to turn the tide of battle?

In this book the best-selling author of *Storm Island* has written a spy story both amazing and, because it is based on fact, totally believable.

Its hero is the British Intelligence officer, William Vandam. The plot he has to solve is intricate: a British soldier murdered in far-off Asyût; the mysterious activities of a beautiful Arab dancer; the discovery of the book, *Rebecca*, on a desert battlefield; the kidnapping of an innocent child—there had to be a pattern, a key to it all somewhere . . . .

Chapter 1

The last camel collapsed at noon.

It was the five-year-old white bull he had bought in Gialo, the youngest and strongest of the three beasts, and the least ill-tempered; he liked the animal as much as a man could like a camel, which is to say that he hated it only a little.

They had climbed the leeward side of a small hill, man and camel planting big clumsy feet in the inconstant sand, and at the top they stopped. They looked ahead, seeing nothing but another hillock to climb, and after that a thousand more, and it was as if the camel despaired at the thought. Its forelegs folded, then its rear went down, and it crouched on top of the hill like a monument, staring across the empty desert with the indifference of the dying.

The man hauled on its nose rope but it would not get up. The man went behind and kicked its hindquarters. Finally he took out a razor-sharp, curved, bedouin knife with a narrow point and stabbed the camel's rump. Blood flowed but the camel did not even look round.

The man understood what was happening. The animal's body, starved of nourishment, had simply stopped working, like a machine that has run out of fuel. He had seen camels collapse like this on the outskirts of an oasis, surrounded by life-giving foliage which they ignored, lacking the energy to eat.

There were two more tricks he might have tried. One was to pour water into its nostrils until it began to drown; the other to light a fire under its hind quarters. He could not spare the water for one nor the firewood for the other, and besides neither method had a great chance of success.

It was time to stop, anyway. The sun was high and fierce. The long Saharan summer was beginning, and the midday temperature would reach 110 degrees in the shade. Without unloading the camel, the man opened one of the saddlebags and took out his tent. He pitched it beside the dying camel, there on top of the hillock .

He sat cross-legged in the open end of the tent, gnawed at some dates, and watched the camel die while he waited for the sun to pass overhead. His tranquillity was practised. He had come more than a thousand miles in this desert. Two months earlier he had left El Agheila, on the Mediterranean coast of Libya, and travelled due south for five hundred miles, via Gialo and Al Kufrah, into the empty heart of the Sahara. There he had turned east and crossed the border into Egypt unobserved by man or beast. He had turned north near El Khârga; now he was not far from his destination. He knew the desert and was afraid of it—all intelligent men were. But he never allowed that fear to take hold of him, to panic him. There were always catastrophies: mistakes in navigation that made you miss a well by a couple of miles; water bags that leaked or burst. The only response was to say, *Inshallah:* It is the will of God.

Eventually the sun began to dip towards the west. He looked at the camel's load, wondering how much of it he could carry. There were three small European suitcases, two heavy and one light, all of them important. There was a little bag of clothes, a sextant, maps, food, the water bag. It was already too much: he would have to abandon the tent, the blanket, the cooking pot.

He made the three suitcases into a bundle and tied the clothes, the food and the sextant on top, strapping everything together with a length of cloth. He could put his arms through the cloth straps and carry the whole lot like a rucksack on his back. He slung the goatskin water bag around his neck. It was a heavy load.

Three months earlier he would have been able to carry it all day then play tennis in the evening, but the desert had weakened him. His bowels were water, his skin was a mass of sores, and he had lost twenty or thirty pounds. Without the camel he could not go far.

He started walking. He followed his compass wherever it led, resisting the temptation to divert around the hills, for he was navigating by dead reckoning over the final miles, and a fractional error could take him a fatal few hundred yards astray.

The day cooled into evening. The water bag became lighter around his neck as he consumed its contents. He knew there was not enough for another day.

Clouds gathered on the horizon as the desert cooled. Behind him, the sun sank lower and turned into a big yellow balloon. A little later a white moon appeared in a purple sky. He thought about stopping. Nobody could walk all night. But he had no tent, no blanket. And he was sure he was close to the well: by his reckoning he should have been there.

He walked on. His calm was deserting him now. He had set his strength and his expertise against the ruthless desert, and it began to look as if the desert would win. He could no longer repress the fear. When death became inevitable he would rush to meet it. Not for him the hours of agony and encroaching madness. He had his knife. He seemed to see his mother in the distance, heard a railway train that chugged along with his heartbeat, slowly. Small rocks moved in his path like scampering rats. He smelled roast lamb. He breasted a rise and saw the fire over which the meat had been roasted, and a small boy beside it gnawing the bones. There were the tents around the fire, the hobbled camels, and the wellhead beyond. He walked into the hallucination. The people in the dream looked up at him, startled. A tall man stood up and spoke. The traveller pulled at his *howli*, unwinding the cloth to reveal his face. The tall man stepped forward, shocked, and said, "My cousin!"

The traveller understood that this was not, after all, an illusion; and he smiled faintly and collapsed.

When he awoke at dawn he thought for a moment that he was a boy again, and that his adult life had been a dream.

Someone was touching his shoulder and saying, "Wake up, Achmed," in the language of the desert. Nobody had called him Achmed for years. He realized he was wrapped in a coarse blanket and lying on the cold sand, his head swathed in a *howli*. He opened his eyes to see the gorgeous sunrise like a straight rainbow against the flat black horizon. The icy morning wind blew into his face. In that instant he experienced again all the confusion and anxiety of his fifteenth year.

He had felt utterly lost, that first time he woke up in the desert. He had thought, My father is dead; and then, I have a new father An Arab father. Snatches of the Koran, newly-learned, had run through his head, mixed with bits of the creed which his mother still taught him secretly, in German, which was also the language of his dead father. He remembered the long train journey, wondering what his new desert cousins would be like, and whether they would despise his pale body and his city ways. He had walked out of the railway station and seen the two Arabs, sitting beside their camels in the dust of the station yard, covered in robes from head to foot except for the slit in the *howli* which revealed only their dark, unreadable eyes. They had taken him to the well. It had been terrifying. But although these were hard men they were not unkind. All these memories had run through his mind as he looked at his first desert sunrise, and they came back again now, twenty years later, with the words, "Wake up, Achmed."

He sat up abruptly, his head clearing. He had crossed the desert on a vitally important mission. He had found the well, and it had not been an hallucination: his cousins were here, as they always were at this time of the year. He suffered a sudden sharp panic as he thought of his precious baggage—had he still been carrying it when he arrived?—then he saw it, piled neatly at his feet.

Ishmael, his boyhood companion, squatting beside him, said, "Heavy worries, Cousin."

Achmed nodded. "There is a war."

Ishmael went away. One of the women subserviently brought him tea. He took it without thanking her and drank it quickly. He ate some cold boiled rice while the unhurried work of the encampment went on around him. It seemed that this nomad branch of the family was still wealthy: there were several servants, many children, many sheep, and more than twenty camels.

Achmed finished his breakfast and checked his baggage. He opened the small leather suitcase, and when he looked in at the switches and dials of the compact radio, he had a sudden vivid memory like a film: the frantic city of Berlin; a tree-lined street called the Tirpitzufer; a four-storey sandstone building; a maze of hallways; an office; a prematurely white-haired admiral who said, "Rommel wants me to put an agent into Cairo."

The case also contained a book, a novel in English. Idly, Achmed read the first line: "Last night I dreamt I went to Manderley again." A folded sheet of paper fell out from between the leaves of the book. Carefully Achmed picked it up and put it back. He replaced the book in the case, and closed it.

Ishmael was standing at his shoulder. "Was it a long journey?"

Achmed nodded. "I came from Libya. From the sea."

"From the sea!" Ishmael was awestruck: he had never seen the sea. He said, "But why?"

"It is to do with this war."

"One gang of Europeans fighting with another over who shall sit in Cairo—What does this matter to the sons of the desert?"

"My mother's people are in the war," Achmed said.

"A man should follow his father."

"And if he has two fathers?"

Ishmael shrugged. He understood dilemmas.

Achmed lifted the suitcase. "Will you keep this for me?"

"Yes." Ishmael took it. "Who is winning the war?"

"My mother's people. They are like the nomads—they are proud, and cruel, and strong. They are going to rule the world."

The two cousins looked at one another. It was five years since the last time they had met. The world had changed. Achmed thought of the things he could tell: the crucial meeting in Beirut in 1938, his trip to Berlin, his great coup in Istanbul. . . . None of it would mean anything to his cousin—and Ishmael was probably thinking the same about the events of *his* last five years. As boys they had loved· each other fiercely, but they had never had anything to talk about.

After a moment Ishmael turned away and took the suitcase to his tent. Achmed fetched a little water in a bowl. He opened the bag of clothes and took out a small piece of soap, a brush, a mirror and a razor. He stuck the mirror in the sand, adjusted it, and began to unwind the *howli* from around his head.

The sight of his own face in the mirror shocked him.

His strong, normally clear forehead was covered with sores. His eyes were hooded with pain and lined in the corners. The dark beard grew matted and unkempt on his fine-boned cheeks, and the skin of his large hooked nose was red and split. He parted his blistered lips and saw that his fine, even teeth were filthy.

He brushed the soap on and began to shave. Gradually his features emerged. They were strong rather than handsome, and normally wore a look which he recognized, in his more detached moments, to be faintly dissolute; but now they were simply ravaged.

He carried the bag into Ishmael's tent. He took off his desert robes and donned a white English shirt, a striped tie, grey socks and a brown checked suit. When he tried to put on the shoes he discovered that his feet had swollen; it was agonizing to attempt to force them into the hard new leather. In the end he slit the shoes with his curved knife and wore them loose.

He wanted more: a hot bath, a haircut, cool soothing cream for his sores, a silk shirt, a gold bracelet, a cold bottle of champagne and a warm soft woman. For those he would have to wait.

When he emerged from the tent the nomads looked at him as if he were a stranger. Ishmael came to him. The cousins embraced.

Achmed took a wallet from the pocket of his jacket to check his papers. Looking at the identity card, he realized that once again he was Alexander Wolff, age thirty-four, of Villa les Oliviers, Garden City, Cairo, a businessman, ancestry—European.

He put on his hat, picked up the two remaining cases—one heavy, one light—and set off to walk across the last few miles of desert to the town. The ancient caravan route led through a mountain pass and at last merged with a modern road. On one side were the yellow, dusty, barren hills; on the other were lush fields of cotton squared off with irrigation ditches, where the peasants bent over their crops. Walking north on the road, smelling the cool damp breeze off the nearby Nile, observing the increasing signs of urban civilization, Wolff began to feel human again. Finally he heard the engine of a car, and he knew he was safe.

The vehicle was approaching him from the direction of Asyût. It was a military jeep. As it came closer he saw the British army uniforms of the men in it, and he realized he had left behind one danger only to face another.

Deliberately he made himself calm. I have every right to be here, he thought. I was born in Alexandria. I am Egyptian by nationality. I own a house in Cairo. My papers are all genuine. I am a wealthy man, a European. I am also a German spy behind enemy lines. . . .

The jeep screeched to a halt in a cloud of dust. One of the men jumped out. He had three cloth pips on each shoulder of his uniform shirt: a captain. He walked with a limp.

The captain said, "Where the devil have you come from?"

Wolff put down his cases and jerked a thumb back over his shoulder. "My car broke down on the desert road."

"I'd better see your papers, please."

Wolff handed them over. The captain examined them, then looked up. "You seem all in, Mr. Wolff. How long have you been walking?"

"Since yesterday afternoon," he said with a weariness that was not entirely faked. "I got a bit lost."

"You've been out here all *night?* Good Lord, you'd better have a lift with us." He turned to the jeep. "Corporal, take the gentleman's cases."

Wolff opened his mouth to protest, then shut it again abruptly. A man who had been walking all night would be only too glad to have someone take his luggage. As the corporal hefted the bags into the back of the jeep, Wolff realized with a sinking feeling that he had not even bothered to lock them. How could I be so stupid? he thought. He knew the answer. He was still in tune with the desert, where the last thing anyone wanted to steal was a radio transmitter that had to be plugged into a power outlet. Now he had to think of policemen and papers and locks and lies. He resolved to take more care, and climbed into the jeep.

The captain got in beside him and said to the driver, "Back into town." To Wolff he said, "Oh, by the way, I'm Captain Newman." He stuck out his hand.

Wolff shook it and looked more closely at the man. He was terribly young—early twenties, at a guess—with a boyish forelock and a ready smile; but there was in his demeanour that weary maturity that comes early to fighting men. Wolff asked him, "Seen any action?"

"Some." Captain Newman touched his lame leg. "Did this at

Cyrenaica—the Western Desert—that's why they sent me to this one-horse town." He grinned. "Where does your accent come from?"

The sudden question took Wolff by surprise. It had been intended to, he thought; Captain Newman was sharp-witted. Fortunately Wolff had a prepared answer. "My parents were Boers who came from South Africa to Egypt. I grew up speaking Afrikaans and Arabic." He hesitated, nervous of seeming too eager to explain. "The name Wolff is Dutch, originally."

Newman seemed politely interested. "What brings you here?"

"I have business interests in several towns up the river." He smiled. "I like to pay them surprise visits."

They were entering Asyût. By Egyptian standards it was a large town, with factories, hospitals, a Muslim university and some sixty thousand inhabitants. Wolff was about to ask to be dropped at the railway station when Newman saved him from that error. "We'll take you to Nasif's garage," the captain said. "He has a tow truck."

Wolff forced himself to say, "Thank you." He swallowed drily. He was still not thinking fast enough. It's the damn desert, he thought; it's slowed me down. He looked at his watch. He had time to go through a charade at the garage and still catch the daily train three hundred miles north to Cairo. He would have to go into the place until the soldiers drove away. He would make inquiries about car parts or something, then walk to the station. With luck, the garageman and Newman might never compare notes on the subject of Alex Wolff.

The jeep drove through the busy, narrow streets. The familiar sights of an Egyptian town pleased Wolff: the women carrying bundles on their heads, the sharp characters in sunglasses, the tiny shops spilling out into the rutted streets, the battered cars and the overloaded asses. They stopped in front of a row of low, mud-brick buildings. The road was half-blocked by an ancient truck and the remains of a cannibalized Fiat.

Newman said, "I'll have to leave you here. Duty calls."

Wolffe shook his hand. "You've been very kind."

"I don't like to dump you this way," Newman continued. "You've had a bad time. Tell you what—I'll leave Corporal Cox to look after you."

Wolff said, "It's kind, but really—"

Newman was not listening. "Get the man's bags, Cox. I want you to take care of him—understand?"

"Yes, sir!" said Cox.

Wolff groaned inwardly. Captain Newman's kindness was becoming a nuisance—could that possibly be intentional? Wolff realized that his plan of slipping unobserved into Egypt might well fail. He and Cox got out, and the jeep pulled away.

Wolff walked into Nasif's garage, and Cox followed, carrying the cases. Nasif, a smiling young man, was working on a car battery by the light of an oil lamp. Wolff spoke to him in rapid Egyptian Arabic. "My car has broken down. They say you have a tow truck."

"Yes. We can leave right away. Where is the car?"

"On the desert road, forty or fifty miles out. It's a Ford. But we're not coming with you." He took out his wallet and gave Nasif an English pound note. "You'll find me at the Grand Hotel by the railway station."

Nasif took the money with alacrity. "Very good!"

Wolff nodded curtly and turned around. Walking out of the garage with Cox in tow, he looked at his watch. He still had time to catch the train. He would be able to get rid of Cox in the lobby of the hotel, then get something to eat and drink while he was waiting, if he was quick.

Cox was a short, dark man with some kind of British regional accent which Wolff could not identify. He looked about Wolff's age, and as he was still a corporal he was probably not too bright.

They entered the hotel. Wolff turned to Cox. "Thank you, Corporal. I think you could get back to work now."

"No hurry, sir," Cox said cheerfully. "I'll carry your bags up."

"I'm sure they have porters here—"

"Wouldn't trust 'em, sir, if I were you."

The situation was becoming more and more like a nightmare or a farce, in which well-intentioned people pushed him into increasingly senseless behaviour in consequence of one small lie. It crossed his mind with terrifying absurdity that perhaps they knew everything and were toying with him. He pushed the thought aside. To Cox he said, "Thank you."

He turned to the desk and asked for a room. He looked at his watch: he had fifteen minutes left. A Nubian porter led them upstairs to the room. Wolff tipped him at the door. Cox put the cases on the bed.

"Well, Corporal," Wolff began, "you've been very helpful—"

"Let me unpack for you, sir," Cox said.

"No, thank you," Wolff said firmly. "I want to lie down."

"You go ahead and lie down," Cox persisted generously. "It won't take me—"

"Don't open that!"

Cox was lifting the lid of the small case. Wolff reached inside his jacket, thinking, damn the man, now I'm blown and can I do this quietly? The little corporal stared at the neat stacks of new English pound notes which filled the case. He said, "My God, you're loaded!" Cox began to turn, saying, "What do you want with all that—"

Wolff pulled out the wicked, curved, bedouin knife, and it glinted in his hand as his eyes met Cox's, and Cox flinched and opened his mouth to shout; and then the razor-sharp blade sliced deep into his throat, and his shout of fear came as a bloody gurgle and he died; and Wolff felt nothing, only disappointment.

Chapter 2

It was May, and the khamsin was blowing, a hot dusty wind from the south. Standing under the shower, William Vandam had the depressing thought that this would be the only time he would feel cool all day. He turned off the water and dried himself rapidly. His body was full of small aches. He had played cricket the day before, for the first time in years. General Staff Intelligence had got up a team to play the doctors from the field hospital—spies versus quacks, they had called it—and Vandam, fielding on the boundary, had been run ragged. He had to admit he was not in good condition. Gin had sapped his strength, and cigarettes had shortened his wind, and he had too many worries to concentrate on the game.

He lit a cigarette, coughed and started to shave. He always smoked while he was shaving—it was the only way he knew to relieve the boredom of the inevitable daily task. Fifteen years ago he had sworn he would grow a beard as soon as he got out of the army, but he was still in the army.

He dressed in the everyday uniform: heavy sandals, socks, bush shirt, khaki shorts, and went downstairs. Gaafar was in the kitchen, making tea. Vandam's servant was an elderly Copt with a bald head and a shuffling walk, and pretensions to be an English butler. That he would never be, but he had a little dignity and he was honest. Vandam said, "Is Billy up?"

"Yes, sir, he's coming down directly."

Vandam nodded. A small pan of water was bubbling on the stove. Vandam put an egg in to boil and set the timer. He made toast, buttered it, then took the egg out of the water and decapitated it. Billy came into the kitchen and said, "Good morning, Dad."

Vandam smiled at his ten-year-old son. "Breakfast is ready."

The boy began to eat. Vandam sat opposite him with a cup of tea, watching. People said Billy was like his father, but Vandam could not see the resemblance. However, he could see traces of Billy's mother: the grey eyes, the delicate skin and the faintly supercilious expression which came over his face when someone crossed him.

Vandam always prepared his son's breakfast. Most of the time the servant looked after the boy, but Vandam liked to keep this little ritual for himself. Often it was the only time he was with Billy all day.

After breakfast Billy brushed his teeth while Gaafar got out Vandam's motorcycle, a fast BSA 350, very practical for snaking through Cairo traffic jams. Billy came back wearing his school cap, and Vandam put on his uniform hat. As they did every day, they saluted each other. Billy said, "Right, sir—let's go and win the war." Then they went out.

MAJOR VANDAM'S office was in one of a group of buildings surrounded by barbed-wire fencing which made up General Headquarters, Middle East, Cairo. There was an incident report on his desk when he arrived. He sat down, lit a cigarette and began to read.

The report came from Asyût, three hundred miles south, and at first Vandam could not see why it had been marked for intelligence. A patrol had picked up a hitchhiking European who had subsequently murdered a corporal with a knife. The body had been discovered last night, several hours after the death. A man answering the hitchhiker's description had bought a ticket to Cairo at the railway station. There was no indication of motive.

The Egyptian police force and the British military police would be investigating already, in Asyût and in Cairo. What reason was there for intelligence to get involved? Vandam frowned and thought again. Then he called Asyût. Eventually the army camp switchboard got Captain Newman to a phone.

Vandam said, "This knife murder looks like a blown cover."

"That occurred to me, sir," said Newman. He sounded like a young man. "That's why I marked the report for intelligence."

"Good thinking. Tell me, what was your impression of the man? I've got your description here—six foot, twelve stone, dark hair and eyes—but that doesn't tell me what he was *like*."

"Well, to be candid," Newman said, "at first I wasn't suspicious of him. He seemed an upright citizen: decently dressed, well spoken, with an accent he said was Dutch, or rather Afrikaans. His papers were genuine."

"But . . . ?"

"He told me he was checking on his business interests in Upper Egypt. But he didn't strike me as the kind of man to spend his life investing in a few shops and cotton farms. He was much more the assured cosmopolitan type. If he had money to invest, it would probably be with a London stockbroker or a Swiss bank. Then it occurred to me that he had, as it were, just appeared in the desert, and I didn't really know where he might have come from . . . so I told poor old Cox to stay with him, on the pretence of helping him, until we had a chance to check his story. I should have arrested the man, of course, but I had only the most slender suspicion—"

"I don't think anyone's blaming you, Captain," said Vandam. "You did well to remember the name and address from the papers. Alex Wolff, Villa les Oliviers, Garden City, right?"

"Yes, sir."

"All right, keep me in touch with any developments at your end." Vandam hung up. Newman's suspicions chimed with his own instincts about the killing. He decided to speak to his superior, Lieutenant Colonel Bogge, a deputy director of military intelligence. Bogge was responsible for personnel security, and most of his time was spent administering the censorship apparatus. Vandam's concern was security leaks by means other than letters. He and his men had several hundred agents in Cairo and Alexandria; he had informants in most clubs and bars and among the domestic staffs of the more important Arab politicians. King Faruk's valet worked for Vandam, and so, on occasion, did Abdullah, Cairo's wealthiest thief, whose services were for sale to any and all sides. Vandam was interested in who was talking too much, and who was listening; and among the listeners, Arab nationalists were his main target. However, the mystery man from Asyût seemed to be a different kind of threat.

Vandam's wartime career had so far been distinguished by one spectacular success and one great failure. The failure took place in Turkey, where Rashid Ali, Iraq's nationalist prime minister, had escaped into exile. The Germans wanted to get him out and use him for propaganda. Vandam's job had been to make sure Ali stayed in Istanbul, but Ali had switched clothes with a German agent and slipped out of the country under Vandam's nose. A few days later Ali was making nationalist speeches to the Middle East on Nazi radio. Vandam had redeemed himself in Cairo, where he uncovered a major security leak: a senior American diplomat reporting to Washington in an insecure code. The code had been changed, the leak stopped up and Vandam promoted to major.

Had he been a peacetime soldier, he would have been proud of his triumph and reconciled to his defeat: "You win some, you lose some." But in war an officer's mistakes killed people. In the aftermath of the Rashid Ali affair an agent had been murdered, a woman, and Vandam had not been able to forgive himself.

He knocked on Lieutenant Colonel Bogge's door and walked in. Reggie Bogge was a short, square man in his fifties, with an immaculate uniform and brilliantined black hair. He had a nervous cough which he used when he did not know quite what to say, which was often. He sat behind a huge curved desk going through his in-tray.

As Vandam took a chair, Bogge said, "More bloody bad news. We expected Rommel to attack the Gazala line head-on. Should have known better. He went around our southern flank and took the Seventh Armoured's headquarters."

It was a depressingly familiar story, and Vandam suddenly felt weary. "When are we going to *stop* him?" he said.

"He won't get much farther." Bogge did not want to criticize the generals. "What have you there?"

Vandam gave him the incident report. "It looks like a blown cover."

Bogge read the report. "You mean he was a spy?" He laughed contemptuously. "How d'you suppose he got to Asyût—by parachute?"

That was the trouble with Bogge, thought Vandam: he had to ridicule the idea, as an excuse for not thinking of it himself. "It's not impossible for a small plane to sneak through. It's not impossible to cross the desert, either."

Bogge sailed the report through the air across the desk. "Not very likely," he said. "Don't waste any time on that one."

"Very good, sir." Vandam picked up the report from the floor, suppressing the familiar frustrated anger. "I'll ask the police to keep us informed of their progress, just for the file."

On the way back to his own office, a woman in a white hospital coat saluted him. He returned the salute absentmindedly. The woman said, "Major Vandam, isn't it?"

He stopped and looked at her. She had been a spectator at the previous day's cricket match, and they had exchanged pleasantries afterwards.

"Dr. Abuthnot," he said. "Good morning." She was tall, about his age, a surgeon with the rank of captain. He was a widower and she was single, and this was the second time in a week they had been seen talking together in public: by now the English colony in Cairo would have them practically engaged.

She said, "You worked hard yesterday."

Vandam smiled. "I enjoyed myself, though."

"So did I," she said, returning his smile.

"How did you manage to become a surgeon?" he asked with interest. "It's not easy for a woman."

"I fought tooth and nail. You're a little unconventional, too, I'm told, bringing up your child by yourself."

"No choice after his mother died. If I had wanted to send him back to England, I wouldn't have been able to—you can't get passage unless you're disabled or a general."

"But you didn't want to."

"He's my son. I don't want anyone else to bring him up—nor does he."

"I understand. I'm ashamed of myself, I've been prying." She smiled and turned away.

Vandam watched her go. She was trim, elegant and self-possessed: she reminded him of Angela, his late wife.

He entered his office, his mind once more on Captain Newman's report. He had no intention of forgetting about the Asyût murder. Bogge could go to hell. Vandam would go to work. First he called the Egyptian police and confirmed that they would be checking the hotels and flophouses of Cairo today. He contacted field security and asked them to step up their spot checks on identity papers for a few days. He told the British paymaster general to keep a special watch for forged currency. He advised the wireless listening service to be alert for a new, local transmitter; and he detailed a sergeant to visit every radio shop in the area and ask them to report any sales of parts and equipment which might be used to make or repair a transmitter.

Then he went to the Villa les Oliviers, the address on Alex Wolff's papers. The house got its name from a small public garden across the street where a grove of olive trees was now in bloom, shedding white petals like dust onto the dry, brown grass.

The house had a high wall broken by a heavy, carved wooden gate. Using the ornamentation for footholds, Vandam climbed over the gate and found himself in a large courtyard. The whitewashed walls were grubby, their windows blinded by closed, peeling shutters. The place had not been lived in for at least a year. He opened a shutter, broke a pane of glass, reached through to unfasten the window, and climbed over the sill into the house.

It did not look like the home of a European, he thought as he walked through the dark, cool rooms. There were no hunting prints on the walls, no rows of smart novels, no furniture imported from Harrods. Instead, the place was furnished with large cushions, low tables, handwoven rugs and hanging tapestries.

Upstairs, behind a locked door which he kicked open, he found a clean and tidy study, with a few pieces of rather luxurious furniture: a wide, low divan covered in velvet, a hand-carved coffee table, a beautifully inlaid desk and a leather chair. In the desk drawer Vandam found company reports from Switzerland, Germany and the United States. Gathering dust on a shelf behind the desk were books in several languages: nineteenth-century French novels; the Shorter Oxford Dictionary; a volume of Arabic poetry, with erotic illustrations, and the Bible in German. There were no personal documents, no letters, not a single photograph.

Vandam sat in the soft leather chair behind the desk and looked around the room. It was a masculine room, the home of a cosmopolitan intellectual, a man who was on the one hand careful, precise and tidy, and on the other hand sensitive and sensual.

Vandam was intrigued. A European name, a totally Arabic house. A wealth of information about a character, but not a single clue which might help find the man. There should have been bank statements, tradesmen's bills, a birth certificate and a will, photographs of parents or children. The man had left no trace of his identity, as if he knew that one day someone would come looking for him.

Vandam said aloud, "Alex Wolff, who are you?"

He got up from the chair and left the house. He climbed back over the gate and dropped into the street. Across the road an Arab in a green-striped *galabia*—as the natives' cotton shifts were called—sat cross-legged on the ground in the shade of the olive trees, watching Vandam incuriously. Vandam thought of other sources from which he could seek information about the owner of this house: municipal records, local tradesmen who might have delivered there when the place was occupied, neighbours. He would put two of his men on it, and tell Bogge some cover story. He climbed onto his motorcycle and kicked it into life. The engine roared and Vandam drove away.

FULL OF ANGER and despair Wolff—wearing the *galabia* he had bought in the native market—sat opposite his home and watched the British officer ride away. The officer, his arrogant face and his prying eyes hidden in the shadow of the peaked uniform cap, had broken in and violated Wolff's domain. Wolff wished he could have seen the man's face; he would like to kill him one day.

He had thought of this place all through his journey. In Berlin

and Tripoli, in the desert crossing, in the fear and haste of his flight from Asyût, the villa had represented a safe haven, a place to rest and get clean and whole again. Now he would have to go away and stay away.

He had remained outside all morning, wearing the *galabia* just in case Captain Newman should have remembered the address and sent somebody to search the house. It had been a mistake to show genuine papers. He could see that, with hindsight. The trouble was, he mistrusted forgeries made by German intelligence. Meeting other spies, he had heard horror stories about obvious errors in their documents: botched printing, misspellings of common English words. Wolff had weighed the alternatives and picked what seemed the least risky. He had been wrong, and now he had no place to go.

He stood, picked up his two cases and began to walk.

He thought of his family. His mother and his stepfather were dead, but he had three stepbrothers and a stepsister in Cairo. It would be hard for them to hide him. They would be questioned as soon as the British realized their connection to him; they might tell lies for his sake, but their servants would surely talk.

He left the Garden City and headed downtown. The streets were even busier than when he had left Cairo two years before. There were countless uniforms—not just British, but Australian, New Zealand, Polish, Yugoslav, Palestinian, Indian and Greek—and the beggars and peddlers were out in force, taking advantage of them. The slow, verminous trams were more crowded than ever, with passengers perched on the running boards and sitting cross-legged on the roofs. There seemed to be a shortage of vehicle parts, for many of the cars had broken windows, flat tyres and ailing engines. The only decent cars were the monstrous American limousines of the wealthy pashas, and the occasional pre-war English Austin. Mixing with the motor vehicles were the horse-drawn gharries, the mule carts of the peasants, and the livestock—camels, sheep and goats.

And the noise—Wolff had forgotten the noise.

The trams rang their bells continuously. In traffic jams all the cars hooted all the time. The drivers of carts and camels yelled at the tops of their voices. Shops and cafés blared Arab music from cheap radios turned to full volume. Street vendors called. Dogs barked. From time to time it would all be swamped by the roar of an aeroplane.

This is my town, Wolff thought; they can't catch me here.

There were a dozen well-known pensions designed for tourists. He rejected them as too obvious. Finally he remembered a cheap lodging house run by nuns at Bulaq, the port district. It catered mainly for the sailors who came down the Nile in steam tugs and feluccas laden with cotton, coal, paper and stone. Nobody would think to look for him there.

The hostel was a large, decaying building which had once been the villa of some pasha. A black-robed nun was watering a tiny bed of flowers in front of the building. Through the arch Wolff saw a cool, quiet hall. He had walked several miles today, with his heavy cases; he looked forward to a rest.

Two Egyptian policemen came out of the hostel.

Wolff's heart sank. He turned his back and walked on. It was worse than he had imagined. The police must be checking *everywhere*. He was beginning to feel as he had in the desert, as if he had been walking forever without getting anywhere.

He saw a taxi, a big old Ford with steam hissing out from under its bonnet. He jumped in and gave the driver an address. The car jerked away in third gear, apparently the only gear that worked. The taxi took him to Coptic Cairo, the ancient Christian ghetto. He paid the driver and went down the steps to the entrance.

The ghetto was an island of darkness and quiet in the stormy sea of Cairo. Wolff walked its narrow passages and went into the smallest of the five ancient churches. The service was about to begin. Wolff put his precious cases beside a pew and sat down.

The choir began to chant a passage of scripture in Arabic. Wolff settled into his seat. He would be safe here until darkness fell. Then he would take off the *galabia* and try his last shot.

Chapter 3

The Cha-Cha was a large open-air nightclub in a garden beside the river. It was packed, as usual. Wolff finally got a table and a bottle of champagne. The evening was warm and the stage lights made it worse. The audience was rowdy and drunk. They began to shout for the star of the show, Sonja Fahzi. Then there was a roll of drums, the lights went off and silence descended.

When the spotlight came on Sonja stood still in the centre of the stage with her arms stretched skywards. She wore diaphanous trousers and a sequined halter, and her body was powdered white. Music began—drums and a pipe—and she started to move. Wolff sipped champagne and watched, smiling. She was still the best.

She jerked her hips slowly, stamping one foot and then the other. Her arms began to tremble, then her shoulders moved and her breasts shook; and then her famous belly rolled hypnotically. The rhythm quickened. She closed her eyes. Each part of her body seemed to move independently of the rest. The audience was silent, perspiring, mesmerized. She went faster and faster, seeming to be transported. The music climaxed with a bang. In the instant of silence that followed Sonja uttered a short, sharp cry; then she fell backwards, her legs folded beneath her until her head touched the boards of the stage. She held the position for a moment, then the lights went out. The audience rose to their feet with a roar of applause. The lights came up, and she was gone.

Sonja never took encores.

Wolff gave the waiter a pound—three months' wages for most Egyptians—to lead him backstage. The waiter showed him the door to Sonja's dressing room, then went away. Wolff walked in.

She was sitting on a stool, wearing a silk robe, taking off her make-up. She saw him in the mirror and spun around. Wolff said, "Hello, Sonja."

Her eyes flashed with anger. "What are you doing here?"

She had not changed. She was a handsome woman. She had glossy black hair, long and thick; large, slightly protruding brown eyes with lush eyelashes; high cheekbones and an arched nose, gracefully arrogant; a full mouth with even, white teeth. Her body was all smooth curves, but because she was taller than average she did not look plump.

Wolff put down his cases and sat on the divan. She rose and stood with her hands on her hips, her chin thrust forward, her breasts outlined in green silk. "You're beautiful," he said.

"Get out of here."

He studied her carefully. She appeared angry and scornful, but did she mean it?

"I need help," he said levelly. "The British are after me. They're watching my house. I want to move in with you."

"Go to hell," she said.

"Give me a minute. Let me tell you why I walked out on you."

"After two years no excuse is good enough." She glared at him a moment, then opened the door. He thought she was going to throw him out. He watched her face as she looked back at him, holding the door. Then she put her head outside and yelled, "Somebody get me a drink!" Wolff relaxed a little.

Sonja came back in and closed the door. "A minute," she said. She went back to her stool and resumed working on her face.

He hesitated. How would he explain why he had left her without saying goodbye and never contacted her since? Reluctant as he was to share his secret, he had to tell her the truth, for he was desperate and she was his only chance.

He said, "Do you remember I went to Beirut in 1938? I went there to see a German army officer. He asked me to work for Germany in the coming war. I agreed."

She turned from her mirror and faced him. He saw in her eyes something like hope. She wanted to believe him.

"They told me to come back to Cairo and wait. Two years ago I heard from them. They wanted me to go to Berlin. I went. I did a training course, then I worked in the Levant. I went back to Berlin in February for briefing on a new assignment. They sent me here—"

"You're a *spy?*" she said incredulously. "I don't believe it."

"Look." He picked up a suitcase and opened it. "This is a radio, for sending messages to Rommel." He closed it again and opened the other. "This is my financing."

She stared at the neat stacks of notes. "It's a *fortune.*"

There was a knock at the door. Wolff closed the case. A waiter came in with a bottle of champagne in a bucket of ice. Seeing Wolff, he said, "Shall I bring another glass?"

"No," Sonja said impatiently. "Go away."

The waiter left. Wolff opened the wine, filled the glass, gave it to Sonja then took a long drink from the bottle.

"Listen," he said. "Our army needs to know about British strength—numbers of men, which divisions are in the field, names of commanders, quality of weapons and equipment, battle plans.

99

We can find these things out. Then when the Germans take Cairo we will be heroes."

"We?"

"You can help, first by giving me a place to live. You hate the British, don't you? You want to see them thrown out?"

"I would do it for anyone but you."

"Sonja. If I had sent you a postcard from Berlin, the British would have thrown you in gaol. You must not be angry." He lowered his voice. "We can bring those old times back. We'll have good food and the best champagne, new clothes and beautiful parties. We'll go to Berlin, you've always wanted to dance in Berlin, you'll be a star there. We—" He paused. None of this was getting through to her. It was time to play his last card. "How is Fawzi?"

Sonja lowered her eyes. "She left."

Wolff put both hands to Sonja's neck. With his thumbs under her chin he forced her to stand. "I'll find another Fawzi for us," he said softly. He saw that her eyes were suddenly moist. "I'm the only one who understands what you need."

Sonja closed her eyes. "I hate you," she moaned.

A FEW NIGHTS LATER in the cool of the evening, Wolff walked along the towpath beside the Nile towards Sonja's houseboat, the *Jihan*. The sores had gone from his face. He wore a new white suit, and he carried two bags full of his favourite groceries.

The island suburb of Zamalek was peaceful. The raucous noise of central Cairo could be heard only faintly across a wide stretch of water. The calm, muddy river lapped gently against the houseboats lined along the bank.

Sonja's was smaller but more richly furnished than most. A gangplank led from the path to the top deck. Wolff boarded the boat and went down the ladder to the interior. It was crowded with chairs, divans, tables, cabinets full of knick-knacks. There was a tiny kitchen in the prow. Floor-to-ceiling curtains of maroon velvet divided the space in two, closing off the bedroom. Beyond the bedroom, in the stern, was a bathroom.

Sonja was sitting on a cushion painting her toenails before going to the Cha-Cha Club. Wolff put his bags on a table and began to take things out.

"French champagne . . . English marmalade . . . German sausage . . . quails' eggs . . . Scotch salmon."

Sonja looked up, astonished. "Nobody can find things like that —there's a war on."

Wolff smiled. "There's a little Greek grocer in Qulali. His shop is the only place in North Africa where you can get caviar."

She dipped into a bag. "Caviar!" She took the lid off the jar and began to eat with her fingers. Wolff put a bottle of champagne in the fridge. He took an English-language newspaper out of one of the bags and began to look through it. "Still nothing about me in here." He had told Sonja of the events in Asyût.

"They're always late with the news," she said through a mouthful of caviar.

"It's not that. The British don't want people to suspect that the Germans have spies in Egypt. It looks bad."

She went into the bedroom to change. She called through the curtain, "Does that mean they've stopped looking for you?"

"No. I saw Abdullah in the marketplace. He says there's a Major Vandam who's keeping the pressure on."

Sonja said, "How does Abdullah know?"

"He's a thief, he hears things." Wolff went to the fridge and took out the bottle. It was not really cold enough, but he poured two glasses. Sonja came out, her face lightly made-up, wearing a sheer cherry-red dress and matching shoes. A couple of minutes later her taxi arrived. She drained her glass and left.

Wolff went to the cupboard where he kept the radio. He took out the English novel and the sheet of paper bearing the key to the code. He studied the key. Today was May 28. He had to add 42—the year—to 28 to arrive at the page number in the novel which he must use to encode his message. May was the fifth month, so every fifth letter on the page would be discounted.

He decided to send, "HAVE ARRIVED. ACKNOWLEDGE." Beginning at the top of page 70 of the book, he looked along the line of print for the letter *H*. It was the tenth character, discounting every fifth letter. In his code it would therefore be represented by the tenth letter of the alphabet, *J*. Next he needed an A. In the book, the third letter after the *H* was an A. The A of HAVE would therefore be represented by the third letter of the alphabet, *C*. There were special ways of dealing with rare letters, like *X*. To

101

decode the message a listener had to have both the book and the key, making the code unbreakable in theory and in practice.

When he had encoded his message he looked at his watch. He was always to transmit at midnight. He had a few hours. He poured another glass of champagne and decided to finish the caviar. He found a spoon and picked up the jar. It was empty. Sonja had eaten it all.

THE RUNWAY was a strip of desert hastily cleared of camel thorn and large rocks. Field Marshal Erwin Rommel looked down as the ground came up to meet him. The Feisler-Storch, a light aircraft used by German commanders for short trips around the battlefield, came down like a fly. The plane stopped and Rommel jumped out.

The heat hit him first, then the dust. It had been relatively cool up in the sky; now he felt as if he had stepped into a furnace. He began to perspire immediately. As soon as he breathed in, a thin layer of sand coated his lips. Von Mellenthin, his intelligence officer, ran towards him across the sand. "Kesselring's here."

"*Auch das noch*," said Rommel. "That's all I need."

Albert Kesselring, the smiling field marshal, represented everything Rommel disliked in the German armed forces. He was a General Staff officer, and Rommel hated the General Staff; he was a founder of the Luftwaffe, which had let Rommel down so often; and he was a snob.

Rommel stumped across the sand towards the command vehicle, with von Mellenthin in tow. They entered the back of the command vehicle, a huge truck. The shade was welcome. Kesselring was bent over a map. He looked up. "My dear Rommel, thank heaven you're back," he said silkily.

Rommel took off his cap. "I've been fighting a battle."

"So I gather. What happened?"

Rommel pointed to the map. "This is the Gazala line." It was a string of fortified "boxes" linked by minefields which ran from the coast at El Gazala due south into the desert for fifty miles. "We made a dogleg around the southern end of the line and hit them from behind. Then we ran out of fuel and ammunition." Rommel sat down heavily, suddenly feeling very tired. "Again," he added pointedly. Kesselring, as commander in chief (South), was responsible for Rommel's supplies. "But I'm winning," Rommel went on. "If I'd had my supplies, I'd be in Cairo now."

"You're not going to Cairo," Kesselring said sharply. "You're going to Tobruk. There you'll stay until I've taken Malta. Such are the Führer's orders."

"Of course." Rommel was not going to re-open that argument; not yet. Tobruk was the immediate objective. Once that fortified port was taken, the supply convoys from Europe could come directly to the front line, cutting out the long journey across the desert. "And to reach Tobruk we have to break the Gazala line."

"What's your next step?"

"I'm going to fall back and regroup."

"The British will chase us, but not immediately," said von Mellenthin. "They are always slow to press an advantage. But sooner or later they will try a breakout."

Rommel said, "The question is, when and where?"

"Indeed," von Mellenthin agreed. He seemed to hesitate, then said, "There is a little item in today's summaries which will interest you, sir. The spy checked in."

"The spy?" Then Rommel remembered. He had flown to the oasis of Gialo, deep in the Libyan desert, to brief the man before the spy began a long marathon walk. Wolff, that was his name. Rommel had been impressed by his courage. "Where was he calling from?"

"Cairo."

"So he got there. If he's capable of that, he's capable of anything. Perhaps he can foretell the breakout."

Kesselring broke in, "My God, you're not relying on spies now, are you? Intelligence from spies is the worst kind."

"I agree," Rommel said calmly. "But I have a feeling this one could be different."

Chapter 4

Elene Fontana looked at her face in the mirror and thought, I'm twenty-three. I must be losing my looks.

She leaned closer to the glass and examined herself carefully, searching for signs of deterioration. Her complexion was perfect.

Her round brown eyes were as clear as a mountain pool. There were no wrinkles. It was a childish face, delicately modelled, with a look of waiflike innocence. She smiled a small, intimate smile, with a hint of mischief about it, one she knew could make a man break out into a cold sweat.

She picked up the note and read it again.

My dear Elene,

I'm afraid it is all over. My wife has found out. Of course you can stay in the flat, but I can't pay the rent any more. I'm so sorry it happened this way—but I suppose we both knew it could not last forever. Good luck—

Your Claud

Just like that, she thought. She tore up the note and its cheap sentiments. Claud was a fat, half-French and half-Greek business-man. He was cultured and kind, but he cared nothing for Elene. He was the third in six years. It was her fault as much as the men's that the affairs broke up. The real cause was always the same: Elene was unhappy.

She contemplated the prospect of another affair. Perhaps he would be an Italian, with flashing eyes and glossy hair and per-fectly manicured hands. She might meet him in the bar of the Metropolitan Hotel, where the reporters drank. She would smile at him, and he would be lost. He would spend more and more time at the flat, and he would begin to pay the rent and the bills. Elene would then have everything she wanted: a home, money and affection. She would begin to wonder why she was so miser-able. There would be rows. She would throw a tantrum if he arrived half an hour late. Finally the crisis would come. His wife would get suspicious, or a child would fall ill, or he would run short of money.

And Elene would be back where she was now: drifting, alone, disreputable—and a year older.

Her eyes focused, and she saw again her face in the mirror. Her face was the cause of all this. Had she been ugly, she would always have yearned to live like this, and never discovered its hollowness. You led me astray, she thought; you pretended I was somebody else. You're not my face, you're a mask. I'm not a beautiful Cairo socialite of independent means, I'm a slum girl from Alexandria. I'm not Egyptian, I'm Jewish. My name is not Elene Fontana. It's Abigail Asnani.

And I want to go home.

THE YOUNG MAN behind the desk at the Jewish agency in Cairo wore a *yarmulka*. Apart from a wisp of beard, his cheeks were smooth. He seemed confused. Elene was used to this; most men got a little flustered when she smiled at them. He said, "But why do you want to go to Palestine?"

"I'm Jewish," she said. "All my family are dead. I'm wasting my life." The first part was not true; the second part was.

"What work would you do in Palestine? It's mostly agricultural."

"That's fine."

He smiled gently. He was recovering his composure. "I mean no offence, but you don't look like a farmhand. What work do you do now?"

"I sing, and when I can't get singing I dance, and when I can't get dancing I wait at tables." She had done all three at one time or another. "Why all the questions? Is Palestine accepting only college graduates now?"

"It's very tough to get in. The British have imposed a quota, and all the places are taken by refugees from the Nazis."

"Why didn't you tell me that before?" she said angrily.

"Two reasons. One is that we can get people in illegally. The other. . . . Would you wait a minute? I must telephone someone."

He went into a back room to phone. Elene waited impatiently. She felt a little foolish. She might have guessed they would ask her questions; she should have prepared her answers. She should have come dressed in something a little less glamorous.

The young man came back. "It's so warm," he said. "Shall we go across the street for a cold drink?"

So that was the game. "No," she said, "you're too young for me."

He was terribly embarrassed. "Oh, please don't misunderstand me. There's someone I want you to meet, that's all."

She had nothing to lose, she thought. "All right."

He held the door for her. They crossed the street, ducked under a striped awning and stepped into a café. The young man ordered lemon juice; Elene had gin and tonic. She said, "You can get people in illegally."

"Sometimes." He took half his drink in one gulp. "One reason we do it, is if people have done a lot for the cause."

"You mean I have to earn the right to go to Palestine?"

"Look, maybe one day all Jews will have the right to go there. But while there are quotas there have to be criteria."

Elene asked, "What do I have to do?"

"We don't like the British much, but any enemy of the Nazis is a friend of ours, so at the moment we're working with British intelligence. I think you could help them."

"For God's sake! How?"

A shadow fell across the table, and the young man looked up. "Ah!" he said. He looked back at Elene. "I want you to meet my friend, Major William Vandam."

He was a tall man, with wide shoulders. Elene guessed he was close to forty and beginning to go a little soft. He had a round, open face topped by wiry brown hair. He shook her hand, sat down, lit a cigarette and ordered gin. He wore a stern expression, as if he thought life was a very serious business.

The young man from the agency asked him. "What's the news?"

"The Gazala line is holding, but it's fierce out there."

Vandam's voice was a surprise. He spoke precisely but softly, with a slight burr on the *r*.

"Where do you come from, Major?" she asked him.

"Dorset. Southwest England. Why do you ask?"

"I was wondering about your accent."

"You're observant. I thought I had no accent."

"Just a trace."

The young man took his leave. "I'll let Major Vandam explain everything. I hope you will work with him. It's very important."

Vandam shook his hand, thanked him, and the young man went out. Vandam said to Elene, "Tell me about yourself."

"No," she said. "You tell me about *your*self."

He raised an eyebrow at her, faintly startled, a little amused. "All right," he said. "Cairo is full of secrets: our strengths, our weaknesses and our plans. The Germans have people in Cairo trying to get those secrets. It's my job to stop them."

"That's simple."

He considered. "It's simple, but it's not easy."

He took everything she said seriously. She rather liked it; men generally treated her conversation like background music.

He was waiting. "It's your turn," he said.

Suddenly she wanted to tell him the truth. "I'm a lousy singer and a mediocre dancer, but sometimes I find a rich man to pay my bills."

He said nothing, but he looked taken aback.

The imp of mischief seized her. "Isn't that what most women do when they get married—find a man to pay the bills? I just turn them around a little faster than the average housewife."

Vandam burst out laughing. Suddenly he looked a different man. He threw back his head and all the tension went out of his body. When the laugh subsided they grinned at one another. Then he was serious again. "My problem is information. Nobody tells an Englishman anything. That's where you come in. Because you're Egyptian, you hear the kind of gossip that never comes my way. Because you're Jewish, you'll pass it to me. I hope."

"What kind of gossip?"

"I'm interested in anyone who's curious about the British army. In particular, I'm looking for a man called Alex Wolff. He used to live in Cairo and he has recently returned. He is certainly making inquiries about British forces."

Elene shrugged. "After all that build-up I was expecting to be asked to do something much more dramatic—waltz with Rommel and pick his pockets."

Vandam laughed again. Elene thought, I could get fond of that laugh.

He said, "Well, mundane though it is, will you do it? I need people like you, Miss Fontana. You're observant, you have a perfect cover, and you're obviously intelligent. Please excuse me for being so direct—"

"Don't apologize, I love it," she said. "Keep talking."

"Most of my people are not very reliable. They do it for the money, whereas you have a better motive—"

"Wait a minute," she interrupted. "I want money, too. What does the job pay?"

"How much do you want?"

"Enough to pay the rent of my flat. Seventy-five a month."

"You'd have to be awfully useful to justify seventy-five a month. But all right, a month's trial."

Elene tried not to look triumphant. "How do I contact you?"

"Send me a message." He took out a pencil and a scrap of paper. "I'll give you my address and phone number, at GHQ and at home. As soon as I hear from you, I'll come to your place."

She wrote down her address. "If I'm asked who you are, I'll say you're my lover."

He looked away. "Very well."

"But you'd better act the part." She kept a straight face. "You must bring armfuls of flowers and boxes of chocolates . . . William."

"I don't know . . ."

"Don't Englishmen give their mistresses flowers and chocolates?"

He looked at her unblinkingly. "I've never had a mistress."

Elene thought, I stand corrected. She said. "Then you've got a lot to learn."

They rose. "I'll look forward to hearing from you," he said. She shook his hand and walked away. Somehow she had the feeling he was not watching her go.

Chapter 5

Alex Wolff wore his *galabia* and a fez, and stood thirty yards from the gate of GHQ—British headquarters—selling paper fans.

The hue and cry had died down. He had not seen the British conducting a spot check on identity papers for a week. This Vandam character could not keep up the pressure indefinitely.

Wolff had gone to GHQ as soon as he felt reasonably safe. Getting into Cairo had been a triumph, but it was useless unless he could get the information Rommel wanted and quickly.

Somewhere inside GHQ there were pieces of paper which gave numbers of troops, names of divisions, numbers of tanks in the field and in reserve, quantities of ammunition, food and fuel, the strategic and tactical intentions of the British high command. It was those pieces of paper Wolff wanted. That was why he was selling fans outside GHQ.

For their headquarters the British had taken over a number of the large houses—most of them owned by pashas—in the Garden City suburb. The commandeered homes were surrounded by a barbed-wire fence. People in uniform were passed quickly through the gate, but civilians were stopped and questioned at length while the sentries made phone calls to verify credentials.

Wolff had spent a lot of time, back in the Abwehr spy school, learning to recognize uniforms, regimental identification marks and the faces of literally hundreds of senior British officers. Here, for several mornings, he had peeked through the windows of staff cars to see colonels, generals, admirals, squadron leaders, and the commander in chief, Sir Claude Auchinleck, himself.

The General Staff travelled by car but their aides walked. Each morning the captains and majors arrived on foot, carrying briefcases. Towards noon some of them left, still carrying their briefcases. Each day Wolff followed one of the aides.

Most of the aides worked at GHQ, and their secret papers would be locked up inside. But a few of them had offices in other parts of the city; and they had to carry their briefing papers with them between one office and another. One of them went to the Semiramis Hotel, which housed something called British Troops in Egypt. Two went to the barracks in the Kasr-el-Nil. A fourth went to an unmarked building in the Shari Suleiman Pasha. Wolff wanted to get into those briefcases. Today he would do a dry run.

When the aides came out Wolff followed the pair that went to the barracks. A minute later Abdullah emerged from a café and fell into step beside him, and asked, "Those two?"

"Those two."

Abdullah was a fat man with a steel tooth. He was one of the richest men in Cairo, but unlike most rich Arabs he did not ape the Europeans. He wore sandals, a dirty robe and a fez. His greasy hair curled around his ears and his fingernails were black. His wealth came from crime. Abdullah was a thief.

Wolff liked him. He was sly, deceitful, cruel, generous, and always laughing; for Wolff he embodied the age-old vices and virtues of the Middle East. His army of children, grandchildren, nephews and nieces had been burgling houses and picking pockets in Cairo for thirty years. He had tentacles everywhere.

They followed the two officers into the modern city centre. Abdullah said, "Do you want one briefcase, or both?"

Wolff considered. One was a casual theft; two looked organized. "One," he said. "It doesn't matter which."

Wolff had considered going to Abdullah for help after the discovery that the Villa les Oliviers was no longer safe. He had decided not to. Abdullah could certainly have hidden him away somewhere, but as soon as he had Wolff concealed, he would have opened negotiations to sell him to the British. Abdullah divided the world in two: his family and the rest. He was utterly loyal to his family and trusted them completely; he would cheat everyone else and expected them to try to cheat him.

They came to a busy corner. The two officers crossed the road, dodging the traffic. Wolff was about to follow when Abdullah put a hand on his arm. "We'll do it here," Abdullah said.

Wolff looked around, observing the buildings, the road junction and the street vendors. He smiled. "It's perfect," he said.

They did it the next day. Abdullah had indeed chosen the perfect spot for the snatch. It was where a busy side street joined a main road. On the corner was a café with tables outside, reducing the pavement to half its width. Outside the café, on the side of the main road, was a bus stop, with people milling about on the already crowded pavement. The side street was a little clearer, but Abdullah had remedied this shortcoming by detailing two acrobats to perform there.

Wolff sat at the corner table and worried that things might go wrong. He was terrified of going to prison. He could live without good food and wine and girls, if he had the vast wild emptiness of the desert to console him; and he could forgo the freedom of the desert to live in a crowded city, if he had the urban luxuries to console him; but he could not lose both. The idea of living in a tiny, colourless cell, among the scum of the earth, eating bad food, never seeing the blue sky or the open plains . . . panic touched him. He pushed it out of his mind.

At eleven forty-five the large, grubby form of Abdullah waddled past the café. His expression was vacant but his small black eyes looked around sharply, checking his arrangements.

At five past twelve Wolff spotted two military caps among the massed heads in the distance. He sat on the edge of his chair. The officers came nearer. They were carrying their briefcases.

Across the street a parked car revved its idling engine. A bus drew up to the stop, and Wolff thought, Abdullah can't possibly have arranged *that:* it's a piece of luck, a bonus.

The officers were five yards from Wolff.

The car across the street, a big black Packard, pulled out suddenly. It came across the road like a charging elephant, motor screaming in low gear, heading for the side street, its horn blaring. On the corner, a few feet from where Wolff sat, it ploughed into the front of an old Fiat taxi.

The two officers stood beside Wolff's table and stared at the crash. The taxi driver, a young Arab in a Western shirt and a fez, leaped out of his car. A young Greek in a mohair suit jumped out of the Packard. The Arab slapped the Greek and the Greek punched the Arab. The people getting off the bus, and those who had been intending to get on it, came closer.

Around the corner, the acrobat who was standing on his colleague's head turned to look at the fight, seemed to lose his balance and fell into his audience. A small boy darted past Wolff's table. Wolff stood up, pointed at the boy and shouted at the top of his voice, "Stop, thief!"

The boy dashed off, running between the two officers. Wolff went after him, and four people sitting near Wolff jumped up and tried to grab the boy. Together they cannoned into the officers, knocking both of them to the ground. Several people began to shout, "Stop, thief!" Some of the newcomers thought it must be one of the fighting drivers. The crowd from the bus stop, the acrobats' audience, and most of the people in the café surged forward and began to attack one or the other of the drivers. Someone picked up a chair from the café and hurled it through the windscreen of the Packard. The waiters, the kitchen staff and the proprietor of the café rushed out and began to attack everyone who swayed, stumbled or sat on their furniture. Everyone yelled at everyone else in five languages. Passing cars halted to watch the melee, the traffic backed up in three directions, and every stopped car sounded its horn. A dog struggled free of its leash and started biting people's legs in a frenzy of excitement. Everyone got off the bus. Drivers who had stopped to watch the fun regretted it when the fight engulfed their cars. Men, women and children jumped on the car roofs, fought on the bonnets, fell on the running boards. A frightened goat ran into the souvenir shop next to the café and began to knock down all the tables laden with china and pottery and glass. A baboon came from somewhere—it had probably been riding the goat, in a common form of street entertainment—and ran across the heads in the crowd. From a window above the café a woman emptied a bucket of dirty water into the melee. Nobody noticed.

At last the police arrived. When people heard the whistles there was a sudden scramble to get away before the arrests began. Wolff, who had fallen over early in the proceedings, picked himself up and strolled across the road to watch the denouement. By the time six people had been handcuffed, there was no one left fighting except for an old woman in black and a one-legged beggar feebly shoving each other in the gutter. The café proprietor and the owner of the souvenir shop were wringing their hands and berating the police for not coming sooner.

When the police tried to move the two crashed cars they discovered that during the fight the street urchins had jacked up the rear ends of both vehicles and stolen the tyres. Every single light bulb in the bus had also disappeared.

And so had one British army briefcase.

Not long afterwards Wolff sat in Abdullah's living room. Like its owner, it was dirty, comfortable and rich. Three small children and a puppy chased each other around the expensive sofas and inlaid tables. Abdullah sat cross-legged on an embroidered cushion with a baby in his lap. He smiled at Wolff. "My friend, what a success we have had!"

Wolff, sitting opposite him, said, "It was wonderful."

"Such a riot! And the bus arriving at just the right moment."

Wolff looked more closely at what Abdullah was doing. On the floor beside him was a pile of wallets, handbags and watches. As they spoke, Abdullah began to rifle a wallet. "You old rogue," Wolff said. "You had your boys in the crowd picking pockets."

Abdullah grinned, showing his steel tooth. "To go to all that trouble and then steal only one briefcase . . ."

"But you have got the briefcase."

"Of course." Abdullah made no move to produce the case. "You were to pay me another fifty pounds on delivery."

Wolff counted out the notes. Abdullah leaned forward, holding the baby to his chest with one arm, and with the other reached

112

under the cushion he was sitting on and pulled out the briefcase.

Wolff took it from him and pried open the lock of the case. Inside were ten or twelve sheets of paper closely typewritten in English. He read the first, then with growing incredulity leafed through the rest. "Dear God," he said softly. He started to laugh. He had stolen a complete set of barracks canteen menus for the month of June.

VANDAM said to Colonel Bogge, "I've issued a notice reminding officers that General Staff papers are not to be carried about the town. One of my informants, the new girl I told you about, heard a rumour that the riot had been organized by Abdullah. He's a kind of Egyptian Fagin. He also happens to be an informant."

"For what purpose was the riot supposedly organized?"

"Theft. A lot of stuff was stolen, but we have to consider the possibility that the main object was the briefcase, in the hope it contained secret papers. Abdullah may have been put up to it by Alex Wolff. The Asyût knife man."

"Oh, now really, I thought we had finished with all that."

"The Asyût murderer is still at large," Vandam said. "It may be significant that soon after his arrival in Cairo a General Staff officer is robbed of his briefcase. I've talked to Abdullah. He denies all knowledge of Alex Wolff, and I think he's lying. We could have field security pull him in and sweat him a little."

Bogge smiled. "If I went to field security with this story of stolen canteen menus I'd be laughed out of the office. We've discussed this enough, Major. I don't believe the riot was organized, I don't believe Abdullah intended to steal the briefcase, and I don't believe Wolff is a Nazi spy. Is that clear?"

"Yes, sir."

"Good. Dismissed."

Chapter 6

Anwar el-Sadat fingered his moustache. He was rather pleased with it. He was only twenty-two years old, and in his Egyptian captain's uniform he looked a bit like a boy soldier; the moustache made him seem older. He needed all the authority he could get, for what he was about to propose was—as usual—faintly ludicrous. At these little meetings he was at pains to talk and act as if the handful of hotheads in the room really were going to throw the British out of Egypt any day now.

He deliberately made his voice a little deeper as he began to speak. "We have all been hoping that Rommel would defeat the British in the desert and so liberate our country. Now we have some very bad news. Hitler has agreed to give Egypt to the Italians."

Sadat was exaggerating; this was not news, it was a rumour. The audience, however, responded with angry murmurs.

Sadat continued, "I propose that the Free Officers Movement should negotiate a treaty with Germany, under which we would organize an uprising against the British in Cairo, and they would guarantee the independence of Egypt after the defeat of the British."

As he spoke, the risibility of the situation struck him afresh: here he was, a peasant boy just off the farm, talking to half a dozen discontented Egyptian subalterns about negotiations with the German Reich. And yet, who else would represent the Egyptian people? The British were conquerors, the Egyptian parliament was a puppet and King Faruk was a foreigner, a fat, licentious Turk.

There was another reason for the proposal: Gamal Abdel Nasser had been posted to the Sudan; his absence gave Sadat a chance to become the leader of the rebel movement. He pushed the thought out of his mind, for it was ignoble. He had to get the others to agree to the proposal, then to agree to the means of carrying it out.

It was Kemel who spoke first. "But will the Germans take us seriously?" The others began to talk about whether it would work. Sadat made no contribution to the discussion. Let them talk, he thought; it's what they really like to do. In fact, he and Kemel had agreed beforehand that Kemel should ask this question, for it was a red herring. The real question was whether the Germans could be trusted to keep to any agreement they made with a group of unofficial rebels; Sadat did *not* want the meeting to discuss that. If the Egyptians did rise up against the British, and if they were then betrayed by the Germans, they would see that nothing but independence was good enough—and perhaps, too, they would turn for leadership to the man who had organized the uprising. Such hard political realities were not for meetings such as this; they were too sophisticated, too calculating. Kemel was the only person with whom Sadat could discuss tactics. Kemel was a policeman, a detective with the Cairo force, a shrewd, careful man.

"But we haven't any means of contacting the Germans." It was Imam speaking, one of the pilots.

Sadat was pleased that they were already discussing *how to* do it rather than *whether to*.

Kemel had the answer. "We might send the message by plane."

"Yes!" Imam was young and fiery. "One of us could go up on patrol, divert from the course and land behind German lines."

One of the older pilots said, "On his return he would have to account for his diversion."

"He could not come back at all," Imam said forlornly.

Sadat said quietly, "He could come back with Rommel."

Imam's eyes lit up, and Sadat knew that the young pilot was seeing himself and Rommel marching into Cairo at the head of an army of liberation. Sadat decided that he should be the one to take the message.

"Let us agree on the text of the message," Sadat said democratically. "I think we should make four points. One: We are honest Egyptians who have an organization within the army. Two: Like them, we are fighting the British. Three: We are able to recruit a rebel army to fight on their side. Four: We will organize an uprising against the British in Cairo, if they will guarantee the independence of Egypt after the British defeat. That leaves only the question of which of us will fly the plane." Sadat looked around the room, letting his gaze rest finally on Imam. After a moment's hesitation, Imam stood up.

Sadat's eyes blazed with triumph.

Two days later Kemel walked the three miles from central Cairo to the suburb where Sadat lived. As a detective inspector, Kemel had the use of an official car whenever he wanted it, but he rarely used one to go to rebel meetings, for security reasons.

Kemel was fifteen years older than Sadat, yet his attitude to the younger man was one almost of hero worship. Kemel shared

Sadat's cynicism, his realistic understanding of the levers of political power; but Sadat had something more, and that was a burning idealism which gave him unlimited energy.

Kemel wondered how to tell him the news.

The message to Rommel had been typed out and signed by Sadat and all the leading Free Officers except the absent Nasser. Imam had taken off in his Gladiator, with a compatriot, Baghdadi, following in a second plane. They had touched down in the desert to pick up Kemel, who had given the message to Imam and climbed into Baghdadi's plane. Imam's face had been shining with youthful idealism.

It was the first time Kemel had flown. The desert, so featureless from ground level, had been a mosaic of shapes and patterns: the patches of gravel, the carved volcanic hills.

After a while both planes had turned due east, and Baghdadi spoke into his radio, telling base that Imam had veered off course and was not replying to radio calls. As expected, base told Baghdadi to follow Imam. This little charade was necessary so that Baghdadi, who was to return, should not fall under suspicion.

They flew over an army encampment. Kemel saw British tanks, trucks, field guns and jeeps. Both planes climbed. Directly ahead they saw signs of battle: great clouds of dust, explosions and gunfire. They turned to pass south of the battlefield. Kemel thought, next we should come to a German base.

Ahead, Imam's plane lost height. Instead of following, Baghdadi climbed a little more and peeled off to the south. Now Kemel saw what the pilots had seen: a small camp with a cleared strip marked as a runway.

Approaching Sadat's house, Kemel recalled how elated he had felt, up there in the sky, the treaty almost in Rommel's hands.

He knocked on the door. It was an ordinary family house, rather poorer than Kemel's home. In a moment Sadat came to the door, wearing a *galabia* and smoking a pipe. He saw Kemel's face. "It went wrong."

"Yes." Kemel stepped inside. They went into the little room Sadat used as a study. There was a desk, a shelf of books, some cushions on the bare floor. They sat down. Kemel said, "We found a German runway. Imam descended. Then the Germans started to fire on him. It was an English plane, you see—we never considered that. He waggled his wings, and I suppose he tried to radio; anyway they kept firing. The tail of the plane took a hit."

"Oh, God."

"He seemed to be going down very fast. Somehow he managed to land on his wheels but he went off the hard surface and into a patch of sand; then his plane blew up."

"And Imam?"

"He could not possibly live through such a fire."

"We must find another way to get a message through."

Kemel stared at him, and realized that his brisk tone was phoney. Sadat tried to light his pipe, but his hand was shaking too much and he had tears in his eyes. "The poor boy," he whispered.

Chapter 7

Wolff was back at square one; he knew where the secrets were, but he could not get at them. He might have stolen another briefcase, but that would begin to look, to the British, like a conspiracy. Besides, he needed regular, unimpeded access to secret papers. That was where Sonja came in.

· She was lying on the bed, eating chocolates from a box. Wolff came out of the bathroom wrapped in a big towel. "I've thought of another way to get into those briefcases," he said. "I'm going to make friends with a British officer. Then I'll bring him here, and go through his briefcase while he is in bed with you."

She sulked. "No. You promised to find us another Fawzi."

"I brought that girl last night from Madame Fahmy's."

"She wasn't another Fawzi. Fawzi didn't ask for ten pounds, and she didn't go home in the morning."

"All right. I'm still looking."

"You didn't promise to *look*, you promised to *find*."

Wolff went into the other room and got a bottle of champagne out of the fridge. He picked up two glasses, took them back into the bedroom. He poured and handed her a glass. "To the unknown British officer who is about to get the nicest surprise of his life."

"I won't have anything to do with an Englishman," Sonja said. "I hate them."

"That's why you'll do it—because you hate them. Just imagine it: while he's in here with you and thinking how lucky he is, I'll be reading his secret papers."

Wolff began to dress. He put on a shirt which had been made for him in one of the tiny tailor shops in the Old City—a British uniform shirt with captain's pips on the shoulders.

Sonja said, "You're going to pretend to be British?"

"South African, I think. If I find a likely one, I'll take him to the Cha-Cha."

He reached into his shirt and drew his knife from its underarm sheath. He went close to her and touched her naked shoulder with its point. "If you let me down, I'll use this."

She did not speak, but there was fear in her eyes.

When Wolff arrived at Shepheard's Hotel it was, as always, packed with people: Levantine merchants holding noisy business meetings, Egyptian girls in their cheap gowns, and British officers —the hotel was out-of-bounds to other ranks. Wolff made his way through the crowded lounge to the long bar at the far end. Here it was a little quieter. Women were banned, and serious drinking was the order of the day. It was here that a lonely officer would come.

Wolff sat at the bar. He was about to order champagne, then he remembered his disguise and asked for whisky and water. He had given careful thought to his clothes. The brown shoes were highly polished; the baggy brown shorts had a sharp crease; the bush shirt was worn outside the shorts; the flat cap was just slightly raked. He had also grown a moustache to complete the disguise. Since he was looking for an officer from GHQ, he would say that he himself was with BTE—British Troops in Egypt—a separate outfit.

There were fifteen or twenty officers in the bar, but he recognized none of them. He was looking specifically for any one of the aides who left GHQ each midday with their briefcases. He had memorized their faces and would recognize them instantly. He hoped it would not take long.

It took five minutes.

The major who walked in was a small man, thin, and probably in his mid-forties. His cheeks had the broken veins of a hard drinker. He had bulbous blue eyes, and thin sandy hair. Every day he left GHQ at midday and walked to an unmarked building in the Shari Suleiman Pasha—carrying his briefcase.

Wolff's heart missed a beat.

The major came up to the bar, took off his cap, and said, "Scotch. No ice. Make it snappy." He turned to Wolff. "Bloody weather," he said conversationally.

"Isn't it always, sir?" Wolff said.

"Bloody right. I'm Smith, GHQ."

"How do you do, sir," Wolff said.

He knew that, since Smith went from GHQ to another building every day, the major could not really be at GHQ; and he wondered briefly why the man should lie about it. He said, "I'm Slavenburg, BTE."

"Jolly good. Get you another?"

"Very kind of you, sir," Wolff said.

"Ease up on the sirs. No bull in the bar. What'll it be?"

"Whisky and water, please."

"Shouldn't take water with it if I were you. Comes straight out of the Nile, they say."

"I'm used to it. Born in Africa, been in Cairo ten years." Wolff was slipping into Smith's abbreviated style of speech. I should have been an actor, he thought.

"Africa, eh? I thought you had a bit of an accent."

"Dutch father, English mother," Wolff explained. He raised his glass. "Cheers."

They drank. Smith said, "You know this place. What's a chap to do in the evening, other than drink in Shepheard's bar?"

Wolff pretended to consider. "Seen any belly dancing?"

Smith gave a disgusted snort. "Once. Fat woman wiggling her hips."

"Ah. Then you ought to see the real thing. Real belly dancing is the most erotic thing you've ever seen."

There was an odd light in Smith's eyes. "Is that so?"

Wolff thought, Major Smith, you are just what I need. He said, "Sonja is the best. Matter of fact, I was toying with the idea of going on to see her act myself. Care to join me?"

"Let's have another drink first," said Smith.

Watching Smith put away the liquor Wolff reflected that the major was, at least on the surface, a highly corruptible man. He seemed bored, weak-willed and alcoholic. Sonja should be able to seduce him easily.

They finished their drinks and set out for the Cha-Cha Club. The place was crowded and hot, again. Wolff had to bribe a waiter to get a table. Sonja's act began moments after they sat down. Smith watched Sonja while Wolff watched Smith. Wolff said, "Good, isn't she?"

"Fantastic," Smith replied without looking round.

"Matter of fact, I know her slightly," Wolff said. "Shall I ask her to join us afterwards?"

This time Smith did look round. "Good Lord! Would you?"

In the storm of applause following her act, Sonja crossed the darkened stage to the wings. She walked quickly to her dressing room, head down, looking at no one. She took off her shoes, her filmy pantaloons and her sequined halter, and put on a silk robe. She sat in front of the mirror to remove her make-up. There was a knock on the door. She called, "Come in." One of the waiters entered with a note. "Table 41. Alex."

She crumpled the paper. So he had found one. That was quick. His instinct for weakness was working again. She understood him because she was like him. She, too, used people. She even used him. He had style, taste, high-class friends and money; and one day he would take her to Berlin. It was one thing to be a star in Egypt, and quite another in Europe. She wanted to be queen of the cabaret in the most decadent city in the world. Wolff would be her passport. It must be unusual, she thought, for two people to be so close and yet to love each other so little. He *would* use his knife, if she did not do what he wanted.

She shuddered, and stopped thinking about it. She put on a white gown with wide sleeves and a low neck, stepped into white high-heeled sandals, and fastened a heavy gold bracelet around each wrist. Around her neck she hung a gold chain with a teardrop pendant which lay snugly in her cleavage.

As she went into the club, people fell quiet. On stage she was separated from them by an invisible wall. Down here they could touch her, and they all wanted to. The danger thrilled her. She reached table forty-one and both men stood up.

Wolff said, "Sonja, my dear, you were magnificent, as always. Allow me to introduce Major Smith."

120

Sonja shook his hand. He was a thin, chinless man with a fair moustache and ugly, bony hands. He looked at her as if she were an extravagant dessert. He said, "Enchanted, absolutely."

They sat down. Wolff poured champagne. Smith said, "Your dancing was splendid, mademoiselle. Very . . . artistic."

"You're very kind, Major."

Wolff was nervous, she could tell. He was not sure whether she would do what he wanted. In truth, she had not yet decided.

Wolff said to Smith, "I knew Sonja's late father."

It was a lie. Sonja knew why he had said it: to remind her. Her father had been a part-time thief. When there was work he worked, and when there was none he stole. One day he had tried to snatch the handbag of a European woman. In the scuffle the woman had been knocked down. She was an important woman, and Sonja's father had been flogged by the British for the offence. He had died during the flogging.

Since then Sonja had hated the British with all her being. She wanted Hitler to humiliate them. She would do anything she could to help. She would even seduce an Englishman.

"Major Smith," she said, "you're a *very* attractive man." Wolff relaxed visibly.

Smith was startled. "Good Lord! Do you think so?"

"Yes, I do, Major."

"I say, I wish you'd call me Sandy."

Wolff stood up. "I'm afraid I've got to leave you. Sonja, may I escort you home?"

Smith said, "You can leave that to me. That is, if Sonja . . ."

Sonja batted her eyelids. "Of course, Sandy."

Wolff excused himself and left. A waiter brought dinner. Sonja picked at it while Smith told her about his successes on the school cricket team. He was very boring. Sonja kept remembering the flogging.

He drank steadily through dinner. When they left he was weaving slightly. She gave him her arm, more for his benefit than hers. They walked in the cool night air. They stopped at the houseboat. "Would you like to see inside?"

"Rather," Smith said. She led him over the gangplank and down the stairs. He looked around, wide-eyed. "I must say, it's very luxurious."

She gave him a drink and sat close to him. He touched her shoulder, kissed her cheek, roughly grabbed her. She shuddered but pulled him to her. She said, "Oh, Sandy, you're so strong."

She looked over his shoulder and saw Wolff watching through the hatch, laughing soundlessly.

Chapter 8

William Vandam was beginning to despair of ever finding Alex Wolff. The Asyût murder was almost three weeks in the past, and Vandam was no closer to his quarry. He knew he was becoming a little obsessed with the man. What fascinated him was something to do with Wolff's *style*, the sideways manner in which he had slipped into Egypt, the sudden murder of Corporal Cox, the ease with which Wolff had melted into the city.

Vandam had made no real progress, but he had gathered some information, and the information had fed his obsession. The Villa les Oliviers was owned by someone called Achmed Rahmha. Achmed had inherited the house from his stepfather, Gamal Rahmha, a wealthy Cairo lawyer. Gamal had married Eva Wolff, widow of Hans Wolff, both German nationals; he'd then adopted Hans and Eva's son, which explained how Achmed Rahmha obtained legitimate Egyptian papers in the name of Alex Wolff.

Interviews with all surviving Rahmhas had produced nothing. Achmed had disappeared two years ago and had not been heard from since. Vandam was convinced that he had been in Germany.

There was another branch of the Rahmha family, but they were nomads, and no one knew where they could be found. No doubt, Vandam thought, they had helped Wolff somehow with his re-entry into Egypt.

Vandam sat in his office, smoking one cigarette after another, worrying about Wolff. The man was no low-grade collector of gossip. The briefcase theft proved he was after top-level stuff. But the spy had his problems, too. He had to explain himself to inquisitive neighbours, conceal his radio somewhere, find informants. One way or another, traces had to appear.

Vandam was convinced that Abdullah, the thief, was involved with Wolff. Vandam had offered him a large sum of money for information. Abdullah still claimed to know nothing of anyone called Wolff, but the light of greed had flickered in his eyes.

Vandam paced the room. Something to do with *style*. Wolff might almost have been a man Vandam had known long ago, but could no longer bring to mind. Style.

The phone rang. He picked it up. "Major Vandam."

"This is Major Calder in the paymaster's office. You sent us a note to look out for forged sterling. We've found some."

That was it—that was the trace. "Good!" Vandam said. "I need to see it as soon as possible."

"It's on its way, along with the names of the people who paid it in."

"Marvellous. I'll ring you back when I've seen the notes."

Vandam hung up. Forged sterling—it fitted. Sterling was no longer legal tender in Egypt. Officially Egypt was a sovereign country. However, people who did business with foreigners usually accepted sterling, then exchanged it for Egyptian money at the office of the paymaster general. Vandam opened his door and shouted along the hall. "Jakes! Bring me the file on forged banknotes."

"Yes, sir!" Jakes shouted back.

Jakes appeared a moment later with a file. The most senior of Vandam's team, Jakes was an eager, reliable young man. Vandam switched on his desk light and said, "Right, show me a picture of Nazi-style funny money."

Jakes flicked through the forgery file. He extracted a sheaf of glossy photographs. Each print showed the front and the back of a forged banknote—money taken from German spies captured in England. Black arrows indicated the errors by which the forgeries might be identified. Jakes said, "You'd think they'd know better than to give their spies funny money."

"Espionage is an expensive business," Vandam replied. "Why should they buy English currency in Switzerland when they can make it themselves? A spy has forged papers, he might as well have forged money."

Vandam's secretary came in. "Package from the paymaster, sir." Vandam signed the receipt and tore open the envelope. It contained several hundred one pound notes. He put a note from the envelope next to one of the photographs. "Look, Jakes."

The note bore the same error as the one in the photograph.

"That's it, sir," said Jakes.

"Nazi money, made in Germany," said Vandam. "*Now* we're on his trail."

A short while later Vandam walked into a small grocery store owned by one Mikis Aristopoulos. The store smelled of spices and coffee but there was not much on the shelves. Aristopoulos himself was a short Greek about twenty-five years old, with a wide, white-toothed smile. He said, "Good morning, sir. How can I help you?"

"You don't seem to have much to sell," Vandam said.

Aristopoulos smiled. "If you're looking for something particular, I may have it in stock. Have you shopped here before?"

So that was the system: scarce delicacies in the back room for regular customers only. Vandam said, "I'm not here to buy. Two days ago you exchanged one hundred and forty-seven English pounds with the British paymaster general. Most of that was counterfeit."

Aristopoulos spread his arms in a huge shrug. "I take the money from English, I give it back to English. What can I do?"

"You can go to gaol for passing counterfeit notes."

Aristopoulos stopped smiling. "Please. How could I know?"

"Was all that money paid to you by one person?"

"I don't know—"

"Think! Did anyone pay for a large order with English pounds?"

"Ah, yes! One hundred twenty-six pounds ten shillings."

"His name?" Vandam held his breath.

"Wolff. I am so shocked. He has been a good customer for many years."

"Listen," Vandam said. "Did you deliver the groceries?"

"We offered to deliver, as usual, to his home, Villa les Oliviers, but this time Mr. Wolff took them with him."

"You haven't delivered there recently?"

"Not since Mr. Wolff came back. Sir, I am very sorry about this bad money. Perhaps something can be arranged . . . ?"

"Perhaps," Vandam said thoughtfully.

Aristopoulos led him into the back room. The shelves here were well laden. Vandam noticed Russian caviar, American canned ham and English jam. Aristopoulos poured thick strong coffee into tiny cups. They drank. Aristopoulos said, "Perhaps, as a gesture of friendship, I could offer you something from my store. Some Scotch whisky?"

"I'm not interested in *that* kind of arrangement. I want to find Wolff. You said he was a regular customer. What sort of stuff does he buy?"

"Much champagne. Caviar. Coffee. Foreign liquor. . . ."

Style, Vandam thought. It was a question of style. "When he comes back I must find out where he lives. I'm going to give you an assistant."

"I want to help you, sir, but my business is private—"

"You've got no choice. It's help me, or go to gaol."

"But to have an English officer working here in my shop—"

"Oh, it won't be an English officer." That would only scare Wolff away. Vandam smiled. "I think I know the ideal person."

That evening after dinner Vandam went to Elene's flat, carrying a huge bunch of flowers, feeling foolish. She lived in a spacious old block near the Place de l'Opéra. The concierge directed him to the third floor. He climbed the curving marble staircase and knocked at 3A. The door opened.

She was wearing a simple yellow cotton dress with a full skirt; the colour looked very pretty against her light brown skin. She gazed at him blankly for a moment, then gave her impish smile. "Well, hello William!" She stepped forward and kissed his cheek. "Come in."

He went inside and she closed the door. "I wasn't expecting the kiss," he said.

"All part of the act. Let me relieve you of your disguise."

He gave her the flowers. He felt he was being teased.

"Go in there while I put these in water," she said. He followed her pointing finger into the living room. The room was comfortable, decorated in pink and gold and furnished with deep soft seats and a table of pale oak. It was a corner room with windows on two sides, and now the evening sun shone in and made everything glow. On a couch was a book which she had presumably been reading when he knocked. He picked it up and sat down. The book was called *Stamboul Train*. It looked like cloak-and-dagger stuff.

She came in with the flowers in a vase, and the smell of wisteria filled the room. "Would you like a drink?"

"Can you make martinis?"

"Yes. Smoke if you want to."

"Thank you." She knew how to be hospitable, Vandam thought. He supposed she had to, given the way she earned her living.

"Do you like this stuff?" He indicated the book.

"I've been trying to find out how a spy should behave."

He saw her smiling, and realized he was being teased again. "I never know whether you're serious."

"Very rarely." She handed him a drink, sat down on the couch and looked at him over the rim of her glass. "To espionage."

He sipped his martini. It was perfect. So was she. The mellow sunshine burnished her skin. Her arms and legs looked smooth and soft. Damn. She had had this effect on him last time.

"What are you thinking about?" she said.

"Espionage."

She laughed. "You must love it," she said, knowing he was lying.

Vandam thought, How does she do this to me? She kept him always off-balance with her teasing and her insight, her innocent face and her long brown limbs. He said, "Catching spies can be satisfying work, but I don't love it."

"Why—because they hang when you catch them?"

"Because I don't always catch them."

"Are you proud of being so hardhearted?"

"I don't think I'm hardhearted. We're trying to kill more of them than they can kill of us." He thought, How did I come to be defending myself? Quickly he changed the subject. "Are your parents alive?"

She looked away from him, and then, seeming to yield to an impulse, began to tell him of her background. She had been the eldest of five daughters in a desperately poor Jewish family in Alexandria. Her parents were cultured and loving people. "My father taught me English and my mother taught me to wear clean clothes," she said. When Elene was fifteen years old her father, a tailor, began to go blind. He could no longer work. Elene went as a live-in maid to a British home and sent her wages to her family. She fell in love with the son of the house and he seduced her. They were found out, the son was sent away to the university and Elene was paid off. She was terrified to return home and tell her father why she had been fired. She had lived on her payoff until a businessman set her up in a flat. Soon afterwards her father was told how she was living, and he made the family sit *Shibah* for her.

"What is *Shibah?*" Vandam asked.

"Mourning."

Since then she had not heard from them, except for a message from a friend to tell her that her mother had died.

Vandam said, "Do you hate your father?"

She shrugged. "I think it turned out rather well." She spread her arms to indicate the apartment.

"But are you happy?"

She looked at him. Twice she seemed about to speak. Then she looked away. It was her turn to change the subject. "What brings you here tonight, William?"

Vandam collected his thoughts. "I'm still looking for Alex Wolff," he began. "I haven't found him, but I've found his grocer. I want to put someone inside the shop in case he comes back."

"Me."

"That's what I had in mind."

"Then, when he comes in, I hit him over the head with a bag of sugar and guard the unconscious body until you come along."

Vandam laughed. "I believe you would." He realized how much he was relaxing, and resolved to pull himself together before he made a fool of himself. "Seriously, you have to discover where he lives. I thought perhaps you might befriend him."

"What do you mean by 'befriend'?"

"That's up to you. Just as long as you get his address."

"I see." Suddenly her mood had changed, and there was bitterness in her voice. The switch astonished Vandam. Surely a woman like Elene would not be offended by this suggestion? She said, "Why don't you have one of your soldiers follow him home?"

"He might realize he was being followed and shake off the tail— then he would never go back to the grocer's. But if you can persuade him, say, to invite you to his house for dinner, then we'll get the information we need without tipping our hand."

"I suppose it's no worse than what I've been doing."

"That's what I thought," said Vandam with relief.

She gave him a very black look.

"You start tomorrow," he said. He gave her the address. "I'll get in touch with you every few days, to make sure everything's all right. By the way, the shopkeeper thinks we're after Wolff for forgery. Don't talk to him about espionage."

"I won't." The change in her mood was permanent. They were no longer enjoying each other's company. Vandam said, "I'll leave you to your thriller."

She stood up. "I'll see you out."

They went to the door. As Vandam stepped out, the tenant of the neighbouring flat approached along the corridor. Vandam did what he had been determined not to do. He took Elene's arm, bent his head and kissed her mouth. Her lips moved briefly in response. The neighbour passed by, entered his flat and closed the door. Vandam pulled away. She said, "You're a good actor."

"Yes," he said. "Goodbye."

He turned away and walked briskly down the corridor. He should have felt pleased with his evening's work, but instead he felt as if he had done something shameful. He heard her door bang shut behind him. Elene leaned her back against the closed door. Vandam had come into her life, full of English courtesy, asking her to do a new kind of work and help win the war. She had really thought he was going to change her life, give her a worthwhile job, something she could believe in, something that mattered. Now it turned out to be the same old game—the one she wanted to stop.

She had been curiously happy to have him in her home, sitting on her couch, smoking and talking. He treated her as a person. She knew he would never pat her and say, "Don't you worry your pretty head."

And he had spoiled it all. He had revealed that he regarded her as nothing but a woman who sold herself.

She thought, But why do I mind so much?

Chapter 9

In the early morning the tiled floor of the mosque was cold to Alex Wolff's bare feet. In the vastness of the pillared hall there was a silence, a sense of peace. A shaft of sunlight pierced one of the high narrow slits in the wall, and at that moment the muezzin

129

began to cry, "*Allahu akbar! Allahu akbar! Allahu akbar!*"

Wolff turned to face Mecca.

He was wearing a long robe and a turban, and the shoes in his hand were simple Arab sandals. He was never quite sure why he did this. He was a true believer only in theory. He had been circumcised according to Islamic doctrine, and he had completed the pilgrimage to Mecca; but he drank alcohol and ate pork and he did not pray every day, let alone five times a day. But every so often he felt the need to immerse himself, just for a few minutes, in the familiar rituals.

He touched his ears with his hands, then clasped his hands in front of him, the left within the right. He bowed, then knelt down. Touching his forehead to the floor at appropriate moments, he recited the *el-fatha:* "In the name of God the merciful and compassionate. Praise be to God, the lord of the worlds, the merciful and compassionate, the Prince of the day of judgment; Thee we serve, and to Thee we pray for help . . ."

He looked over his right shoulder, then his left, to greet the two recording angels who wrote down his good and bad acts.

When he looked over his left shoulder he saw Abdullah. The thief smiled broadly, showing his steel tooth. Wolff got up and went out.

He stopped outside to put on his sandals, and Abdullah came waddling after him.

"You are a devout man, like myself," Abdullah said. "I knew you would come, sooner or later, to your father's mosque."

"You've been looking for me?"

"Many people are looking for you. Knowing you to be a true believer, I could not betray you to the British; so I told Major Vandam that I knew nobody by the name of Alex Wolff, or Achmed Rahmha."

Wolff steered Abdullah into an Arab café. They sat down. Wolff said, "He knows my Arab name."

"He knows all about you—except where to find you. He is patient and determined. If I were you, I should be afraid of him."

Suddenly Wolff was afraid.

"He has talked to your brothers. They said they knew nothing."

The café proprietor brought each of them a dish of mashed fava beans and coarse bread. Abdullah spoke through a mouthful of food. "Vandam is offering one hundred pounds for your address. Ha! As if we would betray one of our own for money."

Wolff swallowed. "Even if you knew my address."

Abdullah shrugged. "It would be a small thing to find out."

"I know," Wolff said. "So I am going to tell you, as a sign of my faith in your friendship. I work in the kitchens at Shepheard's Hotel, cleaning pots. I sleep there on the floor."

"So cunning! You hide under their noses!"

"I know you will keep this secret," Wolff said. "And as a sign of my gratitude for your friendship, I hope you will accept from me a gift of one hundred pounds."

"But this is not necessary—"

"I insist. I will have the money sent to your house."

"Very well." Abdullah wiped his empty bowl with the last of his bread. "I must leave you now. *Allah yisallimak*. May God protect thee." He went out.

Wolff called for coffee and thought about Abdullah. The thief would betray Wolff for a lot less than a hundred pounds, of course. The story about living in the kitchens was no more than a delaying tactic; so was the bribe. However, when at last Abdullah found out that Wolff was living in Sonja's houseboat on Zamalek, he would probably come to Wolff for more money instead of going to Vandam. The situation was under control—for the moment.

Wolff went out and made his way to the central post office to use a telephone. He called GHQ and asked the operator for Major Sandy Smith.

"He's not here at the moment. May I take a message?"

Wolff had known the major would not be in—it was too early. "Tell him, Twelve noon today at Zamalek. Sign it, S." Wolff hung up and headed for Zamalek.

Since Sonja had seduced Smith, the major had sent her a dozen roses, a box of chocolates and two hand-delivered messages asking for another date. Wolff had forbidden her to reply. After a couple of days of suspense Smith would jump at any chance to see her again. When Wolff got to the houseboat Sonja was still asleep. At the far end of the living room, in the prow of the boat, was a tiny open kitchen. It had one large broom cupboard. Wolff could just get inside if he bent his knees and ducked his head. However, he could not see through the doorjamb.

He took a nail and a flatiron and banged the nail through the thin wood of the door at eye level. He used a kitchen fork to enlarge the hole. He got inside the cupboard again, shut the door and put his eye to the hole. He saw the curtains part. Sonja came into the living room. She looked around, surprised that he was not there. She shrugged, came across to the kitchen, picked up the kettle and turned on the tap.

Wolff opened the door and stepped out. "Good morning."

Sonja screamed.

Wolff laughed. "It's a good hiding place, isn't it?"

"What do you need a hiding place for?"

"To watch you and Major Smith. He's coming at noon today."

"Oh, no. Why so early in the morning?"

"Listen. If he's got anything worthwhile in that briefcase, he certainly isn't allowed to go wandering around the city with it. We mustn't give him time to take it to his office and lock it in the safe. What we want is for him to come rushing here straight from GHQ. You'd better start getting ready. I want you to look irresistible."

"I'm always irresistible." She went through to the bedroom. Wolff took out a bottle of champagne, put it in a bucket of ice and placed it beside the bed with two glasses. Then he sat on a divan by a porthole to watch the towpath.

A few minutes after noon Major Smith appeared. He was hurrying, as if afraid to be late. He wore a short-sleeved shirt in the bush-jacket style, khaki shorts, socks and sandals, but he had taken off his officer's cap. He was carrying his briefcase.

Wolff grinned with satisfaction. "Here he comes," he called. He got into the cupboard, shut the door and put his eye to the peephole.

He heard Smith's footsteps on the gangplank and then on the deck. Looking through the peephole, Wolff saw Smith come down the stairs into the interior of the boat.

"Is anybody there?" His voice was full of the expectation of disappointment. "Sonja?"

The bedroom curtains parted. Sonja stood there, her arms lifted to hold the curtains apart. She had put her hair up in a complex pyramid as she did for her act. She wore the baggy trousers of filmy gauze and a jewelled collar around her neck.

Smith dropped his briefcase and went to her. Quickly she undid the buttons on his bush shirt, slipped it off his shoulders and let it drop to the floor. As he embraced her, she drew him into the bedroom and closed the curtains behind them.

Wolff opened the cupboard door and stepped out.

The briefcase lay on the floor just this side of the curtains. Wolff knelt down and tried the catches. The case was locked. His eyes fell on Smith's bush shirt lying in a heap where Sonja had dropped it.

With any luck, the key to the briefcase would be in one of the breast or side pockets of the shirt. Wolff put his hand into the first pocket he came to, and felt for a key. The pocket was empty. He turned the shirt over until he found another pocket. He felt in it. There was a bunch of keys inside. Wolff breathed a silent sigh of relief. He sorted through the keys, found the smallest and tried it in the locks of the case. It worked.

He opened the other catch and lifted the lid. Inside was a sheaf of papers in a stiff cardboard folder. Wolff thought, No more menus, please. He opened the folder. The top sheet read:

OPERATION ABERDEEN
1. Allied forces will mount a major counter-attack at dawn on 5 June.
2. The attack will be two-pronged . . .

"My God," Wolff whispered. "This is it!"

He listened to the noises in the bedroom. They were quite loud now. There was not much time. The report was detailed. Wolff was not sure exactly how the British chain of command worked, but presumably the battles were planned at desert headquarters, then sent to GHQ in Cairo for approval. Plans for the more important battles would be discussed at the morning conferences, which Smith obviously attended. Wolff wondered again what department was housed in the unmarked building in the Shari Suleiman Pasha where Smith went each afternoon. Wolff found a writing pad and a red pencil in a drawer, and began to make notes. The main Allied forces were besieged in an area they called the Cauldron. The 5 June counter-attack was intended to be a breakout. It would begin at 0250 hours with the bombardment, by four regiments of artillery, of the Aslagh Ridge, on Rommel's eastern flank. The spearhead attack by the infantry of the 10th

Indian Brigade would follow. Tanks of the 22nd Armoured Brigade would rush through the gap. Meanwhile the 32nd Army Tank Brigade, with infantry support, would attack Rommel's northern flank at Sidra Ridge.

When he came to the end of the report Wolff realized he had been so absorbed that he had not noticed that the sounds behind the curtain had ceased. Now the bed creaked and a pair of feet hit the floor. Wolff tensed. Sonja said, "Darling, drink a glass of champagne with me before you go."

"Your wish is my command."

Wolff relaxed. She may complain, he thought, but she does what I want! He looked quickly through the rest of the papers, jotting some notes. He was determined that he would not be caught now, Smith was a wonderful find, and it would be a tragedy to kill the goose the first time it laid a golden egg.

A cork popped loudly as he was writing. He wondered how quickly Smith could drink a glass of champagne. He decided to take no chances. He put the papers back in the folder and the folder back in the case. He closed the lid and keyed the locks. He put the bunch of keys back in the pocket of the bush shirt. He got into the cupboard and shut the door. He was jubilant.

It was half an hour before he saw, through the peephole, Smith come into the living room and reach for his shirt. Wolff was feeling very cramped. Sonja said, "Must you go so soon?"

"I'm afraid so," Smith said. "To be perfectly frank, I'm not actually supposed to carry this briefcase around with me. I had the very devil of a job to come here at noon. You see, I have to go from GHQ straight to my office. Well, I didn't do that today. I told my office I was lunching at GHQ, and told GHQ I was lunching at my office. However, next time I'll go to my office, dump the briefcase, and come on here."

Wolff thought, For God's sake, Sonja, say something!

She said, "Oh, but, Sandy, my housekeeper comes every afternoon to clean—we wouldn't be alone."

Smith frowned. "Then, we'll have to meet in the evenings."

"But I have to work—and after my act, I have to stay in the club and talk to the customers." She took Smith's hands and placed them on her hips. "Oh, Sandy, say you'll come at noon."

It was more than Smith could withstand. "Of course."

They kissed, and Smith picked up his case and left. Wolff listened to the footsteps crossing the deck and the gangplank. He got out of the cupboard. Sonja watched with malicious glee as he stretched his aching limbs. "Did you get what you wanted?"

"Better than I could have dreamed."

Wolff cut up bread and sausages for lunch while Sonja took a bath. After lunch he took out the English novel and the key to the code, and drafted his signal to Rommel. That evening when Sonja had gone to the Cha-Cha Club he set up the radio.

At exactly 2400 hours, he tapped out his call sign, Sphinx. A few seconds later Rommel's desert listening post, or Horch Company, answered. Wolff sent a series of Vs to enable them to tune in exactly; then, in code, he began: "Operation Aberdeen. . . ."

Chapter 10

The signal from the spy was only one of twenty or thirty reports on the desk of von Mellenthin, Rommel's intelligence officer at seven o'clock on the morning of 4 June. Von Mellenthin despised spy reports. Based on gossip and sheer guesswork, they were wrong as often as they were right. But this one *looked* different.

The spy, whose call sign was Sphinx, began his message: "Operation Aberdeen." He gave the date of the attack, the brigades involved and their specific roles, the places they would pounce, and the tactical thinking of the planners.

Von Mellenthin was not convinced, but he was interested. As the thermometer in his tent passed the 100-degree mark he began his routine round of morning discussions. In person and by field telephone he talked to the divisional intelligence officers and the Luftwaffe liaison officer for aerial reconnaissance. He told them to look out for the brigades mentioned in the spy's report. He also told them to watch for battle preparations in the areas from which the counterthrust would supposedly come. Von Mellenthin then went to the command vehicle.

The morning discussion there was brief, for Rommel had already made his major decisions and given his orders for the day during the previous evening. Besides, Rommel was not in a reflective mood in the mornings; he wanted action. He tore around the desert, going from one front-line position to another in his staff car or his Storch aircraft, giving new orders, joking with the men and taking charge of skirmishes. Von Mellenthin went with him today, taking the opportunity to get his own picture of the front-line situation, and making his personal assessment of the intelligence reports.

In the early evening the Italian division occupying the Aslagh Ridge reported to von Mellenthin signs of increased enemy air reconnaissance. The Luftwaffe reported activity in no-man's-land which might have been an advance party marking out an assembly point. There was a garbled radio interception in which an Indian brigade requested urgent clarification of the morning's orders with reference to the timing of artillery bombardment. The evidence was building.

Von Mellenthin checked his card index for the 32nd Army Tank Brigade and discovered that they had recently been sighted at Rigel Ridge—a logical position from which to attack Sidra Ridge. He decided to gamble on Sphinx.

At 1830 hours he took his report to the command vehicle. Rommel was there with his chief of staff Colonel Bayerlein and Field Marshal Kesselring. They stood around a camp table looking at the operations map. Rommel's large, balding head appeared too big for his small body. He looked tired and thin. But his slitted dark eyes were bright with enthusiasm.

Von Mellenthin clicked his heels and formally handed over the report, then he explained his conclusions on the map. Kesselring said, "And all this is based on the report of a spy?"

"No, Field Marshal," von Mellenthin said firmly. "There are confirming indications."

Kesselring said, "We really can't plan battles on the basis of information from some grubby little secret agent in Cairo."

Rommel said crossly, "I am inclined to believe this report."

Von Mellenthin watched the two men. They were curiously balanced in terms of power. Kesselring outranked Rommel, but Rommel did not take orders from him, by some whim of Hitler's. Both men had patrons in Berlin. Although Rommel had the last word here in the desert, back in Europe—von Mellenthin knew— Kesselring was manoeuvering to get rid of him. Rommel turned to the map. "Let us be ready, then, for a two-pronged attack."

SIXTEEN DAYS LATER von Mellenthin and Rommel watched the sun rise over Tobruk.

They stood together on an escarpment, waiting for the start of the battle. Rommel was wearing the goggles which had become a kind of trademark of his. He was in top form: bright-eyed, lively and confident. You could almost hear his brain tick as he scanned the landscape and computed how the battle might go.

Von Mellenthin said, "The spy was right."

Rommel smiled. "That's exactly what I was thinking."

The Allied counter-attack of 5 June had come precisely as forecast, and Rommel's defence had worked so well that three Allied brigades involved had been wiped out. Rommel had pressed his advantage remorselessly. On 14 June the Gazala line had been broken and today, 20 June, they were to besiege the vital coastal garrison of Tobruk, with its fuel, dynamite, British trucks and fresh food.

At twenty minutes past five the attack began.

A sound like distant thunder swelled to a deafening roar as the Stukas approached. The first formation flew over, dived towards the British positions and dropped their bombs. A great cloud of dust and smoke arose, and with that Rommel's entire artillery forces opened fire with a simultaneous ear-splitting crash.

AT TEN THIRTY that morning Lieutenant Colonel Bogge poked his head around the door of Vandam's office and said, "Tobruk is under siege."

It seemed pointless to work then. Vandam went on mechanically, trying to think of a fresh approach to the Alex Wolff case, but everything seemed hopelessly trivial. The news became more depressing as the day wore on. The Germans breached the perimeter wire; they bridged the anti-tank ditch; they crossed the inner minefield; they reached the strategic road junction known as King's Cross. By evening the 21st Panzers had entered Tobruk and fired from the quay onto several British ships which were trying, belatedly, to escape to the open sea. A number of vessels had been sunk. Vandam thought of the men who made a ship, and the tons of precious steel that went into it, and the training of the sailors; and now the men were dead, the ship sunk, the effort wasted.

He spent the night in the officers' mess, waiting for news. The sun rose. A cook came in with coffee. As Vandam was drinking, a captain came down with another bulletin. "General Klopper surrendered the garrison of Tobruk to Rommel at dawn today."

Vandam, overwhelmed with despair, left the mess and walked towards his house by the Nile. He felt impotent and useless, sitting in Cairo catching spies while out in the desert his country was losing the war. It crossed his mind that Alex Wolff might have had something to do with Rommel's latest victories; but he dismissed the thought as farfetched. He felt so depressed that he wondered whether things could possibly get any worse, and he realized that, of course, they could.

Chapter 11

After two weeks in the shop Elene was ready to strangle Mikis Aristopoulos.

The shop itself was fine. Elene liked the spicy smells and the rows of gaily coloured boxes and cans on the shelves in the back room. The work was easy, the time passed quickly. But the boss was a pain, always making passes. Every chance he got he would touch her arm or her shoulder; each time he went by her, he would brush against her.

She did not need this. Her emotions were too confused already. She both liked and loathed William Vandam, who talked to her as an equal, then treated her like a kept woman; she was supposed to seduce Alex Wolff, whom she had never met; and she was being harassed by Mikis Aristopoulos. They all use me, she thought; it's the story of my life.

She wondered what Wolff would be like. It was easy for Vandam to tell her to befriend him. But a lot depended on the man. Some men liked her immediately. With others it was impossible. Half of her hoped it would be impossible with Wolff. The other half remembered that he was a German spy, and Rommel was coming closer every day, and if the Nazis ever got to Cairo . . . .

Aristopoulos brought a box of pasta out from the back room. On his way back, as he squeezed past her, he stroked her hip. She moved away. She heard someone come into the shop. She thought, I'll teach the Greek a lesson. As he went into the back room, she called after him in Arabic, "If you touch me again, I'll cut your hand off!"

There was a burst of laughter from the customer. She turned and looked at him. He was a European, but he understood Arabic. He called towards the back room, "What have you been doing, Aristopoulos, you young goat?"

Aristopoulos poked his head around the door. "Good day, sir. This is my niece, Elene." His face showed embarrassment and something else which Elene could not read. He ducked back into the storeroom.

"Niece!" The customer looked at Elene. "A likely tale."

He was a big man in his thirties with dark hair, dark skin and dark eyes. He had a large hooked nose. When he smiled he showed small even teeth—like a cat's. Elene knew the signs of wealth and she saw them here: a silk shirt, a gold wristwatch, tailored cotton trousers with a crocodile belt, handmade shoes.

Elene said, "How can I help you?"

He looked at her, contemplating several possible answers, then said, "Let's start with some English marmalade." She went to the back room to get a jar.

"It's him!" Aristopoulos hissed. "The bad-money man!"

"Oh, God!" Her mind went blank. "What shall I say to him?"

"I don't know—give him the marmalade—I don't know—"

"Yes, the marmalade, right." She took a jar from a shelf and returned to the shop. She forced herself to smile brightly at Wolff. "What else?"

"Two pounds of the dark coffee, ground fine."

He was watching her while she weighed the coffee and put it through the grinder. Suddenly she was afraid of him. He seemed poised and confident: it would be hard to deceive him. "Something else?" she asked.

"A tin of ham."

She moved around the shop, finding what he wanted. She thought, I must talk to him, I can't keep saying "Something else?" I'm supposed to befriend him. "Something else?"

"A half case of champagne."

The cardboard box containing six full bottles was heavy. She dragged it out of the back room. "I expect you'd like us to deliver this order," she said. She tried to make it sound casual.

He seemed to look through her with his dark eyes. "No delivery," he said firmly.

She nodded. "As you wish." She had not really expected it to work, but she was disappointed all the same.

She began to add up the bill. Wolff said, "Aristopoulos must be doing well, to employ an assistant."

"You wouldn't say that if you knew what he pays me."

"Don't you like the job?"

She looked at him. "I'd do *anything* to get out of here."

"What did you have in mind?" He was very quick.

She shrugged, and went back to her addition. Eventually she said, "Thirteen pounds, ten shillings and fourpence."

"How did you know I'd pay in sterling?"

He was *quick*. She was afraid she had given herself away. She had an inspiration. "You're a British officer, aren't you?"

He laughed loudly at that. He took out a roll of pound notes and gave her fourteen. She gave him his change in Egyptian coins. She was thinking, What else can I do? What else can I say? She said, "Are you having a party? I love parties."

"What makes you ask?"

"The champagne."

"Ah. Well, life is one long party."

She thought, I've failed. He will go away now, and perhaps he won't come back for weeks, perhaps never.

He lifted the case of champagne to his left shoulder, and picked up the shopping bag with his right hand. "Goodbye," he said.

"Goodbye."

He turned around at the door. "Meet me at the Oasis Restaurant on Wednesday night at seven thirty."

"All right!" she said jubilantly. Then he was gone.

IT TOOK them most of the morning to get to the Hill of Jesus. Jakes sat in the front next to the driver; Vandam and Bogge sat in the back. Vandam was exultant. An Australian company had taken the hill and had captured a German wireless listening post. It was the first good news Vandam had heard for months.

They took the main road to Alexandria, then the coast road to El Alamein, where they turned onto a barrel track—a route through the desert marked with barrels. Nearly all the traffic was going in the opposite direction, retreating. Nobody knew what was happening. They went through a recent battlefield, littered with wrecked and burned-out tanks, where a graveyard detail was desultorily collecting corpses. The barrels disappeared, but the driver picked them up again on the far side of the gravel plain.

They found the hill at midday. Field intelligence men were already at work. Prisoners were being interrogated in a small tent. Enemy-ordnance experts were examining weapons and vehicles. It was the task of Bogge's squad to go through the material in the captured radio trucks to determine how much the Germans had been learning in advance about Allied movements.

They each took a truck. Vandam's was a mess. The Germans had begun to destroy their papers when they realized the battle was lost. Boxes had been emptied and a small fire started, but the damage had been arrested quickly. There was blood on a cardboard folder: someone had died defending his secrets.

Vandam went to work. They would have tried to destroy the important papers first, so he began with the half-burned pile. There were many Allied radio signals, intercepted and in some cases decoded. As he worked Vandam began to realize that German intelligence's wireless interception was picking up an awful lot of useful information.

At the bottom of the half-burned pile was a novel in English. Vandam read the first line: "Last night I dreamt I went to Manderley again." The title was familiar: *Rebecca* by Daphne du Maurier. Vandam thought his wife might have read it. It seemed to be about a young woman living in an English country house.

It was peculiar reading for the Afrika Korps. And why in English? It might have been taken from a captured English soldier, but Vandam was doubtful: in his experience, soldiers read hardboiled private-eye stories and the Bible. He could think of only one possibility: the book was the basis of a code.

A book code was a variation on the one-time pad, which had letters and numbers randomly printed in five-character groups. Only two copies of each pad were made: one for the sender, one for the recipient. Each sheet was used for one message, then destroyed. Because each sheet was used only once, the code could not be broken. A book code worked the same way, except that the pages were not necessarily destroyed after use. A book had one big advantage over a pad. A pad was unmistakably intended for encipherment, but a book looked quite innocent. This would be important to an agent behind enemy lines. This might also explain why the book was in English. A spy in British territory would need to carry a book in English.

Vandam examined the book more closely. The price had been written in pencil on the endpaper, then erased. Trying to read the impression the pencil had made in the paper, Vandam made out the number 50, followed by esc—fifty escudos. The book had been bought secondhand in Portugal—neutral territory, a hive of low-level espionage.

As soon as he got back to Cairo he would ask the Lisbon intelligence station to check the English-language bookshops in Portugal—there could not be many. At least two copies would have been bought, and a bookseller might remember such a sale. Vandam was pretty sure the other copy was in Cairo, and he thought he knew who was using it.

Bogge, white-faced and angry to the point of hysteria, came suddenly stomping across the dusty sand. He handed Vandam a sheet of paper.

It was a decoded radio signal, timed at midnight on 3 June, call sign, Sphinx. The message bore the heading OPERATION ABERDEEN.

Vandam was thunderstruck. Operation Aberdeen had taken place on 5 June, and the Germans had received a signal about it two days earlier. "My God, this is a disaster."

"Of course it's a disaster!" Bogge yelled. "It means Rommel is getting full details of our attacks before they begin!"

Jakes appeared. "Excuse me, sir—"

Vandam said abruptly, "Not now, Jakes."

"Stay here, Jakes," Bogge said. "This concerns you, too." Then the enraged Bogge turned to Vandam. "They must be getting this stuff from an English officer. Your job is personnel security—this is your bloody responsibility!" Bogge stumped off in a fury.

Vandam sat down on the step of the truck. He lit a cigarette with a shaking hand. Not only had Alex Wolff penetrated Cairo and evaded Vandam's net, he had gained access to high-level secrets from some traitor. It was possible that Wolff had nothing to do with it—but it was hard to believe there might be two like Wolff in Cairo.

Jakes was standing beside Vandam, staring at the decoded signal. Vandam said, "Not only is this information getting through but Rommel is using it. If you recall the fighting on fifth June—"

"It was a massacre," Jakes said.

And Bogge had been right, Vandam thought. It was my fault. One man could not win the war, but one man could lose it. Vandam did not want to be that man.

Jakes snapped his fingers. "I forgot what I came to tell you: you're wanted on the field telephone. It's GHQ. There's an Egyptian woman in your office, asking for you, refusing to leave. She says she has an urgent message."

Elene! She must have made contact with Wolff. Vandam ran to the command vehicle and grabbed the phone.

"Yes?"

"William?"

"Elene!" He wanted to tell her how good it was to hear her voice, but instead he said, "What happened?"

"He came into the shop. I've got a date with him."

"Well done! Where and when?"

"Tomorrow night, seven thirty, at the Oasis Restaurant."

"I'll be there. Elene, I can't tell you how grateful I am."

"Until tomorrow."

"Goodbye." Vandam put down the phone.

Bogge was standing behind him. "What the devil do you mean by using the field telephone to make dates with your girl friends?"

Vandam gave him a sunny smile. "That wasn't a girl friend, it was an informant," he said. "She's made contact with the spy. I expect to arrest him tomorrow night."

Chapter 12

The most important thing in life for Wolff and Sonja was the indulgence of their appetites. They both knew that Wolff was taking a small but unnecessary risk by eating in a restaurant, and they both felt the risk was worth it, for life would hardly be worth living without good food.

After Sonja finished her ice-cream dessert, Wolff called the waiter and asked for coffee, brandy and the bill. He said to Sonja,

"There's some news. You were so good with Major Smith, you deserve a treat. I think I've found another Fawzi."

She was suddenly very still. "Who is she?"

"The grocer's niece. She's a real beauty. She has a lovely, innocent face and a slightly wicked smile."

"And you think she will . . . ?"

"I think so. She's dying to get away from Aristopoulos. I'm taking her to dinner tomorrow night."

"Will you bring her home?"

"Maybe. I don't want to spoil everything by rushing her." Wolff sipped his brandy. He felt good: full of food and wine, his mission going remarkably well and a new adventure in view. When the bill came he paid it with English pound notes.

The restaurant was small but successful. Ibrahim managed it and his brother did the cooking: French-Arab cuisine. They made a good living. But wealth had not made Ibrahim careless.

Two days earlier a friend who was a cashier at the Metropolitan Hotel had told him that the British paymaster general had refused to exchange four of the English pound notes which had been passed in the hotel bar. The notes were counterfeit. What was so unfair was that the British had confiscated the money. Since he had heard the news Ibrahim had been checking carefully every pound note before putting it into the till. His friend from the Metropolitan had told him how to spot the forgeries.

When he received the counterfeit notes from the tall European who had bought the most expensive dishes for the famous belly dancer, he decided to call the British military police. They would prevent the customer running off and perhaps help persuade him to pay by cheque, or an IOU.

Ibrahim went over to the table, carrying the brandy bottle. "Monsieur, madame, I hope you will accept a glass of brandy, with the compliments of the house."

"Very kind," said the man.

Ibrahim poured them brandy and bowed away. That should keep them sitting still for a while longer, he thought.

If I had a restaurant, Wolff thought, I would do things like that. The two glasses of brandy cost the proprietor very little, in relation to Wolff's total bill, but the gesture was effective in making the customer feel wanted. Sonja also enjoyed the attention.

The proprietor had disappeared for a few minutes, then returned. Out of the corner of his eye, Wolff saw the man whispering to a waiter. He guessed they were talking about the famous Sonja. She yawned. It was time to put her to bed. Wolff waved to a waiter and said, "Please will you fetch Madame's wrap." The man went off, paused to mutter something to the proprietor, then continued on towards the cloakroom. An alarm bell sounded in Wolff's mind.

He toyed with a spoon as he waited for Sonja's wrap. The proprietor went out of the front door and came back in again. He approached their table. "May I get you a taxi?"

Wolff said, "I'd like a breath of air. We'll walk a little."

"Very good, sir."

The waiter brought Sonja's wrap. The proprietor kept looking at the door. Wolff heard another alarm bell, this one louder. He said to the proprietor, "Is something the matter?"

The man looked worried. "I must mention an extremely delicate problem, sir." There was the sound of a vehicle noisily drawing up outside. "The money with which you paid. It's counterfeit."

The restaurant door burst open and three military policemen marched in. Wolff stared at them openmouthed. It was all happening so quickly. Military police. Counterfeit money. He was suddenly afraid. He might go to gaol. Those imbeciles in Berlin must have given him forged notes.

The MPs marched up to the table. Two were British and the third was Australian. They wore heavy boots and steel helmets, and each of them had a small gun in a belt holster. One of the British said, "Is this the man?"

"Just a moment," Wolff said, and was astonished at how cool his voice sounded. "The proprietor has, this very minute, told me that my money is no good. I don't believe this, but I'm prepared to humour him. I'm sure we can make some arrangement. It really wasn't necessary to call the police."

The senior MP said, "It's an offence to pass forged money."

"It is an offence *knowingly* to pass forged money." As Wolff listened to his own voice, quiet and persuasive, his confidence grew. "Now then, I will write a cheque to cover my bill, and use Egyptian money for the tip. Tomorrow I will take the allegedly counterfeit notes to the British paymaster general for examination, and if they really are forgeries I will surrender them. That should satisfy everyone."

The MP replied, "All the same, sir, you'll have to come with me. We need to ask you some questions. Those are my orders."

"Very well then," said Wolff. He could feel the fear pumping desperate strength into his arms. As he stood up, he picked up the table and threw it at the MP. Its edge struck one of the English MPs on the bridge of the nose. He fell back and the table landed on top of him.

Wolff grabbed the proprietor and pushed him at the second English MP. Then he jumped at the third MP, the Australian, and punched his face. The Australian took the punch but did not fall. The English MP pushed the proprietor out of the way and kicked Wolff's feet from under him. Wolff landed heavily. His cheek hit the tiled floor. The Englishman jumped on his chest beating him about the head. The Australian sat on Wolff's feet. Then Wolff saw, above him, Sonja's face, twisted with rage. The thought flashed through his mind that she was remembering another beating that had been administered by British soldiers. She raised a heavy chair high in the air, brought it down with all her might. The English MP gave a shout of pain and looked up, turning to ward off the next blow.

The Australian got off Wolff's feet and grabbed Sonja. Wolff threw off the wounded Englishman, then scrambled to his feet.

He reached inside his shirt and whipped out his knife.

The Australian threw Sonja aside, took a pace forward, spotted the knife and stopped. Wolff saw the man's eyes flicker to one side, then the other, where his partners lay on the floor. The Australian's hand went to his holster.

As Sonja threw herself at the Australian, Wolff turned and ran for the door. He flung it open with a crash. A shot rang out.

VANDAM drove the motorcycle through the streets at a dangerous speed. He had ripped the blackout mask off the headlight and drove with his thumb on the horn, weaving through the traffic, ignoring the outraged hooting of the cars, the raised fists.

The assistant provost marshal had called him at home. "Vandam, we've just had a call from a restaurant where a European is trying to pass some of that funny money."

"*Where?*" The APM told him and Vandam ran out of the house. He wanted desperately to get his hands on Alex Wolff.

He swerved to avoid a pothole, then opened the throttle and roared down a quiet street. The address was towards the Old Town. He turned two more corners and was there. The street was narrow and dark. He was halfway down it when he heard the *crack!* of a small firearm and the sound of glass shattering. A tall man ran out of a door. It had to be Wolff.

Vandam felt a surge of savagery. He twisted the throttle and roared after the man, catching him in the beam of the headlight. He was running strongly, steadily, arms and legs pumping. When the light hit him he glanced back over his shoulder. Vandam glimpsed a hawk nose, a moustache, a mouth open and panting. Vandam would have shot him, but GHQ officers did not carry guns.

The motorcycle gained fast. When they were almost level Wolff suddenly turned a corner. Vandam braked, and went into a back-wheel skid, came to a stop and then raced forward again.

He saw Wolff disappear into a narrow alleyway. Without slowing down, Vandam turned the corner and drove into the alley. The bike plunged out into empty space. Vandam's stomach turned over. The white cone of his headlight illuminated nothing. He thought he was falling into a pit. The back wheel hit something. The front wheel went down, then hit. The headlight showed a flight of steps. The bike bounced, landed again, descended the steps in a series of spine-jarring bumps. With each bump Vandam was sure he would lose control and crash. He reached the foot of the staircase. He saw Wolff turn another corner, and followed. They were in a maze of alleys. Wolff ran up a short flight of steps.

Vandam accelerated. A moment before hitting the bottom he jerked the handlebars. The front wheel lifted. The bike bumped crazily up. Vandam reached the top.

He found himself in a long passage with high, blank walls on either side. Wolff was still in front of him, still running. Vandam put on a burst of speed, drew level, eased ahead then braked sharply. He leaped off as the bike fell over, and landed on his feet, facing Wolff. The smashed headlight threw a shaft of light into the darkness of the passage. Without pausing in his stride Wolff jumped over the bike and charged into Vandam. Vandam, still unsteady, stumbled backwards and fell. He reached out blindly in the dark, found Wolff's ankle, gripped and yanked. Wolff crashed to the ground.

The engine of the bike had cut out, and in the silence Vandam could hear Wolff's breathing, ragged and hoarse. He could smell him, too: a smell of booze and perspiration and fear. But he could not see his face.

There was a split second when the two of them lay on the ground, one exhausted, the other momentarily stunned. Then they both scrambled to their feet. Vandam jumped at Wolff. He tried to pin his arms, but he could not hold on to him. Suddenly Vandam let go and threw a punch. It landed somewhere soft, and Wolff said, "Ooff." Vandam punched again, aiming for the face; but Wolff dodged. Something in his hand glinted in the dim light. Vandam thought, A knife!

The blade flashed towards his throat. He jerked back reflexively. There was a searing pain all across his cheek. His hand flew to his face. He felt a gush of hot blood. Suddenly the pain was unbearable. Then he felt himself falling, and he heard Wolff running away, and everything turned black.

Chapter 13

In the hospital a nurse froze half of Vandam's face with anaesthetic, then Dr. Abuthnot stitched up his cheek. She put on a protective dressing and secured it by tying a bandage around his head. "I must look like a toothache cartoon," he said.

She looked grave. She did not have a big sense of humour. "You won't be so chirpy when the anaesthetic wears off. Your face is going to hurt. I'll give you a pain killer."

"No, thanks," said Vandam.

"Don't be a tough guy, Major," she said. "You'll regret it."

He looked at her, in her white hospital coat and her sensible flat-heeled shoes, and wondered how he had ever found her even faintly desirable. She was pleasant enough, but she was also cold, superior and antiseptic. Not like Elene.

"A pain killer will send me to sleep," he told her. "I have some important work that won't wait."

"You can't *work*. You're weak from loss of blood. In a few hours you'll feel dizzy and exhausted."

"I'll be worse if the Germans take Cairo." He stood up.

Jakes was waiting outside with a car. "I knew they wouldn't be able to keep you long, sir. Shall I drive you home?"

"No." Vandam's watch had stopped. "What's the time?"

"Five past two."

"I presume Wolff wasn't dining alone."

"No, sir. His companion is under arrest at GHQ. A real dish. Name of Sonja."

"The dancer?"

"No less."

"Drive me there." The car pulled away.

Wolff was a cool customer, Vandam thought, to go out with the most famous belly dancer in Egypt in between stealing British military secrets. Well, he would not be so cool now. That was unfortunate in a way: having been warned by this incident that the British were on to him, he would be more careful from now on.

They arrived at GHQ and got out of the car. Vandam said, "What's been done with her since she arrived?"

"The no-treatment treatment," Jakes said. "A bare cell, no food, no drink, no questions."

"Good." It was a pity, all the same, that she had been given time to collect her thoughts. Jakes led the way to the interview room. Vandam looked in through the judas. It was a square room, without windows but bright with electric light. There was a table, two chairs. Jakes was right, Vandam thought; Sonja was a dish. However she was by no means *pretty*. She was something of an Amazon, with her ripe, voluptuous body and strong features. She wore a long gown of garish yellow. She was pacing up and down.

Vandam opened the door and went in. He sat down at the table without speaking. This left her standing, which was a psychological disadvantage for a woman. Score the first point to me, he thought. He heard Jakes come in behind him. He looked up at Sonja. "Sit down."

She stood gazing at him, and a slow smile spread across her face. She pointed at his bandages. "Did he do that to you?"

Score the second point to her.

"Sit down." She sat. "Who is 'he'?"

"Alex Wolff, the man you *tried* to beat up tonight."

"And who is Alex Wolff?"

"A wealthy patron of the Cha-Cha Club."

"How long have you known him?"

She looked at her watch. "Five hours."

"What is your relationship with him?"

She shrugged. "He was a date."

"How did you meet?"

"The usual way. Mr. Wolff invited me to his table, gave me a glass of champagne and asked me to have dinner with him. I accepted."

"Why?"

"Mr. Wolff seemed like an unusual sort of man." She looked at Vandam's bandage again, and grinned. "He *was* an unusual sort of man."

"What is your address?"

"*Jihan*, Zamalek. It's a houseboat."

"Age?"

"How discourteous. I refuse to answer."

"You're on dangerous ground—"

"No, *you* are on dangerous ground." Her sudden fury startled Vandam. "At least ten people saw your uniformed bullies arrest me in the restaurant. By midday tomorrow half of Cairo will know that the British have put Sonja in gaol. If I don't appear at the Cha-Cha tomorrow night, there will be a riot. No, mister, it isn't me who's on dangerous ground."

Vandam remained expressionless. He had to ignore what she said because she was right. "Let's go over this again," he said mildly. "You say you met Wolff at the Cha-Cha—"

"No," she interrupted. "I won't go over it again. I'll answer questions, but I will not be interrogated." She stood up, turned her chair around and sat down with her back to Vandam.

Vandam stared at the back of her head. He was angry with himself for letting her outmanoeuvre him, but his anger was mixed with a sneaking admiration for the way she had done it. Abruptly he got up and left the room. Jakes followed. In the corridor he told Jakes, "We'll have to let her go."

Jakes went to give instructions. While he waited, Vandam thought about Sonja. He wondered from what source she had been drawing the strength to defy him. It was true that her fame gave her some protection, but in threatening him with it she ought to have been blustering and a little desperate.

He ran over the conversation in his mind. She had been calm, expressionless, except when she had smiled at his wound. Then at the end, as she raged at him, what had he seen there in her face? Not just anger. Not fear.

Then he had it: hatred. She hated him. But he was nothing to her, except a British officer. Therefore she hated the British. And her hatred had given her strength.

Suddenly Vandam was tired. He sat down heavily on a bench in the corridor. From where was *he* to draw strength? He imagined the Nazis marching into Cairo. People like Sonja looked at Egypt under' British rule and felt that the Nazis had already arrived. Seen through her eyes it had a certain plausibility: the Nazis said that Jews were subhuman, and the British said that blacks were like children; there was no freedom of the press in Germany, and there was none in Egypt either; and the British, like the Germans, had their political police.

The anaesthetic in his face was wearing off. He could feel a sharp, clear line of pain across his cheek, like a new burn.

He thought of Billy. He did not want the boy to miss him at breakfast. Perhaps I'll stay awake until morning, then take him to school, then go home and sleep. What would Billy's life be like under the Nazis? They would teach him to despise the Arabs. His present teachers were no great admirers of African culture, but at least Vandam could do a little to make his son realize that people who were different were not necessarily stupid.

He thought of Elene in the brothel of a concentration camp. He shuddered.

We're not very admirable, especially in our colonies, he thought. But the Nazis are worse. Think about the people you love, and the issues become clearer. Draw strength from that.

Jakes came back. Vandam said, "She's an Anglophobe. She hates the British. I don't believe Wolff was a casual pickup. Take me to the main police station."

When Jakes stopped the car outside police headquarters Vandam said, "We want the chief of detectives."

"I shouldn't think he'll be here at this hour—"

152

"No. Get his address. We'll wake him up."

Jakes went into the building. Vandam stared ahead through the windscreen. Dawn was on its way. The stars had winked out, and now the sky was grey rather than black.

Jakes came back. "Gezira," he said. They drove across the bridge to the island. The sky turned from slate grey to pearl. Jakes stopped the car outside a small, pretty, single-storey house with a well-watered garden. Vandam guessed that the chief of detectives was doing well enough out of his bribes, but not too well. A cautious man, perhaps; it was a good sign.

They walked up the path and hammered on the door. Jakes put on his sergeant major's voice. "Military intelligence—open up!"

A minute later a small, handsome Arab opened the door, still belting his trousers. He said in English, "What's going on?"

Vandam took charge. "An emergency. Let us in, will you?"

"Of course." The detective led them into a small living room. "What has happened?" He seemed frightened.

Vandam said, "There's nothing to panic about. We want you to set up a surveillance, and we need it right away."

"Of course. Please sit down." The detective found a notebook and pencil. "Who is the subject?"

"Sonja Fahzi, the dancer. I want you to put a twenty-four-hour watch on her home, a houseboat called *Jihan* in Zamalek."

As the detective wrote, Vandam wished he did not have to use the Egyptian police for this work. But it was impossible, in an African country, to use conspicuous, white-skinned people for surveillance. The detective said, "And what is the nature of the crime?"

I'm not telling *you*, Vandam thought. "We believe she is an associate of whoever is passing counterfeit sterling."

"So you want to know who comes and goes. . . ."

"Yes. And there is a particular man that we're interested in: Alex Wolff, the man suspected of the Asyût knife murder; you have his description already. If Wolff is seen, I want to know immediately. You can reach Captain Jakes or me at GHQ during the day. Give him our home phone numbers, Jakes."

Vandam stood up. Suddenly he could not see straight. He felt himself losing his balance. Then Jakes was beside him, holding his arm. His vision returned. "I'm all right now," he said.

"You've had a nasty injury," the detective said sympathetically. They went to the door. The detective added, "Gentlemen, be assured that I will handle this surveillance personally. The towpath will be a good place for a beggar to sit. Nobody ever sees a beggar. They won't get a mouse aboard that houseboat without your knowing it."

Vandam shook hands. "By the way, I'm Major Vandam."

The detective gave a little bow. "Superintendent Kemel, at your service, sir."

Chapter 14

Sonja had half expected Wolff to be at the houseboat when she returned towards dawn, but she had found the place empty. At first, when she had been arrested, she had felt nothing but rage towards Wolff for leaving her at the mercy of the British thugs. Being an accomplice in Wolff's spying, she was terrified of what they might do to her. Then she had realized that Wolff had been smart. By abandoning her he had diverted suspicion away from her. It was for the best. Sitting alone in the bare little room at GHQ, she had turned her anger towards the British. She had defied them, and they had backed down.

At the time she had not been sure that the man who interrogated her had been Major Vandam, but when she was being released, the clerk had let the name slip. The confirmation had delighted her. She smiled again when she thought of the grotesque bandage on Vandam's face. Wolff must have cut him. What a glorious night! She wondered where Wolff was now. She would have liked him here, to share the triumph.

She put on her nightdress, poured herself a whisky. As she was tasting it she heard footsteps on the gangplank. She called, "Achmed?" Then she realized the step was not his.

The hatch was lifted and an Arab face looked in. "Sonja?"

"Yes—"

"You were expecting someone else, I think." The man climbed down the ladder. Sonja watched him, thinking. What now? He was a small man with a handsome face and quick, neat movements. He wore European clothes: dark trousers, polished black shoes and a

154

short-sleeved white shirt. "I am Detective Superintendent Kemel, and I am honoured to meet you." He held out his hand.

Sonja turned away and sat down on the divan. "What do you want?"

"I am interested in your friend, Alex Wolff."

"He's not my friend."

Kemel ignored that. "The British have told me two things about Mr. Wolff: one, that he knifed a soldier in Asyût; two, that he tried to pass counterfeit English banknotes. Why was he in Asyût? Why did he kill the soldier? And where did he get the forged money?"

"I don't know anything about the man," said Sonja.

"I do, though," said Kemel. "I know who Alex Wolff is. His parents were German. His stepfather was a lawyer, here in Cairo. I know, too, that Wolff is a nationalist. I know that he used to be your lover. And I know that you are a nationalist."

Sonja had gone cold. She sat still, her drink untouched.

Kemel went on, "Where did he get the forged money? I don't think there is a printer in Egypt capable of doing the work. Therefore the money came from Europe. Now Wolff, also known as Achmed Rahmha, quietly disappeared a couple of years ago. Where did he go? Europe? He came back—via Asyût. Why? Did he want to sneak into the country unnoticed? There is a mystery."

He knows, Sonja thought. Dear God, he knows.

"Now the British have asked me to put a watch on this house-boat. Wolff will come here, they hope; and then they will arrest him; and then they will have the answers."

A watch on the boat! Why, she thought, is Kemel telling me?

"The key, I think, lies in Wolff's nature: he is both a German and an Egyptian." Kemel crossed the floor to sit beside Sonja. "I think he is fighting for Germany and Egypt. I think the forged money comes from the Germans. I think Wolff is a spy. If he is, I can save him."

Sonja looked at him. "What does that mean?"

"I want to meet him. Secretly. You are not the only one who wants Egypt to be free. There are many of us. We want to see the British defeated, and we are not fastidious about who does the defeating. We want to talk to Rommel. If Achmed is a spy, he must have a way of getting messages to the Germans."

Sonja's mind was in a turmoil. From being her accuser, Kemel had turned into a co-conspirator—unless this was a trap.

Kemel persisted gently. "Can you arrange a meeting?"

She could not possibly decide so quickly. "No," she said.

"Remember the watch on the houseboat. The surveillance reports will come to me before being passed on to Major Vandam. If you can arrange a meeting, I in turn can make sure that the reports are edited so as to contain nothing . . . embarrassing."

Sonja had forgotten the surveillance. When Wolff came back—and he would, sooner or later—Vandam would know, unless Kemel fixed it. She had no choice. "I'll arrange a meeting."

"Good." He stood up. "Call the main police station and leave a message saying that Sirhan wants to see me. When I get that message I'll contact you to arrange date and time."

Sonja said, "I'll get in touch just as soon as I can."

"Thank you." He held out his hand. This time she shook it. He went up the ladder and out, closing the hatch behind him.

Sonja felt tired. She finished the whisky in the glass, then went through the curtains into the bedroom. She heard a tapping sound. She whirled around to the porthole on the far side of the boat looking across the river. There was a face behind the glass. She screamed. The face disappeared.

She realized it had been Wolff.

She ran up the ladder and out onto the deck. Looking over the side, she saw him in the water. He appeared to be naked. He clambered up the side of the little boat, using the portholes for handholds. She reached for his arm and pulled him onto the deck. He scampered down the hatch. She followed him. He stood on the carpet, dripping and shivering.

She said, "What happened?"

"Run me a bath," he said.

She went through to the bathroom. There was a small tub with an electric water heater. She turned the taps on. Wolff got in and let the water rise around him. "I didn't want to risk coming down the towpath, so I took off my clothes on the opposite bank and swam across. I looked in and saw that man with you. Another policeman?"

"Yes."

"So I had to wait in the water until he went away. My God,

156

I'm cold. The damned Abwehr gave me dud money. Turn off the water, will you?" He began to wash the river mud off his legs.

"You'll have to use your own money," she said.

"I can't get at it. You can be sure the bank has instructions to call the police the moment I show my face."

So you will have to use my money, Sonja thought. You won't ask, though; you'll just take it. "That detective is putting a watch on the boat—on Vandam's instructions."

Wolf grinned. "So it was Vandam."

"Did you cut him?"

"Yes, but I wasn't sure where. It was dark."

"The face. He had a huge bandage."

Wolff laughed. "I wish I could see him. Did he question you?"

"Yes. I told him that I hardly knew you."

"Good girl." He looked at her appraisingly, and she knew that he was pleased. "Did he believe you?"

"Presumably not, since he ordered this surveillance."

Wolff frowned. "That's going to be awkward. I can't swim the river every time I want to come home."

"Don't worry. The detective is one of us."

"A nationalist?"

"Yes. He wants to use your radio."

"How does he know I've got one?" Wolff said threateningly.

"He doesn't. He deduces that you're a spy, and he presumes a spy has a means of communicating with the Germans. The nationalists want to send a message to Rommel."

Wolff shook his head. "I'd rather not get involved."

"You've got to," she said sharply.

"I suppose I do," he said wearily. "They're closing in. I don't know where to go. Damn."

She sat on the edge of the bathtub, looking at his naked body. He seemed . . . not defeated, but at least cornered. For the first time, he was dependent on her. He needed her money, he needed her home; last night he had depended on her silence under interrogation, and he had been saved by her deal with the nationalist detective. She felt an odd sense of power. It was as if she were taking control. She found it exhilarating.

Wolff said, "I wonder if I should keep my date with that girl, Elene, this evening. It might be safer to lie low."

"No," said Sonja firmly. "I want her."

He looked up at her through narrowed eyes. She wondered if he recognized her newfound strength. "All right," he said finally. "I'll just have to take precautions."

He had given in. She had tested her strength against his, and she had won. It gave her a kind of thrill.

That evening Vandam, in high spirits, sat in the Oasis Restaurant, sipping a cold martini, with Jakes beside him. He had slept all day and had woken up feeling battered but ready to fight back. He had gone to the hospital where Dr. Abuthnot had changed his dressing for a smaller one that did not have to be secured by a bandage around his head. Now, in a few minutes, if Alex Wolff came, he would catch him.

Vandam and Jakes were at the back of the restaurant, able to see the whole place. The table nearest to the entrance was occupied by two hefty sergeants eating fried chicken. Outside, in an unmarked car, were two MPs in civilian clothes with handguns in their jacket pockets. The trap was set: all that was missing was the bait. Elene would arrive at any minute.

Billy had been shocked by the bandage at breakfast that morning. Vandam had sworn the boy to secrecy, then told him the truth. "I had a fight with a German spy. He had a knife. He got away, but I think I may catch him tonight." It was a breach of security, but the boy needed to know why his father was wounded. Billy was thrilled by the story.

Vandam looked at his watch. It was seven thirty. At any moment Alex Wolff might walk through the door. Vandam felt sure he would recognize him—a tall, hawk-nosed European with brown hair and brown eyes, a strong, fit man—but he would make no move until Elene came in and sat by Wolff. Then Vandam and Jakes would move in. If Wolff fled, the two sergeants would block the door. The MPs outside would provide backup.

Seven thirty-five. The restaurant door opened and Elene walked in. She looked stunning. She wore a cream-coloured silk dress. Its simple lines drew attention to her slender figure and its colour and texture flattered her tan skin.

She looked around the restaurant, searching for Wolff and not finding him. Her eyes met Vandam's and moved on without hesitating. The headwaiter seated her at a table close to the door .

158

Vandam caught the eye of one of the sergeants and inclined his head in Elene's direction. The sergeant gave a little nod.

Where was Wolff? Vandam lit a cigarette and began to worry. Suppose that, after last night's scare, Wolff had decided to lie low for a while? Somehow Vandam felt that lying low was not Wolff's style. He hoped not.

A waiter brought Elene a drink. It was seven forty-five. The door of the restaurant opened. Vandam froze, then relaxed again, disappointed: it was only a small boy. The boy handed a piece of paper to a waiter, then went out.

Vandam saw the waiter go to Elene's table and hand her the paper. Vandam frowned. What was this? An apology from Wolff, saying he could not keep the date? Elene looked at Vandam and gave a small, dainty shrug. She picked up her handbag from the chair beside her and stood up. Vandam thought she was going to the ladies' room. Instead, she went out through the door.

Vandam and Jakes got to their feet together. One of the sergeants half rose, looking at Vandam. As Vandam and Jakes hurried across the restaurant to the door, Vandam said to the sergeants, "Follow me." They went through the door into the street. A few yards away Elene was getting into a taxi. Vandam broke into a run. The door of the taxi slammed and it pulled away.

Across the street, the MPs' car roared, shot forward clumsily and collided with a passing bus. Vandam caught up with the taxi and leaped onto the running board. The car swerved suddenly. Vandam lost his grip, hit the road running and fell. He got to his feet. His face blazed with pain: his wound was bleeding again. Jakes and the two sergeants gathered around him. Across the road the MPs were arguing with the bus driver.

The taxi had disappeared.

Chapter 15

Elene was terrified. It had all gone wrong. Wolff was supposed to have been arrested, and now he was here, in a taxi with her, smiling a feral smile. She sat still, her mind a blank.

"Who was he?" Wolff said. "That man who ran after us. I couldn't see him properly, but I thought he was a European."

Elene fought down her fear. "I don't know." Suddenly she was inspired. "He was bothering me. It's your fault, you were late."

"I'm so sorry," he said quickly.

"Why are we in a taxi?" she asked. "Aren't we having dinner?"

"I had a wonderful idea." He smiled again. "We're going to have a picnic. There's a basket in the boot."

She did not know whether to believe him. Why had he sent a boy in with a message unless he suspected a trap? What would he do now, take her into the desert and knife her? She had a sudden urge to leap out of the car. She forced herself to think calmly. If he suspected a trap, why did he come at all? No, it had to be more complex than that. She said, "Where are we going?"

"A few miles out of town, to a little spot by the river where we can watch the sun go down."

"I don't want to go. I hardly know you. I should get out of the car."

"Please don't." He touched her arm lightly. "I have some smoked salmon, a cold chicken, some grapes, and a bottle of champagne. I get so bored with restaurants."

Elene considered. She could leave him now, and she would be safe. But I'm Vandam's only hope, she thought. She *had* to stay with Wolff, try to find out where he lived. She gave him a weak smile. "OK."

He turned his attention to the driver. They were out of the city, and Wolff began to give directions. They passed through a series of villages, then followed a winding track up a small hill and emerged on a little plateau atop a bluff. The river was immediately below them, and on its far side Elene could see the neat patchwork of cultivated fields stretching to the edge of the desert. Wolff said, "Isn't this a lovely spot?"

Elene had to agree. A flight of swifts rising from the far bank of the river drew her eye upward, and she saw that the evening clouds were already edged in pink. A lone felucca sailed upstream, propelled by a light breeze.

The driver got out of the car and walked fifty yards away. He sat down, turned his back on them and unfolded a newspaper. Wolff got a picnic hamper out of the boot and set it on the floor of the car between them. Elene asked him, "How did you discover this place?"

"My mother brought me here when I was a boy." He handed her a glass of wine. "After my father died, my mother married an Egyptian. From time to time she would find the Muslim household oppressive, so she would bring me here."

"Did you enjoy it?"

"At that age I preferred my Arab family. My stepbrothers were wicked, and nobody tried to control them. We used to steal oranges, puncture bicycle tyres. Only my mother minded. She was always saying, "They'll catch you one day, Alex!"

The mother was right, Elene thought. She said, "Where do you live now?"

"My house has been . . . commandeered by the British. I'm living with friends." He handed her a slice of smoked salmon on a china plate, then cut a lemon in half. Elene wondered what *he* wanted from *her*, that he should work so hard to please her.

VANDAM'S FACE HURT, and so did his pride. The great arrest had been a fiasco. He had failed professionally, he had been outwitted by Alex Wolff and he had sent Elene into danger.

He sat at home, his cheek newly bandaged, drinking gin to ease the pain. They had the license number of the taxi. Every policeman and MP in the city had orders to stop it and arrest the occupants. They would find it, sooner or later, and Vandam felt sure it would be too late. Nevertheless he was sitting by the phone.

What was Elene doing now? Perhaps she was in a candlelit restaurant, drinking wine and laughing at Wolff's jokes. What would they do later? If they went to his place, Elene would report in the morning, and Vandam would be able to arrest Wolff with his radio, his code book and perhaps even his back traffic. Professionally, that would be better—but it would also mean that Elene would spend a night with Wolff, and that thought made Vandam more angry than it should have done. Alternatively, if they went to her place, where Jakes was waiting with ten men, Wolff would be grabbed before he got a chance to . . .

Vandam got up and paced the room. He had sent a woman into danger once before. It had happened after his other great fiasco, when Rashid Ali, the Iraqi nationalist, had slipped out of Turkey under Vandam's nose. Vandam had sent a woman to pick up the German agent who had helped Ali to escape. He had hoped to

161

salvage something from the shambles by finding out about the man. But next day the woman had been found dead in a hotel bed. It was a chilling parallel.

There was no point in staying in the house. He could not possibly sleep, and there was nothing he could do here. He would join Jakes and the others at Elene's apartment, despite Dr. Abuthnot's orders. He put on a coat and his uniform cap, went outside, and wheeled his motorcycle out of the garage.

ELENE AND WOLFF stood together, close to the edge of the bluff, looking at the distant lights of Cairo and the nearer, flickering glimmers of peasant fires in dark villages. Then she turned from the view and walked back towards the car. It was time for him to make his pass. They had finished the meal, emptied the champagne bottle, picked clean the bunch of grapes. Now he would expect his reward. He stayed a moment longer on the edge of the bluff, then walked towards her, calling to the driver. He got in beside her. "Did you enjoy the picnic?"

She made an effort to be bright. "Yes, it was lovely."

The car pulled away. Either he would invite her to his place or he would take her to her flat and ask for a nightcap. She would have to find a way to refuse him.

They reached the outskirts of the city. It was after midnight, and the streets were quiet. Wolff said, "Where do you live?"

She told him. So it was to be her place.

Wolff said, "We must do this again." Several miles from her home, he told the driver to stop. He turned to her. "Thank you for a lovely evening. I'll see you soon." He got out of the car.

She stared in astonishment. He bent down by the driver's window, gave the man some money and told him Elene's address. The driver nodded and pulled away. Elene looked back and saw Wolff start walking towards the river.

She thought, What do you make of that? No pass, no invitation to his place, not even a goodnight kiss—what game was he playing? Whatever it was, she was grateful he had left.

The taxi drew up outside her building. Suddenly, from nowhere, three cars roared up. Men materialized out of the shadows. All four doors of the taxi were flung open, and four guns pointed in. Elene screamed. Then a head was poked into the car, and Elene recognized Vandam. "Gone?" Vandam said. "How long ago did you leave him?"

"Five or ten minutes. May I get out of the car?"

He gave her a hand, and she stepped onto the pavement. He said, "I'm sorry we scared you." He looked utterly defeated.

She felt a surge of affection for him. She touched his arm. "Why don't you send your men home and come and talk inside?"

He hesitated, then turned to one of his men. "Jakes, see what you can get out of the driver. I'll see you at GHQ."

Elene led the way inside. It was so good to enter her own home and slump on the sofa. The trial was over, Wolff had gone, and Vandam was here. She said, "What went wrong?"

Vandam sat down opposite her and took out his cigarettes. "We expected him to walk into the trap all unawares—but he was suspicious, or at least cautious. What happened then?"

She rested her head against the back of the sofa and told him about the picnic. She spoke abruptly; she wanted to forget, not remember. When she finished she said, "Make me a drink, and have one yourself." He went to the cupboard. Elene could see that he was angry. For the first time she wondered about the bandage he wore. She said, "What happened to your face?"

"We almost caught Wolff last night."

"Oh, no." So he had failed twice in twenty-four hours; no wonder he looked defeated. She wanted to console him, to put her arms around him, to lay his head in her lap and stroke his hair.

He gave her a drink. As he stooped to hand her the glass she reached up and turned his chin with her fingertips so that she could look at his bandaged cheek. He let her look, just for a second, then moved his head away.

She had not seen him this tense before. He crossed the room and sat opposite her, holding himself upright on the edge of the chair. He was full of a suppressed emotion, something like rage, but when she looked into his eyes she saw not anger but pain.

He said, "How did Wolff strike you?"

"Charming. Intelligent. Dangerous. What are you fishing for?"

He shook his head irritably. "Nothing. Everything." He lit another cigarette. What was the matter with him? There was something familiar in his anger. It was not just that he felt he had failed. It was his attitude towards her.

163

"Wolff said he would see you again?" Vandam asked.

"He said, 'We must do this again'—something like that."

"What do you think he had in mind, exactly?"

She shrugged. "Another picnic, another date. William, what has got into you?"

"I'm just curious," he said. His face wore a twisted grin. "I'd like to know what the two of you did, other than eat and drink; all that time together, in the dark, a man and a woman—"

"Shut up." She closed her eyes. Now she understood. Without opening her eyes she said, "I'm going to bed. You can see yourself out." A few seconds later the front door slammed.

She went to the window and looked down at the street. She saw him leave the building and get on his motorcycle. He kicked the engine into life and roared off down the road at a breakneck speed. Elene was very tired, but she was not unhappy, for she knew the cause of his anger, and that gave her hope. She smiled faintly. "William Vandam, I do believe you're jealous."

Chapter 16

By the time Major Smith made his third lunch-hour visit to the houseboat, on the day after the picnic, Wolff and Sonja had fitted into a routine. Wolff hid in the cupboard when the major approached. Sonja met him in the living room with a drink. She made him sit there, ensuring that his briefcase was put down. After a minute or two she began kissing him, contrived to get his bush shirt off, then soon afterwards took him into the bedroom. As soon as Wolff heard the bed creak, he came out of the cupboard. He took the key out of the side pocket of the shirt and opened the case, his notebook and pencil ready.

Smith's second visit had been disappointing; however, this time Wolff struck gold again. General Sir Claude Auchinleck, the Middle East commander in chief, had taken direct control of the Eighth Army. As a sign of Allied panic, that alone would be welcome news to Rommel. It might also help Wolff, for it meant that battles were now being planned in Cairo rather than in the desert, in which case Smith was more likely to get copies.

The most important paper in Smith's briefcase was a summary

of the Allies' new defence line at Mersa Matrûh. The new line began at the coastal village of Matrûh and stretched south into the desert as far as an escarpment called Sidi Hamza. 10th Corps was at Matrûh; then there was a heavy minefield fifteen miles long; then a lighter minefield for ten miles; then the escarpment; then, south of the escarpment, the 13th Corps.

The picture was fairly clear: the Allied line was strong at either end and weak in the middle. Armed with Wolff's information, Rommel could hit the soft centre and pour his forces through the gap like a stream bursting a dam.

Wolff smiled to himself. He felt he was playing a major role in the struggle for German domination of North Africa; he found it enormously satisfying.

In the bedroom, a cork popped—the sign that it was all over. Wolff put the papers back in the case, locked it and put the key back in the shirt pocket. He no longer got back into the cupboard afterwards—once had been enough. He put his shoes in his trouser pockets and tiptoed soundlessly in his socks up the ladder, across the deck and down the gangplank to the towpath. Then he put his shoes on and went to lunch.

LATE THAT AFTERNOON Elene went shopping. Her flat had come to seem claustrophobic. She had spent most of the day pacing around, unable to concentrate on anything, alternately miserable and happy; so she put on a cheerful striped dress and went out.

She liked the fruit-and-vegetable market. It was a lively place, especially at the end of the day when the tradesmen were trying to get rid of the last of their produce. She bought tomatoes and eggs, having decided to make an omelette for supper. It was good to be carrying a basket of food, more food than she could eat at one meal; it made her feel safe. She could remember days when there had been no supper, when as a ten-year-old she had wondered, secretly, how long people took to starve to death.

She left the market and went window shopping, looking at dresses. She wanted one day to have her own dressmaker. Could William Vandam afford that for a wife? When she thought of Vandam she was happy, until she thought of Wolff. She knew she could escape simply by refusing to make another date with Wolff. She was under no obligation to act as the bait in a trap for a knife murderer. She kept returning to this idea, worrying at it like a loose tooth: I don't have to.

She suddenly lost interest in dresses, and headed for home. When she turned into the entrance to her block of flats a voice said, "Abigail." She froze with shock. It was the voice of a ghost. She made herself turn around. A figure came out of the shadows: an old Jew, shabbily dressed, half-blind, with a matted beard, veined feet in rubber-tyre sandals. Elene said, "Father."

He stood in front of her, as if afraid to touch her, just peering at her. He said, "So beautiful still, and not poor."

Impulsively she stepped forward, kissed his cheek.

He said, "Your grandfather, my father, has died."

She took his arm and led him up the stairs. It was all unreal, like a dream. Inside the flat she said, "You should eat," and took him into the kitchen. She put a pan on to heat and began to beat the eggs. She said, "How did you find me?"

"I've always known where you were," he said. "Your friend Esme writes to her father, who sometimes I see."

Esme was an acquaintance rather than a friend. And she had never let on that she was writing home.

Elene said, "I didn't want you to ask me to come back."

"And what would I have said to you? Come home, it is your duty to starve with your family. No. But I knew where you were."

She sliced tomatoes into the omelette. "You would have said it was better to starve than to live immorally."

"Yes, I would have said that. And would I have been wrong?"

She turned to look at him. The glaucoma which had taken the sight of his left eye years ago was now spreading to the right. He was fifty-five, she calculated; he looked seventy. "Yes, you would have been wrong. It is always better to live."

"Perhaps. I'm not as certain of these things as I used to be."

Elene served the omelette and put bread on the table. Her father blessed the bread. "Blessed art thou O Lord our God . . ." Elene was surprised that the prayer did not drive her into a fury. In the blackest moments of her lonely life she had cursed her father and his religion. For his poverty and what it had driven her to.

Her father was very hungry and wolfed his food. Elene wondered why he had come. She asked about her sisters. After the death of their mother all four of them, in their different ways, had broken

with their father. Two had gone to America, one had married the son of her father's greatest enemy; the youngest, Naomi, had died. It dawned on Elene that her father was destroyed.

He asked her what she was doing. She decided to tell him. "The British are trying to catch a German spy. It's my job to befriend him. But I think I may not help them anymore."

He had stopped eating. "Are you afraid?"

She nodded. "He's very dangerous."

They finished their meal, and Elene got up to make him a glass of tea. He said, "The Germans are coming. It will be very bad for Jews. I'm going to Jerusalem."

"How? The trains are full, there's a quota for Jews—"

"I am going to walk." He smiled. "It's been done before."

"Moses never made it," she said angrily. "You're crazy!"

"Haven't I always been a little crazy?"

"Yes!" she shouted. Suddenly her anger collapsed. "Yes, and I should know better than to try to change your mind."

"I will pray to God to preserve you. You will have a chance here—you're young and beautiful, and perhaps they won't know you're Jewish. But me, a useless old man . . . me they would send to a camp to die. It is always better to live. You said that."

She tried to persuade him to stay with her, for one night at least, but he would not. She gave him a sweater, and a scarf and all the cash she had in the place. She cried, and dried her eyes and cried again. When he left she looked out of the window and saw him walking along the street, an old man going up out of Egypt, following in the footsteps of the children of Israel. When she thought of his courage she knew she could not run out on Vandam.

"SHE'S AN intriguing girl," Wolff said. "I can't quite figure her out." He was sitting on the bed, watching Sonja get dressed. "She's a little jumpy. When I told her we were going on a picnic she acted quite scared. Yet she can be very earthy and direct."

"Just bring her home to me. I'll figure her out."

"It bothers me." Wolff frowned. His instinct was to lie low. But Sonja would insist. "Somebody tried to jump into the taxi with us."

"This town is full of crazy people, you know that." Sonja was brushing her hair. "When am I going to tell Kemel you'll meet him? He must know by now that you're living here."

Wolff sighed. Another claim on him; another danger. "Call him tonight from the club."

"OK." She was ready, and her taxi was waiting. "And you make a date with Elene." She went out.

She was not in his power the way she had once been, Wolff realized. The walls you build to protect you also close you in. And Sonja might be crazy enough to betray him, if she really got angry. He got up from the bed, found paper and pen and sat down to write a note to Elene.

Chapter 17

The message came the day after Elene's father left for Jerusalem. A small boy came to the door with an envelope. Elene tipped him and read the letter.

> My dear Elene, let us meet at the Oasis Restaurant for a late dinner at ten o'clock on Thursday. I eagerly look forward to it.
>
> Fondly, Alex Wolff

Thursday—the day after tomorrow. She did not know whether to be elated or scared. Her first thought was to telephone Vandam; then she hesitated.

She had become intensely curious about Vandam. She knew so little about him. What did he do when he was not catching spies? What was his home like? With whom did he live? She wanted to patch up their quarrel, and she had an excuse to contact him now, but instead of telephoning she would go to his home.

She decided to wear her pale pink dress, the one with puffed shoulders and buttons down the front: that was very pretty. She put on a little perfume, then sat in front of the mirror to comb her short hair. The dark, fine locks gleamed. I look ravishing, she thought.

She left the flat and headed for his house in Garden City. She felt gay and reckless. What a good idea it was to go there—so much better than sitting alone at home. She found the house easily. It was a small French-colonial villa, all pillars and high windows, its white stone reflecting the evening sun with painful brilliance. She walked up the short drive and rang the bell. An elderly, bald Egyptian came to the door. "Good evening, madam," he said, speaking like an English butler.

"I'd like to see Major Vandam. My name is Elene Fontana."

"The major has not yet returned home, madam."

"Perhaps I could wait," Elene said.

"Of course, madam." He led her into a drawing room. "My name is Gaafar. Please call me if there is anything you require."

Elene was delighted to be left alone to look around. The drawing room had a large marble fireplace and very English furniture. Everything was clean and tidy and not very lived-in.

The door opened and a young boy walked in. He was very good-looking, with curly brown hair and smooth skin. He seemed about ten years old. He looked familiar. He said, "Hello, I'm Billy Vandam."

Elene stared in horror. A son—Vandam had a son! She knew now why he seemed familiar: he was a miniature of his father. Why had it never occurred to her that Vandam might be married? A man like that—charming, kind, handsome, clever—was unlikely to have reached his late thirties without getting hooked.

She shook Billy's hand. "How do you do. I'm Elene Fontana."

"We never know what time Dad's coming home," Billy said. "I hope you won't have to wait long. Would you like a drink, or anything?"

He was very polite, like his father, with a formality that was somehow disarming. Elene said, "No, thank you."

"Well, I've got to have my supper. Sorry to leave you alone."

The boy went out, and Elene sat down heavily. She was disoriented, as if in her own home she had found a door to a room she had not known was there. She noticed a photograph on the marble mantelpiece and got up to look at it. It was of a beautiful woman in her early twenties: cool, aristocratic-looking, with a faintly supercilious smile. The woman's eyes were clear and perceptive and light in colour; Elene realized that Billy had eyes like that. This, then, was Billy's mother—Vandam's wife: a classic English beauty with a superior air.

Elene wandered around the room, wondering if it held any more shocks. Against one wall was a small upright piano. Perhaps Mrs. Vandam played in the evenings, filling the air with Chopin while

Vandam sat in the armchair as he sang romantic ballads to her in a strong tenor. She picked up a novel from the top of the piano and read the first line: "Last night I dreamt I went to Manderley again." She read on, wondering whether the book belonged to Vandam's wife.

In a while Billy came back. Elene put the book down, feeling as if she had been prying. "That one's no good," Billy said. "It's about some silly girl who's afraid of her husband's housekeeper. There's no action."

Elene sat down, and Billy sat opposite her. Obviously he was going to entertain her. She said, "You've read it, then?"

"*Rebecca*? Yes. I didn't like it much. I like tecs—detective stories —best. I've read all of Agatha Christie's. I like the American ones most of all—S. S. Van Dine and Raymond Chandler."

"Really? I read detective stories all the time."

"Oh! Who's your favourite author?"

Elene considered. "Georges Simenon. He writes in French, but some of the books have been translated into English."

"Would you lend me one? It's so hard to get new books, I've read all the ones in this house, and in the school library."

"All right, let's swap. What have you got to lend me?"

"I'll lend you a Chandler. The American ones are much more true to life. I've gone off those stories about English country houses and people who probably couldn't murder a fly."

It was odd, Elene thought, that a boy for whom the English country house might be part of everyday life should find stories about American private eyes more "true to life". She hesitated, then asked, "Does your mother read detective stories?"

Billy said briskly, "My mother died last year in Crete."

"Oh!" Elene put her hand to her mouth; she felt the blood drain from her face. So Vandam was *not* married! She said, "Billy, how awful for you. I'm so sorry."

"It's all right," Billy said. "It's the war, you see."

And now he was like his father again. The mask was on: the mask of courtesy, formality. *It's the war, you see.* He had heard someone else say that, and had adopted it as his own defence. She decided to talk of other things.

She said awkwardly, "I suppose, with your father working at GHQ, you get more news of the war than the rest of us."

"I suppose I do, but usually I don't really understand it. When he comes home in a bad mood I know we've lost another battle." He started to bite a fingernail, then stuffed his hands into his shorts pockets. "I wish I was older."

"You want to fight?"

He looked at her fiercely, as if he thought she was mocking him. "It's just that I'm afraid the Germans will *win*. Then it would all have been for nothing." He bit his nail again, and this time he did not stop himself. Elene wondered *what* would have been for nothing: the death of his mother? His own struggle to be brave?

Billy looked at the clock on the mantelpiece. "I'm supposed to go to bed at nine." Suddenly he was a child again. He stood up.

"May I come and say goodnight to you, in a few minutes?"

"If you like." He went out.

What kind of life did they lead in this house? Elene wondered. The man, the boy and the old servant lived here together, each with his own concerns. Billy's young-old wisdom was charming, but he seemed like a child who did not have much fun. She experienced a rush of compassion for him, a motherless child in an alien country besieged by foreign armies.

She left the drawing room and went upstairs. One of the bedroom doors was open, and she went in, expecting to see model planes, sports gear, clothes on the floor. But the place might almost have been the bedroom of an adult. The clothes were folded neatly on a chair, schoolbooks were stacked tidily on the desk and the only toy in evidence was a cardboard model of a tank. Billy was in bed, his striped pyjama top buttoned to the neck, a book on the blanket beside him.

"What are you reading?" Elene said.

"*The Greek Coffin Mystery.*"

She sat on the edge of the bed. "Don't stay awake too late."

"I have to put out the light at nine thirty."

She leaned forward suddenly and kissed his cheek.

At that moment Vandam walked in.

The familiarity of the scene shocked him: the boy in bed with his book, the woman leaning forward to kiss the boy goodnight. Vandam stood and stared, feeling like one who knows he is in a dream but cannot wake up.

"Goodnight, Billy." Elene stood up. "Hello, William."

"Hello, Elene."

She went past Vandam and left the room. Vandam sat on the edge of the bed. "Been entertaining our guest?"

"Yes. I like her—she reads tecs. We're going to swap books. She's ever so pretty, isn't she?"

"Yes. She's working for me—it's a bit hush-hush, so . . ."

Billy lowered his voice. "Is she, you know, a secret agent?"

Vandam put a finger to his lips. "Walls have ears."

The boy looked suspicious. "You're having me on."

Vandam shook his head silently.

Billy said, "Gosh!"

Vandam said goodnight and went out. As he closed the door it occurred to him that Elene's goodnight kiss had probably done Billy a lot of good.

He found Elene in the drawing room, shaking martinis. He felt he should have resented more than he did the way she had made herself at home in his house, but he was too tired to strike attitudes. He sank gratefully into a chair and accepted a drink. He said, "What made you come here?"

"I've got a date with Wolff."

"Wonderful! When?"

"Thursday." She handed him a sheet of paper.

He studied the message. "How did this come?"

"A boy brought it to my door. What will we do?"

"The same as last time, only better." Vandam tried to sound more confident than he felt. Wolff was unpredictable. He might try another trick.

As if reading his mind, Elene said, "I don't want to spend another evening with him. He frightens me. If he tries to seduce me, I'm afraid he won't take no for an answer."

Vandam felt guilty—*remember Istanbul*—and suppressed his sympathy. "We've learned our lesson," he said with false assurance. "There'll be no mistakes this time." Secretly he was surprised by her simple determination not to go to bed with Wolff. He had assumed that such things did not matter much to her, one way or the other. He had misjudged her, then. Seeing her in this new light somehow made him very cheerful.

Gaafar came in and said, "Dinner is served, sir." Vandam smiled. Gaafar was doing his English butler act.

"What have we got, Gaafar?"

"For you, sir, clear soup, scrambled eggs and yoghurt. But I took the liberty of grilling a chop for Miss Fontana."

Elene said to Vandam, "Do you always eat like that?"

"No, it's because of my cheek, I can't chew." He stood up.

They went into the dining room and Gaafar served the soup.

Elene said, "Your son is old beyond his years."

"He's been through a couple of things that ought to be reserved for adults."

"Yes." Elene hesitated. "When did your wife die?"

"May the twenty-eighth, nineteen forty-one, in the evening."

"Billy told me it happened in Crete."

"Yes. She worked on cryptanalysis for the air force. She was on a temporary posting to Crete at the time the Germans invaded the island. The British lost and decided to get out. Apparently she was hit by a stray shell and killed instantly. Of course, we were trying to get live people away then, not bodies, so . . . There's no grave, you see. No memorial. Nothing left."

Elene said quietly, "Do you still love her?"

"I think I always will. It's like that with people you really love. If they go away, or die, it makes no difference."

"Were you very happy?"

"We . . ." He hesitated, thinking of the diplomat's daughter, graceful, imperious, who had married an unknown junior army officer. "Ours wasn't an idyllic marriage. It was I who was *devoted*. Angela was fond of me."

"Do you think you will marry again?"

He shrugged. He did not know the answer. Elene seemed to understand, for she fell silent and began to drink her soup.

Afterwards Gaafar brought them coffee in the drawing room. At this time of day Vandam usually began to hit the bottle, but tonight he did not want to drink. He sent Gaafar to bed, and they drank their coffee. Vandam smoked a cigarette.

He felt the desire for music. He had loved music at one time, although lately it had gone out of his life. Now, with the mild night air coming in through the open windows, he wanted to hear clear, delightful notes and sweet harmonies. He went to the piano and began to play Beethoven's "Für Elise". The ability to play came back to him instantly, almost as if he had never stopped. His hands knew what to do in a way he always felt was miraculous.

When the song was over he went back to Elene, sat next to her and kissed her cheek. Her face was wet with tears. She said, "William, I love you with all my heart."

Chapter 18

Rommel could smell the sea. At Tobruk the heat and the dust and the flies were as bad as they had been in the desert, but it was all made bearable by that whiff of dampness in the breeze.

Von Mellenthin came into the command vehicle with his intelligence report. "Good evening, General Field Marshal."

Rommel smiled. He had been promoted after the victory at Tobruk, and he was not yet used to the full new title. "Anything new?"

"A signal from the spy in Cairo. He says the Mersa Matrûh line is weak in the middle."

Rommel took the report and glanced over it. "If this is correct, we can burst through the line as soon as we get there."

"I'll be doing my best to check the spy's report, of course," said von Mellenthin. "But he was right last time."

The door to the vehicle flew open and Kesselring came in.

"Field Marshal!" Rommel said. "I thought you were in Sicily."

"I was," Kesselring said. He stamped the dust off his handmade boots. "I've flown here to see you. Damn it, Rommel, this has got to stop. Your orders were to advance to Tobruk and no farther."

Rommel sat back in his canvas chair. He had hoped to keep Kesselring out of this argument. "The circumstances have changed."

"But your original orders have been confirmed by the Italian Supreme Command," said Kesselring. "Your air and sea support is now needed for the attack on Malta. After we have taken Malta your communications will be secure for the advance to Egypt."

"You people have learned nothing!" Rommel said. "While we are digging in, the enemy, too, will be digging in. I did not get this far by playing the old game of advance, consolidate, then advance again. They are running now, and now is the time to take Egypt."

Kesselring turned to von Mellenthin. "How many tanks and men do we have?"

Rommel suppressed the urge to tell von Mellenthin not to answer; he knew this was a weak point.

"Sixty tanks, General Field Marshal. Two thousand five hundred men. The Italians have six thousand men and fourteen tanks."

Kesselring turned back to Rommel. "And you're going to take Egypt with a total of seventy-four tanks? Von Mellenthin, what is our estimate of the enemy's strength?"

"Allied forces are three times as numerous as ours, but we are well supplied and the men are in tremendous spirits."

Rommel said, "Von Mellenthin, go to the communications truck and see if any message has arrived."

Von Mellenthin went out. Rommel said, "The Allies are regrouping at Mersa Matrûh. They expect us to move around the southern end of their line. Instead we will hit the middle, where they are weakest—"

"How do you know all this?" Kesselring interrupted.

"Our intelligence assessment, based on a spy report—"

"My God! You've no tanks, but you have your spy!"

"He was right last time."

Von Mellenthin came back in, carrying a radio message pad.

Kesselring said, "All this makes no difference. I am here to confirm the Führer's orders: you are to advance no farther."

Rommel smiled. "I have sent a personal envoy to the Führer. I am a general field marshal now, and I have direct access to him. I think von Mellenthin may have his reply."

Von Mellenthin read the message. "'It is only once in a lifetime that the goddess of victory smiles. On to Cairo. Adolf Hitler.'"

Chapter 19

When Vandam got to his office on Thursday morning he learned that the previous evening Rommel had advanced to within sixty miles of Alexandria. Rommel seemed unstoppable. The Mersa Matrûh line had broken in half like a matchstick. The Allies had fallen back once again. The new line of defence stretched across a thirty-mile gap between the sea and the impassable Qattara Depression, and if that line fell, there would be no more defences. Egypt would be Rommel's.

The news was not enough to dampen Vandam's elation. It was more than twenty-four hours since he had awakened at dawn, on the sofa in his drawing room, with Elene in his arms. Since then he had been suffused with a kind of adolescent glee.

In the office he was visited early by a Captain Brown from the special liaison unit of military intelligence. Brown leaned on the edge of the table and spoke around the stem of his pipe. "Are you being evacuated, Vandam?"

Vandam said, "What? Evacuated? Why?"

"Our lot's off to Jerusalem. So's everyone who knows too much. Keep people out of enemy hands. Now then, I've got a little snippet for you. We all know Rommel's got a spy in Cairo."

"How did you know?" Vandam said.

"Stuff comes through from London, old boy." The special liaison unit had an ultrasecret source of intelligence. "The chap has been identified as 'the hero of the Rashid Ali affair.' Mean anything to you?"

Vandam was thunderstruck. "It does!" he said.

"Well, that's all," Brown said. "Good luck. I may not see you for a while."

"Thanks," Vandam muttered distractedly as Brown went out.

The hero of the Rashid Ali affair. It was incredible that Wolff should have been the man who outwitted Vandam in Istanbul. Yet it made sense: Vandam recalled the odd feeling he had had about Wolff's *style,* as if it were familiar. The girl Vandam had sent to pick up the mystery man had had her throat cut.

And now Vandam was sending Elene in against the same man.

A corporal came in with an order. Vandam read it with mounting disbelief. All departments were to extract from their files those papers which might be dangerous in enemy hands, and burn them. Clearly the brass thought the Germans might soon be taking Egypt.

It's going to pieces, Vandam thought; it's falling apart.

It was unthinkable. Thousands of men had died in the desert. After all that, was it possible that we could turn and run away?

He called Jakes in and watched him read the order. Jakes nodded, as if he had been expecting it. "We'll have the bonfire in the yard at the back, sir."

After Jakes went out, Vandam opened his file drawer and began

177

to sort through his papers: names and addresses, security reports on individuals, details of codes, a little file on Alex Wolff. Jakes brought in a big cardboard box, and Vandam began to dump papers into it, thinking, This is what it is like to be the losers.

The box was half full when Vandam's corporal sent in a Major Smith, a small man with bulbous blue eyes and an air of being rather pleased with himself. He shook hands and said, "Sandy Smith, SIS."

"What can I do for the Secret Intelligence Service?" asked Vandam.

"I'm the liaison man between SIS and the General Staff," Smith explained. "Your inquiry about a book called *Rebecca* got routed through us." Smith produced a piece of paper with a flourish.

Vandam read the message. The SIS head of station in Portugal had sent one of his men to visit all the English-language bookshops in the country. In the holiday area of Estoril he had found a book-seller who recalled selling six copies of *Rebecca* to one woman— the wife of the German military attaché in Lisbon.

Vandam said, "This confirms something I suspected. Thank you for taking the trouble to bring it over."

"No trouble," Smith said. "I'm over here every morning, any-way. Glad to help." He went out.

Vandam reflected on the news while he went on with his work. There was only one plausible explanation of the fact that the book had found its way from Estoril to the Sahara. Undoubtedly it was the basis of a code. It was a pity the key to the code had not been captured along with the book.

When the cardboard box was full Vandam hefted it onto his shoulder and went outside. Jakes had the fire going in a rusty steel water tank propped up on bricks. A corporal was feeding papers to the flames. Charred scraps of paper floated up on a pillar of hot air. Vandam dumped his box and turned away.

He wanted to think, to walk. He left GHQ and headed down-town. His cheek was hurting. He thought he should welcome the pain, for it was supposed to be a sign of healing. He was growing a beard to cover the wound so that he would look a little less un-sightly when the dressing came off.

He thought of Elene. It was, of course, a disaster that the two of them had fallen so joyfully in love. His parents, his friends and the army would be aghast at the idea of his marrying an Egyptian and a Jew. But Vandam decided not to worry over all that. He and Elene might be dead within a few days. We'll bask in the sunshine while it lasts, he thought. He kept thinking of the girl whose throat had been cut, apparently by Wolff, in Istanbul. He was terrified that Elene might find herself alone with Wolff again that evening.

Looking around him, he observed that there was a festive feeling in the air. He passed a hairdresser's salon and noticed that it was packed with women standing and waiting. The dress shops seemed to be doing good business. Vandam realized that the Egyptians were looking forward to being liberated.

He could not escape a sense of impending doom. Even the sky seemed dark. He looked up; the sky *was* dark. There seemed to be a grey swirling mist, dotted with particles, over the city: smoke mixed with charred paper. All across Cairo the British were burning their files, and the soot had darkened the sun.

Vandam was suddenly furious with himself and the rest of the Allied armies for preparing so equably for defeat. What had happened to that famous mixture of obstinacy, ingenuity and courage which was supposed to characterize the British nation? What, Vandam asked himself, are *you* planning to do about it?

He turned around and walked back towards GHQ. He visualized the map of the El Alamein line, where the Allies would make their last stand. This was one line Rommel could not circumvent, for below it was the vast, impassable Qattara Depression. Rommel would have to break the line. But where? Immediately behind the line was the heavily fortified Alam Halfa Ridge. Clearly it would benefit the Allies if Rommel spent his strength attacking Alam Halfa. Furthermore, the southern approach to the ridge was through treacherous soft sand. It was unlikely that Rommel knew about the quicksand, for he had never penetrated this far east before, and only the Allies had good maps of the desert.

So, Vandam thought, my duty is to prevent Alex Wolff telling Rommel that Alam Halfa is well defended and cannot be attacked from the south. Then it hit him: suppose I capture Wolff, get his radio, find the key to his code. Then I could impersonate Wolff, get a message to Rommel saying the El Alamein line was weak at the southern end and that Alam Halfa itself was weakly defended.

The temptation would be too much for Rommel to resist.

He would break through the line at the southern end and swing north towards Alam Halfa. Then he would hit the quicksand. While he was struggling through it, our artillery would decimate his forces. When he reached Alam Halfa he would find it heavily defended. At that point we would bring in more forces from the front line and squeeze the enemy like a nutcracker.

If the ambush worked well, it might not only save Egypt but annihilate the Afrika Korps. Vandam began to feel elated. He thought: I've got to put this idea up to the brass. I'll write a memo to Bogge, who, of course, will block it. But I'll send a copy to the brigadier. He hurried for his office. Suddenly the future looked different. Perhaps the jackboot would not ring out on the tiled floors of the mosques. Perhaps Billy would not have to join the Hitler Youth. Perhaps Elene would not be sent to Dachau.

We could all be saved, he thought. If I catch Wolff.

ONE OF THESE DAYS, Vandam thought, I'm going to punch Bogge on the nose. Today he was at his worst: indecisive, sarcastic, touchy.

"Too risky," he said. "You don't seem to realize, laddie, that—"

There was a knock at the door and the brigadier walked in. Vandam and Bogge stood up. "At ease, gentlemen," the brigadier said. "I've been looking for you, Vandam."

Bogge said: "We were just working on a deception plan—"

"Yes, I saw the memo."

"Ah, Vandam sent you a copy," Bogge said.

The brigadier turned to Vandam. "You're supposed to be catching spies, Major, not advising generals on strategy."

Vandam's heart sank.

"However, since this is such a splendid plan, I want you to come and sell it to Auchinleck. You can spare him, Bogge, can't you?"

"Of course, sir," Bogge said through clenched teeth.

"All right, Vandam. Let's go."

Chapter 20

Major Smith came to the houseboat at lunchtime. The information he brought with him was the most valuable yet.

Wolff and Sonja went through their now familiar routine. Sonja and Smith began on the couch and moved into the bedroom. When Wolff emerged from the cupboard there on the floor were Smith's briefcase and his bush shirt, with the key ring poking out of the pocket. Wolff opened the briefcase and began to read.

Once again Smith had come to the houseboat straight from the morning conference at GHQ, at which Auchinleck and his staff discussed Allied strategy and decided what to do.

After a few minutes' reading Wolff realized that what he held in his hand was a complete rundown of the Allies' last-ditch defence on the El Alamein line: artillery on the ridges, tanks on the level ground and minefields all along. The Alam Halfa Ridge, five miles behind the centre of the line, was heavily fortified. The southern end of the line was weaker, both in troops and mines.

Smith's briefcase also contained an enemy-position paper. Allied intelligence thought Rommel would probably try to break through at the southern end. Beneath this, written in pencil, in what was presumably Smith's handwriting, was a note which Wolff found more exciting than all the rest: "Major Vandam proposes deception plan. Encourage Rommel to break through at southern end, lure him towards Alam Halfa, catch him in quicksand, then nutcracker. Plan accepted by Auchinleck."

What a discovery! Not only did Wolff hold in his hand the details of the Allied defence line—he also knew their deception plan. And the plan was Vandam's!

This was the greatest espionage coup of the century. Wolff himself would be responsible for Rommel's victory in North Africa. They should make me king of Egypt for this, he thought.

He looked up and saw Smith standing between the curtains, wearing only his shorts, staring down at him. Smith roared, "Who the devil are you?"

Wolff realized angrily that he had not been paying attention to the noises from the bedroom. Something had gone wrong, there had been no champagne-cork warning.

Smith said, "That's my briefcase!" He took a step forward. Wolff reached out, caught Smith's foot and heaved sideways. The major toppled over and hit the floor with a heavy thud. Wolff and Smith scrambled to their feet.

Smith was a small man, ten years older than Wolff and in poor shape. He stepped backwards, fear showing in his face. He bumped into a shelf, glanced sideways, saw a cut glass fruit bowl on the shelf, picked it up and hurled it at Wolff. It missed, fell into the kitchen sink, and shattered loudly. The noise, Wolff thought, if he makes any more noise, people will come to investigate. He moved towards Smith.

Smith, with his back to the wall, yelled, "Help!"

Wolff hit him once, on the point of the jaw, and he collapsed, sliding down the wall to sit, unconscious, on the floor.

Sonja came out and stared at Smith. "What are we going to do about him?"

"I don't know." He needed time to think. To kill Smith might be dangerous. The death of an officer—and the disappearance of his briefcase—would cause a terrific rumpus throughout the city.

Smith groaned and opened his eyes. "You. You're Slavenburg." He looked at Sonja, then turned back at Wolff. "It was you who introduced . . . in the Cha-Cha . . . this was all planned. . . ."

"Shut up," Wolff said mildly.

"You're damned spies," Smith said. His face was white.

Sonja said nastily, "And you thought I was crazy about you."

"Stop it!" Wolff said. "Got any rope to tie him with?"

Sonja thought for a moment. "Up on deck, in the locker."

Wolff took from the kitchen drawer the heavy steel rod for sharpening the carving knife. He gave it to Sonja. "If he moves, hit him with that," he said.

Wolff went up the ladder and onto the deck. He opened the locker and took out a coil of rope. Then he heard Sonja's voice, from below, raised in a shout. There was a patter of feet on the ladder. Wolff whirled around. Smith came up through the hatch at a run. Sonja must have missed him with the steel rod.

Wolff dashed across the deck to the gangplank to head him off.

Smith turned, ran to the other side of the boat, and jumped into the water.

Wolff looked all around quickly. There was no one on the decks of the other houseboats—it was the hour of the siesta. The towpath was deserted except for the "beggar" he presumed Kemel had stationed there. Kemel would have to deal with him. On the river there were a couple of feluccas, at least a quarter of a mile away.

Wolff ran to the side. Smith surfaced, gasping for air. He began to swim, inexpertly, away from the houseboat. Wolff stepped back

182

several paces and took a running jump into the river. He landed, feet first, on Smith's head.

For several seconds all was confusion. Wolff went under in a tangle of arms and legs and struggled to push Smith down. When Wolff could hold his breath no longer he wriggled away and came up.

He sucked air and wiped his eyes. Smith's head bobbed up in front of him, coughing and spluttering. Wolff got behind him and crooked one arm around his throat while he used the other to push down on the top of his head. Smith continued to thrash around underwater, flailing his arms, kicking his legs.

This was no good, it was taking too long. Wolff pulled out his knife. Grabbing Smith by the hair he stabbed him. The river water turned muddy red all around them. Sheathing the knife, Wolff pulled the body over to the houseboat. Sonja, wearing a dressing gown, stared over the side. "Is he dead?"

"Yes. We have to sink the body. Get that rope!"

She disappeared from view for a moment, and returned with the rope. "Now find something heavy. That spare anchor up in the bow will do."

She went forward to where the rusty anchor lay on the deck. She dragged it, scraping all the way, to where Wolff was clinging to the side. "What now?" she said.

"Tie the end of the rope around the stock of the anchor."

Her fingers moved quickly.

"Now throw me the rope," Wolff said.

She threw down the other end of the rope. Treading water, he pulled in the slack, threaded the rope under the dead man's armpits, wound it around the torso twice then tied a knot.

"Throw the anchor into the water," he told Sonja.

She heaved the anchor over the side. It splashed a couple of yards away from the houseboat and went down. The rope became taut, then the body went under. Wolff kicked his legs underwater where the body had gone down: they did not contact anything. The body had sunk deep.

Wolff climbed on deck. Looking back down, he saw that the pink tinge was rapidly disappearing from the water. They went below.

Sonja slumped on the couch and closed her eyes. Wolff stripped off his wet clothes.

Sonja said, "It's the worst thing that's ever happened to me."

"You'll survive," Wolff said.

"At least it was an Englishman."

Wolff went into the bathroom and turned on the taps of the bath. When he came back Sonja said, "Was it worth it?"

"Yes." Wolff pointed to the military papers which were still on the floor, where he had dropped them when Smith surprised him. "That stuff is red-hot. With that, Rommel can win the war."

"When will you send it?"

"Tonight, at midnight."

"Tonight you're going to bring Elene here."

He stared at her. "How can you think of that when we've just killed a man and sunk his body?"

She stared at him defiantly. "I don't know, I just do. You *will* bring her home tonight. You owe it to me."

Wolff hesitated. "I'd have to broadcast while she's here."

"I'll keep her busy. Damn it, Alex, you *owe* me!"

"All right." Wolff went into the bathroom. Sonja was unbelievable, he thought. She took depravity to new heights of sophistication. He ran hot water and got in.

"But now Smith won't be bringing you any more secrets," she called to him.

"I don't think we'll need them after the next battle," Wolff replied. "He's served his purpose."

He picked up the soap and began to wash off what little blood remained on him.

Chapter 21

Vandam knocked at the door of Elene's flat an hour before she was due to meet Alex Wolff. She came to the door wearing a black cocktail dress and high-heeled black shoes with silk stockings. Around her neck was a slender gold chain. Her face was made up, and her hair gleamed. She had been expecting him.

He smiled at her. She looked astonishingly beautiful. "Hello."

"Come in." She led him into the living room. "Sit down."

He wanted to kiss her, but she did not give him a chance. He sat on the couch. "I want to tell you the details for tonight."

"OK." She sat on a chair opposite him. She had not even returned his smile. "If you want a drink, help yourself."

He stared at her. "Is something wrong?"

"Nothing. Give yourself a drink, then brief me."

Vandam frowned. He stood up, went across to her and knelt in front of her chair. "Elene, what is it?"

She glared at him. She seemed close to tears. She said loudly, "Where have you been for the last two days?"

"I've been at work."

"And where do you think I've been?"

"Here, I suppose."

"Exactly!"

He did not understand what that meant. He said, "I've been working and you've been here, and so you're mad at me?"

"Yes! You could have sent me a note or a bunch of flowers!"

"Flowers? What do you want with flowers? We don't need to play that game any more."

"Oh, really? We made love the night before last, in case you've forgotten. You brought me home and kissed me goodbye. Then—nothing."

He sat on the floor and looked away from her. "In case *you* have forgotten, a certain Erwin Rommel is knocking at the gates with a bunch of Nazis in tow, and I'm one of the people who's trying to keep him out."

"You could have taken five minutes to send me a note."

"What *for*?"

"Well, exactly. What for—I'm a loose woman, am I not? I give myself to a man the way I take a drink of water. An hour later I've forgotten. Damn you, William, you make me feel cheap!"

It still made no sense, but now he could hear the pain in her voice. He turned to face her. "You're the most beautiful thing that's happened to me for a long time, perhaps ever. Please forgive me for being a fool. " He took her hand in his own.

She bit her lip, fighting back tears. "Yes, you are," she said. She looked down at him and touched his hair. "You bloody fool," she whispered, stroking his head.

"I've such a lot to learn about you," he said.

"And I about you."

He looked away, thinking aloud. "People resent my equanimity

—always have. Those who work for me don't, they like it. They know I don't panic and they feel reassured. Exactly the same attitude often infuriates others—my superiors, my friends, my wife, Angela, you. I've never understood why."

"Because sometimes you *should* panic, fool," she said softly. "Sometimes you should show that you are frightened, or obsessed, or crazy for something. It's human, it's a sign that you care."

Vandam said, "Well, people should know better. Lovers should know better, and so should friends and bosses if they're any good." He said this honestly, but in the back of his mind he realized that there was an element of coldheartedness in his famous equanimity. "I *do* care, but I refuse to make symbolic gestures. Either we love each other or we don't, and all the flowers in the world won't make any difference. But the work I did today could affect whether we live or die. I *did* think of you, all day; but I don't worry about you when I know you're OK. Can you imagine yourself getting used to that?"

She gave him a watery smile. "I'll try."

"What I want to say, after all that, is—forget about tonight, don't go, we'll manage without you. But I can't. We need you, and it's terribly important."

"That's OK, I understand."

"But first of all, may I kiss you hello?"

Kneeling beside the arm of her chair, he took her face in his big hand and kissed her. Her mouth was soft and yielding and slightly moist. He savoured the feel and the taste of her. Eventually she drew back, took a deep breath and said, "My, my, I do believe you mean it."

"You may be sure of that."

She laughed. "When you said that, you were the old Major Vandam for a moment. Brief me, Major."

"I'll have to get out of kissing distance."

Vandam crossed the room to the drinks cabinet and found the gin. "A major in intelligence has disappeared—along with a briefcase full of secrets. It turns out he has been disappearing at lunchtimes recently, and nobody knows where he's been going. I've a hunch that he might have been meeting Wolff."

"What was in his briefcase today?"

"A rundown of our defences which was so complete that we

think it could alter the result of the next battle. So we'd better catch Wolff tonight."

"But it might be too late already!"

"No. We found the decrypt of one of Wolff's signals. It was timed at midnight. Spies generally report at the same time every day. At other times their masters won't be listening—at least, not on the right wavelength. I think Wolff will send this information tonight at midnight unless I catch him first."

He hesitated, then decided she ought to know the full importance of what she was doing. "There's something else. He's using a code based on a novel called *Rebecca*. If I can get the key to the code—"

"What's that?"

"A piece of paper telling him how to encode signals. If I can get the key to the *Rebecca* code, I can impersonate Wolff over the radio and send false information to Rommel. It could save Egypt. But I must have the key."

"All right. What's tonight's plan?"

"It's the same as before, only more so. I'll be in the restaurant with Jakes, and we'll both have pistols."

Her eyes widened. "You've got a gun?"

"I haven't got it now, but I will have. There will be two other men in the restaurant, six more outside, and civilian cars ready to block all exits from the street. No matter what Wolff does tonight, if he wants to see you, he's going to be caught."

There was a knock at the door.

Vandam said, "What's that? Are you expecting someone?"

"No, of course not. It's almost time for me to leave."

Vandam frowned. "I don't like this. Don't answer."

"I have to. It might be my father. Or news of him."

Elene went out of the living room. Vandam sat listening as she opened the door. He heard her say, "Alex!"

He heard Wolff's voice. "You're all ready. How delightful." It was a deep, confident voice, with only a trace of an accent.

Elene said, "But we were to meet in the restaurant—"

"I know. May I come in?"

Vandam leaped over the sofa and lay on the floor behind it.

Wolff's voice came closer. "This way?"

"Um . . . yes. . . ."

Vandam heard the two of them enter the room. Wolff said, "What a lovely flat. Mikis Aristopoulos must pay you well."

"Oh, I don't work there regularly. It's family, I help out."

"Well. These are for you."

"Oh, flowers. Thank you."

Vandam thought, Damn you.

Wolff said, "May I sit down?"

Vandam felt the sofa shift as Wolff lowered his weight onto it.

Vandam thought, I could jump him now. They were about the same weight, and evenly matched—except for the knife. If they fought, and Wolff had the knife, Wolff would win. It had happened before, when they had grappled in the alley. Vandam thought, Why didn't I bring the gun?

If they fought, and Wolff won, then what? Wolff would know Elene had been trying to trap him. In Istanbul, in a similar situation, he had slit the girl's throat.

Wolff said, "I see you were having a drink. May I join you?"

"Of course," Elene said. "What would you like?"

"What's that?" Wolff sniffed. "A little gin would be nice."

Vandam thought, That was my drink. Thank God Elene didn't have a drink as well—two glasses would really have given the game away.

"Cheers!" Wolff said.

"Cheers."

She was coping so well, Vandam thought. What does she think I'm planning to do? She must have guessed by now where I'm hiding. Poor Elene! Once again she had got more than she bargained for. Vandam hoped she would be passive and trust him.

Wolff said, "You seem nervous, Elene. Did I confuse you by coming here? If you want to finish getting ready or something, just leave me here with the gin bottle."

"No, no. . . . Well, we did say we'd meet at the restaurant."

"And here I am, altering everything at the last minute again. To be truthful, I'm bored with restaurants. I arrange to have dinner with people, then when the time comes I can't face it, and I think of something else to do."

So they're not going to the Oasis, Vandam thought. Damn. That means no help from Jakes and the others.

Elene said, "What do you want to do?"

189

"May I surprise you again?"

Vandam thought, Make him tell you!

Elene said, "All right."

Vandam groaned inwardly. If Wolff would reveal where they were going, Vandam could contact Jakes and have the ambush moved.

Wolff said, "Shall we go?" The sofa creaked as he got up. Vandam thought, I could go for him now! Too risky.

He heard them leave the room. Wolff, in the hallway, said, "After you." Then the front door was slammed shut.

Vandam stood up. He would have to follow them, and take the first available opportunity to contact Jakes. He went to the front door and listened. He heard nothing. He opened it a fraction; they had gone. He hurried along the corridor and down the stairs.

As he stepped out of the building, he saw them across the road. Wolff was holding open a car door for Elene to get in. It was not a taxi; Wolff must have rented, borrowed or stolen a car for the evening. Wolff closed Elene's door and walked around to the driver's side. Vandam climbed on his motorcycle.

The car pulled away, and Vandam followed.

The city traffic was heavy. Vandam was able to keep five or six cars behind without losing his quarry. He still did not know where Wolff was going.

He began to suspect the answer when they crossed the bridge to Zamalek, where the dancer, Sonja, had her houseboat. It was surely not possible that Wolff was living there. The place had been under surveillance for days, and Kemel had reported nothing unusual.

Wolff parked in a street and got out. Vandam stood his motorcycle against a wall and followed Wolff and Elene to the towpath. From behind a bush he watched as they walked to one of the boats and Wolff helped Elene onto the gangplank. Wolff followed her onto the deck. Then they disappeared below.

This was surely his best chance to send for help, Vandam thought. There must be a policeman around here. "Hey!" he said in stage whisper. "Is anybody there? Police?"

A dark figure materialized from behind a tree. An Arab voice said, "Yes?"

"I'm Major Vandam. Are you watching the houseboat?"

"Yes, sir."

"The man we're chasing is on the boat now. Do you have a gun?"

"No, sir."

"Hell." Vandam considered whether he and the Arab could raid the boat on their own, and decided they could not: in that confined space Wolff's knife could wreak havoc. "I want you to go to the nearest telephone, ring GHQ and get a message through to Captain Jakes: his men are to come here immediately. Is that clear?"

"Captain Jakes, GHQ. Yes, sir."

The Arab left at a trot. He had been instructed to report to his superior officer and no one else on this case. He would go to the station house and call Superintendent Kemel at home. Kemel would know what to do.

Anxiously Vandam found a position in which he was concealed but could still watch the houseboat and the towpath. A while later the figure of a woman came along the path. She looked familiar. She boarded the houseboat, and Vandam realized she was Sonja.

He was relieved; at least Wolff could not molest Elene while there was another woman on the boat. He settled down to wait.

Chapter 22

Elene stepped off the ladder and looked nervously around the interior of the houseboat. She had expected the decor to be sparse and nautical. In fact, it was luxurious, if a little overripe. There were thick rugs, low divans, occasional tables and rich velvet floor-to-ceiling curtains which divided this area from what was presumably the bedroom. Opposite the curtains, where the boat narrowed to its stern, was a tiny kitchen.

"Is this yours?" she asked Wolff.

"It belongs to a friend," he said. "Do sit down."

Elene felt trapped. Where was William Vandam? Several times she had thought there was a motorcycle behind the car, but she had been unable to look carefully for fear of alerting Wolff. Now he was going to the refrigerator, taking out caviar, a bottle of champagne, finding two glasses, pulling the cork with a loud pop. He set the caviar on a table before her and poured the champagne.

She was terrified of Wolff. What kind of game was he playing? She shuddered.

"Are you cold?" Wolff said as he handed her a glass.

"No, I wasn't shivering."

He raised his glass. "Your health."

Her mouth was dry. She sipped the cold wine, then took a gulp. It made her feel a little better.

He sat beside her on the couch. "I enjoy your company so much," he said. "You're an enchantress." He put his hand on her knee.

She froze. Here it comes, she thought.

"You're enigmatic," he said. "Desirable, rather aloof, very beautiful, sometimes naïve and sometimes so knowing." With his fingertip he traced the silhouette of her face: forehead, nose, lips, chin. He said, "Why do you go out with me?"

What did he mean? Was it possible he suspected what she was really doing? Or was this just the next move in the game?

She looked at him and said, "You're a very intriguing man."

"I'm glad you think so." He leaned forward to kiss her. She offered him her cheek. His lips brushed her skin, then he whispered, "Why are you frightened of me?"

There was a noise up on deck—quick, light footsteps—and then the hatch opened. Elene thought, William!

A high-heeled shoe and woman's foot appeared. The woman came down and Elene recognized her as Sonja, the belly dancer.

She thought, What on earth is going on?

"ALL RIGHT, Sergeant," Kemel said into the telephone. "You did exactly the right thing in contacting me. I'll deal with everything myself. In fact, you may go off duty now."

"Thank you, sir," said the sergeant. "Goodnight."

Kemel hung up. This was a catastrophe. The British had followed Alex Wolff to the houseboat, and Vandam was trying to organize a raid. The consequences would be twofold. First, there would be no possibility of using the German's radio on the houseboat to contact Rommel. Second, once the British discovered that the houseboat was a nest of spies, they would quickly figure out that Kemel had been protecting it. What was he going to do?

He went back into the bedroom, dressed quickly. From the bed his wife said softly, "What is it?"

"Work," he whispered.

"Oh, no." She turned over.

He took his pistol from the locked drawer in the desk and put it in his jacket pocket, then he kissed his wife and left the house quietly. He got into his car and started the engine. He had to consult Sadat about this, but in the meanwhile Vandam might grow impatient, waiting at the houseboat, and do something precipitate. Vandam would have to be dealt with first, quickly.

Kemel drove to Zamalek and parked near the towpath. From the boot of the car he took a length of rope. He carried his gun in his right hand, holding it reversed, for clubbing.

He reached the riverbank. He looked at the silver Nile, the black shapes of the houseboats. Vandam would be in the bushes somewhere. Kemel stepped forward, walking softly.

Vandam turned at the sound of footsteps behind him. "Who is it?" he hissed. "Jakes?"

A dark figure emerged from the bushes and raised an arm. Vandam said, "Who—" then he realized that the arm was sweeping down. The blow landed squarely on Vandam's left temple.

Kemel knelt beside the prone figure. Working quickly, he took off Vandam's sandals, removed his socks and stuffed them into his mouth. That should stop him from calling out. Next Kemel rolled Vandam over, crossed his wrists behind his back and tied them together with the rope. Then he bound Vandam's ankles. Finally he tied the rope to a tree.

Vandam would come around in a few minutes, but he would find it impossible to move or cry out. Kemel decided to take a quick look at the houseboat. He walked light-footedly along the towpath to the *Jihan*. There were lights on inside, but little curtains were drawn across the portholes. He was tempted to go aboard, but he wanted to consult with Sadat first, for he was not sure what should be done. He turned around and headed back towards his car.

SONJA SMILED. "Alex has told me all about you, Elene."

Elene smiled back. Was this the friend of Wolff's who owned the houseboat? Had he not expected her back so early? Why was neither of them angry or embarrassed?

Wolff handed Sonja a glass of champagne. She took it without looking at him, and said to Elene, "So you work in Mikis' shop?"

"No, I don't," Elene said. "I helped him for a few days, that's all. We're related."

"So you're Greek?"

"That's right."

The small talk was giving Elene confidence. Her fear receded. Whatever happened, Wolff was not likely to rape her at knife-point in front of one of the most famous women in Egypt. Sonja gave her a breathing space, at least. William was determined to capture Wolff before midnight—Midnight!

She had almost forgotten. At midnight Wolff was to contact the enemy by wireless, and hand over the details of the defence line. But where was the radio? Was it here on the boat? Would he send his message in front of her and Sonja?

Wolff sat down beside Elene. She felt vaguely threatened, with the two of them sitting on either side of her.

He said, "What a lucky man I am, to be sitting here with two such beautiful women."

Elene looked straight ahead, not knowing what to say.

Wolff said, "Isn't she beautiful, Sonja?"

"Oh, yes." Sonja touched Elene's face, then took her chin and turned her head.

"Do you think I'm beautiful, Elene?" she asked.

"Of course." Elene frowned. This was getting weird.

"I'm so glad," Sonja said. She put her hand on Elene's knee.

And then Elene understood.

Everything fell into place: Wolff's patience, his phoney court-liness, the houseboat, the unexpected appearance of Sonja. Elene realized she was not safe at all. The pair of them wanted to use her. Her fear of Wolff came back, stronger than before.

Stop it.

I won't be afraid. I can stand being mauled by two fools. There's more at stake here. Forget about yourself, think about the radio, and how to stop Wolff from contacting Rommel.

This threesome might be turned to advantage.

She looked furtively at her wristwatch. It was a quarter to midnight. Too late now to rely on William. She, Elene, was the only one who could stop Wolff. And she thought she knew how.

She calmly proceeded to make Wolff and Sonja fight each other —without success—for her attentions.

Chapter 23

It was long past midnight. Beside Elene on the bed, Wolff and Sonja lay fast asleep. It was a game that they obviously knew well. In the denouement, Wolff had rejected Elene and chosen Sonja instead. It had not been pleasant, but Elene had escaped unscathed— and she had succeeded in making Wolff forget all about his midnight transmission to Rommel.

She wondered what had happened to Vandam. Had he lost sight of Wolff's car in the traffic or had an accident? Whatever the reason, Vandam was no longer watching over her. She was on her own. What was to stop Wolff sending his message another night? If his radio was here on the houseboat, that might make all the difference.

She remembered something Vandam had said: "If I can get the key to the *Rebecca* code, I can impersonate him over the radio . . . it could turn the tables completely."

Elene thought, perhaps I can find the key. Vandam had said it was a sheet of paper explaining how to use the book to encode messages. She had to search the houseboat.

Wolff's breathing was quiet and even. Sonja did not stir.

Slowly Elene eased off the bed. Where should the search start? She decided to begin at the front and work backwards. She tiptoed into the tiny bathroom. Here there was a basin, a small bath, and a cupboard contained shaving gear, pills. The radio was not in the bathroom.

She passed through the bedroom into the living room. A divan couch was screwed to the floor. The radio would not be there. Next there was a tall cupboard. She opened it gently. There was a broom, and some dusters and cleaning materials. No radio.

She moved into the kitchen. She opened six small cupboards. They contained crockery, canned food, saucepans, glasses. There were several drawers. She opened one. The rattle of cutlery shredded her nerves. Another, bottled spices and flavourings. Another, kitchen knives.

Next to the kitchen was a small writing desk with a fold-down desk top. Beneath it was a small suitcase. Elene opened it. There was the radio. Her heart skipped.

The radio fitted inside the suitcase exactly, as if it had been designed that way. On top of the radio there was a book. Elene lifted it out. It was *Rebecca*. In the middle there was something between the pages. She let the book fall open and a sheet of paper dropped to the floor. She bent down and picked it up. It was a list of numbers and dates, with some words in German. This was surely the key to the code.

She held in her hand what Vandam needed to turn the tide of the war. She had to go, now, with the book and the key. Her dress was on a chair. As she slipped it over her head, the bed creaked. From behind the curtains came the unmistakable sound of someone getting up.

She went to the ladder and ran up the narrow wooden steps. Glancing down, she saw Wolff appear between the curtains and glance up at her in astonishment. His eyes went to the suitcase opened on the floor. Elene turned to the hatch. It was secured on the inside with two bolts. She slid them back. From the corner of her eye she saw Wolff dash to the ladder. She pushed up the hatch and climbed out. Wolff was scrambling up the ladder. She bent swiftly. As Wolff grasped the rim of the opening, Elene slammed the hatch down on his hand with all her might. There was a roar of agony. Elene ran across the deck and down the gangplank, stopped, picked up the end of the plank, and threw it into the river.

Wolff came up through the hatch, his face a mask of pain and fury. Elene panicked as she saw him come across the deck at a run. She thought, He's naked, he can't chase me! He took a flying jump over the rail of the boat, landed on the edge of the riverbank, arms windmilling for balance. With a sudden access of courage Elene rushed at him and pushed him backwards into the water. She turned and ran along the towpath.

When she reached the lower end of the pathway that led to the street she stopped and looked back. Her heart was pounding. She felt elated when she saw Wolff, dripping wet and naked, climbing out of the water up the muddy riverbank. It was getting light; he could not chase her far in that state. She spun around towards the street, broke into a run and crashed into someone.

Strong arms caught her in a tight grip. She struggled desperately. The man holding her got an arm around her throat before she could scream. Wolff came up and said, "Who are you?"

196

"I'm Kemel." He was back from talking to Sadat. "You must be Wolff."

"Thank God you were there. You'd better come aboard." Wolff slid down the bank and into the water, grabbed the floating plank, shoved it up onto the shore and climbed up after it. He laid it across the gap between the houseboat and the bank. Kemel marched Elene across the deck and down the ladder. He pushed Elene over to the couch and made her sit down.

Wolff went through the curtains and came back a moment later with a big towel. He proceeded to rub himself dry with it, then wrapped it around his waist and sat down. He examined his hand. "She nearly broke my fingers," he said. He looked at Elene with a mixture of anger and amusement.

Kemel said, "Where's Sonja?"

"In bed," Wolff said, jerking his head towards the curtains. "She sleeps through earthquakes."

"You're in trouble," Kemel said.

"I know," Wolff said. He glanced at his watch and cursed as he saw the time. "I suppose this girl's working for Vandam."

"I don't know about that. I got a call from my man on the towpath. Vandam had come alone and sent my man for help."

Wolff was shocked. "We came close! Where's Vandam now?"

"Out there still. I knocked him on the head and tied him up."

Elene's heart sank. Vandam was incapacitated—and nobody else knew where she was. It had all been for nothing.

Wolff nodded. "Vandam must have followed her. That's two people who know about this place. If I stay here, I'll have to kill them."

"Not good enough," Kemel said. "If you kill Vandam, the murder will eventually be blamed on me." He paused, watching Wolff with narrowed eyes. "And if you were to kill me, that would still leave that guard who called me last night."

"So . . ." Wolff frowned. "I have to go. Damn."

Kemel nodded. "If you disappear, I think I can cover up. But I want something from you. Remember the reason we've been helping you. We want to talk to Rommel."

"I'll be sending again tonight. Tell me what to say, and I'll—"

"No. We want to do it ourselves. We want your radio." Sadat's instructions had been clear on that point.

198

Wolff frowned. Elene realized that Kemel was a nationalist rebel, trying to co-operate with the Germans.

Kemel added: "We could send your message for you."

"Not necessary," Wolff said. He seemed to have reached a decision. "I have another radio."

"It's agreed, then."

"There's the radio." Wolff pointed to the case, still open on the floor. "It's already tuned to the correct wavelength. All you have to do is broadcast at midnight, any night."

Kemel went over to the radio and examined it. Elene wondered why Wolff had said nothing about the *Rebecca* code. Wolff was playing safe, she decided; to give Kemel the code would be to risk that he might give it to someone else.

Wolff said, "Where does Vandam live?"

Kemel had done some checking. He told Wolff the address.

Elene thought, *Now* what is he after?

Wolff said, "He's married, I suppose."

"A widower. His wife was killed in Crete last year."

"Any children?"

"Yes," Kemel said. "A small boy called Billy. Vandam drives him to school every morning. Why?"

Wolff shrugged. "I'm a little obsessed with the man who's come so close to catching me." Elene was sure he was lying.

Kemel closed the suitcase, apparently satisfied. Wolff said, "Keep an eye on her for a minute, would you?" Wolff had noticed that Elene still had *Rebecca* in her hand. He reached down and took it from her. He disappeared through the curtains. He came back without the book, carrying his clothes. He began to dress.

Kemel said to him, "Do you have a call sign?"

"Sphinx," Wolff said shortly.

"A code?"

"No code."

"What was in that book?"

Wolff looked angry. "A code. But you can't have it. You'll have to take your chance and broadcast in clear."

Suddenly Wolff's knife was in his hand. "Don't argue," he said. "I know you've got a gun. But if you shoot, you'll still have to deal with the girl. Why not leave her to me?"

Kemel turned without speaking, picked up the radio and went

199

up through the hatch. Wolff went to the porthole and watched him walk off.

Wolff put his knife away and buttoned his shirt over the sheath. He got the book from the next room, extracted the paper bearing the key, crumpled it, dropped it into a glass ashtray, took a box of matches from a kitchen drawer and set fire to the paper.

He must have another key with the other radio, Elene thought.

Wolff made sure the paper was entirely burned. Then he opened a porthole and dropped the book into the river.

He found a small suitcase and began to pack a few things.

"Where are you going?" Elene said.

"You'll find out—you're coming."

"Oh, no." What would he do with her? He had caught her deceiving him—and now she knew too much. She felt very afraid. Nothing she had done had turned out well.

Wolff continued packing his case. When he was ready he took a last look around. He said, "I hate to disturb Sonja's beauty sleep." He grinned. "Let's go."

They walked along the towpath. Why was he leaving Sonja behind? Elene wondered. Wolff was completely unscrupulous, she realized; and the thought made her shudder.

He carried his case in his left hand and gripped her arm with his right. They turned onto the footpath, walked to the street and went to his car. He made her climb in the driver's side and over the gear lever to the passenger side. He got in beside her and they drove away.

Elene wondered where they were going. Wherever it was, Wolff's second radio was there, along with another copy of *Rebecca* and another key to the code. When we get there I'll have to try again, she thought wearily. Now that Wolff had left the houseboat, there was nothing Vandam could do even after somebody untied him. Elene, on her own, had to try to stop Wolff from contacting Rommel, and if possible steal the key to the code. The idea was ridiculous. All she really wanted was to get away from this evil, dangerous man, to go home, to feel safe again. But she thought of her father, walking to Jerusalem, and she knew she had to try.

Wolff stopped the car. Elene said, "This is Vandam's house!" She gazed at Wolff. "But Vandam isn't here."

"No." Wolff smiled bleakly. "But Billy is."

Chapter 24

Anwar el-Sadat was delighted with the radio. He plugged it in to test it, and told Kemel it was very powerful. They hid it in the oven in Sadat's kitchen. Then Kemel drove back to Zamalek, rehearsing the story he had prepared to cover up his role in the events of the night.

He parked his car, went cautiously down to the towpath, and slipped into the bushes thirty or forty yards from where he had left Vandam. He rolled on the ground to make his clothes dirty, and smeared some of the sandy soil on his face. Then, rubbing his wrists to make them look sore, he went in search of Vandam. He was sure the Englishman could not have recognized his attacker.

He found him exactly where he had left him. The bonds were still tight and the gag still in place. Kemel bent down; Vandam looked at him with wide, staring eyes. Kemel said, "My God, they got you, too!"

He removed the gag and began to untie Vandam. "The sergeant contacted me," he explained. "I came down here looking for you, and the next thing I knew, I woke up bound and gagged with a headache. I just got free." Kemel threw the rope aside. Vandam stood up stiffly. Kemel said, "How do you feel?"

"I'm all right."

"Let's board the houseboat and see what we can find."

As soon as Kemel turned, Vandam hit him as hard as he could with an edge-of-the-hand blow to the back of the neck. It might have killed Kemel, but Vandam did not care. He knew that Kemel had betrayed him. He had been bound and gagged, but he had been able to hear, "I'm Kemel. You must be Wolff." Since then, Vandam had been seething, and all his pent-up anger had gone into the blow.

Kemel lay on the ground, stunned. Vandam rolled him over, searched him and found the gun. He used the rope that had bound his own hands to tie Kemel's hands behind his back. Then he slapped Kemel's face until he came around. "Get up," he said.

Fear came into Kemel's eyes. He struggled to his feet. Vandam took hold of Kemel's collar with his left hand, keeping the gun in his right. "Move."

They walked to the houseboat. Vandam pushed Kemel ahead, up the gangplank and across the deck. Awkwardly, with his hands tied, Kemel descended the ladder. Vandam bent down to look inside. There was nobody there. He went quickly down the ladder. Pushing Kemel to one side, he pulled back the curtain. He saw Sonja in bed, sleeping. "Get in there."

Kemel went through and stood beside the bed. "Wake her."

Kemel touched Sonja with his foot. She opened her eyes and sat up. She recognized Kemel, then saw Vandam with the gun. She and Vandam said simultaneously, "Where's Wolff?"

Vandam was sure she was not dissembling. It was clear now that Kemel had warned Wolff, and Wolff had fled without waking Sonja. Presumably he had taken Elene with him for some reason.

Vandam said, "Has Wolff sent a radio message tonight?"

"No," Sonja replied. "No, he hasn't."

Thank God for that, at least.

"What *did* happen here?" Vandam asked, dreading the answer.

"We went to bed."

"Who did?"

"We all did."

So that was it. And Vandam had thought Elene was safe, because there was another woman around! He put the thought out of his mind. "Get dressed," he told Sonja.

She got off the bed and hurriedly put on a dress. Keeping both of them covered with the gun, Vandam went to the prow of the boat and looked through the little doorway. He saw a tiny bathroom. He ordered Kemel and Sonja inside, then locked the door on them and began to search the houseboat. He found a glass ashtray full of charred paper, but it was completely burned up. After half an hour he was sure that the houseboat contained no radio, no copy of *Rebecca* and no code key.

He found rope. He got the two prisoners out of the bathroom, tied Sonja's hands, then roped Sonja and Kemel together. He marched them off the boat and up to the street, where he hailed a taxi. He put Sonja and Kemel in the back. Keeping the gun pointed at them, he got in the front. "GHQ," he told the wide-eyed, frightened Arab driver.

The two prisoners would be interrogated, but really there were only two questions: Where was Wolff? And where was Elene?

SITTING IN THE CAR, Wolff took hold of Elene's wrist. He drew out his knife and ran its blade lightly across the back of her hand. The knife was very sharp. Elene stared at her hand in horror. At first there was just a line like a pencil mark. Then blood welled up and there was a sharp pain. She gasped.

Wolff said, "You're to stay very close to me and say nothing."

Suddenly Elene hated him. "Otherwise you'll cut me?" she said with scorn.

"No," he said. "Otherwise I'll cut Billy."

He got out of the car. Elene sat still, feeling helpless. What could she do against this ruthless man? She took a handkerchief from her bag and wrapped it around her bleeding hand. Wolff came around to her side of the car, and, taking her arm, made her get out.

They walked up the drive to Vandam's house and rang the bell. Gaafar opened the door. He said, "Good morning, Miss Fontana."

Wolff said, "Good morning. I'm Captain Alexander. The major asked me to come around. Let us in, would you?"

"Of course, sir." Gaafar stood aside. Wolff, gripping Elene's arm, stepped into the tiled hall. Gaafar said, "I hope the major is all right."

"Yes, he's fine. But he can't get home this morning, so he asked me to drive Billy to school."

Elene was aghast. Wolff was going to kidnap Billy. She must not let it happen! She wanted to shout, No, Gaafar, he's lying, take Billy and get away, run, run! But Wolff had the knife, and Gaafar was old, and Wolff would get Billy anyway.

Gaafar seemed to hesitate. Wolff said, "All right, Gaafar, snap it up. We haven't got all day."

"Yes, sir," Gaafar said. "Billy is just finishing his breakfast. Would you wait in here for a moment?" He opened the drawing-room door for them.

Wolff propelled Elene into the room and at last let go of her arm. He sat down at the desk, found paper and a pencil and began to write.

"Why did you bring me here?" Elene cried.

Wolff looked up from his writing. "To keep the boy quiet. We've got a long way to go."

"Leave Billy here," she pleaded. "He's a child."

"Vandam's child," Wolff said with a smile. "Vandam may be

able to guess where I'm going. I want to make sure he doesn't come after me." He continued to write.

Elene forced herself to concentrate. They were going on a long journey. At the end, surely, was the spare radio, with a copy of *Rebecca* and a copy of the key to the code. Somehow she had to help Vandam follow them. Where would Wolff have kept a spare radio? He might have hidden it somewhere in the desert, or somewhere between Cairo and Asyût. Maybe . . .

Billy came in. "Hello," he said to Elene. "Did you bring me that book?"

"Book?" She stared at him, thinking that he was still a child, despite his grown-up ways. He wore grey flannel shorts, a white shirt and a school tie. He was carrying a school satchel.

"You were going to lend me a detective story by Simenon."

"I forgot. I'm sorry."

Wolff had been staring at Billy like a miser looking into his treasure chest. Now he stood up. "Hello, Billy," he said with a smile. "I'm Captain Alexander."

Billy shook hands and said, "How do you do, sir."

"Your father asked me to tell you that he's pretty busy coping with old Rommel and I'm to take you to school."

"Has he been in another fight?"

Wolff hesitated. "Matter of fact he has, but he's OK. He got a bump on the head." Billy seemed more proud than worried.

Wolff spoke to Elene in rapid Arabic. "Keep the boy quiet for a minute." He turned back to the desk.

Elene looked at Billy's satchel and had the glimmer of an idea. "Show me your schoolbooks," she said. The satchel was open, and an atlas stuck out. She reached for it. "What are you doing in geography?"

"The Norwegian fjords."

Elene saw Wolff finish writing, then put the sheet of paper in an envelope. He sealed the envelope and stuffed it in his pocket.

"Let's find Norway." Elene flipped the pages of the atlas.

Wolff picked up the telephone and dialled. He looked at Elene, then looked away, out of the window.

Elene found the map of Egypt. Billy said, "But that's—"

Quickly Elene touched his lips with her finger. He stopped speaking and frowned at her. "That's Scandinavia, yes, but Norway is in Scandinavia, look." She unwrapped the handkerchief from around her hand. With her fingernail she opened the cut and made it bleed. Billy turned white.

Elene had been almost sure Wolff was going to Asyût. He had said he was afraid Vandam would guess their destination, and it was likely Vandam would associate that town with Wolff. Just then she heard Wolff say into the phone, "Hello? Give me the time of the train to Asyût."

I was right! she thought. She dipped her finger in the blood from her hand. With three strokes, she drew an arrow in blood, pointing to the town of Asyût, three hundred miles south of Cairo. She closed the atlas. She used her handkerchief to smear blood on the cover, then pushed the book behind her. Billy seemed dumbstruck. He was staring at Elene's hand.

Wolff put down the phone. "Let's go. You don't want to be late for school, Billy." He went to the door and opened it.

Billy, frowning, picked up his satchel and went out. Elene followed. There was a little pile of letters on a table in the hall. Wolff dropped his envelope on top of the pile and they left the house.

Wolff asked Elene, "Can you drive?"

"Yes," she answered, then realized she should have said no.

"You two get in the front." Wolff got in the back.

As she pulled away, Wolff leaned forward. He said, "See this?" He was showing the knife to Billy .

"Yes," Billy said in an unsteady voice.

Wolff said, "If you make trouble, I'll use it on you."

Billy began to cry.

Chapter 25

In the interrogation room, Vandam said, "Listen, Kemel. As things stand you're going to be shot for spying. If you tell us all you know about Alex Wolff, you could get off with a prison sentence. Be sensible. Now, you came to the towpath and knocked me out, didn't you?"

"No, sir."

Vandam sighed, Kemel had his story and he was sticking to it.

Even if he knew, or could guess, where Wolff had gone, he would not reveal it while he was pretending innocence.

Vandam said, "What is your wife's involvement in all this?"

Kemel said nothing, but he looked scared.

"If you won't answer my questions, I'll have to ask her."

Kemel's lips were pressed together in a hard line.

Vandam stood up. "All right, Jakes," he said. "Bring in the wife on suspicion of spying."

Kemel said, "Typical British justice."

Vandam looked at him. "Where is Wolff?"

"I don't know."

Vandam went out. When Jakes came out Vandam said, "He's a policeman, he knows the techniques. He'll break, but not today." And Vandam had to find Wolff and Elene today.

They walked a few yards to another cell. Vandam opened the door and went in. Sonja sat on a hard chair, wearing a coarse grey prison dress. Beside her stood a woman army officer who would have scared Vandam, had he been her prisoner. She was short and stout, with a hard masculine face and short grey hair.

Vandam and Jakes sat down. Vandam had interrogated Sonja once before, and she had been stronger than he. This time Elene's safety was in the balance, and Vandam had few scruples left. He said, "Where is Alex Wolff?"

"I don't know."

"Wolff is a German spy, and you have been helping him."

"Ridiculous." Vandam watched her face. She was proud, confident, unafraid.

"Wolff betrayed you," Vandam said. "Kemel, the policeman, warned Wolff of the danger; but Wolff left you sleeping and went off with another woman. Are you going to protect him after that?"

She said nothing.

"Wolff kept his radio on your boat. You knew this, so you were an accessory. You're going to be shot for spying."

"All Cairo will riot! You wouldn't dare!"

"You think so? What do we care if Cairo riots now? The Germans are at the gates—let them put down the rebellion."

"You can't touch me."

"I think I'd better prove to you that I can." Vandam nodded to the woman officer.

The woman held Sonja still while Jakes tied her to the chair. She struggled for a moment, but it was hopeless. For the first time there was a hint of fear in her eyes. The woman officer took a large pair of scissors from her bag. She lifted a hank of Sonja's long, thick hair and cut it off.

"You can't do this!" Sonja shrieked.

The woman continued to cut. As the heavy locks fell away, she dropped them in Sonja's lap. Sonja's screams subsided into tears. Vandam said, "You see, we don't care much about Egyptian public opinion anymore. We've got our backs to the wall. We may all be killed soon. We're desperate."

The woman took soap and a shaving brush and lathered Sonja's head, then began to shave her scalp. Finally the woman took a mirror from her bag and held it in front of Sonja. Sonja gasped when she saw the reflection of her totally bald head. "No. It's not me." She burst into wilder crying.

All the hatred was gone now; she was completely demoralized. Vandam said softly, "Where was Wolff getting his information?"

"From Major Smith," Sonja replied. "Sandy Smith."

Vandam glanced at Jakes. That was the name of the major from SIS who had disappeared. "How did he get the information?"

"Sandy came to the houseboat in his lunch break to visit me. While we were in bed Alex went through his briefcase."

As simple as that, Vandam thought. God, I feel tired. Smith was liaison man between the Secret Intelligence Service and GHQ. He had been privy to all strategic planning. Smith had been going straight from the morning conference at GHQ to the houseboat, with a briefcase full of secrets.

Vandam said, "Where is Smith now?"

"He caught Alex going through his briefcase. Alex killed him. He's in the river by the houseboat."

Vandam nodded to Jakes, and Jakes went out.

Vandam said to Sonja, "Tell me about Kemel."

She was in full flood now, eager to tell all she knew, her resistance quite crushed; she would do anything to make people be nice to her. "He came and told me he would censor his surveillance reports if I would arrange a meeting between Alex and Anwar el-Sadat. He's a captain in the army."

"Why did Sadat want to meet Wolff?"

"So the Free Officers Movement could send a message to Rommel."

Vandam said to the woman officer, "Go and find the address of Captain Anwar el-Sadat."

"Yes, sir." The woman went out.

Vandam said, "Do you know where Wolff might have gone?"

"The thief, Abdullah. He might have gone to Abdullah."

"Good idea. Any other suggestions?"

"His cousins in the desert."

"And where would they be found?"

"No one knows. They're nomads."

"Might Wolff know their movements?"

"I suppose he might."

Vandam sat looking at her. She was totally broken, not only willing but eager to betray her friends and tell all her secrets.

"I'll see you again," Vandam said, and went out.

The woman officer handed him a slip of paper with Sadat's address on it. Jakes was waiting in the muster room. "The navy is lending us a couple of divers," Jakes said. "They're on their way."

"Good. I'm going to arrest this Sadat fellow. Has everyone been briefed?"

Jakes nodded. "They know we're looking for a wireless transmitter, a copy of *Rebecca* and a set of coding instructions."

"I want you to raid Abdullah's place. Then meet me at the houseboat."

SADAT LIVED in a suburb three miles out of Cairo in the direction of Heliopolis. Four jeeps roared up outside, and the soldiers immediately surrounded the house and began to search the garden. Vandam rapped on the front door. The door was opened. "Captain Anwar el-Sadat?"

"Yes." Sadat was a thin, serious young man of medium height. His curly brown hair was already receding. He wore his uniform and fez, as if he was about to go out.

"You're under arrest," Vandam said, and pushed past him into the house. "Which is your room, Captain?"

Sadat pointed. He was calm and dignified, but hiding some tension. He's afraid, Vandam thought; but not of going to prison; he's afraid of something else.

Vandam went into the room. It was a simple bedroom with a mattress on the floor and a *galabia* hanging from a hook. Two soldiers began to search.

"You know Alex Wolff," Vandam said to Sadat. "He also calls himself Achmed Rahmha, but he's a European."

"I've never heard of him."

Clearly Sadat was a fairly tough personality, not the kind to break down and confess everything just because a few burly soldiers started messing up his room.

A shout came from another part of the house, "Major Vandam!"

Vandam followed the sound into the kitchen. A sergeant MP was lifting a suitcase radio out of the oven. Vandam looked at Sadat, who had followed him into the kitchen. The Arab's face was twisted with bitterness and disappointment. So the rebels had warned Wolff, and in exchange they had got his radio. Did that mean he had another?

"Well done, Sergeant. Take Captain Sadat to GHQ."

"I protest," Sadat said. "The law states that officers in the Egyptian army may be detained only in the officers' mess and must be guarded by a fellow officer."

"The law also states that spies are to be shot," Vandam said. He turned to the sergeant. "Finish searching the house. Then have Sadat charged with espionage."

He looked again at Sadat. The bitterness and disappointment had gone from his face, to be replaced by a calculating look. He's going to make the most of all this, Vandam thought; he's preparing to play martyr. Very adaptable—he should be a politician.

Vandam went out to his jeep. "To Zamalek," he told the driver.

When Vandam reached the houseboat, the divers had done their work. Two soldiers were hauling the body out of the Nile. Jakes came over. "Look at this, sir." He handed Vandam a waterlogged book. It was *Rebecca*.

The radio went to Sadat; the code book went into the river. Vandam remembered the ashtray full of charred paper in the houseboat. Had Wolff burned the key to the code? But why, when he still had a vital message to send to Rommel? The conclusion was inescapable: Wolff had *another* radio, book and key hidden away somewhere.

The soldiers got the body onto the bank. Vandam stood over

it. "Ugly, isn't it," he said to Jakes. "Stabbed, then dumped in the river. Wolff's damn quick with that knife." Vandam touched his cheek: the dressing had been taken off now, and several days' growth of beard hid the wound. *But not Elene, not with the knife, please.* "I gather you haven't found Wolff."

"There was no sign of him at Abdullah's house."

"Nor at Captain Sadat's." Suddenly Vandam felt utterly drained. It seemed that Wolff outwitted him at every turn. He rubbed his face. He had not slept in the last twenty-four hours. And he only had till midnight.

"I think I'll go home and get some rest," he said. "It might help me think more clearly. This afternoon we'll interrogate the prisoners again."

On the way home, Vandam recalled that Sonja had mentioned another possibility: Wolff's nomad cousins. But who could tell where they would be except Wolff himself. The jeep stopped outside Vandam's house. He got out and dismissed the driver.

There was mail on the hall table. The top envelope had no stamp, and was addressed to Vandam in a vaguely familiar hand. It had "Urgent" scribbled on it. Vandam picked it up.

There was more he should do, he realized. Wolff could well be heading south now. Roadblocks should be set up on the route. There should be someone at every stop on the railway line, looking for him. Vandam was finding it hard to concentrate. He went into the drawing room, looking for a letter opener. Somehow the search had to be narrowed down. He remembered where all this had started: Asyût. That seemed to be where Wolff had come in from the desert, so maybe he would go out that way. Maybe his cousins were in that vicinity. Where was that damned letter opener? He went to the door and called, "Gaafar!" He came back into the room, and saw Billy's school atlas on a chair. It looked mucky. The boy had dropped it in a puddle, or something. Vandam picked it up. It was sticky. He realized there was blood on it. He felt as if he were in a nightmare. What was going on?

Gaafar came in. Vandam said, "What's this mess?"

Gaafar looked. "I'm sorry, sir, I don't know. They were looking at it while Captain Alexander was here—"

"Who's they? Who's Captain Alexander?"

"The officer you sent to take Billy to school, sir."

210

A terrible fear cleared Vandam's brain in an instant. "A British army captain came here this morning and took Billy away?"

"Yes, sir, he took him to school. He said you sent him—"

"Gaafar, *I sent nobody.*"

The servant's brown face turned grey.

Vandam said, "Didn't you check that he was genuine?"

"But, sir, Miss Fontana was with him, so it seemed all right."

"Oh, my God." Now he knew why the writing on the envelope was familiar: it was the same as that on the note that Wolff had sent Elene. He ripped open the envelope. Inside was a message.

Dear Major Vandam,

Billy is with me. Elene is taking care of him. He will be quite all right as long as I am safe. I advise you to stay where you are and do nothing. I have no wish to harm the boy. All the same, the life of one child is as nothing beside the future of my two nations, Egypt and Germany; so be assured that if it suits my purpose I will kill Billy.

Alex Wolff

It was a letter from a madman: the polite salutation, the correct English, the attempt to justify the kidnapping of an innocent child. Wolff was insane. And he had Billy.

Vandam handed the note to Gaafar, who put on his spectacles with a shaky hand. What was the point of the kidnap? Where had they gone? And why the blood? Gaafar was weeping openly. Vandam said, "Who was hurt? Who was bleeding?"

"There was no violence. Miss Fontana had cut her hand."

And she had smeared blood on Billy's atlas and left it on the chair. It was a sign, a message. Vandam held the book and let it fall open. Immediately he saw the map of Egypt with a blotted red arrow pointing to Asyût.

If I report this to GHQ, Bogge will order Wolff arrested at Asyût. There will be a fight. Wolff will know he has lost. What will he do then? He will kill my son.

He felt paralysed by fear. Of course that was Wolff's aim in the kidnap, to paralyse him. There was only one option. He had to go after them alone. Wolff had come from Asyût by train. Vandam would gamble that he would return by train.

Vandam went into the hall, put on his motorcycle goggles, then found a scarf and wound it around his mouth and neck. He left the house, climbed onto his motorcycle and kicked the bike into life. Gaafar had followed him, still weeping. Vandam touched the old man's shoulder. "I'll bring them back," he said. He rocked the bike off its stand, drove into the street and turned south.

Chapter 26

Billy is so pale, Elene thought. He's trying to be brave. They were riding in a first-class carriage with Wolff towards Asyût. What am I going to do? she wondered. She got a chill every time she looked at Wolff. The way he stared at Billy. The gleam in his eye, the look of triumph. Perhaps she could take Billy's mind off things by playing a game. What a ridiculous idea. Perhaps not so ridiculous. Here was his school satchel. Here was an exercise book. He looked at her curiously. What game? Noughts-and-crosses. Four lines for the grid; her cross in the centre. He took the pencil, and put a nought in the corner. I believe he's going along with this idea in order to comfort me! she thought. Wolff snatched the book, looked at it, shrugged and gave it back. Her next cross, Billy's next nought . . . the game was a draw.

I have to get Billy away from that knife, thought Elene. Billy made a cross in the centre of a new grid. She made a nought, then scribbled hastily: *We must escape—be ready*. Billy made another cross, and: *OK*. Her nought. *Next station*. Billy's third cross made a line. He smiled up at her jubilantly. He had won. The train slowed down. The thing to do was to give Billy a chance to run, then try to prevent Wolff from giving chase.

Elene looked around the carriage. Think quickly! They were in an open carriage, with fifteen or twenty rows of seats. She and Billy sat side by side, facing forward. Wolff was opposite them. Beside him was an empty seat. Behind him was the exit door to the station platform beginning to slide into view. The other passengers were a mixture of Europeans and wealthy Egyptians, all of them in Western clothing. Everyone was hot and weary. Several people were asleep.

The train stopped .

212

Not yet, Elene thought; not yet. The time to move would be when the train was about to pull out again—that would give Wolff less time to catch them. She sat feverishly still.

A priest in Coptic robes boarded the train and took the seat next to Wolff. Elene murmured to Billy, "When the whistle blows run for the door and get off the train."

Wolff said, "What was that?" The whistle blew. Billy looked at Elene, hesitating.

Wolff frowned.

Elene threw herself at Wolff, reaching for his face. He put up his arms protectively, but they did not stop her furious rush. She raked his face with her fingernails. The priest gave a shout of surprise. Over the back of Wolff's seat she saw Billy run to the door and struggle to open it. She collapsed on Wolff and tried to scratch his eyes.

At last he found his voice, and roared with anger. He pushed himself out of his seat, driving Elene backwards. She caught hold of his shirtfront. His fist came up, struck the side of her jaw. She fell back into her seat. When her vision cleared she saw Wolff heading for the door. She stood up. She saw Billy fling the door open and jump onto the platform. Wolff leaped after him. Elene ran to the door.

Billy was racing along the platform. Wolff was charging after him. The few Egyptians standing around were looking on, mildly astonished, and doing nothing. Elene ran after Wolff. The train shuddered, about to move. Wolff put on a burst of speed. Elene yelled, "Run, Billy, run!" Billy was almost at the station exit. The train was inching forward, and Wolff had to get back on it. She thought. We did it! Then Billy slipped and fell, hitting the ground hard. Wolff was on him in a flash, bending to lift him. Elene caught up with them and jumped on Wolff's back. Wolff stumbled, losing his grip on Billy. Elene clung to Wolff. The train was moving slowly but steadily. Wolff broke Elene's grip and threw her to the ground. Then he lifted Billy across his shoulder. The boy was yelling and hammering on his back. Wolff ran alongside the moving train for a few paces, then jumped in through an open door.

Elene struggled to her feet. She could not leave Billy. She ran, stumbling, alongside the train. Someone reached out a hand to her. She took it, and jumped. She was aboard, back where she started. She felt crushed. She followed Wolff to their seats. She did not look at the faces of the people she passed. She saw Wolff give Billy one sharp smack on the bottom and dump him into his seat. The boy was crying silently.

Wolff turned to Elene. "You're a crazy girl," he said loudly, for the benefit of the other passengers. He grabbed her arm and slapped her face. The priest stood up, touched Wolff's shoulder and said something.

Wolff let her go and sat down. She looked around. They were all staring at her. None of them would help her, for she was an Egyptian woman, and women, like camels, had to be beaten from time to time. As she met the eyes of the other passengers, they looked away, embarrassed. She fell into her seat. Useless, impotent rage boiled within her. They had almost escaped. She put her arm around the child and pulled him close. She began to stroke his hair. After a while he fell asleep.

Chapter 27

Vandam knew that he was—by now—well ahead of the train. He had stopped at four stations to ask if the train had passed through yet. It had not. He drove very fast, his goggles and the scarf around his mouth and neck protecting him from the worst of the dust. He knew what he was going to do, but he needed time. He would stop at the next station and put his plan into effect.

Somewhere along the road he had made a decision. He had set out from Cairo to rescue Billy and Elene; but then he had realized that that was not his only duty. There was still the war.

Vandam was almost certain that Wolff had another radio, another copy of *Rebecca* and another key to the code; and that they were all hidden at Asyût. To implement the plan for deceiving Rommel, Vandam had to have the radio and the key—and that meant he had to let Wolff get to Asyût and retrieve his spare set. Only then could he rescue Billy and Elene. It would be tough on them, but living under Nazi rule would also be tough.

Having made the decision, Vandam now needed to be certain that Wolff was on that train. He might just be able to make things a little easier for Billy and Elene at the same time.

When Vandam reached the next town he pulled up outside the police station. It was in a central square, opposite the railway station. He gave a peremptory blast on the horn of his bike. Two Arab policemen came out of the building: a grey-haired man and a boy of eighteen or twenty. Vandam got off the bike and bawled, "Attention!" Both men stood straight and saluted. Vandam returned the salute. "I'm chasing a dangerous criminal, and I need your help," he said dramatically. "Let's go inside."

Vandam led the way. He said to the older man, "Call British headquarters in Cairo for me." The man picked up the phone from a table. Vandam turned to the younger policeman. "Could you ride my motorcycle?"

The boy was thrilled by the idea. "I ride it very well."

"Go out and try it."

The older man, who had been shouting into the telephone, held it out to Vandam. "This is GHQ."

Vandam spoke into the phone. "Connect me with Captain Jakes, fast." Jakes's voice came on the line. "Hello?"

"This is Vandam. I'm in the south, following a hunch. In order to assure the maximal support of the indigenous constabulary—" he spoke like this so that the policeman would not understand—"I want you to do your Dutch uncle act."

Vandam gave the phone to the grey-haired policeman. The policeman unconsciously stood straighter as Jakes instructed him, in no uncertain terms, to do everything Vandam wanted. "Yes, sir!" the policeman said, several times. Finally he said, "Please be assured, sir and gentleman, that we will do all in our power."

Vandam went to the window. The young policeman was driving around the square on the motorcycle, hooting the horn and over-revving the engine. A small crowd had gathered to watch. The boy was grinning from ear to ear. He'll do, Vandam thought.

"I'm getting on the Asyût train when it stops here," he said to the older man. "I want your boy to drive my bike to the next station and meet me there."

"Yes, sir!"

Vandam could not hear the train yet. He had time for one more phone call. He picked up the receiver and asked the operator for Captain Newman at the army base in Asyût. After a long wait, Newman came on the line.

"This is Vandam. I think I'm on the trail of your knife man."

"Jolly good show, sir!" said Newman. "Anything I can do?"

"I'll be arriving in Asyût by road in a few hours. I need a taxi, a large *galabia* and a small Arab boy. Will you meet me?"

"I'll be at the city limits, how's that?"

"Fine." Vandam heard a distant *chuff-chuff-chuff*. "I have to go." He hung up. He put a five-pound note on the table beside the telephone: a little baksheesh never hurt. He went out into the square. Away to the north he could see the approaching smoke of the train. The younger policeman drove up to him on the bike. Vandam said, "I'm getting on the train. You drive the motorcycle to the next station and meet me there. OK?"

"OK, OK!" He was delighted.

Vandam took out a pound note, tore it in half, and gave him half the note. "You get the other half when you meet me."

The train was almost in the station. Vandam crossed the square and ran along the platform so that he could board at the front of the train without being seen by the passengers. The train came in, billowing smoke. Vandam climbed aboard.

He found himself in an economy carriage. Wolff would surely travel first-class. Vandam began to walk along the train, picking his way over the people sitting on the floor with their boxes and crates and animals. He passed through three economy carriages, then he was at the door to a first-class coach. Suddenly he was not sure that he had the nerve to go through with this. Wolff had never had a good look at him—they had fought in the dark in the alley, and the gash on his cheek was almost completely covered now by his beard. But Billy was the real problem. Vandam had to warn his son, somehow, to pretend not to recognize his father. He took a deep breath and opened the door.

Stepping through, he glanced quickly and nervously at the first few rows of seats; no Billy. He spoke to the passengers nearest him. "Your papers, please."

"What's this, Major?" said an Egyptian army colonel.

"Routine check, sir." Vandam moved slowly along the aisle, checking people's papers. By the time he was halfway down the carriage he was sure that Wolff, Elene and Billy were not there. He began to wonder whether his guesswork might have gone wrong. He reached the end of the carriage and passed through the door into the space between the coaches. Ahead was the last carriage. If they were on the train, I'll know now, he thought.

He opened the door. He saw Billy immediately. He felt a pang of distress like a wound. The boy was asleep in his seat, his feet only just reaching the floor, his body slumped sideways, his hair falling over his forehead. Elene had her arm around him. She looked up. Her eyes widened. Vandam quickly raised a finger to his lips. She dropped her eyes; but Wolff had caught her look, and he was turning his head to find out what she had seen. Vandam said to Wolff, "Papers, please."

It was the first time Vandam had seen his enemy face to face. Wolff was a handsome fellow, with strong features. Only around the eyes and the corners of the mouth was there a hint of weakness, of depravity. He handed over his papers then looked out of the window, bored. The papers identified him as Alex Wolff, Villa les Oliviers, Garden City. Vandam said, "Where are you going, sir?"

"Asyût. To visit relations."

"Are you people together?"

"That's my son and his nanny," Wolff said.

Vandam took Elene's papers and glanced at them. He wanted to take Wolff by the throat. *My son and his nanny*. You bastard.

He gave Elene her papers. "No need to wake the child," he said. He looked at the priest sitting next to Wolff, and took the proffered wallet. The priest said, "I'm going to Asyût, too."

"I see," said Vandam. He returned the papers. "Thank you." He backed away, along the aisle to the next row of seats, and continued to examine papers. When he looked up Wolff was staring out of the window again.

Vandam reached the end of the carriage. He was handing back the last of the papers, when he heard a cry that pierced his heart: *"That's my dad!"*

He looked up. Billy was running along the aisle towards him, stumbling, bumping against the seats, his arms outstretched. *Oh, God*. Beyond Billy, Vandam could see Wolff and Elene standing up, watching: Wolff with intensity, Elene with fear. Vandam opened the door behind him, pretending to take no notice, and backed through it onto the coach platform. Billy came flying through. Vandam slammed the door. He took Billy in his arms.

218

"It's all right," Vandam said. "It's all right."

Wolff would be coming to investigate.

"They took me away!" Billy said. "I missed school and I was really really scared!"

"It's all right now." Vandam felt he could not leave Billy now; he would have to kill Wolff, to abandon his deception plan and the radio and the code. No, it *had* to be done. He fought down his instincts. "Listen," he said. "I have to catch that man, and I don't want him to know who I am. He's the German spy I'm after, do you understand?"

"Yes, yes . . ."

"Can you pretend I'm not your father? Can you go back to him?"

Billy stared, openmouthed. His whole expression said *no, no!*

"This is a real-life tec story, Billy, and we're in it, you and I. You have to pretend you made a mistake. I'll be nearby, and together we'll catch the spy."

The door opened. Wolff came through. "What's all this?"

Vandam made his face bland. "He seems to have woken up from a dream and mistaken me for his father. We're the same build. You did say you were his father, didn't you?"

"What nonsense, Billy!" Wolff said. "Come back to your seat."

Billy stood still.

"Come on, lad," Vandam said. "Let's go and win the war."

The old catchphrase did the trick. Billy gave a brave grin. "I'm sorry, sir," he said. "I must have been dreaming."

Vandam felt as though his heart would break.

Billy turned away and went back inside the coach. Wolff and Vandam followed. As they walked along the aisle, the train slowed down. They were approaching the next station where Vandam's motorcycle would be waiting. Billy reached his seat and sat down. Elene was staring at Vandam uncomprehendingly. Billy touched her arm and said, "It's OK, I made a mistake." A strange light came into her eyes; she seemed on the point of tears.

Vandam paused at the carriage door. "Have a good trip," he said to Billy.

"Thank you, sir."

The train pulled into the station and stopped. Vandam got off and walked forward along the platform a little way. He stood in the shade of an awning and waited. There was a whistle, and the train began to move. Vandam's eye was fixed on the window next to Billy's seat. As it passed him, he saw Billy raise his hand in a little wave. Vandam waved back, and Billy's face was gone.

Vandam realized he was trembling all over.

When the train was almost out of sight he left the station. Outside was the young policeman from the last town sitting astride the motorcycle. Vandam gave him the other half of the pound note, climbed on the motorcycle and took the road south. He would reach Asyût thirty or forty minutes ahead of the train, he calculated. Captain Newman would be there to meet him.

He pulled ahead of the train which carried Billy and Elene, the only people he loved. He explained to himself again that he had done the best thing for everyone, the best thing for Billy; but in the back of his mind a voice said, Cruel, cruel, cruel.

Chapter 28

The train entered the station and stopped. Elene saw a sign which said, in Arabic and English: ASYÛT. She realized with a shock that they had arrived.

Vandam must have some scheme to rescue her and Billy and also get the key to the code. She wished she knew how. Fortunately Billy did not seem to be troubled by such thoughts. He had perked up, taking an interest in the countryside through which the train was passing, and had even asked Wolff where he got his knife. Elene wished she had as much faith in William Vandam.

She glanced at Wolff. He seemed full of nervous excitement. Some kind of change had occurred in him in the last twenty-four hours, she thought. When she first met him he had been a poised, suave man. Now all that had gone. He fidgeted, he looked about restlessly, and every few seconds the corner of his mouth twitched almost imperceptibly. It was curious that Wolff, the ruthless one, was getting desperate while Vandam just got cooler.

Elene and Billy followed Wolff from the train and onto the crowded platform. Suddenly a dirty boy in bare feet and green striped pyjamas snatched Wolff's case, shouting, "I get taxi!" Wolff gave a good-humoured shrug and let the boy lead him to the gate.

They went out into the square. Elene looked around. There was no sign of Vandam. Wolff told the Arab boy, "I want a motor taxi." There was one such car behind the horse-drawn cabs. The boy led them to it.

"Get in the front," Wolff told Elene. He gave the boy a coin and got into the back with Billy. The driver wore dark glasses and a *kaffiyeh*—an Arab headdress. "Go south," Wolff told him in Arabic.

"OK," the driver said.

Elene's heart missed a beat. She knew that voice. She stared at the driver. It was Vandam.

VANDAM DROVE AWAY from the station, thinking, So far, so good. His knowledge of Arabic was rudimentary, but he was able to give—and therefore to understand—directions. Captain Newman had come through with everything Vandam had asked for, even adding a six-shot Enfield .380 revolver. Having studied Newman's map of the Asyût area, Vandam knew how to find the southbound road out of the city. He drove through the marketplace, honking his horn continually in Egyptian fashion, steering dangerously close to the great wooden wheels of the carts, nudging sheep out of the way with his fenders.

Pretending to adjust his rearview mirror, Vandam stole a glance at Billy, wondering if he had recognized his father. Billy was staring at the back of Vandam's head with an expression of delight. Vandam thought, Don't give the game away!

They left the town behind and headed south on a straight desert road. On their left were irrigated fields and groves of trees; on their right, a wall of granite cliffs, coloured beige by a layer of dusty sand. Wolff said, "*Ruh alyaminak*."

Vandam knew this meant "Turn right." Up ahead he saw a turnoff which led straight to the cliff. He took the turn, then saw that he was headed for a pass through the hills. The road began to climb, and the old car struggled. At the summit Vandam looked out across the apparently endless Western Desert.

The road became a track. Directly ahead, the sun rolled down the edge of the sky. Wolff sat up in his seat and began to look about him. Soon afterwards the road intersected a wadi. Cautiously Vandam let the car roll down the bank of the dried-up river. Wolff said, "*Ruh ashshimalak*."

Vandam turned left. The going was firm. He was astonished to see groups of people, tents and animals in the wadi. It was like a secret community. A mile farther on they saw the explanation: a wellhead, marked by a low circular wall of mud brick. Beyond it was a large encampment where Wolff made Vandam stop. There were tents in a cluster, hobbled camels and cooking fires.

Wolff reached into the front of the car, switched off the engine and pulled out the key. Without a word he got out.

By a fire, Ishmael sat making tea. He looked up and said, "Peace be with you," as casually as if Wolff had dropped in from the tent next door.

"And with you be health and God's blessing," Wolff replied.

Ishmael handed him a cup. Wolff drank. The tea was sweet and very strong. Ishmael asked, "What of your friends?" He nodded towards the taxi.

"They are not friends," Wolff said.

Ishmael nodded. He was incurious. "You will join us in eating?"

"Alas, no. Already the sun is low, and I must be back in the city before night falls."

Ishmael shook his head sadly. "You have come for your box."

"Yes. Please fetch it, my cousin."

Ishmael spoke to a man standing behind him, who brought the case. Wolff opened it. A great sense of euphoria flooded over him as he looked at the radio, the book and the key to the code. He felt intoxicated with the sense of power and imminent victory. He stood up. "I thank you, my cousin. May God protect thee."

"Go in safety."

Wolff was walking towards the taxi with the suitcase in his hand. "He's coming back," Elene said. "What now?"

"He'll want to go back to Asyût," Vandam said, not looking at her or Billy. "Those radios have no batteries, they have to be plugged in. He has to go somewhere where there's electricity."

Wolff got into the car. "Asyût," he said. He handed Vandam the key. Vandam started the car and turned it around. They went along the wadi and turned onto the road. The sun was low behind them now. Evening clouds were gathering over the hills ahead.

"Go faster," Wolff said in Arabic. "It's getting dark."

Vandam increased speed. The car bounced and swayed on the unmade road. Billy said, "I feel sick."

Elene turned around to look at him. His face was pale and he was sitting bolt upright. "Go slower," she said in Arabic.

Vandam slowed down for a moment, but Wolff said, "Go faster." He said to Elene, "Forget about the child."

Vandam went faster.

Elene looked at Billy again. He was as white as a sheet and on the brink of tears. "Damn you," she said to Wolff.

"Stop the car," Billy said.

Wolff ignored him, and Vandam had to pretend not to understand English. The car hit a bump in the road, rose into the air and came down hard. Billy yelled, "Dad, stop the car! Dad!"

Vandam slammed on the brakes. The gear lever bent in his hand. Elene braced herself and turned to look at Wolff.

For a split second he was stunned with shock. His eyes went to Vandam, then to Billy, then back to Vandam. She knew he was thinking about the incident on the train, and the Arab boy at the railway station, and the *kaffiyeh* that covered the taxi driver's face; and then she saw that he understood it all.

The car was grinding to a halt. Wolff threw his arm around Billy and pulled the boy to him. Then he pulled out the knife.

The car stopped. Elene saw Vandam's hand go towards the side slit of his *galabia*—and freeze as he looked into the back seat. Elene turned around.

Wolff held the knife an inch from Billy's throat. Billy was wild-eyed with fear. Vandam looked stricken. At the corners of Wolff's mouth there was the hint of a mad smile.

"You almost had me," he said.

Vandam removed the *kaffiyeh*. They all stared at Wolff.

"Let me guess," said Wolff. "Major Vandam." He was enjoying the moment. "What a good thing I took your son for insurance." Then he turned to Elene. "Underneath the *galabia*, Major Vandam is wearing khaki trousers. In one of the pockets or possibly in the waistband, you will find a gun. Take it out."

Elene found the gun and took it out.

Wolff said, "Break the back of the gun, take out the cartridges and drop them outside the car." She did. "Put the gun on the floor." She put it down. Now, once again, Wolff held the only weapon—his knife. He spoke to Vandam. "Get out of the car." Vandam sat motionless.

"Get out," Wolff repeated. With a sudden precise movement he nicked the lobe of Billy's ear with the knife. A drop of blood welled out. Vandam got out of the car.

Wolff said to Elene, "Get into the driver's seat."

She climbed over the wobbly gear lever. Vandam stood beside the car, staring in.

"Drive," Wolff said.

Elene forced the gear into neutral. She pushed the starter button. The engine caught and roared. She pulled away. Looking in the mirror she saw Wolff put the knife away and release Billy. Behind the car, already fifty yards away, Vandam stood on the desert road, his silhouette black against the sunset. He was quite still. Elene said, "He's got no water!"

"No," Wolff replied.

Then Billy went berserk.

Elene heard him scream, "You can't leave him behind!" She turned around, forgetting about the road. Billy had leaped on Wolff like an enraged wildcat, punching and scratching and kicking. Wolff had relaxed, thinking the crisis was over. He raised his arms to protect himself.

Elene looked back to the road. The car had gone off course, and the left front wheel was ploughing through the sandy scrub beside the road. She struggled to turn the steering wheel and stamped on the brake. The rear of the car began to slide sideways. Too late, she saw a deep rut running across the road immediately in front. The car hit the rut with an impact that jarred her bones, and skidded off the far side of the road into soft sand. It tilted sideways and began to roll. Elene wrestled with the wheel and the gear lever. The car was now perched on its left side like a coin dropped edgeways into the sand. The gear lever came off in her hand. She fell against the door, banging her head. The car was still.

She got to her knees, holding the broken-off gear lever. She had one knee on the car door and the other on the window. She looked into the back seat. Wolff and Billy had fallen in a heap with Wolff on top. Billy seemed to be unconscious.

Wolff got to his feet. Standing on the inside of the left rear door, he threw his weight against the floor of the car. The car rocked. He did it again. On his third try the car tilted and fell on all four wheels with a crash. Wolff opened the door and got out of the car.

He crouched and drew his knife. Elene saw Vandam approaching. Vandam crouched also ready to spring, his hands raised protectively. He was red-faced and panting: he had run after the car. They circled. Wolff was limping slightly. The sun was a huge orange globe behind them.

Vandam advanced, then hesitated. Wolff lashed out with the knife, but he had been surprised by Vandam's hesitation, and his thrust missed. Vandam's fist shot out. Wolff jerked back.. His nose was bleeding. They faced each other again.

Vandam jumped forward. Wolff dodged, the knife striking Vandam's shoulder. Vandam kicked out. Wolff jabbed again, and the knife ripped through Vandam's trousers. A dark stain appeared on his trouser leg. Vandam went down on one knee. His left arm hung limply from a shoulder covered with blood. He held his right arm up defensively. Wolff approached him.

Elene jumped out of the car. She still had the broken gear lever in her hand. She saw Wolff bring back his arm, ready to slash at Vandam once more. She rushed up behind Wolff, raised the gear lever high in the air and brought it down with all her might on the back of Wolff's head. He stood for a moment, quite still.

She hit him again. He fell. She dropped the gear lever and knelt beside Vandam.

"Well done," he said weakly. He put a hand on her shoulder and struggled to his feet. "It's not as bad as it looks. Help me with this." Using his good arm, he took hold of Wolff's leg and pulled him towards the car. Elene grabbed the unconscious man's other leg and heaved, until Wolff was lying beside the car.

Vandam leaned into the back of the car and put a hand on Billy's chest. "Alive," he said. "Thank God."

He got into the front seat. "Where's the gear lever?"

"It broke off. That's what I hit him with."

Vandam pressed the starter. The car jerked. "Good—it's still in gear." He pressed the clutch and turned the key again. The engine fired. He switched off. "We're mobile," he said.

"What will we do with Wolff?"

"Lock him in the boot."

Vandam took another look at Billy. He was conscious now, his eyes wide open.

"It's all over, son," said Vandam. "How are you?"

"I'm sorry," Billy said, "but I couldn't help feeling sick."

Vandam looked at Elene. "You'll have to drive," he said. There were tears in his eyes.

Chapter 29

There was the sudden roar of nearby aircraft. Rommel saw British bombers approaching low from behind the nearest line of hills. "Take cover!" he yelled. He ran to a slit trench and dived in.

The noise was so loud it was like silence. Rommel lay with his eyes closed. He had a pain in his stomach. They had sent him a doctor from Germany, but Rommel knew that the only medicine he needed was victory.

Today was 1 September, and everything had gone terribly wrong. What had seemed to be the weak point in the Allied defence line was looking more and more like an ambush. The minefields were heavy where they should have been light, the ground beneath had been quicksand where a hard surface was expected, and the Alam Halfa Ridge, which should have been taken easily, was being mightily defended. Rommel's strategy was wrong; his intelligence had been wrong; his spy had been wrong.

The bombers passed overhead. Rommel got out of the trench. His aides and officers emerged from cover and gathered around him again. He raised his field glasses and looked out over the desert. Scores of vehicles stood still in the sand, many of them blazing furiously. The Allies, well dug in, were picking off the Panzer tanks like fish in a barrel.

It was no good. His forward units were fifteen miles from Alexandria, but they were stuck. Another fifteen miles, he thought, and Egypt would have been mine. He looked at the officers around him. He saw in their faces what they saw in his: defeat.

*

HE KNEW IT WAS a nightmare, but he could not wake up.

The cell was six feet long by four feet wide, and half of it was taken up by a bed. The walls were of smooth grey stone. A light bulb hung from the ceiling by a cord. In one end of the cell was a door. In the other end was a small square window, set just above eye level: through it he could see the bright blue sky.

In his dream he thought, I'll wake up soon, and there will be a beautiful woman beside me, and she will kiss me, and we will drink champagne. . . . But the dream of the prison cell came back and he was so horrified that he forced his eyes open.

He woke up.

He looked around him, not understanding. He was wide awake and the dream was over; yet he was still in a prison cell. It was six feet long by four feet wide, half of it taken up by a bed. He stood up. Quietly and calmly he began to bang his head against the wall.

*

Jerusalem, 24 September 1942

My dear Elene,

Today I went to the Wailing Wall. I stood before it with many other Jews, and I prayed. I wrote a *kvitlach* and put it into a crack in the wall. May God grant my petition.

This is the most beautiful place in the world, Jerusalem. I crossed the desert in a British army truck. I sleep on a mattress on the floor in a little room with five other men. I am very poor, like always, but now I am poor in Jerusalem, which is better than rich in Egypt.

I must tell you that I am dying. My illness is quite incurable, and I have only weeks left. Don't be sad. I have never been happier in my life.

I should tell you what I wrote in my *kvitlach*. I asked God to grant happiness to my daughter Elene. I believe he will. Farewell.

Your Father

*

THE SMOKED HAM was sliced thin. The bread rolls were fresh that morning. There was potato salad made with real mayonnaise, a bottle of wine, a bottle of soda water and a bag of oranges. Elene began to pack the food into the picnic basket.

She had just closed the lid when she heard the knock at the door. She went to open it. Vandam stepped inside, closed the door and put his arms around her painfully tightly. He always did this, but she never complained, for they had almost lost each other, and now when they were together they were just so grateful.

They went into the kitchen. "What's the news?" Elene asked.

"Axis forces in full retreat, and I quote." She thought how relaxed he was these days. A little grey was appearing in his hair, and he laughed a lot.

227

They went out. The afternoon sky was curiously black, and Elene said in surprise, "I've never seen it like this."

They got on the motorcycle and headed for Billy's school. The sky became even darker. The first rain fell as they were passing Shepheard's Hotel. The raindrops were enormous; each one soaked right through her dress to the skin. Vandam turned the bike and parked in front of the hotel. As they dismounted the clouds burst.

They stood under the hotel canopy and watched the storm. The sheer quantity of water was incredible. Within minutes the gutters overflowed and the pavements were awash. Opposite the hotel the shopkeepers waded through the flood to put up shutters. Cars had to stop where they were. Elene said, "What about Billy?"

"They'll keep the kids at school until the rain stops."

At last the storm ended and the sun came out. The roads began to steam as they drove up to the school. Billy was waiting outside. "What a storm!" he said excitedly. He climbed onto the bike between Elene and Vandam.

They drove out into the desert. Holding on, eyes half closed, Elene did not see the miracle until Vandam stopped the bike. The three of them got off and looked around, speechless.

The desert was carpeted with flowers.

"It's the rain, obviously," said Vandam. "But . . ."

Millions of flying insects had also appeared from nowhere, and now butterflies and bees dashed frantically from bloom to bloom, reaping the sudden harvest.

Billy said, "The seeds must have been in the sand, waiting."

"That's it," Vandam said. "The seeds have been there for years, just waiting for this."

The flowers were all tiny, like miniatures, but brightly coloured. Billy walked a few paces from the road and bent down to examine one. Vandam put his arms around Elene and kissed her. It started as a peck on the cheek, but turned into a long, loving embrace. Eventually she broke away from him, laughing. "You'll embarrass Billy," she said.

"He's going to have to get used to it," Vandam said.

Elene stopped laughing. "Is he?" she said. "Is he, really?"

Vandam smiled, and kissed her again.

Ken Follett

Of all the many strange things that successful authors claim have started them on their careers, a broken-down car must be one of the strangest. But Ken Follett clearly recalls the time a few years ago when he was a hard-up reporter on the London Evening News and desperately needed extra money with which to pay for repairs to his car. A friend of his had recently earned £200 writing a mystery novel in his spare time, so Follett decided to do the same.

He wrote his novel (in six weeks), earned himself £200, and from such small beginnings climbed steadily to his present position as a worldwide bestseller.

As the rewards for his writing have increased, so has the time he puts into it. In particular, the time he spends in research, creating that impressive authenticity that is his hallmark. "*The Key to Rebecca*," he says, "is based on a true story. I had been in Cairo before, but I went back again while writing the book. There *was* a German spy ring there in 1942; they *did* use a belly-dancer to seduce a British major so that they could go through his briefcase; the belly dancer *did* live in a houseboat on the Nile; Anwar el-Sadat *did* borrow the spy's radio and attempt to negotiate with Rommel; and they *were* all caught as a result of passing forged currency. Subsequently the British *did* use the *Rebecca* code as part of a deception plan for the battle of Alam Halfa...."

Ken Follet and his wife and two daughters now live in the south of France. Life there, he says, is very pleasant. But he isn't letting it get in the way of his determination to continue to write a best-seller a year. Already the new book is shaping up nicely, and by way of a complete change it's a thriller set in Edwardian London. His next bestseller? Well, given the special Follet touch, there's really no doubt of that at all.

Horowitz and Mrs. Washington

A CONDENSATION OF THE BOOK BY

HENRY DENKER

ILLUSTRATED BY TED LEWIN

PUBLISHED BY W. H. ALLEN

What could an elderly Jewish gentleman possibly
have in common with some ghetto-raised black
nurse? Nothing, thought Samuel Horowitz.
Besides, he had never approved of blacks.

A stroke had left Horowitz partially paralyzed,
so his children had hired Mrs. Washington to
care for him. Aggravate him was more like it.
But his son and daughter-in-law had threatened
to put him in a nursing home if he didn't
co-operate, and that was more than the
cantankerous old man could endure.

For her part, Mrs. Washington saw Horowitz
as a challenge. As tough in spirit as her patient,
she was determined to get him out of his
wheelchair and walking again.

In this poignant story set in New York City,
Henry Denker portrays an extraordinary
friendship between two unforgettable characters
—a friendship made all the richer by their
obstinate pride in their different backgrounds.

Chapter One

"MISTER, a man your age does not resist muggers! You could have got yourself killed!" The irritated cop rebuked Samuel Horowitz in a forceful tone.

Horowitz sat silent while a nervous black intern attempted to suture the ugly wound. But he could not keep from thinking, Where did anyone ever get the idea that a black kid could be a good doctor? History, from Maimonides on, proved that the best doctors are Jewish. No wonder this intern is nervous. He knows his work is being judged by an expert, a maven on doctors!

Then a strange, terrifying feeling overcame him. He lost consciousness. The last thing he remembered was the young intern saying, "Not this! Not now!"

WHEN Horowitz came to, he found himself in bed, in a private room. The nurse avoided his questions, gave him a shot, and he went off to sleep. Hours later he woke to find his son, Marvin, staring down at him.

"Marvin?" Horowitz asked, puzzled. Marvin Hammond, born Horowitz, partner in the Washington and New York law firm of Judd, Bristol, Crain and Hammond, should be in Washington, in his big office there.

"You're okay, Pa. Don't worry. It's going to be all right," Marvin reassured.

"What's so bad that you have to tell me it's going to be all right?"

"You had what the doctors say was a minor stroke. It's lucky you were in the emergency room at the time."

"Some *gedillah!*" Horowitz said bitterly. "There I was, bleeding like a stuck pig from a razor slash and I was lucky enough to have a stroke at the same time."

"Pa . . ." Marvin tried to interrupt.

"That black intern, did he discover that I had a stroke? Or did he give me one? Just to finish up what his dear 'brothers' failed to do with the razor?"

"Pa, please . . ."

Sam Horowitz was silent for a moment. "So what's the damage? Give me the straight honest facts. Don't lie to me, Marvin."

"Well . . . they think there's a minor involvement of your left leg and arm. If that proves true, you've got a good chance of recovering almost complete mobility with physical therapy. And it's obvious you haven't lost your power of speech."

His father stared off grimly. "And the stitches on my face?"

"They expect them to heal very well. Oh, by the way, I called Mona. She's planning to come."

"Tell her not to bother," Horowitz said. "There's nothing she can do here. And she has so much to do back there. How are they going to run San Diego without Mona Fields?" he asked sarcastically, reflecting on the three times he had seen his daughter in the past four years.

"She suggested your going out there to recuperate."

"I will recuperate in my own home!" Sam Horowitz said staunchly. "Charity she can do through one of her organizations. Not through me!"

"Pa, please . . ."

"Marvin, do something for me. Go to the apartment. Find my reading glasses. And my toothbrush. Bring them."

"Sure, Pa."

After Marvin left, Sam Horowitz tried to move his left leg. It responded only partially, as if some overwhelming force gripped it. He tried to diminish the importance of that. After all, he argued, he was exhausted from his shattering experience. He attempted to raise his left hand to his face, to find the wound. But again the invisible force weighed on him.

His right leg functioned as usual. His right hand and arm—no problem. So he reached to the bedside table and found the button. He pressed it. After what he impatiently considered a reasonable time, no nurse appeared. This time he pressed his finger down on the button and kept it there.

Soon the door was thrust open. A large woman, red-faced, red-haired, of obvious Celtic extraction, demanded, "What seems to be the emergency in here? And take your finger off that button!"

Horowitz felt a bit sheepish as he said, "I would like a mirror."

"A mirror, is it?" the nurse responded. "Even at two hundred and eighty-five dollars a day, you do not ring like that just to ask for a mirror! You can darn well wait!" She tried to slam the door behind her, but the air-pressure door check prevented her.

Sam Horowitz was alone. Helpless. Yet he needed to see the wound the muggers had inflicted. There must be a mirror in the bathroom. He rolled onto his side, pushed himself up until he was in a sitting position, then slid his right leg onto the shiny tile floor. With an assist from his right hand he eased his left leg down and pushed himself up from the bed. For the first time in his life he discovered that his legs would not sustain him. He toppled forward and struck the floor, unconscious.

When he came to, he was back in bed. The red-haired nurse was standing over him, staring down angrily. Horowitz closed his eyes to blot out her reproving stare.

"Don't you ever, ever, get out of bed without assistance! Do you understand, Mr. Horowitz?"

Opening one eye, Horowitz responded, "What's your name?"

"Copeland."

"Copeland?" Horowitz questioned. "You look Irish."

"I am," she declared belligerently, as if any question were an invitation to a fight. "My maiden name was McMennamin."

"Then, Ms. McMennamin, go blow up some buildings in Belfast! But before you do, give me a mirror! I want to see what they did to me."

That seemed to soften the burly nurse. She left the room and returned moments later with a hand mirror. Gently she lifted the taped edge of the gauze pad on his face. Horowitz stared into the mirror, shocked by the angry red scar and the black thread of sutures crisscrossing his left cheek.

The nurse consoled him. "When it heals, you'll hardly notice it."

Horowitz shook his head sadly. "It's no longer a world for people. Only for animals."

"I hear you tried to fight back," she said disapprovingly.

"I should give up without a fight? That's a lie that Jews don't fight back! Remember the Six-Day War? And what happened in '73? They hit us with a sneak attack on Yom Kippur, but in the end we had the Egyptians surrounded. And don't you forget it!"

"Okay," Copeland conceded, hoping to end his tirade. "I won't forget it." She turned to leave.

"Where are you going?" Horowitz demanded.

"I have patients who are really sick," she said pointedly.

"What's the matter? I'm not sick?" Horowitz glared at her. She glared back. Then she could no longer maintain her angry gaze.

He smiled. "You're pretty fresh. But I like that. My Hannah, she was fresh too." He beckoned her closer with the forefinger of his still functioning right hand. "I want to ask you something."

"What?"

"Doctors lie. Relatives lie. But someone like you, an honest woman, I would believe. What's going to happen to me?"

"They'll make an evaluation of your condition. Then give you physical therapy. You'll slowly regain the use of your leg, your arm, your hand. After a while it'll be like it never happened."

"It always works, this therapy?" He tried to pin her down.

"Well, in medicine nothing always works. But you're in pretty good condition for a man your age. You can overcome almost anything. If you try."

Once she was gone, he picked up the mirror and stared at his face. Samuel Horowitz, sixty-eight years old, with a scar on his cheek and a left arm and leg that would not respond.

He frowned. Then he smiled. He was still a fairly handsome man. At least Hannah had thought so. And he appeared quite benign until impatience betrayed itself in his pursed lips and deep blue eyes. He had always been stubborn. But since Hannah's death three years ago he had grown irritable as well. He was quick to argue, easy to antagonize, and had appointed himself the arbiter of all public questions.

He read *The New York Times* every morning mainly for the sheer enjoyment of disagreeing. He was given to a loud singsong Ho-ho-ho! every time his view of common sense was egregiously violated by the *Times*. He had his own opinion of what constituted all the news that's fit to print.

Horowitz was a man of great pride. He had come to this country as a child, and poverty had forced him to leave school at an early age. He had gone into the paper and twine business on his own when he was twenty-three, and had succeeded well enough to marry, live comfortably, and send two children to prestigious colleges. He had provided Hannah with a maid, two vacations a year, and a new mink coat every fourth year. And all their life Hannah had never known want or wanted for love.

Being a prideful man, Horowitz did not find it easy to apologize, even when he knew he was wrong. Forced to do so, he always had to seek a roundabout way, which he usually couched in a manner reminiscent of the Talmudic logic of the rabbis of old. He closed both eyes as if in deep thought. Then finally he would open his right eye to glance at his opponent. Thus, one eye open, one closed, he would worm his way into an apology that usually ended short of confessing his error.

Horowitz put down the mirror and thought, Damn it, they are going to put me in a cage. They'll call it a wheelchair. Or a nursing home. But it will be a cage.

And my son, his wife, and two children will come to stare at me at decent intervals. Not to assure me but to salve their own consciences. Mona will come from San Diego, and perhaps Bruce and Candy will come down from Boston to visit during school breaks. Leave it to Mona to send her children to school in Boston. Harvard yet. It was a mark of distinction in Mona's West Coast circle to have children who could make it at Harvard.

Mona, Mona, Mona, he lamented. She had achieved everything in this life that she had ever wanted. Then why did he always think of her with a touch of sorrow?

Right now he had other more pressing problems. What would happen to *him*? If only Hannah were still alive . . . she would be by his side now.

He could recall reading somewhere that once one mate died, the other was sure to follow shortly thereafter. And why not? What was there to live for?

Two DAYS later a young black man, wearing glasses and attired in a starched white hospital uniform, came to see Sam Horowitz. "I'm the physical therapist," he said. "I'm here to assess how much of an insult has occurred."

"When they grab you from behind and hold a razor to your throat, I don't call that an insult. I call that an attempted murder."

"Mr. Horowitz," the young man explained, "I used insult as a medical term. It means the body has suffered a trauma. My job is to evaluate the damage, so I can prescribe the proper therapy."

"Okay," Horowitz said. "Insult me. Evaluate me."

The therapist threw back the sheet. "I'm going to exert some pressure on your leg. I want you to push back. Hard as you can."

He lifted Horowitz's left leg and pushed against it, waiting for Horowitz to resist. The old man tried but did not succeed too well. The young therapist nodded gravely, then put him through similar tests to discover the degree of mobility and resistance in his left hip, arm, and shoulder.

"Now the left hand, Mr. Horowitz, close it. Make a fist."

With all the will and effort at his command Horowitz tried to make a fist. But he couldn't. The hand resembled an open claw.

"How does it feel?" the young man asked.

"Like . . . like rubber bands are attached to my fingers and won't let them close."

The therapist nodded again. "I'll map out a course of exercise that will begin tomorrow."

"What's the evaluation?" Horowitz demanded.

"You show a degree of loss of function of the left leg, hip, arm, hand, and shoulder. There is apparently a lack of ability to dorsiflex the foot, which will create drag in attempting to walk. You have not lost sensation in your arm or leg. And that's good.

238

But there is loss of mobility, which we must begin to overcome at once, or else spasticity will set in."

Although he did not understand much of what the therapist had said, Horowitz responded with an agreeable, "Now that's what I call a civil answer."

To himself he said, Smart aleck! A little education and he right away becomes better than anyone.

Later that day Horowitz received his first bitter taste of reality when they rolled a wheelchair into his room.

Mrs. Copeland and an orderly assisted him into the chair. She gave him instructions on how to use his good right hand to make the chair go forward and back. Then she left him to practice, saying, "You're free to go down the hall to the solarium. It's a lovely summer day. You'll enjoy talking to other patients."

Left alone, Samuel Horowitz sat motionless in the wheelchair. After some minutes, hating the chair and the world at large, he put his right hand on the wheel. He moved the chair forward slightly.

Then he stopped suddenly, thinking, If I learn to do this well, I'll be doomed to do it for the rest of my life. I want to walk! I refuse to become a prisoner of this chair! Tears slowly traced down his cheeks. He had not cried since Hannah died.

Soon Horowitz learned to operate the chair proficiently enough to get to the solarium. There he could look out over Central Park. He could even see his own home.

When other patients tried to engage him in conversation, he was curt. In every way possible he tried to dissociate himself from the sick and helpless. He had been an active man all his life. He would not be content with less than the man he had been.

Eventually the therapist brought him a quad cane. It was a shiny metal cane with a padded black handle. It rested on a small square platform, supported by four rubber-tipped metal feet, which gave him a more secure base on which to lean. Grudgingly he exercised with it until he was able to take as many as ten steps. Emotionally he was never able to accept it at all.

The day finally came when Samuel Horowitz was ready to go home. He was glad to get out of the hospital, but when Marvin came to get him, Horowitz realized that going home was a difficult matter. He was not permitted to go by taxi. The trip would require a special car called an ambulette, which would accommodate his wheelchair. He dreaded the whole idea.

Chapter Two

THE ambulette pulled up before the canopy of the old apartment house on Central Park West. Marvin and the driver lifted out the wheelchair. While they settled financial matters, Horowitz slowly turned the chair about to face the building.

It had been almost new when he, Hannah, and the two children had moved in twenty-nine years ago. Now it appeared shabby. The canvas canopy was frayed in places, and one wall bore traces of graffiti, a sign of how the neighborhood had deteriorated.

Still, this old building had served them well. Mona and Marvin had both grown up here. From here they had gone off to college and here they returned with their degrees. Mona with a husband too. In a bold decision, the newlyweds had left for California, where Albert went into real estate and amassed a fortune. Now Mona lived extremely well and had two children of her own.

Bruce. And Candy. Some names for Jewish children, Horowitz thought. Yet they went well with the name to which Mona's Albert had changed before they moved to San Diego. From Feldstein to Fields.

But Horowitz was quick to remind his conscience that neither Mona nor Albert ever denied being Jewish. Quite the reverse; Mona was extremely active in Hadassah and Albert was a heavy contributor to the United Jewish Appeal out there in San Diego.

All these thoughts flashed through Horowitz's mind. But now he had to address himself to the present. In a moment Juan, the doorman, would come rushing out to greet them. Juan would smile and appear cheerful, though Horowitz knew that secretly the Cuban refugee resented having to do menial work.

How different, Horowitz thought, from the days when my father brought us over to escape the danger of the First World War. Jews were used to deprivation, and did not hold themselves to be above any honest work. But these new immigrants wanted

240

to start at the top. As for the blacks, don't even mention their pretensions. Some world!

At the same time Horowitz realized that what he resented most was having Juan see him in his present condition.

"Mr. Horowitz!" Juan exclaimed warmly as he rushed out.

The doorman insisted on helping with the wheelchair, down the front stairs, into the elevator, and right up into the apartment. When Marvin offered Juan a tip, the man refused.

"Not for somethin' like this," Juan said.

He's faking, Sam Horowitz thought bitterly. He's faking because he can see me as the source of lots of big tips from now on.

Finally Juan was gone. Horowitz was free to look about the apartment he had inhabited for twenty-nine years. But instead of feeling relieved, he was depressed.

"Pa . . ." Marvin began, with a rising inflection which made it clear that this was the preamble to a serious discussion.

Horowitz thought, He better not lay down the law to me. I've seen it too many times. A parent grows old or sick and right away his children start to make his decisions for him. But he replied with a barely indulgent, "Yes, Marvin?"

"Mona and I talked it over, and, well, we think this apartment is too big for you now. But for the time being, you'll be better off here in a familiar place. So we'll let moving go till later."

Thank you very kindly, my dear children, Sam Horowitz observed to himself. Aloud he said, "What else did you and Mona talk over?"

"You're going to need a woman," Marvin said.

"That's very thoughtful. I would like a nice *zaftik* twenty-two-year-old blonde," Horowitz taunted. "Your mother could tell you that I always liked a woman with a little flesh on her bones."

"Dad, be serious! After talking to the doctors, Mona and I decided that what you need is a woman who can help with your physical therapy, yet won't mind doing housework, preparing your meals, things like that."

"So?" Horowitz asked belligerently.

"So," Marvin ventured, "Mona and I decided to look for such a woman. They're not easy to find. I had my secretary call dozens of nurses' registries."

241

"I see," Horowitz said. "And what's wrong with Bernadine? She worked for your mother eleven years and for me ever since your mother died!"

"Bernadine is a very competent cleaning woman," Marvin granted. "But she doesn't know anything about therapy. We found a fine woman. Good references. With hospital experience."

Horowitz did not respond at once. Finally he asked, "What's her name, this gem of a woman?"

"Harriet Washington," Marvin said.

"Is she married or not?"

"She's a widow," Marvin replied.

"Ho-ho-ho! Save me from widows! I had enough of them in the months right after your mother died."

"She is a grandmother, and she has other things on her mind than marrying a man like you."

"Okay," Horowitz accepted. "As long as we get that clear. . . ." He paused. "Washington. That's not a common name. Hey, wait a minute! Washington *is* a common name among colored people. Tell me, she's a *shvartze?*"

"Yes."

Horowitz exploded. "I don't want her in this house!"

"But, Pa, Bernadine is black too."

"Bernadine is different. She's a fine, warm human being. You don't have to count the silverware when she leaves."

"Pa . . . please, keep your voice down," Marvin pleaded.

"I will *not* keep my voice down!" Horowitz shouted. Addressing the front door, he called out, "Mrs. Washington, don't you dare come here! I have twenty-two stitches in my face because of black strangers. I don't want to see another black stranger as long as I live!"

At that moment Samuel Horowitz heard a woman's voice behind him. It was soft but quite firm. And a bit angry.

"Mr. Hammond, may I talk to you?" the voice asked.

Slowly Samuel Horowitz turned his wheelchair around. Standing in the archway that led to his bedroom was a small, mature black woman. Her shiny ebony hair was braided and wound about her head like a glistening tiara. Her face was neatly featured behind silver-rimmed glasses. She was compactly built, and attired

242

in a white nurse's uniform. She carried a fresh pillowcase in her hand, betraying that she had been making up the bed.

Horowitz felt deeply embarrassed. She stared at him, not angrily but almost pityingly. He resented the pity so much that he spun his wheelchair around again.

"Mr. Hammond?" the woman repeated to Marvin.

"Yes, of course," Marvin said. He and the woman went into the dining room to talk privately.

"He should have been told before today," Mrs. Washington said. "You shouldn't have thrown it at him so suddenly."

"I'm sorry."

"Now, if it's going to cause a problem, I'll only stay a day or two until you can find a replacement. A white woman."

"It won't be easy to find a woman equipped for this particular job, white *or* black," Marvin explained. "Give it a try, please?"

"That depends more on him than on me," she pointed out.

Marvin returned to his father and wheeled the chair close to the large living-room window. He raised the shade to allow the midmorning sun to stream into the room and at the same time give access to an extravagant view of Central Park.

"Pa, this time you have to listen to me," Marvin began.

"I'm listening," Horowitz declared impatiently. "Though I don't know why I can't still have Bernadine. She's practically a member of the family."

"Pa, you need therapy every day. Bernadine can't do that. And you need someone to make you three balanced meals a day. Mona and I agreed—"

"Ho-ho-ho!" Horowitz exclaimed sadly at the mention of his daughter's name. "So what did the pride of San Diego agree to?"

"If you can't get the care you need at home, and if you refuse to go out and stay with her, Mona and I decided that we will have to put you in a nursing home."

"*You* will put *me* in a nursing home? If it were not so insulting, I would laugh. I'll go back to the hospital first!"

"They won't take you back. You're not sick enough to occupy a hospital bed. You need a more normal life."

"Some normal life. In a nursing home," Horowitz retorted. "I'd rather be dead."

"Pa, dying is easy. Living takes a little effort."

"Ho-ho-ho! The Talmud according to Marvin Hammond."

"Pa, one thing I've always admired about you is your independence. It was no great trick for me to become a partner in a law firm. Because you handed me my education on a silver platter. But you don't know how often I've asked myself, if I had been a refugee kid with no advantages, would I have had the guts and the ability to set up my own business?"

Making a pretense at modesty, Samuel Horowitz protested, "IBM I wasn't."

"But you did it by yourself. On your own. And now you need help. There's no shame in admitting it or accepting it."

Horowitz was silent for a moment before he asked, "Marvin, what the doctors said to me is true? I can get better?"

"Right!" Marvin said. "But you'll need help until you do."

"Or else a nursing home," Horowitz said sadly.

"It's the only alternative."

Horowitz considered. "That woman seems *balebatish*, decent, clean." He closed both his eyes. Then after a moment he opened his right eye and said, "Okay."

"Good!" Marvin was relieved. "Now I have to go. She has all the instructions, and she knows the stores you shop at."

Marvin was at the door when Horowitz called out, "One thing, Marvin. What about Bernadine?"

"I gave her four weeks' salary and let her go."

"A woman is with this family so many years, and you gave her four weeks' salary? A woman her age, who won't be able to get another job easily?"

"She'll have social security," Marvin countered.

"Social security you can put in your eye these days! I want that woman on a pension! You take it out of my money."

"Pa, you're not required—"

"Stop being a lawyer and become a human being for a change!" Horowitz exclaimed angrily.

"Okay, okay, Pa," Marvin relented. "I'll arrange it."

When Marvin had left, Horowitz looked around the living room, dwelling on pieces of furniture that Hannah had assembled so joyously. He rolled himself to the large graceful breakfront of mellow walnut and rubbed his fingers across it. He stared at the comfortable sofa, covered in a brocade of gold and white. In the corner was the handmade bridge table, with its four armchairs carved by an old Italian craftsman and upholstered in red leather. At that table Horowitz had fought many a pinochle war with Hannah or Phil Liebowitz in the old days.

With great difficulty Horowitz wheeled himself to the bedroom and stared in, but only briefly, because that woman was in there, tidying up. So he pushed himself slowly past the dining room and kitchen, back into the living room, thinking, Lonely as this apartment has been since Hannah died, still it is home.

He became aware of the woman as she bustled from his bedroom toward the foyer. He called to her, "What's your name again?"

She called out, "Mrs. Harriet Washington."

"Well, Harriet—"

"*Mrs. Washington*, if you don't mind," she reproved firmly.

"What's wrong with Harriet?" he demanded, irritated.

"If you wish to address a maid by her first name and she permits it, that may be all right. But I am a nurse and my professional dignity demands that I be called Mrs. Washington!"

"Not *Ms.* Washington?" Horowitz taunted.

"I was married to a fine man named Horace Washington. I don't intend to forget it. Nor do I want anyone else to forget it. So it's *Mrs.* Washington!"

"Well, okay, Mrs. Washington!"

SAMUEL Horowitz knew that he would have to make his peace with this woman. The only question was how. He decided it would be best if he did not have to look into her reproachful face when he did it. So he looked out the living-room window and called, "Mrs. Washington?"

Evidently she had not heard him, so he spoke more loudly. "Mrs. Washington!"

When she did not respond, he exploded. "Where is that woman?"

She whispered, "Right here."

He half turned his head to find her behind him. He realized he had not detected her footsteps on the thickly carpeted living-room floor.

"You don't have to go tiptoeing around here. I don't like surprises!" he declared.

"Do you want me to wear bells on my shoes?" she asked.

Horowitz slowly turned his wheelchair around to face her. "Tell me, Mrs. Washington," he said, trying to sound courteous, "what do you know about bells on shoes?"

"Well, Mr. Horowitz, as I understand it, there was once a famous rabbi, a . . . I forget the word. . . ."

"*Zaddik*," Horowitz supplied. "A *zaddik* is not only a scholar and a philosopher but a great human being. With an enormous love for all of God's creatures, even the smallest."

"And the blackest?" she asked provocatively.

Horowitz changed the subject. "What about bells on shoes?"

"Well, the way I heard it, this *zaddik* felt so responsible for all God's creatures that he did not want to kill even the lowliest ant. Consequently he had bells put on his shoes so that when he walked, the ants could scurry out of the way."

"Hmm," Horowitz remarked in surprise. "Tell me, where did you come across such a bit of obscure information?"

"For a time, before I studied nursing, I worked for the Rosen-gartens. Mister was president of a *shul* on West Seventy-ninth Street. So we had the rabbi to dinner very often. One night I heard the rabbi tell that story."

"Hmm!" Horowitz remarked again. "Interesting. But are you trying to tell me that some of your best employers were Jewish, to make your presence here more acceptable?"

"I told you that because you accused me of sneaking up on you," Mrs. Washington said.

Reminded, Horowitz responded with, "I see. In the future, don't come in without announcing yourself. Now please go fix my lunch."

"It's ready," she said, taking him by surprise.

"How could it be ready? I didn't even tell you what I want."

"What would you like?"

"What I would like is hummingbirds' wings on toast. But my doctor said I can't have toast," Horowitz replied sarcastically.

Suddenly he turned his head away.

"Mr. Horowitz?" she asked gently.

He did not reply, for if he had, he knew he would begin to weep. Finally he said, "What I would really like is for Hannah to be here, making me one of the dishes she made so well. She had a genius for cooking. And a genius for people. People loved her. . . . Sometimes I think they tolerated me just to be near her."

He found himself sniffling, and brushed the moistness from his eyes. "Mrs. Washington, you will find as you get older that your eyes tear up for no good reason."

"Yes, Mr. Horowitz," she said, then added, "Your lunch is set up in the dining room."

"Dining room?" Horowitz challenged. "I haven't eaten in the dining room since Hannah. I'd be better off with a tray in the bedroom. Besides, there's no television in the dining room."

"You don't have to watch television in order to eat."

"Maybe President Carter will be having a press conference. He's the midafternoon Johnny Carson."

"You don't like President Carter?"

"I haven't liked any President since Roosevelt. And if you want to know the truth, I wasn't crazy about him either. Now, what's for lunch?" he asked, rolling himself toward the dining room.

Once there, he stared at the table. "Hannah's best china? For a measly little lunch? She would turn over in her grave."

"Then we won't tell her," Mrs. Washington replied, smiling.

He glared up at her. She had a warm smile. Bright, sparkling ebony eyes set in a glistening black face, with white even teeth, and skin so smooth it seemed to have been hand-rubbed like fine mahogany. He could not resist her smile.

"Have your tomato juice," she said, starting for the kitchen.

"I don't like tomato juice! It gives me heartburn."

"Your son said your wife served it all the time," she replied.

"Oh, that," Horowitz said sheepishly. "Well, Hannah's tomato juice was different. She did something to it."

He lifted the glass and took a sip, intending to hate it. He stopped, disbelieved his taste buds, then took another sip.

"You put something in here," he accused. "What?"

"A dash of lemon, a touch of anise."

"It's . . . it's not bad. In fact, it's"—he hated to make such a concession—"it's very much like Hannah's."

"It's exactly like Hannah's," Mrs. Washington corrected. "I found her recipe file when I was here yesterday."

"You were here, prowling?" he demanded indignantly.

"Don't worry, Bernadine helped me get acquainted with the place," she said, adding pointedly, "So you don't have to count the silverware."

Embarrassed, Horowitz remarked irritably, "I thought you said lunch was ready."

Mrs. Washington went back to the kitchen, and he heard her taking out plates and glasses. She called, "Oh, by the way, a man phoned this morning. Phil Liebowitz. Said he was a friend of yours. He wants to come by."

"So what did you say?" Horowitz asked defensively.

"That you would call back when you arrived."

"In the future, Mrs. Washington, if I am in need of a social secretary, I will hire one. Meantime, don't you go promising people I will call back! Next time he calls, don't answer."

"Of course," Mrs. Washington replied, appearing through the swinging door with a large dish. She set it down before him.

He glared at the food, then asked in a sarcastically sweet voice, "*Mrs.* Washington, did someone tell you I was a millionaire?"

"I never ask my employers for bank references," she replied.

"Steak for lunch?" he complained. "Am I made of money?" As Horowitz had a habit of doing from time to time, he addressed the world at large. "The woman is crazy. Steak for lunch."

He turned back to her. "*Mrs.* Washington, if you are thinking to ingratiate yourself with me by such little tricks, forget it. Between a nursing home and you, you are presently the lesser of two evils. But don't press your luck, as they say."

She waited patiently through his tirade, then said simply, "Your steak is getting cold."

He picked up his knife in his right hand and tried to pick up

248

the fork in his left. He could not quite force his fingers to grip the fork securely. When he tried to pin down the steak, the fork slipped from his damaged hand and dropped to the carpet.

She retrieved the fork, wiped it carefully on her apron, and handed it back to him. Again he could not grip it.

"Mrs. Washington, for lunch you serve a simple dish like a sandwich that can be eaten with one hand. Take this steak away and throw it out. Or, if you want, eat it yourself. Is that what you had in mind all along? Well, I'm on to your game. No, don't take it away! *You* cut it! *You* feed it to me!"

She turned abruptly and went back to the kitchen. When she returned, she carried a second fork. This one had a thick foam-rubber pad taped around the handle.

"Try this," she said, holding out the fork to him.

Reluctantly he closed his left fingers around the thick handle. This time he could grasp it and hold the steak securely in place while he cut a bite-sized piece with his right hand. He then repeated the entire maneuver.

Needing something to criticize, he said, "I like my steak a little better done."

"I have to get used to your broiler," she explained, and walked back into the kitchen. When she returned with his salad, he was still grasping the padded fork, but this time in his right hand.

"You served me steak on purpose," he accused. "So you could point out that I am a cripple! I never want to see this fork again! Never!"

He hurled the fork across the room. It hit the far wall and dropped to the carpeted floor. He wheeled his chair about and slowly rolled himself out of the dining room, trying to maintain an air of dignity.

He wheeled into his bedroom, to the window that looked over the park. He brought his right hand to his face, and he wept.

In the kitchen, Harriet Washington was on the phone. "Dr. Tannenbaum, he resisted every step of the way. Especially the steak. He does not want to be reminded that his left hand is damaged."

"How did he handle the padded fork?"

"Pretty well. But he resents it."

"What about his general attitude?" the doctor asked.

"Hostile, resistant," she reported. "He's a man with a great deal of pride."

"Well, pride can be helpful if it gives him the will to recover," the doctor said. "If it doesn't, it can be fatal."

Chapter Three

Mrs. Washington had done the dinner dishes and seen Horowitz safely in bed. Before she departed she was careful to point out, "If you have to get up during the night, put the light on. And be very careful with your quad cane. This carpet's a little too high-piled for safety."

"Thank you, *Mrs.* Washington," Horowitz replied. "This carpet was personally selected by Hannah. I am sure she would not pick out a carpet that was dangerous to my life."

Mrs. Washington shrugged and said a soft good-night.

Samuel Horowitz settled down in his bed, determined to enjoy his privacy. With his right hand he reached for the remote-control instrument of his television set. Secretly he resented the gadget, believing that all the troubles of the human race could be traced to soft living. If people did not appreciate a miracle like television enough to cross a room to change the channels, then they did not deserve to have it. Nevertheless, he had to grant that, for a sick man, a remote-control television set was a necessity.

The first program he watched did not intrigue him. The police were in search of a killer. In the second program a killer was in search of someone to kill. The third one was a situation comedy about a black family. It only mobilized his resentment against that fresh Mrs. Washington.

He must have drifted off to sleep, because the next thing he knew, the sound of great activity caused him to open his eyes. It was morning.

He listened to furniture being moved about, while a vacuum cleaner droned. It must be that Washington woman. Surely it was possible to clean without making such a racket so early.

His fury mounted until he glanced at the bedside clock. Nine twenty-two. He had not slept this late in years.

Slowly he got out of bed. With halting steps, dragging his left foot and using his quad cane, he made his way to the bathroom.

He realized he would have to shave himself. In the hospital there was a barber who made rounds every morning. Now Horowitz had to resume shaving himself. He already had more than a day's growth of white, bristly beard.

He wet his face and squeezed some cream from the tube by pressing his right thumb against it—even though they had instructed him to use his left hand whenever possible. Now he had the awkward job of rubbing the lather into his face with his left fingers. He would have been wiser, he realized, to have squeezed with his left thumb and applied the stuff with his right hand.

The first few strokes of the razor told him that the blade was old and dull. He would need a fresh one. Carefully he picked up the blade cartridge in his left hand and the razor in his right. But he could not sufficiently control the left thumb to slide out a fresh blade. Defeated, he called angrily, *"Mrs. Washington!"*

The bathroom door opened swiftly. "What's wrong? Did you fall?" She was relieved when she realized that he was on his feet, leaning against the edge of the washbasin for balance.

"Why, of course not," he said bitterly. "Look at me. A handsome figure of a man. All right, a little beard. But that covers the scar your fine young men put there. Twenty-two stitches!"

Mrs. Washington stared into his eyes. "I'm sorry," she said simply. "If there were anything I could do . . ."

"Yes, there is something you can do! You can bring up your young savages to have respect for human life!" Horowitz raged. "Look, I think that you and I are not going to get along. I think I should find someone else. You can find another job."

"I'd rather stay on," she said simply.

"Why? To do penance for what your savages did to me?"

"This job has special inducements for me. And because it does, I am willing to work for a mean old man who is trying to blame everybody but himself for his present condition." With that, Harriet Washington glared at Samuel Horowitz.

"If that isn't the best reason in the world for quitting, I don't know what is," Horowitz grumbled.

"I will explain it to you so you *will* know," Harriet Washington said with impatience in her voice. "I have a daughter who has two

252

children. Very fine children, I might add, before you make any re-
marks. The boy is twelve, the girl eight. During the day my daughter is home. But in the evening she works as night supervisor of
nurses in a hospital. Someone has to be with those children. To
make sure they do their homework. To see that they are not out
on the streets. To see that they do not become savages, Mr. Horowitz. This job fits ideally into that situation."

"You don't look old enough to be a grandmother."

"I'm old enough," she said. "Sixty-one."

A new thought assailed Horowitz. "You didn't mention your
daughter's husband. Did she—"

"She's a widow!" Harriet Washington interrupted sharply. "He
was killed by one of the savages. He was a cop, trying to stop a
holdup in a supermarket."

"Oh, I'm sorry," Horowitz said.

"So you can insult me, get angry, shout, yell, rant, and rave. But
I am here to stay! So get used to me!"

"You think you're a pretty tough cookie," Horowitz mocked.

"I *know* I'm a tough cookie," Harriet Washington corrected.
"Now, you were calling. What did you want?"

Horowitz admitted painfully, "I need a fresh blade in my razor."

Mrs. Washington inserted the new blade, then asked, "Why
don't you use the electric razor I suggested your son buy for you?
Most men in your condition use one. It's much easier."

"First, I am not in any 'condition.' Second, with the energy shortage I am not going to use an electric razor. And third, I don't like
the idea of you telling my son what I should do. Besides, shaving
with an electric shaver is not shaving. It is a close massage. Now
do me the extreme honor of getting out."

She was gone, thanks God. He could at last give himself up to
the luxury of a slow, meticulous shave. He tried to draw the razor
across his face, but realized that his habit had been to hold his
cheek taut with his left hand while applying the razor with his
right. He could no longer use his left hand in that manner.

When he was done, he examined his face in the mirror. He could
still see patches of white stubble.

He grasped his cane and slowly made his way out into the
living room. By the time he arrived there, he was breathless. He

had to admit the thick carpet did prove a hindrance to walking.

Mrs. Washington was just finishing dusting.

"Uh . . ." he began, "Mrs. Washington, I am going to demonstrate that I am a man with an open mind. I will risk experimenting with that electric razor. Where is it?"

"I'll get it for you," she said, careful not to look at him and embarrass him.

He watched as she plugged the cord into the bathroom wall socket. Then he accepted the razor from her and started it. He passed it over his cheek, as he had seen done on television commercials. Then he felt his face. It was unbelievably smooth.

He labored into the bedroom, where Mrs. Washington was making the bed.

"Well?" she asked. "How did it go?"

"Not exactly a shave," he said. "But a convenience. I . . . I'll try it a few more days. I am not given to snap judgments. But I guess you have already observed that."

"Yes," she lied. "Now, how about some breakfast? And it's such a nice day, maybe we'll go out for a little fresh air."

SAM Horowitz was forced to face the most humiliating moment of his convalescence: he had tried to close the zipper of his pants while holding down the fabric with his clawlike grasp, but each time the material slipped, bunching up the zipper, making it impossible to close. Finally he called sheepishly, "Mrs. Washington?"

She came into the bedroom and took one long look at him. "You're not going out looking like that, are you?"

"Certainly not. That's why I called for you." He tried to sound casual. "I . . . I want you should help me with . . . with my zipper, please?"

"Of course. Here." Then she stood back and shook her head sadly. "That outfit."

"What's wrong with my outfit?" he demanded indignantly.

"That is the oldest, baggiest pair of slacks I've ever seen. I simply will not take you out looking like that."

"Where are we going? To a reception at the White House? Well, never mind. I don't want to go out at all! There! Settled. Now leave me alone!"

She did not move. She knew what was at work here—it had happened with other patients. Consciously, or otherwise, Horowitz was contriving to avoid going out and being seen in a wheelchair. His shabby, outfit, his oldest slacks, a revolting combination of colors, all reflected his now depreciated assessment of himself.

"Mr. Horowitz, we are going out in the park. But I am not going to have people think that I permitted you to appear in public that way. I have a reputation to maintain."

"So you can sit on another bench," he argued. "Make believe you don't know me. Which would suit me fine!"

"Get out of that shirt and those slacks," she ordered.

He glared at her defiantly. "Even Hannah never dared to talk to me like that!"

"I'll bet you never dressed this way when Hannah was alive!"

"Please call her Mrs. Horowitz," he said angrily.

"Okay. Mrs. Horowitz!"

"That's better," he approved. Still grumbling, he struggled with the top button of his shirt and finally had it open.

"And while you're at it, you might tie your shoelaces," Mrs. Washington suggested firmly.

"I already tied my shoelaces!" he protested. But when he looked down, he found them dangling. The puzzlement was so clear on his face that she felt obliged to explain gently.

"It happens, Mr. Horowitz. A left hemi—"

He interrupted. "What is a left hemi, half a Communist?"

"Left hemiplegics," she explained, "are people who have had strokes on the right side of the brain, and thus have left-sided impairments. At first, left hemis tend to forget routine things like tying shoelaces and buttoning shirts. But you'll get the hang of it."

Sadly he said, "The last time someone had to tell me to tie my shoelaces, I was seven years old."

When he had changed into well-pressed slacks, a fresh white shirt, and with fumbling fingers had managed to knot an expensive silk necktie, he shuffled out into the foyer to the wheelchair. He was exhausted and welcomed sitting down. Twenty-one steps he had taken, and he was sweating. Time was when he would walk briskly down to Columbus Circle before taking the subway to his place of business.

255

His place of business, he recalled sadly. Abe Gottshall was taking care of things. Abe was a nice man, an honest man, but no genius. As soon as they let him, Horowitz decided, he must go and see how things were going.

He and Mrs. Washington got into the elevator, and there was Angelo, the elevator man, smiling brightly.

"Good morning, Mr. Horowitz. Is nice to see you gettin' out."

Horowitz thought he detected a bit of smug superiority in that bright smile.

When they reached the street floor, Angelo worked meticulously to make sure the car was exactly level with the floor. At last he was satisfied, and Horowitz rolled the chair out with ease.

He propelled himself along until they arrived at the three steps before the tall glass-and-iron front doors. Those miserable three steps, Horowitz said to himself. The architect who designed this building should rot in jail!

Juan, the doorman, and Angelo each seized a side of the chair and lifted it up the steps. Horowitz then wheeled it through the door without touching either side. At least he had been able to carry that off.

He looked about. The street was the same as it had always been. Even old lady Goldstein was in her place in the sun near the corner, wheeled there by her companion. He rolled next to her, and she said, "Mr. Horowitz, I heard and I am terribly sorry." Then she stared at his scarred face. "God, what they did to you! Never fight back," she advised. "That's one thing my grandson Sheldon told me. He's in the district attorney's office. He said too many people get killed resisting muggers."

"There are worse things than getting killed," Horowitz said sadly, clearly referring to his confinement.

"You won't always feel that way," the woman said consolingly. "Think of your grandchildren. You want to see them grow up and become something. You have grandchildren, don't you?"

"I have grandchildren," Horowitz said. "At Harvard."

"Harvard, that's nice." Then, to even the score, she added, "I have a grandson in Cornell Medical School."

"Well," Horowitz said, "got to be going." He slowly rolled himself to the curb, Mrs. Washington right behind him.

When they had crossed the street and entered Central Park, Horowitz wheeled along until he found a place clear of trees and open to the midday sun. He remembered that Hannah had always said he looked especially handsome when he acquired a tan down in Florida.

Mrs. Washington sat on a bench close to him. She made no effort to engage him in conversation.

After some silence, during which the street noises seemed unusually loud, he said, "That Mrs. Goldstein is a very gabby woman. Talk, talk, talk! A man in my situation has got to stay away from widows. They're always scheming to get their hooks into you." He added quickly, "Of course, present company excepted." He paused. "You never wanted to marry again?"

"Not particularly," Mrs. Washington said.

"You're an exceptional woman."

"No, *he* was an exceptional man."

Another long silence followed. Horowitz sat, eyes closed, face raised to the warm sun. Suddenly he opened his right eye and asked, "Do black people get sunburned?"

"Yes, but not like you. We have a built-in shield. Why?"

"With white people, you can tell how well-to-do a man is by his sunburn in the winter. How do you tell about black people?"

"Cadillacs," Mrs. Washington responded.

There was another silence.

"What did your husband do for a living?" Horowitz asked.

"In good times Horace was a welder. But twice he had to take jobs as a janitor. I couldn't stand to see him do menial work. That's why I decided to study practical nursing."

"Then what did he do while you worked?" Horowitz asked.

"Took care of the children, the house. Did odd jobs."

"That's no way for a man to live out his life," Horowitz commented. "How long has he been dead?"

"Nine years," she responded. "He died right before Christmas. My daughter was expecting her second child. Horace was lucky to get a job in a department store. He was planning what he would buy the new baby for Christmas. And suddenly he was dead."

"Very sad," Horowitz said, truly compassionate.

"I don't know," she said strangely. "He lay in his casket with a peaceful look on his face, as if the struggle and the failure were over. I said to him, 'Don't worry, Horace, I always knew what you were, and what you could have been.' "

"You said that? To a dead man?"

"Didn't you say anything to Mrs. Horowitz?"

He did not respond at once, but after a while he admitted, "While the rabbi was talking, saying such nice things about her, I was thinking, Hannah, darling, what can any stranger say about you that will come close to the truth? No one knew you like I knew you. How tender and kind you were. How you could encourage a man with your words, yet you had a golden gift of knowing when a man needed silence. I will never forgive the Lord for taking you, Hannah, never."

Horowitz realized it was the first time he had said this to anyone. And to Mrs. Washington, of all people.

Suddenly there was an explosion of sound down the block—loud shouts, raucous laughter, boasting of youngsters free on their lunch hour. They were teenagers from the high school on Columbus Avenue: a tidal wave of black boys and girls.

At the sight of them approaching, Horowitz involuntarily drew back. Mrs. Washington noticed but said nothing.

Horowitz said grimly, "I think I've had enough sun for today."

Chapter Four

HE SUFFERED the indignity of being carried down into the lobby again, and was relieved, finally, to reach his bedroom. He sank, exhausted, onto the bed, and in a few moments was asleep.

Mrs. Washington was gently waking him a short time later. "Hmm? What?" He came to, startled. "Oh, it's you."

"Who did you expect? Zsa Zsa Gabor?"

"Hattie McDaniel," he shot back.

"Sorry. But then you're not Clark Gable either," she said. "Time for lunch."

"I don't want lunch."

"I didn't want to make lunch, but I did, so you'll eat it," she said firmly. "Now hurry, your blintzes will get cold."

"Blintzes?" His eyes lit up in anticipation. But he refused to let

258

her know how pleased he was. "I don't like frozen blintzes! I tried them once, after Hannah was gone. Like rubber." But he slowly got off the bed and reached for his quad cane.

When he entered the dining room, Horowitz could smell the warm fragrance of frying blintzes. His taste buds responded nostalgically to the memory of the ones Hannah used to make. Each started as a magnificent thin crepe, a perfect circle. And her fillings! She could take a pound of ordinary cottage cheese, a raw egg, some vanilla, a touch of sugar, lemon rind, and spice and turn those crepes into a golden delight. She would fill them and fold them, and fry the blintzes to a delicate golden brown on both sides.

Some people liked to add jam or syrup to blintzes, but with Hannah's, most people ate them plain, to savor the taste. Or with only a dab of sour cream to add a bit of tartness.

Mrs. Washington swung open the kitchen door and entered, carrying a plate and a small dish of sour cream which she set before him. Horowitz stared down with a connoisseur's critical eye.

"This is blintzes?" he asked disparagingly.

"What's wrong?"

"For one thing, they're a little too brown."

"Taste them," she urged.

He leaned forward to inhale their perfume, aloof as a sommelier appraising the cork of a freshly opened bottle of wine.

"What did you fry them in? Not butter," he accused.

"Your doctor doesn't want you to have too much butter," she explained. "I used low-cholesterol margarine. Try them!"

He took the fork in his right hand and cut into the lightly browned delicacy. The crepe was tender, the inside steamy white and tempting. He brought the first forkful to his mouth with more anticipation than he had intended to betray. He chewed slowly, savoring it. He took a second forkful. Then a third.

Finally he was willing to admit, "Well, not Hannah's exactly, but not bad. At least they're not the frozen kind."

He was attacking the last of the three when he asked casually, "That's all? I mean, Hannah used to give me four or five."

"The doctor said three, at the most."

He was down to the last forkful when he asked, "Where did you learn to make such blintzes?"

"From Mrs. Rosengarten."

"But the taste, just like Hannah's. A coincidence, I suppose?"

She did not respond to that, but said instead, "While you were napping your daughter called."

"Why didn't you tell me before?"

"And let your blintzes get cold?"

"A wise decision," he granted. "I have a daughter, Mona," he began to complain, "the Perle Mesta of San Diego. She is a doer. And also a crier. When crying is required, she can *cry*. She is the perfect Jewish woman, wife, and mother. But as a daughter, she leaves a little to be desired."

"She sounded very concerned, asked a lot of questions about how you're getting along," Mrs. Washington pointed out.

"Oh, sure," he scoffed.

"She said when you woke up to call her back."

"It costs too much to call California during the day."

"She left an 800 number, it won't cost you anything."

Deprived of his last excuse, Horowitz surrendered. "Okay, I'll call her."

He got up and struggled across the thick carpet to the armchair in his bedroom. Mrs. Washington came with him and handed him the phone.

The 800 number was direct to the offices of Albert Fields Associates. The operator there put Horowitz through to the Fields's home. His daughter's maid answered and made it known to Horowitz that Mrs. Fields was in a meeting with one of her ladies' committees but had left orders to be interrupted just as soon as her father called.

Despite that, it took a long time before Mona came to the phone. Which caused Horowitz to say to Mrs. Washington, "My Mona is always busy. Hadassah. United Jewish Appeal. Hebrew Home for the Aged. Israel bonds. My Mona has been a president more times than Roosevelt. Lucky for the Pope, she's not Catholic. Otherwise he would be out of a job!"

At that instant Samuel Horowitz heard his daughter exclaim, "Dad!" And she began to cry. "Oh, Dad . . . Dad . . ."

"Mona, Mona, darling, there's no reason to cry. I feel fine. I just had a good lunch. Blintzes! Delicious!"

260

"Blintzes?" Mona asked, horrified. "Do you know how much cholesterol there is in one blintz? How many did you have?"

To avert a national crisis, Horowitz admitted to only two.

"Two blintzes!" she exclaimed, outraged. "Does your doctor know about this?"

"He said it was okay as long as they were fried in margarine."

"A man who's had one stroke can have another. You've got to cut out cholesterol. You've got to keep your blood pressure down. You've got to live on a safe diet. I'm calling Marvin. And I want to have a long talk with your doctor." Suddenly it occurred to her. "Oh, Dad! Don't tell me you had sour cream with your blintzes!"

For a moment Horowitz debated. If he told her, who could know what steps she would take? A judicious lie was in order.

"Mona, darling," he said solemnly, "there was no sour cream."

"Good!" she exulted, greatly relieved.

Horowitz tried to terminate the conversation. "Mona, I don't want to keep you from your meeting."

"School integration in San Diego can wait a few more minutes when my father's life is involved. First, you will come out here as soon as you're able to travel. American Airlines has nonstop flights, New York to San Diego. They have special accommodations for people in wheelchairs. Albert plays golf with one of American's executives, so you'll go VIP all the way."

"Mona, darling . . ."

But she overrode any objection. "Now I insist on talking to that woman Marvin told me about. Mrs. Washington. Put her on!"

Horowitz turned to the nurse. "She wants to talk to you."

Harriet Washington hesitated, then took the phone. "Hello."

"Do I understand that you fed my father blintzes?" Mona asked, with the measured delivery of a prosecuting attorney.

"Yes. He is allowed to eat everything, in moderation."

"What kind of a doctor does he have?" Mona demanded.

"A doctor who believes there's no point in torturing a patient who's in fairly good health. Your father's cholesterol count is within normal limits. I would say that the only thing wrong with him is his attitude. He is an irascible man."

Horowitz glared up at her, but she ignored him.

Mona lowered her voice to a conspiratorial hush. "Mrs. Washington, take care of my father and call me several times a week. I want a detailed report on how he is doing! We just won't let him know that we talk. Okay?"

"I don't make promises like that," Mrs. Washington demurred.

Mona lowered her voice even more. "I'll make it worth your while. Say, twenty-five dollars a week?"

"I'm afraid I can't do that," Harriet Washington replied. "I report to the doctor. And I understand your brother talks to him several times a week."

"I see," Mona said, frustrated and annoyed. "I'll have to handle this in my own way!" And she hung up.

Horowitz commented, "A living doll, no?" He reached out his right hand to seal a bargain. "Mrs. Washington, we have got to make an agreement. You are never going to tell Mona that I am well enough to travel. Okay?"

But she would not take his hand yet. "Mr. Horowitz, an agreement has to be two-sided. You have to agree to something too."

"Okay. Name it! Anything. Just protect me from Mona."

"Mr. Horowitz, *you* are going to get well. If not for your sake, for mine. I have a professional reputation to maintain."

"Get well?" Horowitz asked. "What for? I have children I don't have anything in common with. Grandchildren I hardly know. What is the big value in living? These days, old people are not afraid of dying. They are afraid of living. So what's the big *gedillah* to get well? That's a word that means—"

She anticipated him. "Great joy. Mr. Rosengarten told me."

"Okay, wise guy," Horowitz granted sourly. "So life is no more a *gedillah*, but for your sake, I'll try to get well. Now?" He extended his hand again.

"Not the right one, the left. You must use it whenever possible."

Reluctantly and with effort he reached up to take her left hand, which she deliberately held too high for him to reach easily. "Press! Every chance you get, press. Hard as you can," she reminded.

He made the effort, but it was feeble.

"And now we'll do our exercises," she announced. "Get into bed and lie on your back."

"Exercises," he disparaged as he got up. "Torture, you mean!"

"One exercise you don't need is speech therapy. Okay. Now let's begin. Reach your left arm high above your head until your hand touches the wall behind you. Reach! Slowly! Far as you can go!"

"I'm trying, I'm trying," he protested belligerently.

"You can do better than that!" But she could see that his damaged nerves prevented him from coming closer than ten or twelve inches from the wall.

After more arm exercises she said, "Now bend your knees!"

Reluctantly he assumed the position.

"Raise the toes on your left foot," she commanded.

He made a halfhearted attempt before he said, "Can't."

"Can," she insisted.

"Can't!" he fought back.

She seized his foot and pressed his toes upward.

"Ow! You hurt me!" he protested.

"Good! Where there's sensation there's the promise of increased motor ability."

"Okay, okay, I'll try by myself." And he did, several times, with a slight but perceptible increase in flexibility.

She put Horowitz through an entire series of exercises. He was breathing hard, perspiration shining on his brow. She would have to put him through the ordeal twice again before bedtime. She was not satisfied with his progress. He was not trying. Obeying, yes, only if forced to.

The phone rang. Mrs. Washington answered it and Horowitz braced himself for some new intrusion.

"Dr. Tannenbaum wants to talk to you," Harriet Washington said, handing him the phone.

"Hello, Doctor! I have never felt better in my whole life. In fact, I am thinking of marrying a nineteen-year-old girl and going on a honeymoon cruise to the South Seas."

"Mr. Horowitz," Dr. Tannenbaum said, "your daughter called me. She is very upset."

"She was born upset," Horowitz reported. "With her first breath she started talking, and she reorganized the whole delivery room."

"She feels that you're not getting the right treatment, and that if things continue that way, she wants to have you come out there," the doctor went on. "She says otherwise she'll have you placed in a nursing home."

"Nobody is going to put me in any nursing home! You hear, nobody!" Indignantly he tried to slam the phone down, but was wide of the mark by half a foot. Without a word Mrs. Washington took it and silently settled it in its cradle.

From his attitude of defiant belligerence he was reduced suddenly to sad anxiety. "Do you think she could put me in a nursing home?" he asked Mrs. Washington.

"I don't think so. After all, there's your son. . . ."

"Mona could convince anyone of anything."

"Why not practice your walking?" Mrs. Washington suggested to divert his mind.

"Good idea," he agreed unenthusiastically.

He got out of bed, gripped his metal quad cane, and began walking. Mrs. Washington stood off, watching him.

The ultimate aim of the therapy was equal strides between left foot and right. But he was far from accomplishing that goal. Twice he failed to plant the legs of the cane properly and almost toppled forward. But he labored on, mumbling as he went, "Those hoodlums should have killed me. I'd have been better off."

Finally he made his way into the living room, where the bright light of a summer afternoon flooded the room. Tired, he sank into the easy chair near the window and sighed. "A day like this I used to walk home from business."

"You will again," she said encouragingly. She walked to the bridge table in the corner, where she had assembled a group of objects. A new deck of cards. A jar of marbles. A small cardboard box. And a copy of *The New York Times*.

"What's all that?" he asked.

"Sit at the table and open the deck of cards," she commanded.

"I don't play cards," he said dogmatically. Then under her questioning gaze he admitted, "A little pinochle maybe."

He moved to a bridge chair and took the box of cards in his right hand. He tried to tear off the paper with his left, but could not close his fingers tightly enough to do it. So he switched hands and was able to grasp the box in his left while removing the paper with his right. "There!" he said.

"Now open it and shuffle them," she said.

Horowitz got the cards out and slowly tried to shuffle them in

264

the conventional manner. But some of them escaped his grasp and spewed across the carpet.

Mrs. Washington said nothing, just gathered up the cards and presented them to him. "Do it again," she ordered.

"Anything you say, Mrs. Legree." He scowled at her, but he did it again. And again. Then he turned his gaze toward *The New York Times,* but Mrs. Washington shoved forward the jar of marbles. She poured some of them out, guarding them from rolling off the table.

"Marbles?" Horowitz scoffed.

"Marbles," Mrs. Washington confirmed. "Now gather them up, one at a time, with your left hand and put them back into the jar."

Grumbling, he nevertheless commenced the task. Occasionally a marble skidded from between his fingers and shot off the table like a projectile. Mrs. Washington recovered the strays, and stood over him until he completed the exercise.

He leaned back and eyed the *Times* again. "I'm tired," he declared. "I would like to rest and do a little reading."

"Two more exercises to go," she announced. She opened the cardboard box and poured out an array of buttons of all types and sizes—plastic, horn, metal, dull, shiny, round, square.

"Pick those up, one at a time, with your left hand and put them back in the box."

"I'm not in the button business. Paper and twine I know. Not buttons. A man my age picking up buttons like a child of five."

"Mr. Horowitz," she said patiently, "in a way, you *are* like a child. You have to reeducate certain of your muscles again. So start picking up those buttons!"

He glared at her, he glared at the buttons, but in a while he reached out his left hand and began. When the large buttons had been collected, he attempted one of the smaller ones, but could not grasp it. He sat there, helpless and inept, staring straight ahead. Mrs. Washington felt sorry for him.

"All right, now for the *Times,*" she said.

In great relief he asked, "My reading glasses? I left them on the bedside table."

"This *Times* is not for reading, it's for exercising," she informed him. "What we do is take one whole sheet and crumple it in toward the center until it is one big ball of paper. In the process we use our hands, *both* of them, and our fingers, *all* of them."

"And when do we get to read the damn thing? After all, I cannot read and crumple at the same time. Can you?"

"I don't have to," she replied, and her face, which could be warm and pleasant in repose, was now set as grimly as his.

Horowitz closed his eyes. Then he opened his right eye stealthily. "Since no one ever said that a newspaper that has already been read has lost its exercise power, I suggest the following. First, I will read *The New York Times*. And when I am done, I will, with both these hands, crumple every sheet. What do you think of that?"

"Well, this one time . . ." she granted, though not too willingly.

"I'll need my reading glasses, Mrs. Washington."

"Of course, Mr. Horowitz. They're in the bedroom."

"A little thing like getting a man's reading glasses," he bemoaned, "is that too much to ask?"

"A little walk into the bedroom and back, is that too much to do?" she countered.

How could a woman be so stubborn? he protested silently to himself. No matter how much he talked and how little she talked, he always wound up doing exactly what she wanted him to do.

When he returned with his glasses, he was still muttering.

"Do you know that we Jews were slaves long before your people? In Egypt, Mrs. Washington."

Unmoved by his plaint, she observed, "Let my people go."

"Exactly," Horowitz said. "The first big freedom movement in the history of the world. So you see, we should be allies, not enemies. It wouldn't do any harm if you were not such a tyrant."

By now he had his reading glasses on and was sitting down with the *Times*. Mrs. Washington was free to go prepare his dinner.

Even from the kitchen she could hear his bursts of outrage at some item or editorial he was reading. Every so often the air was punctuated with a "Ho-ho-ho!" or else it was "Let the *Times* run this country, we'd be bankrupt." But he kept his promise. When she returned to the living room, he was crumpling the paper into balls. He did not accomplish it easily, but at least he was trying.

He announced, "I'm saving the editorial page for last. Oh, will I give *it* a crumple!"

HE HAD EATEN HIS light dinner. Lamb chops that required considerable two-handed cutting, a baked potato, and a salad. With his Sanka she served him fresh peaches over a slice of plain cake.

During the meal he called to her, "Mrs. Washington?"

She appeared in the doorway, curious.

"Would you sit down there, please?"

Puzzled, she sat in the chair opposite him. "Well?"

"Just sit there," he said softly, before confessing, "After Hannah died I couldn't eat in here anymore, alone. It's a terrible thing to be lonely."

"I know," she said sympathetically.

"You don't know," he corrected. "You have a daughter and grandchildren to take care of."

"You have a son, a daughter, and four grandchildren."

"Yes, but they don't need me. Hannah and I, when we sat down to dinner at this table, we were a family. She needed me, I needed her." He paused. "Mrs. Washington, could I ask you a favor?"

"Of course."

"Would you have dinner with me every evening?"

"Mr. Horowitz, please understand . . ."

He shook his head sadly. "As soon as someone says, 'Please understand,' then the answer is no. I must have offended you. You take me too seriously. Do you really think, Mrs. Washington, that I blame you for this?" He pointed to the scar on his cheek.

"It's my grandchildren," she explained. "We always have dinner together. It gives them a sense of family, even though their father is not there and their mother is off working. It wouldn't be fair to upset that routine."

"No," he was forced to agree, "it wouldn't be fair." But he could not conceal his disappointment.

"Of course," she volunteered, "there's no reason why I can't just *sit* here while you're having your meals."

"That would be nice," he agreed. "And maybe have a cup of coffee? Would that be all right?"

"I think so." She went into the kitchen and returned with a steaming cup. She sat down opposite him. He glanced at her over his own cup. And he smiled.

It was the first time Mrs. Washington had seen him smile.

Chapter Five

FROM the moment she arrived the next morning, Mrs. Washington knew that Mr. Horowitz had experienced a difficult night. There was evidence that he had come out into the living room after she had made sure he was in bed. In front of an easy chair was a rough swirl in the carpet, betraying a struggle. He must have fallen.

She tiptoed to the bedroom, eased the door open slightly, and listened. He was breathing steadily, deeply, in sleep. Reassured, she went to the kitchen and there she found a shattered cup and a large, dried stain of Sanka spread across the linoleum. By the time she finished tidying up, Horowitz was awake.

She mentioned nothing about the kitchen and the living-room carpet. For breakfast she made a simple meal, but reduced the padding on his fork by half. He had trouble handling it, but silently managed. He had yet to say good morning. He ate and stared off into space.

Finally she barked at him, "Good morning, Mr. Horowitz!"

"What's good about it?" he asked.

"You had a bad night?" she questioned gently.

He did not reply. Later, he proved most uncooperative during his exercises, which she had to force on him. He muttered uncomplimentary epithets, ranging from Idi Amin to Andrew Young.

She observed, "If your arm and hand showed as much resistance as your mean temper, you'd be cured by now."

Thus, insulting each other, they gradually got through the first exercise session of the day.

"Now get dressed," Mrs. Washington said when they'd finished. "We're going out to the park."

THEY had been sitting in the sun without speaking for almost an hour. The sounds of traffic, more oppressive in the city during summer days, were all that could be heard. Occasionally from the playground came the sound of children laughing, or the sudden anguished outcry of a child injured at play.

Horowitz spoke first. "I used to take Mona to that playground when she was small. Even then she used to tell the other kids what to play, and how to play. You think kids are born with all the characteristics they're going to have later?"

"Yes," Mrs. Washington said. "My grandson, Conrad, he was like that from the first. He would reach for a finger and hold on as if his life depended on it. And he's like that to this day. Tightfisted. He won't spend a penny if he can save it. He'll be a success."

"Conrad . . . a nice name," Horowitz said. "And evidently he's a nice boy."

"Oh, yes, and he's going far, far!" Mrs. Washington said with pride and determination. "He's already first in his class."

"That's nice. You must be proud. And the girl?"

"Louise," Mrs. Washington said. "She's very bright too. Her record in second grade was every bit as good as Conrad's."

The traffic noises and the sounds of children at play took over for a moment. Finally Horowitz said, "Mrs. Washington, you must have guessed that I fell last night in the living room. And you saw the spill in the kitchen?"

"Yes."

"I want you to know I appreciate that you didn't mention it. You are a very considerate woman."

"Thank you."

"I don't want anyone to know that I fell. You won't tell Marvin, will you? Or Mona?"

"Not if you promise not to get into such situations again."

"I . . . I couldn't sleep last night," he tried to explain, and then with a gesture of his hand dismissed the subject.

Back at the apartment, Mrs. Washington sat across from him while he ate, and sipped her Sanka. He now used the fork more easily. But he still seemed troubled by some secret burden. And later, during his exercises, he was as uncooperative as ever.

To make amends he offered, "If I shuffled the cards every time, if I used my left hand a lot, would you learn pinochle?"

"I guess I could learn," she acceded.

Eagerly he pointed to the large walnut breakfront. "In the top drawer you will find a deck of pinochle cards. They've been there ever since Hannah . . ." He did not say the word.

Mrs. Washington brought the cards to him and he began to shuffle them laboriously. "In the pinochle deck there are forty-eight

cards. And only aces, kings, queens, jacks, tens, and nines. Two of each suit. Now there are two ways you can make points in this game. You can win tricks. And you can meld."

"Meld?" Mrs. Washington asked.

"Lay down combinations, like in rummy," Horowitz explained. "But you can only meld after you win a trick. There are two kinds of melds. There's runs, like a flush in trump—ace, king, queen, jack, ten. And there's a marriage—a king and queen of the same suit. That's worth twenty points. But a royal marriage is worth forty. A royal marriage is a king and queen of trump."

"What's a trump?" she asked.

Impatiently he declared, "I'm getting to that. First, about tricks! Each trick you win gives you points, because each card has a point value. For instance, an ace is worth eleven, a king, four, a queen, three, a jack, two, and a ten is worth ten."

Mrs. Washington shook her head, saying softly, "Strange game, where a ten is worth more than a king and queen."

"Take my word for it!" Horowitz bellowed. He regained his composure, and assuming the air of a reasonable man, he continued. "Now, the dealer hands out twelve cards, three at a time."

He proceeded to deal. "The top card in the pack we turn over, and it is called trump. That answers your question." Then he finished up. "After we play out the hands, we add up melds and tricks and whoever has the highest number of points is the winner. Understand?"

"Understand," she said, to avoid any further outbursts.

"So let's play," he said, picking up his hand and arranging his cards, while she watched furtively to see how well he used his left hand in the process.

In the midst of the game Horowitz paused. "I would like to say something . . ." he began, but halted.

"Yes?" she encouraged.

He looked into her face. "Last night, after I fell asleep, I woke up suddenly. Something was bothering me. What, I didn't know. I couldn't fall asleep again. And then just when the first light was showing through the shutters, it came to me. Yahrzeit! You know what means Yahrzeit, Mrs. Washington?"

She shook her head slightly.

He then proceeded to explain. "Yahrzeit means the time of year for a most unhappy anniversary. The day a loved one died. My Hannah, she should rest in peace, died on the tenth of June, 1974. Which on the Jewish calendar was the twentieth day of Sivan. This year the twentieth day came out on the sixth of June.

"So why was I so troubled last night? Because Hannah's Yahrzeit was while I was in the hospital. So I had done nothing. Nothing! Do you hear? I shamed her memory. Not I said *Kaddish*, not Marvin said *Kaddish*, you know, the prayer for the dead. We didn't light a Yahrzeit candle the night before. We didn't go to *shul* the next morning. Of course, Marvin is too high class to go to *shul*. He goes to temple. And then only for board meetings. He's a trustee. And Mona, well, women do not go to *shul* on Yahrzeit. So who is left to honor Hannah's memory? Me."

He fell silent for a moment, then reproached himself. "I should have remembered! Because in that bag of groceries I was carrying when I was mugged were two Yahrzeit candles. But once I was in

271

the hospital, I . . . somehow I forgot all about Yahrzeit. So Hannah Horowitz was like she never lived. Nobody went before God and said, Remember this good woman. She was an angel. Maybe even make up to her for the nuisance I was during her lifetime."

He looked at Mrs. Washington and in all seriousness said, "Frankly, Mrs. Washington, I can tell you that I am sometimes very difficult to get along with."

"*No*," she said, attempting to portray surprise.

"Oh, yes," he insisted. "So that was what woke me in the night. Hannah. And no Yahrzeit this year. And that's what made me so grumpy today. I hope you understand."

"I do."

"I would like to go lie down. I need to be alone for a while."

Later, when she knocked on his door, he did not reply. She opened the door gingerly and peeked in. The room was dark. He had closed the shutters before lying down. But he was not asleep. He said softly, "Yes, Mrs. Washington, I know. Exercise time."

It was not till she began working with him on the resistance exercises that she saw his eyes were red from weeping. "Mr. Horowitz, does it make any difference what day Yahrzeit is?"

"Of course!" he replied, trying to raise his left leg against the pressure of her hand. "After all, Yahrzeit is Yahrzeit. It's not like Congress passes a law and says, This year Fourth of July is on the fifth of August. Nobody fools around with Yahrzeit!"

"I was thinking about Yom Kippur. When I worked for the Rosengartens, they lit special candles in jelly glasses, as early as the twelfth of September and sometimes as late as the tenth of October," she recalled.

"Because that's the day Yom Kippur fell that particular year," he explained impatiently, while trying to raise his left foot.

"So if you can light a Yom Kippur candle sometimes in September and sometimes in October, God is not such a stickler for dates. Especially for a man with a good excuse like yours."

"What are you suggesting?" he asked.

"That tomorrow is as good a day as any for going to *shul*."

"There are no excuses before God!" he scoffed.

"Oh, I don't know," she differed. "I remember one Yom Kippur when Mrs. Rosengarten was sick with the flu. The mister said,

272

even though she fasted every year, this year, because she was sick, I was allowed to give her a little chicken soup."

"Well," Horowitz conceded, "that's different."

They were completing the exercises when he granted, in his grumbling voice, "However, it is possible that tomorrow morning they might need an extra man in *shul* to complete the *minyan.* That's the minimum number—ten—needed for a prayer service, in case you didn't know. Yes, I will go and offer my services."

"What time tomorrow?" Mrs. Washington asked.

"Early. Seven thirty. So men who have Yahrzeit can fulfill their duty and still get to work on time," he explained.

"I'll be here early," Mrs. Washington said simply.

THE next morning, at seven twenty-five, Mrs. Washington wheeled Samuel Horowitz in through the double doors of the synagogue. The sexton, a short, portly man with a small white goatee and wearing a black silk yarmulke, greeted them.

"Ah, Mr. Horowitz, I've missed you. What happened?" he inquired, staring at the wheelchair.

"I . . . I had a little stroke," Horowitz admitted.

"A stroke," the sexton lamented. "At that, you're very lucky. Remember Mishkin? The lawyer? Gone. Cancer. Every day it's someone else. You're one of the lucky ones."

"Thank you," Horowitz responded acerbically.

Mrs. Washington wheeled him to the door of the sanctuary. Some nine or ten men were gathered in the first two rows. As she started to push the chair through the door, Horowitz raised his hand to forbid it. He got up from the chair, and using the back of each pew for support, he labored down the aisle to the other men. He selected a prayer shawl and book and took his place.

During the service, though it required great effort, he rose and sat at the appropriate times. At the end, when the time came to say the prayer in remembrance of the dead, Horowitz spoke more loudly than the others who had Yahrzeit.

Mrs. Washington was wheeling him home when he commented, "I hope I didn't hurt your feelings in synagogue. It wasn't that I didn't want you there because you're not Jewish. It was because I didn't want Hannah to see me this way. Needing your help."

273

AT HOME, HE ATE his breakfast
with more appetite than usual.
The morning's prayer had obviously eased his conscience.

As she cleared the table Mrs.
Washington asked him, "Do you
want to light the Yahrzeit candle now?"

"Who's got a Yahrzeit candle?"
he demanded.

"We have one," she said.

Rising, he hobbled after her
into the kitchen. There on the
drainboard were two white
Yahrzeit candles in small jelly
glasses, alongside a box of
kitchen matches.

Leaning against the sink to
support himself, he struck a
match and lit one of the tiny
wicks. "How come we happen to
have them?" he asked.

"On my way home, I happened
to be passing a supermarket."

"Tell me, Mrs. Washington, do
many supermarkets up in Harlem
carry Yahrzeit lamps?"

"It happens."

"How many stores did you have to go to before it 'happened'?"

"One or two. Maybe three," she admitted, smiling.

He patted her cheek tenderly. "If only for your sake, I don't
think God will mind that I was a little late this year."

He took several steps with his cane before he stopped and looked
back at her. "Next year," he said, "I would like to go there on my
own. Walk down that aisle without holding on to the pews."

As he started back to the living room, she made herself a solemn
promise. Yes, Mr. Horowitz, next year you *are* going to that synagogue on the right day, and under your own power!

274

Chapter Six

IN THE physical therapy department of the hospital, Samuel Horowitz was going through his weekly evaluation.

Mrs. Washington stood watching the physical therapist, a brisk
young woman, put Horowitz through the tests. He complied with
her commands with a bored lack of enthusiasm. At last she said,
"Okay, Pop, let's see if you can put your shoes back on."

"In the first place, I am not your pop. In the second place, I can
put my shoes on like I have been doing for sixty-eight years!"

Whereupon he proceeded to demonstrate, a bit awkwardly,
tying the shoelace into a creditable knot. "There! Okay?" he said.

"You forgot to tie your other shoe," the PT pointed out.

He glanced down. True, he had forgotten again.

The physical therapist then turned him over to the occupational
therapist, who made him shuffle cards and perform a number of
other exercises and tests. Mrs. Washington saw that he was doing
them defiantly and not nearly so well as at home.

When the OT finished, she asked them to wait, and she and the
PT conferred privately with the department head, Mrs. Wolff. A
tall woman with the physique of an Amazon and golden braids
wound Germanically about her head, Mrs. Wolff finally came to
her door and asked Mrs. Washington to come in.

The department head studied the two reports she held. "Not
very good, you know. The trouble with you nurses is that either
you baby the patient, or else you keep him sedated so he won't
become a nuisance."

"I don't baby him," Mrs. Washington protested. "And if you
think he's sedated, just talk to him."

"He's not making much progress. You have to drive him more."

"He does better at home than he did here. He resents coming."

"Well, he'll have to get used to it. He is not improving and I will
have to report that to his doctor."

ON THE way home in the cab, neither Horowitz nor Mrs. Washington spoke. But once inside the apartment, Horowitz asked, "So
what did Brünnhilde have to say?"

276

"Brünnhilde?"

"The lady giant," Horowitz explained. "With the blond hair."

"She doesn't like your negative attitude," Mrs. Washington said. "She thinks it's interfering with your rehabilitation. You're not making progress with your exercises."

"Exercises? Soon I'll be ready for the Olympics!" he protested. Then he said bitterly, "Ah, *bobe meises!* You know what means *bobe meises?* Fairy tales! Once my friend Kantrowitz had his stroke, he never got out of his wheelchair. These things don't get better. They only keep you doing those exercises to fool you into thinking that they do."

He turned his head aside, ostensibly to look out the window but actually to hide his tears. In a moment he sniffled back to his usual crusty self. "You know," he said, making every effort to seem gruff again, "when you get older, your eyes tear. Especially in the sunshine. I should wear sunglasses." Then he demanded, "So what's the matter, today is Yom Kippur? No lunch?"

HE WAS just finishing his meal when the phone rang. Mrs. Washington came into the dining room. "It's her."

"Mona," he said, resigned, and wheeled himself to the kitchen telephone.

"Dad, it's me," Mona said sternly. "Now, what's this I hear?"

"Since you heard and I didn't, you tell me."

"Marvin got a call from Dr. Tannenbaum, who got a call from your physical therapist. She says you're not making progress."

"So?"

"So unless you show some improvement, we'll have to take steps."

"You mean, if *I* don't soon take steps, *you* will take steps."

"Dad, this is serious! The therapist said that nurses tend to baby their patients. They don't drive them enough. So Mrs. Washington may have to go."

"Believe me," Horowitz defended, "this nurse is a tyrant. She's the nastiest person I have ever met."

He noticed Mrs. Washington glaring at him, and putting his hand over the phone, explained, "I'm defending you, believe me."

"Dad, this is nothing to joke about!" he heard Mona say.

277

"Okay, darling, I'm sorry. She is a nice, conscientious woman, who is doing her best."

"I hope so. Because if things don't change for the better, and soon, I'm going to have to come east and take charge," Mona said. "So try, please, Dad, try! Work hard!"

"Yes, dear, I'll work. Otherwise, steps!"

As he hung up, he realized how little time it had taken for that nosy therapist to call his doctor, his doctor to call Marvin, Marvin to call Mona, and Mona to call him. Messages had flashed instantaneously across three thousand miles and back, so the whole world would know that Samuel Horowitz had failed his test at the physical therapist's.

Feeling empty and purposeless, he wheeled himself back to the living room. Mrs. Washington followed, announcing, "Now, back to the marbles and the buttons, and I don't want any complaints!"

THE next morning they made their prelunch visit to the park. The oppressive humidity warned of a heat wave of the kind that one encountered only in New York.

Mrs. Washington allowed Horowitz to sit in the sun briefly before wheeling him into an area shaded by wide-spreading leafy trees. They passed the time in silence, listening to the cries and laughter of children, and the sound of an occasional bird presumptuous enough to make itself heard above the other noises.

Finally Horowitz said, "Hannah loved this park. Of course, in her last years I never let her go in here alone. Too dangerous. But it was nice just to be able to look out the window and see it.

"In winter, when it snowed, it was a fairyland. At night the lights would make everything sparkle. Came spring, near the Metropolitan Museum, there were magnificent trees with pink flowers. When a breeze made them drop their blossoms, it was like standing in a pink rain. But fall, fall Hannah loved best. The red and golden leaves under your feet—it was a shame to walk on them they were so beautiful. All that we enjoyed together, Hannah and me."

He paused and then said, "You and your husband must have shared such pleasures too."

"Yes," she said softly. "At Easter time we used to buy the children new clothes and stroll proudly up Lenox Avenue to the

278

church. Or Christmas. If he'd been working and got paid well, we always made sure to have a good Christmas, because we knew he would be laid off right after. Except during the war, when he worked steady. It's sad, isn't it, that people have to yearn for war because it means a decent job."

Horowitz felt free to stare at her, for she was turned away from him. Hers was a strong face. But one could find there the lines that a lifetime of care and worry had left. Her hair, which seemed so ebony, had silver strands running through it. Behind her spectacles her eyes were not as combative as usual. They were a bit moist.

"It'll get better," he consoled. "Our generation was the one that had the struggle and the fear, so that our children would have it better. And they *do* have it better."

"The grandchildren, if they grow up right, they can have it better," she agreed.

"With a grandmother like you for an example, they'll grow up right," he assured.

"It's the things they're exposed to. The violence, the drugs. Girls becoming pregnant at thirteen. Boys learning how to push drugs and steal. How do you keep them from being tempted?"

"It's a problem," he agreed, but could offer no solution.

They were silent. Finally Mrs. Washington said, "It's getting too hot out here. I better get you upstairs to the air conditioner."

THAT evening after his dinner Horowitz watched television while Mrs. Washington bustled about the kitchen cleaning up.

On the news the weather indicated no letup in the heat wave. The forecaster issued a warning from Con Edison to keep power consumption at a minimum. Horowitz comforted himself with the fact that he kept his air conditioner on a nice even low. He considered himself a reasonable man with modest needs.

When Mrs. Washington was ready to leave, he invited her to sit awhile and get cool. But she begged off, saying that she did not want the children to be alone. "On a night like this," she said, "they'll want to be out. It gets hot in that little apartment."

"I can imagine," Horowitz said. "When we were kids in Brooklyn, a night like this Mama would put out blankets and we would sleep on the fire escape. Sometimes in the middle of the night would come up a sudden storm, and we would get drenched and have to come inside. But in the morning the air would be fresh and there would be a breeze. So I know," he recalled. "I know."

IT was the middle of the night. Horowitz woke with a start, as if someone had nudged him. His air conditioner had stopped, disturbing his slumber. He reached for the switch on the bedside lamp. No response. He clicked it again, then again. Nothing.

For a moment he was terrified. A sudden sweat covered his body. Had some burglar made his way into the apartment and cut off all lights to render him defenseless?

Then he became aware that there was no light coming from the outside either. He made his way to the window. The city was in total darkness. He was not so fearful any longer, for he recalled the warnings on the news about power shortages.

He groped about his night table for the battery radio that Marvin had brought him in the hospital. He found it and flipped on the switch. His suspicions were confirmed. The news announcer was talking about a city-wide blackout.

He remembered the last blackout, ten or twelve years ago, when he had been working late and had to walk home. But there had been a bright moon and people took the emergency kindly, helping each other, cheerfully walking in groups, making jokes. By the time he got home, Hannah was terribly worried, but he had kissed away her fears.

He recalled, too, that Hannah had produced candles that night, using her Friday-night candles and the ones she decorated the table with for small dinner parties.

But for three years now there had been no dinner parties, no Friday-night candles. Then he remembered. There *was* a candle. That second Yahrzeit candle Mrs. Washington had brought.

He reached for his quad cane and, feeling his way about, walked carefully to the kitchen. He found the Yahrzeit candle in the cabinet over the sink. He struck a match and held it to the wick.

You see, Hannah, he said silently, you have provided me with a candle this time too.

He wrapped his left hand around the glowing glass, and with a secure right-hand grip on his cane, he returned to the bedroom.

The radio announcer was now talking more rapidly, describing an outbreak of looting and rioting in Harlem. Men and boys, women and young girls had come streaming out of their tenements and were shattering store windows, and even driving cars through the shops' metal grilles, to steal any merchandise that could be carried off. Television sets, hi-fis, jewelry, liquor.

"The police," Horowitz kept muttering, "where are the police?"

But it became apparent from ensuing reports that the police had been ordered not to intervene lest they create a race riot. The looting continued all night; even fires were being set.

Samuel Horowitz stared into the darkness, listening, as the city which he loved and was determined not to abandon was being destroyed. He heard endless police sirens and fire trucks racing beneath his window. A city had gone mad.

Finally he drifted off to sleep. When he woke, it was morning. The air in the apartment was heavy and dank. Obviously power had not yet been restored. His phone rang.

"Dad?" It was Marvin calling from Washington. "Are you okay?"

"I'm fine, yes, why?"

"When I heard the news this morning, I was worried," Marvin said. "Is Mrs. Washington there?"

"No, not yet."

"Dad, it's nine fifteen. Well, maybe she had trouble getting downtown. Things must be a mess in New York this morning. But at least you're all right. Call me if you need anything. I'll be in the office all day."

"Of course, yes, if I need anything," Horowitz echoed. He hung up the phone, worrying about Mrs. Washington. Terrible things could have happened to her. Perhaps looters had broken into her apartment. Of course she would have resisted. And when she did, some black hoodlum would have hit her over the head, splitting her skull open, killing her.

The phone rang again. He answered at once, "Yes? Hello?"

"Mr. Horowitz?" It was her voice, thanks God.

"Are you all right?" he asked.

"Yes, yes, I'm all right. I'm sorry I'm late, but I'll be there within the hour."

As concerned as Horowitz had been about Mrs. Washington's

safety, by the time she arrived he was critical and disapproving. He greeted her sarcastically. "Some show last night. You people can be very proud of yourselves."

Mrs. Washington did not answer but proceeded to the kitchen to prepare his breakfast.

He taunted again loudly, "A man works all his life to build up a business. Everything he has in the world is invested in one little store and they break in and destroy him in one night."

Still she did not respond.

"Something has to be done," he went on when she appeared in the dining room. "Else we are living in a jungle. Last night was only the beginning."

She did not answer, except to remind him that he might want to take a shower after his long hot night.

"Okay, a shower," he acquiesced gloomily. Then he added, "And later, maybe we will *dare* go out in the park. Hmm?"

"Not today," she said quietly. "The elevators are not running. The power hasn't been restored yet."

"But you came up," he began to protest, until it dawned on him. "You mean . . . Mrs. Washington, did you walk up all ten flights?"

She did not answer, but silently turned and left the room.

An hour later his air conditioner came on softly. The power was flowing again. He turned on the television set. Regular programming had been suspended in favor of special news coverage of the looting. On-the-scene footage taken the night before showed mostly black marauders bursting into stores and carrying off furniture, bedding, and electric appliances of all kinds.

Horowitz could not contain himself and called out, "Mrs. Washington! Come in here and look! See for yourself! Animals!"

She did not answer or appear. With the support of his quad cane, he slowly dragged himself into the foyer. She was not in the living room or the dining room. For an instant he feared that she had deserted him. Perhaps he had been too harsh.

The kitchen door was closed, but he thought he could hear the sound of sobbing. He pushed open the swinging door cautiously.

Mrs. Washington sat at the small table, her elbows resting on it. In her hands was a damp handkerchief, which she held to her eyes while she sobbed so that her whole body shook.

Horowitz realized he had to make amends. "Mrs. Washington," he ventured, "I'm sorry about what I said. Even if it's the truth, I shouldn't have said it."

She continued to weep, whispering, "Oh, God, oh, God."

"Mrs. Washington, please, if it would make you feel better to holler at me, holler. I'll understand." He stood there, waiting, like a recalcitrant little boy.

She shook her head forlornly. Whatever it was, it was too painful to talk about.

"So you were a little late today. So what? Never in all my years in business did I dock an employee because of a storm, or something that was not his fault. So don't cry. Please?"

She kept on crying, catching her breath in short gasps.

"What's wrong? There's nothing so bad that you can't tell me," he pleaded. "After all, we are not exactly strangers."

Finally she said, "I had to go to court this morning."

"Court?"

"Yes. Last night . . . once the blackout started . . . the street was full of people. They were laughing, cheering, breaking windows."

"Yes. So?" Horowitz asked.

"My grandson . . . Conrad . . . He watched, he listened. Then suddenly he said, 'I'm going to get ours!' I held on to him. But he pushed me away. And he was gone. He never got home last night."

"They arrested him?" Horowitz ventured.

She nodded. "When they caught him, he was trying to steal an air conditioner."

"I see," Horowitz said sadly. "Yes, I see."

"This boy, a good student, the son of a policeman. A religious boy. And in one night he became one of them," she said tearfully.

"Were you able to get him out of jail?"

"Yes. One of the officers there had worked with his father. He helped. But he'll have to go back for a hearing."

"I'll call Marvin. Someone in his law firm's New York office will handle the case. Without a fee!" Horowitz promised.

"It was my fault," she accused herself. "For days now I kept complaining how hot it was. How much better it would be if we had an air conditioner."

He patted her on the head. "I promise you, he'll get the best legal advice. We'll make sure the judge knows why he did it. Nothing bad will happen to him."

"It's already happened," she said sadly. "Just living in this city is a disease. A child is exposed and can catch it. All the years of bringing up, gone in one night." She fell to weeping again.

"Mrs. Washington, when the whole world goes crazy, you expect one small boy to remain sane? Now, what's the boy's full name?"

"Bruton. Conrad Bruton," Mrs. Washington informed him.

Horowitz hobbled to the kitchen phone. He dialed Marvin's number, and when he reached him, he explained the problem.

"Stealing an air conditioner?" Marvin exploded. "Dad! How would you have contact with someone who steals air conditioners?"

"In the first place, it was just one air conditioner. In the second place, we are not conceding he was stealing it. In the third place, he is the grandson of a very good friend of mine and I want to see that he gets off! He is a good boy. So do something about it!"

"Dad! We do not practice criminal law."

"What about those corporate clients of yours? Those price-fixing cases I read about in the *Times?*"

"That's different," Marvin protested. But finally he conceded, "I'll see what I can do."

"Don't *see*. Just *do!*" Horowitz commanded. "And if there is a bill, if you want to charge your own father, who put you through Harvard Law School, okay by me!" He hung up and turned to Mrs. Washington. "There! Don't worry!"

"Thank you, Mr. Horowitz," she said.

"What kind of thanks? It's little enough to do for a friend."

Chapter Seven

SOME days later they made their usual visit to the park. This time, however, Mrs. Washington took him to the small lake near the open-air Shakespeare-in-the-park theater.

"You ever been in there?" Horowitz asked.

"No," Mrs. Washington said.

"Must be interesting to see theater at night under the stars. Hannah and me talked about going. But we never did." They were silent for a time. Then he asked, "Would you like to go?"

"At night? I couldn't."

"Of course, the grandchildren." He hesitated before asking, "When does Conrad's case come up?"

"Tomorrow."

"Did he say how he likes the young lawyer Marvin sent him?"

"He likes him. But they say the judges have been given orders to be very tough on looters," she said grimly.

"It'll be all right," he promised. After a pause he asked, "If it could be arranged one night that someone was with the children, you think we could go to the Shakespeare?"

"We might," she said, evading, not promising.

"Try. I would like to go, so when I meet Hannah again, I can tell her how it was."

"You're not going to meet her for a long time."

"How do you know?" he asked.

"When the angel of death comes for you, you'll be too damn stubborn."

THE next afternoon the phone rang in the apartment. This time it was for Mrs. Washington.

"Yes, darling, now go home. Straight home," Horowitz heard her say. When she hung up, she smiled at him. "The judge let Conrad off with a warning. Because of his school record and what two of his teachers wrote about him."

"Good!" Horowitz said. "I must tell Marvin they have at least one bright young lawyer in his firm."

Later, when she was putting him through his therapy, he asked abruptly, "Conrad and Louise, they ever been to see Shakespeare?"

"No. Why?"

"Then what would be so terrible, you should bring them down here? We all have dinner together, then go to the Shakespeare."

She would only promise, "I'll think about it."

"Mrs. Washington, no thinking. I want your word. Now! We'll go! Right?"

Because he had never shown such determination and optimism before, Mrs. Washington said, "Right!"

"Good!" he said, then gloated in anticipation. "And the next day I'll call Mona. And I'll just casually toss off, 'Last night I went

285

to see Shakespeare.' That should keep her from coming here and trying to organize me."

Horowitz laughed, and Mrs. Washington joined him.

On the day of their visit to the theater, Samuel Horowitz rooted through the drawers of his chest, searching for something. When Mrs. Washington inquired if she could help, he muttered that he had to learn to do things for himself.

After his nap he selected a pair of navy slacks, a long-neglected, brightly colored sport shirt, and a blue-and-white checked sport jacket. "Not bad," he concluded. "What do you think?"

"Not bad," Mrs. Washington agreed.

That evening, in a little French restaurant on Columbus Avenue, Horowitz acted the host with all the officiousness of which he was capable. He ordered the waiter about. He held forth over the menu, suggesting one dish after another for Conrad and Louise. He was more animated than Mrs. Washington had ever seen him.

Mainly he studied the children. Conrad was a lean, tall boy, with his grandmother's bright black eyes. He was polite and respectful. And no wonder, Horowitz said to himself, with such a tyrant for a grandmother. Louise, four years younger than Conrad, was a slight child of eight. Pretty despite her glasses, she, too, looked as if she would grow up tall and graceful. She carried herself well for a child so young.

When the main course was finished, Horowitz summoned the waiter. "*Garçon,* I want you should bring a tray of the richest, fanciest desserts you have!"

The waiter presented a tray of delicacies abounding in chocolate and whipped cream. Horowitz watched with pride and enjoyment while the youngsters consumed their dessert. He glanced across the table at Mrs. Washington and nodded warmly, giving his approval to her bringing up of the children.

The play, one of Shakespeare's Kings, was loud and theatrical, filled with swordplay and finally death. The street sounds, so close, were miraculously blotted out by the action on the stage. Even a distant storm, which filled the night with flashes of lightning and rumbles of thunder, did not intrude.

Afterward the audience filed out quickly. Horowitz made his way in his wheelchair—with the unasked-for assistance of Conrad, who tried to appear casual so as not to offend the old man's pride.

When they returned to his apartment, Horowitz insisted they all come inside for a while. He rolled himself into the living room and to the bridge table near the window. There he rested his hand on a ruby-red cut-glass box, and turned to the two children.

"Conrad . . . Louise . . ." he began, "I want you both to remember this night. Not because you had a delicious meal. Believe me, your grandmother cooks better. Not because we saw a big show by Shakespeare. You will see other shows in your life. And not because you made an old man feel a little less lonely. That was very nice of you.

"I want you to remember it because this world is changing. Things you can achieve, your grandfather couldn't. Just like I had opportunities here that *my* grandfather didn't have." He touched Conrad's arm. "But, my boy, you do not take advantage of opportunity by rushing out into the night and saying, 'I'm going to get mine!' and then taking what belongs to another man.

"Don't think I don't know that feeling of impatience. When I was a boy, I used to watch my mother working hard at home, and helping my father in the little grocery we had. I wanted to do something bold and desperate to show her how much I resented what the world had done to her.

"But that's not the way. Fight the world, it will crush you. Outsmart the world, it will reward you. You will have plenty of time to do good things for your mother and your grandmother. But do it right. So you can look them in the eye."

He opened the glass box and took out a small coin. It was worn but shiny. He carefully placed the coin in Conrad's hand.

"My boy, this is a five-dollar gold piece. The date says 1901. It was given to me by my father when I was bar mitzvahed. That means thirteen years old. Not much different than you are now. And he said, 'This is only a promise of what you can have if you work hard.' So I say the same to you."

He closed the boy's hand into a tight fist. "Keep it. Always. Until the time comes to give it to *your* son."

"Thank you," the boy said. "Thank you very much."

287

Horowitz turned to the young girl. "And for you, my dear Louise, I also have something."

He reached back into the box and brought out a small gold pin encrusted with tiny seed pearls. He gazed at it fondly.

"This pin," he began, "cost twelve and a half dollars when that was a whole lot of money. I was working as an office boy for sixteen dollars a week. At Christmastime I was promoted to a salesman and raised to twenty dollars a week. On my way home, I bought this pin for my mother. Now I want you to have it. Look at it often and remember this night."

He closed her hand over the gift and said softly, "I wish my grandchildren had less, so they would appreciate little things more. I used to think of giving these to them, but it wouldn't have mattered." Thoughtful and sad, he patted Louise's hand. Suddenly the girl leaned close and kissed him on the cheek.

Horowitz said, "That, my dear, is the nicest kind of thanks."

FOR the third time since they had returned home, Mrs. Washington listened at the door of the children's room. Before, they had been chattering away, but this time all was quiet.

She eased the door open. Conrad was sleeping on his left side, his right hand resting on the small night table. Mrs. Washington drew closer, to discover that his fingers protected the gold coin Mr. Horowitz had given him.

WHEN Mrs. Washington arrived the next morning, she found that Horowitz was not only up but had dressed himself.

He proudly announced, "Today, Mrs. Washington, we are having company!"

"Good!" she exclaimed, encouraged that he was finally seeking contact with the outside world.

"Marvin is in New York. A client of his is in federal court here. My Marvin," he boasted, "does not practice in state courts anymore. Only federal! When he's finished in court today, he'll come up for drinks and hors d'oeuvres! You know how to make hors d'oeuvres?"

"Of course." She was delighted. She had never seen him so enthusiastic.

288

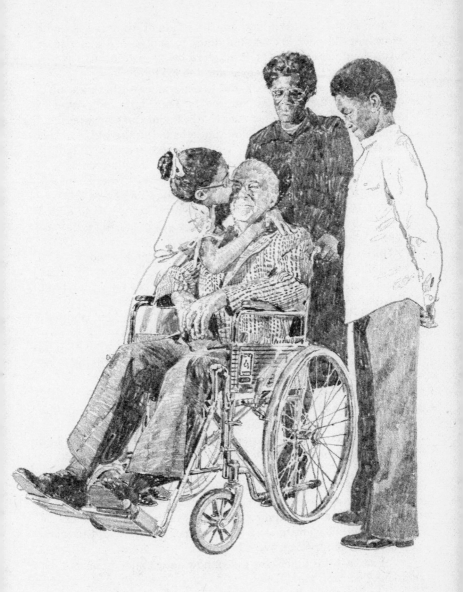

"You know, Mrs. Washington," he suddenly admitted, "maybe as we get older we become too quick to find fault. I mean, after all, I shouldn't criticize Marvin. Here he is, such a busy lawyer, but he makes the time to come and see his father."

He paused, as if he were about to make an earthshaking confession. "And if the truth be told, maybe I'm a little too critical of Mona also. If you could see the awards, the plaques she's received from charities she's worked on. And letters? Hundreds! From kids she straightened out with her youth projects."

"You have a right to be proud of her," Mrs. Washington said.

"If only she didn't treat *me* like a project," Horowitz lamented.

That afternoon he hovered over Mrs. Washington as she prepared all Marvin's favorite hors d'oeuvres. Cream cheese dotted with pink smoked salmon on squares of black bread. Slices of toast with a cheese topping. And chopped liver.

Horowitz was sampling the liver when Marvin phoned.

"Hello, Marvin," Horowitz said. "Listen, don't worry if you are late. These days, the courts so overcrowded. So take your time. What? Not coming? I see. . . ."

For a moment Mrs. Washington feared that Mr. Horowitz might drop the phone, his hand trembled so.

"Listen, Marvin, no apologies necessary. I know how it is. So go, have drinks and dinner with your client. And next time you come to New York we'll get together."

Horowitz hung up the phone. Before Mrs. Washington could utter a word of consolation, he said, "After all, he's one of the busiest lawyers in the country. He can't help it. . . ."

But he avoided Mrs. Washington's eyes and hobbled away into the living room to read the *Times*.

A FEW days later Horowitz finished reading his paper just as Mrs. Washington completed her vacuuming.

"If you want me to crumple the pages, get me another paper!" he said to her. "I want to save this one. For all the world to know when this country began to come apart."

"What is it this time?" she asked, now accustomed to his ranting about *The New York Times*.

"The *Times* is yelling for détente. Do you know what détente is,

Mrs. Washington? It is a French word for what they don't dare say in English. Surrender! Imagine, this was once the greatest country in the world! Now we are making détente with the Russians, who are building up their missiles so they can destroy us."

She took the first page from him. "Crumple!" she said.

"Crumple," he grumbled. "Where should I start? The financial page? The economy is crumpled enough. The sports pages? It's the only place in the *Times* where you can expect at least a little honesty. Or maybe the cooking section? If I want cooking, I will read the *Ladies' Home Journal*."

"Crumple," Mrs. Washington repeated.

"Why not pinochle? Twenty-five cents a hand," he proposed.

"You already owe me twelve dollars and seventy-five cents," she reminded.

"So we'll play double or nothing."

"Crumple! Then the marbles. After that, buttons! Then if there's time left before lunch, a little pinochle."

"Crumple! It's the only word she knows. It doesn't even sound medical!" He held up a page. "Look at this article! It's by a black college professor who is in favor of affirmative action! When we Jews came over to this country, nobody gave *us* any affirmative action. We didn't even speak the language.

"I'll never forget the first day I went to school. Seven years old. And didn't speak a word of English. But my mother knew one thing. I had to go to school. Every Jewish child knows learning is the important thing. So the first day, my mother took one of my father's books. She put a drop of honey on it and said, '*Ess, mein kind.*' Eat! Because a child must know that learning is sweet.

"They put me in a class with a Miss McLanahan. A day went by. Another day. I didn't understand what she was saying. So I never raised my hand. But finally one day she called on me. I sat there feeling stupid. I didn't even understand what the question was, how could I know the answer? The other kids laughed at me. And then I . . . Mrs. Washington, I started to cry."

"I don't blame you," Mrs. Washington said sympathetically.

"When the class was over, she took me by the hand and we went to a small office where a tiny dark-haired woman sat. She was very thin, with small features. She drew me close and spoke in the softest, friendliest voice I have ever heard. *'Farshstast Yiddish, mein kind?'*

"I began to cry again. This time, out of relief. She said that every day after school, for one hour, she would go over with me in Yiddish what the other children had learned that morning. By the end of the term I could speak as well as any of them!" he concluded proudly. "It was something people did by themselves. You didn't need laws and bureaus and a whole megillah!"

Mrs. Washington glared at him and he resumed crumpling the *Times,* tossing the balls across the room with his right arm.

"I wouldn't mind picking them up, if you would throw that far with your left arm," she said.

"Even when I was in school I was a right-handed pitcher," he countered. "But for you, I will throw left-handed." He fashioned another ball and threw it with his left hand.

While he was so engrossed, Mrs. Washington began to dust and at the same time to voice her own opinion.

"Some people forget that for hundreds of years in this country it was against the law to teach a black person to read. No wonder we are so far behind and need the government's help. Or do we just say to young people, because your great-grandfather was a slave you are going to start off behind everyone else and stay there? Is that what you want me to tell my grandchildren?"

Horowitz fought back. "I never owned a slave in my life. My family wasn't even in this country hundreds of years ago. How is it my responsibility?"

Before Mrs. Washington could respond, the phone rang. She went to the kitchen to answer it.

Horowitz was fully expecting her to call out, It's your daughter. But instead, a strange quiet engulfed the kitchen.

In a moment Mrs. Washington appeared, tears starting down her cheeks. "Oh, Mr. Horowitz, it's Conrad . . ." she began. "Conrad was in a street fight. Got stabbed."

"Stabbed? Good God!" Horowitz said. "Where is he?"

"Harlem Hospital."

"Then go! Here." He took a fistful of bills out of his pocket. "Take a cab! Call me as soon as you know anything!"

"What about you?"

"Don't worry about me. I'll get along!"

She was gone.

Gradually, distressed by the fear of what Mrs. Washington might find at the hospital, Horowitz began getting angry at the boy. His mother and grandmother work hard to get him an education, and he has to go get into fights. He might even have been trying to rob somebody when he got into that fight!

After an hour there was still no call from Mrs. Washington. That miserable boy, to bring such grief to a woman as fine as his grandmother. Children, Horowitz lamented, should be a source of joy, but how often they became a cause of sorrow.

It was now past one. He would get himself lunch. He made his way to the refrigerator, where he found some eggs. He decided to soft-boil two of them, but in the process his unsteady left hand betrayed him. One egg fell to the floor and burst, spreading a yellow-and-white blob across the linoleum.

He cursed himself for his ineptitude. And he cursed that boy, Conrad, who had thrust this difficulty on him.

Horowrrz shaved, and then, out of respect for Mrs. Washington's feelings, he selected a plain dark suit to wear.

Slowly, laboriously, he dressed and then examined himself in the long mirror on the closet door. He seemed a fair semblance of the Samuel Horowitz of some months ago. Even the scar on his cheek had faded sufficiently so that it did not anger him as much.

He put twenty dollars in his pocket and picked up his four-footed cane. He was ready to set out on the longest solo expedition he had undertaken since he had suffered his stroke.

He felt a certain pride in entering the elevator on his own two feet and seeing the surprise in Angelo's eyes.

"Hey, Mr. Horowitz, we makin' progress!" Angelo exclaimed.

Horowitz managed a casual smile. "Every day a little better."

But he had not anticipated that traversing the lobby would prove to be so taxing. His days of practice with the quad cane had limited him to the length of the living room and the foyer—twenty-three strides in all. The lobby was more than forty steps. But when Juan, the doorman, came to assist him, Horowitz brushed his hand aside, saying, "Don't worry about me."

Outside, the sun was bright and hot. Juan hailed him a cab and gently assisted him in.

"Where to, mister?" the cabby asked.

"Harlem Hospital."

"Harlem Hospital?" the cabby asked dubiously. "Are you sure?"

"Do I look like a man who's not sure?" Horowitz demanded.

"Okay, mister," the cabby agreed reluctantly.

The cab was not air-conditioned. The breeze was hot and dusty, and Horowitz could feel soot sting his cheeks.

He hated this journey, hated the boy whom he had tried so hard to befriend and who had turned out to be another street bum. Conrad must have had himself a good laugh all through that lecture Horowitz had delivered about hard work. Well, street justice had evidently caught up with the gangster. Good!

The driver stopped at the entrance to Harlem Hospital, and Horowitz began the difficult task of extricating himself from the cab. He couldn't push the door open far enough for the catch to hold. It slammed shut. The cabby bounded out of the front seat, came around the cab, and helped him out.

Near the hospital entrance stood several groups of young black men. With the Pavlovian reflex instilled by a dozen years of recent city history, Horowitz reacted in fear and suspicion. Nevertheless, determined, he started on his labored walk toward the doors of the hospital. No one molested him or even noticed him.

Inside, he approached the information desk. The receptionist looked at him and his cane. "The outpatient department is around to the side," she volunteered.

"And who asked you about the outpatient department?" Horowitz shot back. "I am here to see a patient. His name is Conrad Bruton."

The receptionist dialed a number on her phone and repeated the information. Then she looked up at Horowitz. "He's in the surgical ward. Second floor." She pointed to an elevator.

"About his condition, what did they say?" Horowitz asked.

"Guarded," the woman replied.

"He *should* be guarded! He's a hoodlum!"

He took the elevator to the second floor, where he saw a sign on a door that announced QUIET PLEASE. SURGICAL WARD. He stared in through the glass panel. There were six beds, but one had curtains drawn around it. Conrad must be in that one. Below the curtains he noticed a pair of feet shod in sturdy white shoes. Mrs. Washington's!

He walked into the room and pushed aside the curtain. There Conrad lay, eyes closed. He had an oxygen tube in his nose, and his chest was heavily bandaged. He looked so benign and pitiful that Horowitz thought, The faker! He is trying to look like an angel, but he is really a bum. His grandmother sat by the side of the bed, weeping silently, unaware of Horowitz's arrival.

Cry, Mrs. Washington, cry aloud, Horowitz thought bitterly. All your work, all your hopes, all your dreams end up here.

Now, however, was the moment to decide on his opening salvo. Should he begin with a loud, accusatory Aha? Or a more direct, You are a disgrace to do this to your grandmother!

Yes, Horowitz decided angrily, that should do it. "So?" he bellowed. His voice reverberated throughout the ward.

Startled, Mrs. Washington leaped to her feet. "Mr. Horowitz, what are you doing here?"

Without lowering his voice one decibel, he retorted, "What am *I* doing here? Better to ask what is *he* doing here."

From a bed across the room a voice called out, "Someone get that maniac out of here!"

Knowing Horowitz as she did, Mrs. Washington could imagine the conclusion he had jumped to. She interceded in a low but firm voice. "Mr. Horowitz, don't say anything you'll be sorry for."

"Sorry?" Horowitz demanded, loud as ever. "I should be sorry? For speaking the truth?"

The door to the ward was flung open and a nurse crossed swiftly to Conrad's bed. She said to Horowitz, "You'll have to get out. Right now."

"Not till I say what I came to say!" Horowitz defied.

"Mr. Horowitz, please," Mrs. Washington begged. "There's something you should see."

"I've seen enough," Horowitz said grimly.

Mrs. Washington turned and spoke softly to the boy. "Conrad? Can you hear me?"

Without opening his eyes, the boy nodded.

"Show him," was all his grandmother said.

The boy opened his fist. Horowitz looked down. There in Conrad's palm lay the gold piece he had given him several nights ago. Horowitz raised his questioning eyes to Mrs. Washington.

"He was so proud of that coin that he took it with him every day. Two boys tried to steal it from him. He fought back."

"So . . . so that's how he was knifed?"

"He wouldn't give it up. It meant too much to him."

"He . . . he . . ." Horowitz tried to say, but sniffled instead. "Old age," he explained to the nurse, "the teary eyes of age."

"You have to leave," the nurse persisted, more gently now.

"Okay, okay, I'll go," a chastened Horowitz replied meekly. "But one moment, please?" She granted permission with a nod.

"Conrad, my boy, can you hear me?" he asked. "I'm very sorry for all the things I almost said. Because even to think what I was thinking is something to be sorry for. So, forgive me. Just get strong again. You're a fine boy."

He turned to Mrs. Washington. "Will I ever see you again after the spectacle I made of myself here today?"

"Yes, of course. Tomorrow."

"Good, good. Tomorrow. And thanks. Thanks for not letting me say things that would have been hatred and anger talking."

Chapter Eight

How was I to know? Horowitz kept repeating to himself as the cab made its way down the hot sunbaked avenue. How could I know the boy was only trying to defend what was rightfully his?

Mrs. Washington would surely hate him now for having given the boy the coin that was the cause of it all. He couldn't blame her. After all, her world is built around that boy and his sister.

The process of getting out of the cab, paying the driver, and making his way into the apartment house now occupied all his concentration. Awkwardly he waved Juan aside. Juan dropped back, but stayed within range so that if Horowitz tottered, he could catch him. "I'm all right!" Horowitz said belligerently.

He was able to negotiate the three steps down into the lobby, though he wavered a bit. He made it to the elevator, where Angelo greeted him, smiling. "Walkin' by yourself, Mr. Horowitz, tha's very good!"

Big deal, Horowitz grouched. One of the insults of old age, that a man should be complimented for doing what he had been doing since he was a year old.

Safely back in the apartment, he was relieved to lie down in his unmade bed, fully clothed. He fell asleep, thinking to himself that not to wake up wouldn't be the worst thing in the world.

The persistent ringing of the phone rudely awakened him. He seized it, dropped it, had to pull it up by its cord.

"Dad? Are you all right?" Mona's voice said frantically. "What happened?"

"What happened was, you woke me up, I reached for the phone in my sleep, and dropped it."

"I mean all afternoon. I called and called, and no answer. Where were you?"

He didn't want to tell her. But you could more easily keep a secret from the CIA. So he told her what had happened to Conrad.

Mona's only response was, "You mean Mrs. Washington isn't there to take care of you?"

"I mean she is where she ought to be. With her grandson."

"I think I should come to New York!" Mona declared.

Oh, God, not that! Horowitz thought. Diplomatically he said, "There's nothing to be concerned about. I'm fine! In fact, Mrs. Washington being away for the day is giving me a chance to get along on my own."

"But how will you get dinner? Who's going to make it?"

"I will call Fine and Schapiro and have them send up some chicken soup with matzo balls, and some boiled chicken."

"Good!" Mona agreed. "But tell them to skim the fat off the soup. And take the skin off the chicken. That's where all the cholesterol is!" she pointed out expertly. "And no sour pickles!"

"Sour pickles? I wouldn't dream," Horowitz assured her.

Finally she hung up. He immediately dialed the number of the delicatessen.

A man greeted, "Fine and Schapiro!"

"Irving?" Horowitz asked. "Sam Horowitz."

"Well, hello, Mr. Horowitz! What can I do for you?"

297

"Irving, a nice, thick corned-beef sandwich. Heavy on the meat, thin on the bread. You know how I like it."

"I know, I know. Lean in the middle but don't trim the fat off the edges."

"Right!" Horowitz said. "A nice, new dill pickle too. Some potato salad, some cole slaw, and a cold bottle of beer!"

"Any special brand?"

"Yes," Horowitz said righteously. "A beer that doesn't have any cholesterol in it."

"There's no cholesterol in beer, Mr. Horowitz."

When the doorbell rang announcing his dinner, he almost tripped on the carpet in his haste to reach the door. He tipped the night elevator man, eagerly took his cherished package, and made his way into the kitchen. There he opened the bag with

all the excited expectation of a child opening a holiday gift.

Ah, the warm, pungent aroma of kosher corned beef! He opened the foil wrapping that kept the meat hot. He lifted the top slice of rye bread and dabbed on some mustard from the container that Irving had sent along. He opened his containers of cole slaw and potato salad. Then, with no small effort, he sliced the pickle in half, lengthwise. His feast was ready.

He sat down at the kitchen table and bit into the warm sandwich. It satisfied his every anticipation. If this is cholesterol, he thought, and I was a young man again, I would go into business and put a new flavor on the market called cholesterol and clean up a fortune!

It was the finest meal he had had in months. Years! To add to the enjoyment there was the clandestine air that surrounded it. He had outwitted Mona. And his doctor. To say nothing of Mrs. Washington.

Mona, he thought, with all your money you couldn't buy such corned beef in San Diego. And you want me to come out there and live. Not on your life.

After his dinner he decided to phone Mrs. Washington at her home and inquire about Conrad's condition, but the resolve was not equal to the embarrassment involved. What could he say after making such a fool of himself that afternoon?

Four times Horowitz reached for the phone, four times hesitated. Finally, out of indecision, he abandoned the idea of calling. Having done so, he picked up the phone and dialed.

Mrs. Washington's daughter answered.

"Do you want to talk to my mother, Mr. Horowitz?"

"If you don't mind," he said meekly.

She turned from the phone and called out, "Mama, it's him."

Horowitz closed his eyes. Is that what they call me, *him?*

Mrs. Washington came to the phone. "Mr. Horowitz?"

He was tempted to say, No, it's *him.* Instead, more solicitously, he inquired, "Conrad, is he all right?"

"So far, so good," the gentle woman said.

"I'm glad for him, glad for you, glad for Louise. This must have been terrible for her."

"She can't stop crying. She's terrified."

"Can you blame her? Listen, I would like to send her a little something. Maybe a doll. A toy. Pick it out. Say it's from me. Let me know what it costs. There must be something she's dreamed about. . . ." He had run out of words.

"What she would like," Mrs. Washington said softly, "is for her father to come back. When she gets frightened, she calls for her daddy."

"Ah, yes, some world," Horowitz lamented. "Get her something anyhow. Please. And tomorrow, don't come in. You got too much on your mind to take care of a foolish old man."

"My sister is coming to stay with Louise. Then my daughter can be with Conrad during the day. So I'll be in."

"You don't have to do it for my sake," he protested.

"I'm not doing it for you. I'm doing it for *me*," she explained firmly. "When things go wrong, the best medicine is to do what you are obligated to do."

He had to ask, "You forgive me about this afternoon?"

"I forgive you," she said gently.

He hung up, with a sense of great relief. A remarkable woman, Mrs. Washington, strong, yet very sensitive. Hannah had that same quality. But somehow between Hannah and Mona something had been lost. Mona, too, was strong. But she had not inherited her mother's sensitivity. Mona could run a revolution, but never take time to feel a moment of sorrow for the victims.

He turned to the refuge of the twentieth century, his television set. Talk to me, he said silently, show me pictures, amuse me, fill up my time. Wipe out my feelings.

He tuned in a drama show that had been on for half an hour. At the moment the only feeling he had was a slight heartburn from the pickle. Well, he consoled himself, it was worth it.

He started flicking the remote-control device, going from channel to channel, seeking something that might engage him. He settled for a night baseball game at Yankee Stadium. The Yankees were ahead—a matter of no special comfort. Horowitz had not accepted that there were any legitimate Yankees since Babe Ruth and Lou Gehrig. Today what do you have? Hired hands. At very fancy salaries. They're not playing for the team, they're playing for the dollars. Where's the old pride?

He fell asleep. When he woke up, the screen was blank and only a loud hum could be heard. The garlic from that pickle now burned more. He knew he would have to take something for it.

In the medicine chest there should be some Alka-Seltzer. If not, there was always bicarbonate of soda in the kitchen. He could remember so vividly his father drinking down baking soda to quench the fire that his mother's fried onions had ignited. Next time, he vowed penitently, corned beef, but no pickle.

He made his way slowly on his quad cane to the bathroom. He searched the medicine cabinet. No Alka-Seltzer. He headed for the kitchen, concentrating on his left foot so it would clear the thick pile of the foyer carpet. It was dark, and suddenly one metal foot of his cane became tangled in the carpet, enough to throw him off stride.

He pitched forward, his head striking the door. By the time he slid to the floor he was unconscious.

Chapter Nine

AT EIGHT o'clock Mrs. Washington stepped off the elevator, and was surprised to find *The New York Times* still on Horowitz's doormat. He must have overslept, she thought. Undoubtedly he had a restless night.

She tried to open the door, but discovered that something blocked her way. She peeked in through the narrow opening. Horowitz lay on the foyer floor.

For a moment she almost gave way to panic and was about to scream. But she regained control and pushed gently at the door until she was able to slip into the apartment.

She dropped to her knees and reached for his pulse. It was slow but palpable. She turned him over and saw a large bruise on his forehead.

"Mr. Horowitz," she whispered. "Mr. Horowitz?"

He moaned, coughed slightly, and finally opened his eyes. He looked about and became aware of the daylight. "It's morning?"

"What happened to you?" Mrs. Washington replied, a bit more dictatorial now that she was sure he was alive and well.

Reluctantly he explained, without mentioning the real cause

of his heartburn. He was fine, it was all the fault of the carpet. Mrs. Washington took a close look at the wound on his forehead.

"We'll have to call the doctor," she said.

"Doctor?" Horowitz protested. "I'm fine!"

"It's my duty as a nurse to report this incident," she said firmly. Then she helped him to his feet and picked up his cane for him.

"You're getting even with me because of all those nasty things I almost said about Conrad," Horowitz said. "I apologized, didn't I? What more do you want? Blood?"

She dismissed his accusation with an appropriate stare of impatience and proceeded to the kitchen, where she phoned Dr. Tannenbaum.

Mrs. Washington had discovered the empty Fine and Schapiro kosher delicatessen bag in the waste can when she went to put out the garbage. She marched into the living room, where she had set Horowitz to work on his marbles after breakfast.

"What's the meaning of *this*?" she demanded, waving the bag.

"I ordered a little something for supper last night," he evaded, applying himself overdiligently to his marbles. "A little chicken soup and matzo balls."

"Really?" she asked. "When Fine and Schapiro sends chicken soup and matzo balls, they send it in a jar. I saw no jar."

"How do you know so much about Fine and Schapiro? No, don't tell me! The Rosengartens!"

"Exactly."

"My luck!" he complained. "I should have known. All right, so it wasn't chicken soup! It was a sandwich."

"What else?" she asked, drumming her fingers impatiently on the wrinkled bag.

"Possibly a little potato salad. After all, what's a sandwich without a little potato salad?"

Finally, looking down at his hated marbles, he confessed, "Cole slaw. Corned beef. Mustard." Belatedly he admitted, "And a piece or two of sour pickle." Then he added defensively, "It's not a crime to eat a little corned beef. You want to know why I did it?"

"Okay, tell me why you did it."

"Mona called. She insisted I order chicken soup, skimmed. And boiled chicken, naked. The skin is the best part. Well, I said, I'll teach her to run my life!"

Mrs. Washington could see it all clearly now. She was about to comment angrily when the doorbell rang.

"Tannenbaum!" Horowitz said, identifying the enemy.

Dr. Tannenbaum, a tall, thin man with a flowing mustache and thick glasses, spent considerable time examining the wound on Horowitz's head. Then he had him cough and breathe, deeply and shallowly. All the while Horowitz kept asking himself, How is it possible in the middle of summer for a stethoscope to be so cold? Do they keep them in a freezer all day?

Finally Tannenbaum said, "So far everything seems fine."

Horowitz made a defiant grimace at Mrs. Washington.

"However . . ." Tannenbaum said.

"Ho-ho-ho, the howevers," Horowitz lamented. "The howevers could kill you."

"However, I'll have to stop by tomorrow and maybe the day after, just to make sure nothing develops."

"I won't be here!" Horowitz threatened.

Tannenbaum looked at him through his thick glasses. "Where will you be? Playing second base for the Mets?"

Defeated, Horowitz said softly, "Look, you want to come, that's okay. Though first you should warm up your stethoscope a little. And do me another favor. Don't tell Marvin."

"You suffered a serious fall, Mr. Horowitz. I can't withhold that from your son. I feel it's my duty."

"Duty . . . duty . . ." Horowitz complained. "Everybody has a duty to everybody, except to me."

"It's for your own good," Tannenbaum consoled.

"Tell me, Doctor, at what age does a man lose his right to decide what's for his own good? Is there some law? Something written in the Bible? In the Constitution?"

"Just take my word for it," Tannenbaum said.

"Take your word?" Horowitz echoed, shaking his head sadly. "We took Jimmy Carter's word that he knew how to run the country and look what happened. Believe me, whatever General Sherman did to Georgia, we are now even!"

THE NEXT MORNING the phone rang and Mrs. Washington hastened to answer.

Horowitz cautioned, "Don't rush. It's only Mona."

"How can you tell?"

"If you know Mona, you know her ring."

"That's ridiculous."

"Ridiculous or not, I'll bet it's Mona."

Mrs. Washington picked up the phone.

"Is my father there?" a stern female voice asked.

Mrs. Washington nodded to Horowitz. "Mona," she admitted.

He took the phone. "Mona, darling. And how are you today?"

"I was fine until I heard from Marvin. What's this about a fall and hurting your head?"

"Well," Horowitz began, "you saw that new dance they're doing on TV, the hustle? Well, I was teaching Mrs. Hess, the widow from the third floor, how to do the hustle, when somehow our feet got tangled up and I accidentally fell."

"Dad, this is serious!" Mona said impatiently.

"With Mrs. Hess? Don't be silly. She's a terrible cook."

"Now, Dad, exactly what happened?" she demanded.

"It was really nothing. I got up in the middle of the night to get an Alka-Seltzer and I fell."

"Why did you need an Alka-Seltzer?" Mona demanded.

"I don't know," he avoided. "Unless it was the chicken soup."

"Nobody, absolutely nobody, has ever had a heartburn from chicken soup," Mona declared. "Dad, it is quite obvious to me that you're not getting the kind of attention you need. You should not be left alone during the night!"

"I'm not going to be saddled with nurses all night long! It's enough I put up with Mrs. Washington during the day," he declared, making a gesture to indicate he was only arguing his case.

"What you need is a household where there is full-time staff. Albert and I have a sleep-in couple. If you were here, and something happened in the middle of the night, all you would have to do is buzz. Why . . . you could have . . . died!" she said, and began to weep.

Horowitz whispered angrily to Mrs. Washington, "You see what you did by calling the doctor? Now she's crying. Crying is what she does best. It's how she got Albert to move to San Diego. She cried four straight days."

Into the phone he consoled, "Mona, darling, there's nothing to cry about. I'm getting better every day. You know, for example, that as I am talking to you I am holding this phone in my left hand? And to prove to you how well I can do that, without any assistance from my right hand, I am going to hang up this phone!"

Whereupon he hung up, cutting off her desperate "Dad, no!"

"You see, Mrs. Washington, what you have done? You will have that on your conscience for the rest of your life."

"Don't go dramatic on me, Mr. Horowitz."

"Dramatic? You call that dramatic? They take a poor defenseless man and put him in prison. That's what it would be out there. An elegant prison. Who would I have to talk to? Nobody. Who would there be to play pinochle with? Nobody! I would shrivel up and die from loneliness. There's no Central Park in San Diego. There's no Fine and Schapiro!"

"And no heartburn!" Mrs. Washington reminded.

"Heartburn?" he seized on the word. "The air out there is so thick with smog, you get heartburn just from breathing!"

The phone rang again. "Don't answer it!" he commanded.

"It must be your daughter calling back."

"You see?" he pointed out. "Already you're able to recognize her ring."

He picked up the phone and said sweetly, "Hello, darling!"

"Dad! I don't ever want you to hang up on me again!"

"I thought we were finished. What more is there to say?"

"I am coming east!" she declared. "And I am taking you back with me. So make plans to close the apartment."

"When are you coming?" he asked with great concern.

"I've called a friend of ours who has his own Lear jet. He promised to put it at my disposal a week from Monday. I'll fly in, spend a day or two taking care of details, and we can be back here by Wednesday evening."

"Mona . . ." he tried to interrupt.

"Dad, I can't let you continue on your own. Mother would never forgive me." She began to weep again. "She always said to me, 'If I go first, take care of your father.'"

"Mona," he said sadly, "I *like* it here. This is my home. I want to live here until I die."

At the word die he was greeted with a fresh torrent of tears.

"A week from Monday!" This time it was Mona who hung up.

ALL through lunch, though Mrs. Washington had tried to tempt him with fresh blintzes, Horowitz ate morosely. He finished one, had barely cut into the second, when he pushed back his plate, declaring, "We've got to keep her from coming here!"

"How?"

"I don't know." Then his face lit up in a big smile. "I *have* it!" he exulted. "I *have* it!"

"What?"

"Mrs. Washington, would you do me the honor to marry me? And also at the same time to save my life!"

Mrs. Washington stared, totally taken aback. "That's a ridiculous idea! Besides, how would it save your life?"

"Let me explain. Suppose we get married. Mona arrives. She wants to take me back to San Diego. I say, 'My darling Mona, you must talk this over with my nurse. Then you two fight it out.' "

"I couldn't win any arguments with her," Mrs. Washington said.

"Look! This is like pinochle! Whoever holds the most trump wins. And you, Mrs. Washington, are holding all the trump."

"I am?" she asked gingerly, suspicious of his next words.

"Mona overcomes you, outargues you, outinsists you. All of which she will certainly do. So you say, 'I can see your point of view. Samuel and I have just gotten married and I agree it would be best for him if we moved to your home in San Diego.' "

"Why should I say that?" Mrs. Washington asked.

Horowitz sang out in great glee, "Because when my Mona hears that her father is moving to her house with a black wife, she will be so stunned she will forget to cry. She will be glad to go back to San Diego alone. She will not even call me anymore. Fantastic, no?" he asked, smiling broadly.

Then he noticed the strange look on Mrs. Washington's face. Tears welled up behind her silver-rimmed glasses.

His sense of victory vanished. "What's the matter? What's wrong?"

She turned away to hide her tears. "I think it's very cruel of you," she finally managed.

"What did I do?" he asked in all innocence.

"You made me the butt of this ridiculous game. You used me."

"I never meant . . ." he started to protest.

"You never meant, but you did it just the same. Used me, used my blackness, as a threat against your daughter. I am not a threat, Mr. Horowitz. I am a human being with feelings. I do not like to be reminded that your daughter would not think me fit to live in her house."

"You don't understand . . ." he tried to plead.

"Oh, but I do. Well, I have my own kind of pride. And it does not tolerate such cruel jokes."

She left the room quickly.

Horowitz brooded in the living room for almost an hour, then made his way to the kitchen. Mrs. Washington sat at the table, her lunch before her untouched.

"Mrs. Washington . . ." he tried to open the conversation. "It *was* cruel. I'm sorry. The only excuse I can give is that I am a desperate man fighting to retain his last ounce of freedom and self-respect. I want to be on my own in my last days. I think I have earned that much out of life. But Mona won't let me. So I had to think of some way . . ."

He was about to turn away when he asked, "Mrs. Washington, suppose, just suppose, that I had asked you to marry me, not for that reason but because I have grown genuinely fond of you, what would you have said?"

Slowly she turned to face him. "I would have felt greatly honored. But the answer would still have been no."

When she arrived the next morning, Mrs. Washington discovered the living room in disarray. Her first thought was that the place had been burglarized.

"Mr. Horowitz!" she cried out, racing toward the bedroom.

The room was in turmoil. His muffled voice came from the bedroom closet. There he stood, leaning on his cane with one hand while trying to reach an overhead shelf.

"What's going on here?" Mrs. Washington demanded.

"I am getting ready," he declared dramatically.

She ordered him out of the closet with a commanding fore-finger. "How did you ever manage to turn this apartment into such a mess? Have you been up all night?"

"Not all night. But mostly," he admitted.

"You had a pill on your night table to help you sleep."

"And sleep away my few remaining days of freedom?" he asked in martyrlike anguish. "I am not going into slavery without a word of protest. Remember what your relative Booker T. Washington said. 'Give me liberty, or give me death!'"

"Booker T. Washington was not related to me and he never said that," she replied. "Patrick Henry said it."

"Well, Washington could have said it," he protested.

Mrs. Washington stared at all the clothing, bric-a-brac, and personal memorabilia scattered around. "It'll take a month to get this place in order again," she complained.

"A month?" he lamented. "My time is measured in days. Hours!" Dramatically he extended his left hand to point out the vistas of time that stretched before him. "Some men, in the goodness of a merciful God, are struck down without even a warning. But me, I am doomed to know that a week from Monday comes Mona. The Hebrew Home for the Aged! That's where she'll put me!"

"Whatever gave you that idea?"

"I remember when she was raising money for it!" Horowitz replied. "She said they would make it the best, most up-to-date home in this country! I do not wish to be confined with a lot of aged people. I am not aged. I am not even old. I am, at the most, a man with a little trouble with his left foot."

He ended up waving his right hand and letting go of his quad cane. For a moment he wavered. Then, as he was about to fall, he cried out, "Mrs. Washington!"

She reached out to keep him on his feet. Once she had restored his cane, he regained his dignity.

"Mrs. Washington, what you see strewn about is my life. Things Hannah and I brought back from trips we made. Little things, of no value to anyone but us.

"Last night I tried to make a list of people who might like to have something to remember Hannah and me. I couldn't. Hannah's valuable jewelry is already gone. To Mona, to Candy. To Marvin's wife and his daughter. Of my possessions, not much more. I was never one for rings or expensive watches. Just some cuff links. A collection of odd coins that piled up on trips to Europe."

He stirred the items that lay on the coverlet of his bed.

"You could take them with you," Mrs. Washington suggested.

"What for?" he asked. "To show the other Hebrews in the home for the Hebrew aged? No, it's better if I give it all away."

He turned to her. "You see anything you want, take it!"

"First, I'll make your breakfast," she said, to change the subject.

HOROWITZ was at the table when she entered with his freshly squeezed orange juice. He asked, "So?"

"So what?"

"So are you going to make me guess what happened yesterday?"

She was taken by surprise. "Yesterday?"

"Yesterday!" he repeated impatiently. "A boy is in the hospital. Wounded. Thanks God, he recovers. And yesterday he is due to come home. So! *Did* he come home?"

"Yes, he's home. And he's fine! Aside from a scar on his chest, he'll be good as new, the doctor said. And Conrad says thanks very much for the chemistry set."

"What chemistry set?" It was Horowitz's turn to be puzzled.

"I kept asking Louise what she wanted as a gift, and she said a chemistry set. I thought it was strange. But it turns out that Conrad always wanted one and this was her way of getting it for him as a welcome home."

"Now that's what I call a sweet, considerate sister. And such a sister deserves a gift of her own. So you will . . ."

Before he could discuss it further, she left the room.

Horowitz finished his breakfast in silence. Then he labored into the living room and started his fine-hand-movement exercises, with Mrs. Washington watching him. After a while he said softly, "Mrs. Washington, I am going to miss you. Very much."

She did not respond.

"I want you to know that I appreciate everything you have done for me. And, even more, the things you tried to do and I wouldn't cooperate. I am a stubborn old man. I know that." Sud-

309

denly he exploded in frustration and despair. "That damned pickle! If not for that damned pickle, I would never have fallen and this whole thing would never have happened. To think a man's freedom is taken away from him over one lousy pickle!"

With that he rose, lifted his quad cane, and thrust it forth, only to unbalance himself and totter. But for Mrs. Washington's swift assistance he would have pitched forward onto the carpet.

Gently she said, "Now you see why you should go with Mona. You do need care."

"What about you?"

"I'll find another job."

"Like this one?"

She did not reply.

He was shuffling cards when he called out to her, "Mrs. Washington, come in here!"

"Yes?" she asked, coming in from the kitchen.

"Mrs. Washington," he intoned, "what I am about to say cannot be said in mere words. It needs music! Now, name this tune and you will win an extra week's salary! Listen carefully!" He began to chant a wordless atonal tune, *"Dydle di di deedee di deedeldo! Deedeldo. Deedeldo!"* He waited expectantly.

When she did not respond, he said in disgust, "It's a good thing we're not on television. You would just have lost ten thousand dollars. I'm afraid I will have to give you the answer."

Whereupon he sang, " *'Joshua fit the battle of Jericho. Jericho. Jericho!'* Now do you get it, Mrs. Washington?"

"Yes, I get it. Is that what you called me in here for?"

"It's the significance!" Horowitz pointed out impatiently. "I am sitting here thinking, What can this Hebrew do to escape the Hebrew Home for the Aged? And I am remembering some other aged Hebrews. There was Abraham, Isaac, Jacob. No great escapes there. But who was the first hero to win the first big battle against great odds? Joshua! So I said, What did he do that I couldn't do? Hmm?"

"Well, for one thing, Mr. Horowitz, he walked around that Jericho so many times that the walls fell down."

"Bingo!" Horowitz called out. "You hit it right on the nose.

Now, because I fell down one night, Mona is sure I need to be confined. But I will prove to her that I can walk perfectly well. That I can do everything I need to do without any help at all! Then she won't have a leg to stand on."

"How are you going to prove that to her?"

"How?" he asked indignantly. "By doing what I said. By walking without help. Eating without help. Everything without help!"

"That would be a miracle," she said.

"And you, Mrs. Washington, are going to help me! My exercises instead of four times a day, I will do eight times a day. Cards? No more pinochle! Just exercise! Together we will outsmart her. Your job will be safe. And I will have my freedom."

"We only have ten days," she reminded.

"So? God created a whole world in six days."

Chapter Ten

"STREEEEETCH," Mrs. Washington said as she applied extra effort to force Horowitz's arm up and over his head. He made himself extend his arm farther than he ever had before. Finally, on the tenth try, he succeeded in touching the wall.

"Ho-ho-ho!" he exclaimed. "Not bad, not bad. Next!"

She put him through another set of exercises. "Do them again. But faster, with more zip!" she insisted.

"Zip? What am I training for, the heavyweight championship? I'm the great white hope?"

"Mona!" she threatened.

"Okay, okay." No more threats were necessary.

When they had finished, she prepared his breakfast. She served him a poached egg on toast so that he would have to use both knife and fork. And today his fork had no padding at all.

He hesitated to pick it up, for fear of failing. Finally he made an effort. The fork fell to the floor with a clatter.

"Maybe we're going too fast," he said.

She pulled a fresh fork from her apron pocket. "When you're on the plane to San Diego and they give you your lunch, you'll probably be able to manage it," she said sarcastically. "Again!"

On the eighth try he retained his hold on the fork handle. He held it, stared down at it, admired his grip, and commenced to eat.

"How did you happen to have so many forks handy?" he asked.

She reached into her pocket and brought out four more.

"You thought it would take me twelve times?" he asked, then added a bit proudly, "And I did it in eight! Goes to show!"

After breakfast he practiced walking with his quad cane.

"Mrs. Washington!" he declared suddenly. "It is time for me to get rid of this four-footed animal. We are going downtown to buy a nice, gentleman-type cane."

"There's an orthopedic supply store on Eightieth Street."

"I do not want an orthopedic cane, I want something that will impress Mona," he said. "Saks Fifth Avenue!"

"Okay," she finally acceded. "Right after lunch."

THE young clerk at Saks took one look at Horowitz's quad cane and produced an aluminum cane first. Horowitz banished it with a look of disdain.

"I wish something to use on informal occasions, yet shouldn't look out of place in the evening if a person is going to the theater," he said loftily.

The clerk took three more canes out of the rack: one with a shiny bone handle, a second of fine light-colored malacca, the third with a padded leather handle. Horowitz leaned on each. To Mrs. Washington he seemed to be a bit unsteady on them.

He had narrowed it down to the malacca and the one with the leather handle when he suddenly spied a gnarled Irish cane.

"Let me see that one!" he commanded suddenly.

"This is more a shillelagh than a cane," the clerk protested as he handed it to him.

Horowitz fondled it, then leaned on it, while staring at himself in the mirror. "Sir Harry Lauder!" he exclaimed.

Both Mrs. Washington and the clerk were baffled.

"Harry Lauder, the entertainer," Horowitz explained. "I saw him when he made his twelfth farewell appearance in New York. He used a cane like this."

Horowitz began to sing, *"Didi di di didi,"* and attempted to imitate the Scotsman's jig. "Don't you recognize that song? It's 'Roamin' in the Gloamin'.'"

Suddenly he realized that other customers had gathered to observe him. He stopped his jig and briskly told the clerk, "I'll take this one!"

"Charge and send?" the clerk asked.

"What's the matter, cash has gone out of style?" Horowitz demanded. "And I'll take it with me. I have a little practicing to do."

"TRY it once more," Mrs. Washington said. She watched critically as Horowitz started across the foyer carpet, leaning on his gnarled Irish cane. He walked with a labored gait, better than he did a week ago but still with that inevitable drag of his left foot. Mrs. Washington shook her head sadly.

Dejected, Horowitz shuffled into the living room and sank into an easy chair. "Mrs. Washington," he began, "I'm a very stubborn man, as you know. But there comes a time when a man has to ask himself, Am I being *too* stubborn? Too . . . proud?"

She knew how much it cost him to ask this question, so she was thinking carefully before responding.

He mistook her silence for an answer. "Okay, admit it, you think I should just pack it in, go west with Mona, and get ready to die."

"No, Mr. Horowitz, I don't think so."

"Then tell me, why can't I do it? Why do I have this terrible picture in my mind that in three days Mona will ring the doorbell, I will try to go to the door, and then right in the middle of the foyer I will trip and fall. And she will find me, her father, a helpless cripple, lying on the floor."

Mrs. Washington's eyes were firm and honest behind her silver-rimmed glasses. "I think," she said, "you are tired from trying too hard. But if you think first, I believe you can make it."

"Mrs. Washington, if you believe I can do it, then I will try again. Let's rehearse!"

"No. I think you should just sit quietly and rest for a while."

"Will you sit here with me and rest too?"

"If you wish."

"I wish," he replied. "I need company, Mrs. Washington. I am actually," he hesitated to confess, "a lonely man. It was one thing when I was able to get about on my own. I could walk in the park, go to the zoo, watch the animals. Watch the children watching the animals. I wasn't part of their lives, but I was part of life. Now . . ."

There was a moment of silence. From far below they could hear the traffic of midday.

"Mr. Horowitz," she finally said gently, "you've made *yourself* a lonely man these past weeks. Your friend Phil Liebowitz has called six times. Mrs. Braun on the fourth floor called to ask if she could come up and say hello. That Mrs. Clevenger asked you to come to dinner. You refused."

When he replied, it was in a soft voice that pleaded for understanding. "Mrs. Washington, I can't face these people. Liebowitz, a man I have known for forty-four years. We played pinochle together a thousand times. Went to *shul* together. Our wives were friends. He has never seen me like this. I don't want him staring at my scar when he should be looking at his cards. I don't want him to see me try to pick up a card and fail. Can you understand?"

"Yes."

"So what do you think?"

"I think it is time to exercise again."

He glared at her, then smiled. "Mrs. Washington, you are a tyrant. But a very smart tyrant." He rose from his chair and asked, "You think maybe I was pitying myself a little there?"

"A little," she said.

He glanced at her bright black eyes but said nothing.

SAMUEL Horowitz crossed off another day on his calendar. Two days, only forty-eight hours, before Mona arrived.

He evaluated his chances. Certain things he did better, considerably better. But walking with that cane still presented a problem. If his foot would only respond as it should.

When it was time for the park, he found his wheelchair waiting near the door. Damn it, he said to himself, no more chair for going out! "Mrs. Washington," he announced. "No more chair."

"If you think you can do it, fine!" she agreed.

With dignity, Horowitz entered the elevator, then made his way slowly across the lobby, with Mrs. Washington at his side. He negotiated the three steps cautiously and came out to the street level. His journey to the corner was slow and thoughtful. Though

314

Horowitz did not make it across the street on a single green light, the drivers respected his difficulty and waited.

In the park, they found a bench in the sun. "Did you decide on the menu for lunch with Mona?" he asked suddenly. "It has to look and taste healthy."

"How about fish? Fresh broiled fish with just a touch of margarine has practically no cholesterol at all."

"And no taste either. *Oy,*" Horowitz complained. "I can remember Hannah's flounder. She would bread it and fry it in sweet butter. It was so delicious. But okay, some plain fish. What else?"

"Low-fat cottage cheese on lettuce. We can start with a nice strawberry and orange salad."

"With a little sugar and cream?" he asked. Then corrected himself. "No, Mona sees white sugar and cream, she would get a court order to make me go to California. So, dry fish, dry cottage cheese, and dry lettuce. Settled!"

But in a moment he had an afterthought. "Mrs. Washington, what if you served a little butter? Just to help the fish go down."

"Butter?" she questioned critically. "What would Mona say?"

"Well, just suppose we take an empty little tub, the kind that margarine comes in, and put butter in it? Who's to know it's not margarine? Hmm?"

"I'll see," was all she would say.

When they returned to the lobby, it was his misfortune to run into Mrs. Fine, the widow on the second floor, whom he had not seen since his difficulties began.

"Mr. Horowitz!" she exclaimed. "You look like you just came back from Florida. Such a color! And I heard you weren't doing so well. Just goes to show, you can't believe anybody."

"I'm doing fine, Mrs. Fine!" he said staunchly, and proceeded to march, straight and proud, toward the elevator.

SUNDAY was a bright morning. Samuel Horowitz woke early. He lay on his back, thinking, Mona. Tomorrow is Monday.

He heard Mrs. Washington's key in the front door. He called out, "Mrs. Washington!"

When she appeared in the bedroom, he announced, "Today is the day."

"*Tomorrow* is the day," she corrected.

"Today is the *crucial* day. Today, my dear Mrs. Washington, you are going to be a critic. And I am going to be an actor. We are going to have a dress rehearsal of a play titled *Hello, Mona!*"

He turned on his side to face her. "In twenty-six hours she will arrive. I want to be sure that every detail is perfect. For example, there are many questions we have not even asked ourselves."

"To wit?" She smiled a little, getting into his mood.

"To wit," he repeated, "who goes to the door when Mona rings? You? Or me? And if it is you, where am I? That's a very, very important first impression."

"Let's discuss it at breakfast," she commanded. "Up, wash, brush your teeth, and get in there!"

"Mrs. Washington, you could make moving to San Diego a pleasure!" he shot back. But he compliantly got out of bed.

At the breakfast table he spent more time holding forth on strategy than he did eating. While she sat at the other end of the table having a cup of coffee, he nibbled his margarined toast.

"Every detail counts!" he exclaimed. "For example, if *you* answer the door, am I sitting at the window looking out? Or reading? All those things invalids do. A man who has not seen his dearly beloved daughter for almost a year should rush to the door to greet her, *if* he is healthy enough."

"*You* are going to *rush* to the door?" Mrs. Washington asked skeptically. "Can you also do tricks with loaves and fishes?"

"Mrs. Washington, your reference to the New Testament does not escape me. And I might remind you that the fellow who did that was also Jewish. So we are old hands at miracles. In this case, it calls for a relatively simple miracle. Down at the front door there is a worthy man named Juan. If he calls up here to say that Mona is on the way, I can make it to the door without rushing before she is there. She rings. I slowly count to four, then I open the door! She wants to think it's a miracle, I can't stop her!"

"So what else do you have in mind?" she asked, unconsciously adopting his intonation.

"Well, there is the matter of lunch. I should practice with the equipment. I mean it would add a little touch of class if, when I have my Sanka, I pick up the saucer with the cup."

"Can you?" she asked.

He admitted sheepishly, "Yesterday when I was alone, I practiced. You will notice there are now three less saucers." To cover his embarrassment he said, "But watch this." He applied a layer of marmalade to his piece of toast.

His left hand was a bit unsteady, and she had to caution, "Not so fast. Take your time. It makes you look more confident."

Horowitz simulated eating the entire lunch they had planned. Then, once the breakfast dishes had been cleared, he suggested, "Time to raise the curtain!"

Used to his dramatics, Mrs. Washington said, "You mean from the moment that Juan calls from the front door?"

"Exactly!" he said. He looked around. "Let's see! Where will I be when the buzzer rings? Most likely sitting near the window, reading the *Times*. Actually I will just hold it. Because if I start to read it, by the time she gets here I will be so furious I'll forget everything we practiced. So . . . you go downstairs!"

"Why?"

"So we can time it. I want to know exactly how long it takes you to come from the downstairs switchboard up here!"

She left. He sat in his chair and waited. Several minutes later he could hear the buzzer sound out in the kitchen. He took up his cane, rose, and started across the living room. By the time he reached the foyer, he had hit a good smooth stride, his left foot barely skimming across the carpet's nap. He was at the door when the doorbell rang. He counted to four and opened the door with enthusiasm.

"Mona, my darling!" he exclaimed as Mrs. Washington entered. Then, "How did I do?"

"Perfect!" she cried. "Sidney Poitier couldn't have done better."

"Okay, good. So much for that. Now Mona kisses me. Maybe she throws her arms around me. That could be a problem, because when my Mona throws her arms around you, believe me, an octopus could take lessons. So you will go outside. I will open the door. I will say, 'Mona, my darling!' and you will throw your arms around me and kiss me on the cheek."

"*I* . . . will throw my arms around you and kiss you?"

"Nothing personal! It's only a rehearsal!" he argued.

317

"I'll do my best," she said, far from enthusiastic.

She went outside, she rang, Horowitz counted to four, and flung open the door. "Mona, my darling!" This time Mrs. Turtletaub, the widow from 10A, was about to enter her apartment just as Mrs. Washington threw her arms about Horowitz and kissed him on the cheek.

"Oh, my God!" said Mrs. Turtletaub, horrified.

Horowitz closed the door. "Good, excellent, Mrs. Washington! So much for greetings. Now she is in the apartment and I say to her, 'Come, Mona, darling, let me see you in the light.'" He led the way from the foyer into the brighter light of the living room.

"Turn around, let me see. It's been so long," he said, and gestured for her to turn. Smiling, Mrs. Washington complied, twirling like a dancer.

"Good, good! Better than Mona!" Horowitz exclaimed, then hurried on. "Okay, now lunch rehearsal we have already been through. When lunch is over, how about a little cards?"

"Mona plays pinochle?" Mrs. Washington asked, surprised.

"Of course not. But I could just take the cards out of the box, nonchalantly, of course, and shuffle them and play a little solitaire, like it is something I do every day."

"That sounds like a good idea," Mrs. Washington agreed.

"Okay! Meantime, she is talking a blue streak about San Diego, and then I'll tell her, very clearly, that it was nice of her to come and see how well I am getting along, but I am not going with her. She'll protest, but I'll say . . ."

As Mrs. Washington listened to him, she felt quite sad. He was like a small boy with a daydream. Except that small boys change dreams from day to day, and time takes care of all of them. But men as far along in years as Mr. Horowitz were not permitted many dreams, and each was precious.

HOROWITZ had a restless night but finally drifted off to sleep. He woke to find Mrs. Washington staring down at him.

"It's past nine o'clock," she said. "You must have overslept."

"I didn't close an eye all night. Not a wink," he groaned.

"I didn't sleep all night either," she commiserated. "Tossed and turned. So I had an idea."

"Aha! We run away from home together, right?"

"Wrong! Get washed, have your breakfast, and I'll show you."

He glared at her. "Just because you now have roots does not mean you own the world, Mrs. Washington!" Nevertheless, he got out of bed.

After he had eaten, she led him to the living room. There he stopped, stared, and let out a shriek.

"What have you done? Hannah's living room! She redecorated it only six years ago. And you have destroyed it!"

Calmly, and a bit weary of his hyperboles and histrionics, Mrs. Washington said, "I just moved the furniture around a bit."

Horowitz glared at her. "So this is your big idea?" he disparaged. "Overnight she becomes an interior decorator."

"Try coming into the room."

Slowly, using his gnarled cane, he made his way into the room. Determined to display his disapproval of what she'd done, he began to concentrate less on his walking. His foot caught in the carpet and for an instant he thought he would fall. Instinctively his hand went out seeking support—and rested assuringly on the wing chair, which now seemed so conveniently close.

Looking about, he realized that the furniture had been cleverly rearranged so that there was always a convenient place to grasp, hold on to, or lean against if he faltered. He walked to the window, touching each piece as he went.

He turned to face Mrs. Washington. "Not bad, not bad." It was the utmost in praise from Samuel Horowitz.

IT HAD been more than an hour since Horowitz executed his rehearsal with the new furniture arrangement. He had done all his exercises and was now staring at his watch. Mona was on her way and nothing could stop her. Horowitz's nerves began to show the strain.

Mrs. Washington had set the table with the finest linen mats, the good china, the solid silver service. She had planned everything in the kitchen so that cooking and serving lunch would take only half an hour.

As the appointed time approached, she began to feel as tense as Horowitz. She went into the living room, and found him at the open window, looking down, scanning every passing cab, wondering whether it would stop at his canopy.

To distract him she suggested, "How about a game of pinochle? Remember, you now owe me nine dollars and fifty cents."

"Nine dollars and fifty cents," he roared. "We played double or nothing the last time!"

"And you lost," she reminded.

"Oh, yeah." He sat down and dealt out the cards. Aside from a trace of nervousness, he did it well. She took the first trick and melded one hundred aces. As she neatly laid down the four aces, heart, club, diamond, and spade, he glared at her. "You're doing this to upset me!" he accused.

They played the hand out, and though he had melded fewer points than she had, she deliberately made an error in playing that led to his winning the hand. That seemed to mollify him, until he turned the cards face up and realized what she had done.

"Ho-ho-ho, Mrs. Washington . . ." he reproved.

Caught, she could only smile.

"Doesn't count," Horowitz said. "I still owe you nine dollars and fifty cents. But I appreciate what you tried to do. Yes, I need every little bit of confidence." Suddenly he exclaimed, "Dress! I wanted to be specially dressed for her. I forgot!"

He made his way to the bedroom with Mrs. Washington close behind. "A white shirt," he ordered, "from the top shirt drawer." He turned to the tie rack on the closet door. "And for a tie . . ." He selected his newest, a blue-and-red foulard.

"And this suit," he said, picking out a blue one he had not worn in months. "Now, Mrs. Washington, you will leave me alone."

"Right now you may need help more than modesty."

"It isn't a matter of modesty, my dear Mrs. Washington, but I want to do this alone. Including zip up the trousers. I not only want *her* to know, but I want *myself* to know that I did it."

A few minutes later Samuel Horowitz presented himself for inspection. "Well?" he asked. "Perfect?"

"Not quite perfect," she declared with a connoisseur's air. "I think it would look better if you had a handkerchief in your breast pocket."

"You and Hannah," he said. "Okay, a handkerchief."

Mrs. Washington had just opened the drawer of the chest when they heard the buzzer ring insistently in the kitchen.

"That's Juan!" Horowitz exclaimed. "Mona is here!"

In his excitement he turned too quickly, dropped his cane, and was about to fall when Mrs. Washington caught him.

"Now, remember," she said, "*slowly, carefully, think first!*"

Chapter Eleven

SAMUEL Horowitz was planted at the front door, his left hand resting on the doorknob.

He heard the heavy elevator door slide back. He heard Mona's sharp heels on the tiled hallway floor. He heard the doorbell. As he had rehearsed, he took a long count of four and opened the door, exclaiming, "Mona, darling!" while steeling himself for her catapulting embrace.

Instead, Mona stared at him. No embrace. Nothing but that stare. Then she broke down. "Oh, Dad, Dad!" she moaned between great gushes of tears.

"Mona, what is it?"

"Your face, what they did to your face!"

"You mean the scar? It's nothing. Mona, please," he implored, reaching for his fresh white handkerchief. "Here, Mona, dry your tears. Now, darling, come into the living room, sit down, relax."

He led the way, hoping that she would give up crying long enough to admire the skillful way in which he traversed the distance from the foyer to the living-room window. But when he turned around, he saw that she was only wiping away her tears.

She looked about the room. "It isn't the same," she commented in disapproval.

"We rearranged the furniture a little," he admitted.

"I don't think Mother would have liked it this way," Mona said. Then came a new outburst of tears. "Mother!"

Horowitz waited through her second outburst. When she had tapered off, he said, "Darling, this is life and things happen, and we have to accept them and live with them."

"I know," she assented, sniffling down to a more quiet state. "Dr. Drees says the same thing. He's my psychoanalyst. He says that I tend to become too emotionally involved. Not that that's always bad. He says that one of the reasons I am so effective raising money and working for causes like the Hebrew Home for the Aged is that I get emotionally involved."

To himself Horowitz commented, She has mentioned that place!

She continued, "The home is a magnificent new building. In the last report on homes for the aged, ours was judged the newest, best-equipped in the entire country. You'll see!"

Horowitz thought, Mona, darling, you should live so long.

Mona talked on. "I don't believe that just raising money is enough. If you care, really care, about those old folks, you want to spend time with them. This Passover I went to the first night's Seder. It would have warmed your heart to see those old folks around that long, long table. Those faces! Right out of the Bible! Such character! Well, they just loved it. Their eyes brimmed over with tears. I couldn't help myself, I cried too."

It seemed the memory of it would cause another flood. But Mona managed to remain in control.

"Mona, darling," Horowitz ventured, "did it ever occur to you that maybe the tears in their eyes were because they were thinking how much better it would be to celebrate with their own, instead of with strangers?"

Before Mona could answer, Mrs. Washington came in and announced, "Luncheon is ready!"

THE fish was sufficiently dry to impress Mona with its healthful qualities. With great aplomb Horowitz reached for the butter in the margarine cup and dabbed some on his portion to lubricate it.

"Try some, darling," he invited.

Mona added a bit to her own fish and tasted it. "Marvelous!" she exclaimed. "What brand of margarine is this?"

"It's not exactly margarine. It's an imitation margarine."

"So tasty. I must ask Mrs. Washington what brand it is."

"I think it's only sold in this neighborhood," Horowitz said.

"Too bad. I've got Albert on a low-cholesterol diet and he always complains about the taste of things. He'd love this!"

With considerable flair Horowitz chose a slice of toast from within the folds of the napkin in the silver bread tray. He broke off a piece. Holding the bread in his left hand, he buttered it lavishly with the knife he held in his right hand.

"Hmm," he remarked. "And to think a month ago I couldn't have done that. It goes to show. Remarkable woman, that Mrs. Washington. She made it possible."

As if to conceal it from earshot of the kitchen, he leaned toward Mona and whispered, "A strict disciplinarian. Tough? Don't ask! But worth her weight in gold. When she came here, I was a sick man in a wheelchair. Now we go for strolls in the park."

He hoped he would evoke some enthusiasm from Mona. But his daughter kept eating with a determination that revealed that she had not been swayed.

When she had finished her fish and her low-fat cottage cheese on lettuce, Horowitz asked, "A little dessert, Mona, darling? A little Sanka?"

With his left hand he reached for the silver bell that had not been used since Hannah gave her last dinner party. Mrs. Washington answered his ring promptly. "Yes, Mr. Horowitz?"

"Mrs. Washington, an excellent meal. And now we are ready for dessert, which I hope," he said in a kindly but pointed manner, "is not full of sugar and cholesterol. I mean, just because we have company is no reason to change our usual style of eating."

"I think you'll find it quite satisfactory, sir," she said.

She served slices of low-calorie angel food cake and Sanka. Mona ate her cake and sipped her coffee in silence.

Horowitz knew that when she was most silent she was most determined. Her mother used to refer to her as *farbissen*. Determined, dogged, unswerving to a point beyond all reason.

She has that *farbissener* look, Horowitz warned himself.

When they finished lunch, they returned to the living room. Mona began, "Dad, we have to have a talk. A very serious talk."

He had seated himself at the card table near the window. He suggested casually, "No reason why a man can't play a little solitaire while talking, is there, Mona, darling?"

With the air of an experienced gambler, he then shuffled the cards. Three different ways. Thumbs dug down, regular shuffle, and shuffle in the hands for the final cut. Then he began to lay out the cards for solitaire, always careful to use his left hand.

'Yes, my dear, you were saying?"

"Marvin and I have had several long talks in the past week."

"That's nice," he said, trying to seem casual. But his heart began to sink. "Your mother and I were always worried that, you living way out in San Diego and Marvin living in Washington, you would lose touch."

Undiverted, Mona continued, "And we have decided that the most sensible thing is for you to come back to San Diego with me. We don't want you to be alone anymore. If you get sick again, you'll have family right there. And if you need it, there is the Hebrew Home for the Aged."

"Mona," he began, "twenty-nine years I have lived here—"

"I already have a broker who'll come in and take over this whole place for a flat sum. The personal things you want we can have shipped. In fact, if you like, we can do it now. Meantime, tomorrow at ten the broker is coming up here to look the place over and make us an offer."

"Make *us* an offer?" Horowitz responded, his anger overcoming his fear and concern. "My life! My marriage! My home! And he is going to make *us* an offer? Absolutely not!"

"Dad," she persisted, "it's a matter of your health and safety. What if something happens?"

"What could happen?" he fought back.

"Another stroke," she warned. "The home has special provisions for stroke victims."

"I don't want special provisions," he protested. "I want my own home. . . . Mona, darling, I want my freedom."

"Your freedom to be *mugged?*" she asked.

"My freedom to come and go as I please."

"Dad, we have three cars. And a chauffeur who will be available at all times. You'll have all the freedom you want."

"Mona, darling," he began, pushing aside the cards, "let me explain something to you. What good is the freedom to go anywhere I want, if there's no place I want to go? Here, I have places I know and love. A park. A synagogue. A few stores. Friends! Like Liebowitz. He calls a couple of times a week to play pinochle. Who am I going to play pinochle with in San Diego? Who in San Diego ever even heard of pinochle?"

"At the home there must be some men who know how to play!" she insisted with that *farbissener* quality.

His fear was beginning to undermine his resolve. He asked himself, Am I sicker than I thought? Weaker than I thought? All the work, the exercises we did, Mrs. Washington and I, is that all going to be swept away by this iron-willed daughter of mine?

"Dad, you have to be realistic. This place is too big for you alone. And it can only remind you of Mother."

"I like to be reminded of your mother. She was the best thing that happened to me in my whole life!" he declared. "Loneliness does not mean that the answer is to run away from memories, from the life I have lived. To some place I don't know, where there will always be the threat that one day, when it suits you, I will be shipped off to a Hebrew Home for the Aged. In a big limousine, with a chauffeur, of course. But shipped off nevertheless."

"Dad," she began, and he knew at once that he had not softened her one bit. "Marvin and I . . ."

"It's a free country!" he shouted. "I have a right to vote too! And I don't care what you and Marvin have decided!"

At the sound of his voice, Mrs. Washington hurried out of the kitchen. "Mr. Horowitz? Something wrong?"

"Wrong?" he asked sarcastically. "There's nothing wrong except they want to tie me hand and foot and drag me off to San Diego, that's all."

He rose from his chair in such a precipitate, unthought-out action that the gnarled cane slipped from his hand. He wavered, finally sprawling forward across the table, helpless.

Mrs. Washington raced to his side and helped him stand up again. He tried to strike a pose of relative calm and dignity. But he could read the judgment in Mona's eyes.

"Well, Dad, I guess I don't have to say any more, do I?"

With the taste of ashes in his mouth, he cursed himself for having forgotten the one rule that Mrs. Washington had tried to drum into him. Think first, move later. He had lost the battle.

Mona turned to Mrs. Washington. "My dad is coming back to San Diego with me tomorrow. You will get the apartment in order for a secondhand dealer to take over."

Mrs. Washington spoke up quietly. "If I may say so, this should

326

be a doctor's decision. I think before you force Mr. Horowitz to leave here—"

Mona interrupted sharply, "I am not forcing my father to do anything. After this last little demonstration, I think even he realizes what's best for him."

Mrs. Washington refused to be deterred. "He has made remarkable progress in the last ten days. So I think he shouldn't make any decisions until he's had a chance to talk to Dr. Tannenbaum."

"I've already talked to Dr. Tannenbaum!" Mona protested. "He favors the whole idea!"

"Dr. Tannenbaum has not seen the patient in almost two weeks," Mrs. Washington pointed out. "I think he should see him now."

"Oh, I understand," Mona concluded. "You've got a good thing going here and you don't want to lose it!"

"Don't you dare!" Horowitz interceded loudly. "She is a very fine woman! Sweet! Loyal! And very considerate!"

"I'm sure," Mona said acidly. "However, she does not give the orders around here."

Mrs. Washington interposed herself between Mona and Horowitz. "I can't let anything happen to my patient without his doctor being notified and having a chance to express an opinion!"

"And just what do you propose to do about it?" Mona demanded.

"I am going to call Dr. Tannenbaum and have him come up and examine Mr. Horowitz!"

"It won't change anything, but do whatever you feel your professional duty calls for," Mona said. "Meantime, Dad, let's get on with picking out the things you want to save. Household things of sentimental value we can have shipped to San Diego."

Household things of sentimental value, he thought. They are all of sentimental value! Each item Hannah spent so many hours selecting. So go select, pick up a bit of memory here, another there, consign the rest to a secondhand dealer.

In the old days, the days of Horowitz's boyhood in Brooklyn, a man came along the streets, with a sagging bag in one hand and several hats piled on his head. He called out, "Cash! I cash clothes!" Women would come out of the tenements carrying shabby old garments and worn-out shoes. The secondhand man would give them small coins in exchange.

Now Samuel Horowitz's entire life was going to be traded away like old clothes, for a handful of small coins. He would become a man without a home, a man without warm possessions. He would no longer be Samuel Horowitz, human being, individual. He would be Mona Fields's father, or Albert Fields's father-in-law. Or the man in room who-knows-what in the Hebrew Home for the Aged.

He had lost. He might as well set about doing as Mona wanted.

For three and a half hours—between the time Mrs. Washington called Dr. Tannenbaum's office and the time the doctor arrived—Samuel Horowitz applied himself to the slow, wrenching process of separating his belongings into three groups. There were those he would take with him, those he would give away, and those he would put into the hands of the secondhand dealer.

Horowitz was on his knees digging through a bottom chest drawer when the doorbell rang. Mrs. Washington came into the bedroom a moment later and helped him to his feet. "It's the doctor," she said, adding in a strong whisper, "Confidence! Think first, go at it slowly, and you can do it!"

The look in Horowitz's moist eyes betrayed his sense of insecurity and failure. She raised her hand and gently wiped the corners of his eyes. "Those teary eyes of age may give the wrong impression," she said softly.

Suddenly Horowitz grasped her hand and with desperate resolve said, "I'll do it for you. To save your job. You'll see!"

When they came out of the bedroom, Dr. Tannenbaum was asking Mona, "Where is he? What's the emergency?"

"Coming, Doctor," Horowitz called, crossing the living room.

"What happened? Another fall?" Tannenbaum asked.

"No, Doctor," Horowitz said. "We called you because we have a little difference of opinion here."

"You called me away from an important case to settle a little difference of opinion?"

"You needn't worry, Doctor. Send the bill to me!" Mona said crisply. "Now the problem is this: my brother and I think that my dad should come back to San Diego with me. We have a large house. Live-in help. He will have his own room and bath. He'll be very well cared for."

"I don't want to be cared for!" Horowitz protested. "I am not an infant, or an animal in the zoo. I want to stay here and live my own life. Mrs. Washington and I get along fine, thank you!"

He seized her hand and held it tightly to demonstrate the unity that existed between them.

"Uh-huh," Tannenbaum declared thoughtfully. "Well"—he brushed back the wings of his thick mustache—"if the patient has such a strong feeling, we have to take that into account."

Horowitz and Mrs. Washington exchanged glances of hope.

"But frankly," Tannenbaum continued, "the last time I saw the patient"—and here the doctor turned to Mona—"he seemed resistant to treatment. He was not coming along as well as one would expect."

"Exactly," Mona agreed.

"Well, now, let us see!" Tannenbaum declared. "First, we must admit that the climate in San Diego is much milder than the harsh New York winters, where the temperatures can stay below freezing for days—"

Horowitz interrupted. "Doctor, weather reports I expect on the eleven-o'clock news. Right now I would like your permission to stay in my own home instead of being shipped off to the ends of the earth!"

"Dad, please!"

Horowitz exploded. "No more pleases! You want me out of here, your Albert will have to buy this building and tear it down!"

"Mr. Horowitz," Tannenbaum said, "we must not get excited."

"It's my life. And if I want to get excited, I will get excited. Now, Doctor, you and Mona sit down."

When they were both seated, Horowitz said, "My dear judges, I would like you to witness a little demonstration. First, notice that the patient is no longer using a wheelchair. He is not even using a quad cane. This patient is using a simple cane. And yet the patient gets around pretty well on it. Watch!"

Whereupon Horowitz walked back and forth, summoning up every ounce of determination. In so doing he was able to keep his left foot from dragging on the carpet. Oh, those days of double exercises, he gloated inwardly, they are paying off now.

"Mrs. Washington! Buttons, marbles, and cards!" he called.

While she produced them, Horowitz proceeded to untie his tie and then tie it again. When he had finished with that, he said, "Notice the shoelaces! Tied! Both shoes! And the shirt, every button buttoned. With these two hands!"

Mrs. Washington laid out the paraphernalia on the bridge table. Horowitz sat down and faced his judges.

"What will it be, Doctor?" he asked. "You wish to see a grown man of sixty-eight pick up a few buttons? Look!"

Horowitz used his left hand to pick up a dozen buttons, favoring the small ones to demonstrate his newly acquired skill.

"Now perhaps a little pinochle, Mrs. Washington?" he invited gallantly. She sat down. He shuffled and dealt the cards.

"Dad!" Mona rose impatiently. "The doctor is not here to watch you play games!"

"Games?" Horowitz disputed, and turned to Tannenbaum. "Doctor, do you call this games?"

Tannenbaum was forced to agree. "Not games, Mrs. Fields, exercises!" He seemed quite impressed. "How long have you been doing that so well, Mr. Horowitz?"

"The last week," Horowitz said.

"Uh-*huh*," Tannenbaum said, with special significance. "It's not necessary to continue playing." He turned to Mona. "Mrs. Fields, this is quite remarkable."

"It is?" Mona asked, puzzled.

"Two weeks ago, when I examined your father last, he was not making the kind of progress we like to see. Because patients who do not progress by the third month usually do not progress at all. Whether it's a lack of physical ability or a lack of will, by the end of the third month their future is generally sealed. That's why I agreed that it would be best for Mr. Horowitz to go back to San Diego with you. But what I see today presents a quite different picture. I think he is functioning well. If he wanted to, I think he might still carry on with his business. So he must be allowed to exercise his own judgment as to where he wants to live."

"But, Doctor," Mona protested, "we can do so much for him."

"Mrs. Fields, the real purpose of all our therapy is to prepare the patient to do everything for *himself*."

"Well, I never . . ." Mona said, but never finished.

HOROWITZ DID HIS best to pretend great sadness at Mona's departure. He nodded in agreement with everything she said.

"And you'll come out for the High Holidays," she went on. "Maybe you'll stay the whole ten days."

Horowitz nodded.

"And at Passover you must come too. We have a very impressive Seder in the temple. Six hundred people!"

"That's almost as many Jews as left Egypt. Except, of course, when Cecil B. De Mille made the picture," Horowitz said, trying to seem impressed.

At the door, Mona broke down and cried once more as she traced her finger along the healed scar on her father's cheek. "Oh, Dad, Dad!"

Finally the door was closed. Horowitz leaned against it, listening until the elevator door slid open and closed. Even then he did not trust his luck. He made his way to the living-room window and looked down. Only when he saw Mona step into the waiting limousine did he breathe his first sigh of relief.

He turned from the window to find Mrs. Washington looking at him. "Don't just stand there!" he cried out jubilantly. "Sing!" And he burst into *"California, here she comes!"* Then he added triumphantly, "But without Samuel Horowitz!"

When he realized that Mrs. Washington did not join in his ecstasy, he insisted, "Cheer up! Mrs. Washington, this is as much your victory as mine! Tonight we are going to celebrate. We are going to go out and have the greatest dinner anyone could have!"

"There are the children," she reminded.

"Bring them! Go, get into a cab right this minute and get them. We will eat out and maybe go to a movie. I heard about a new one, *Star Wars.* They say kids are crazy about it. Today I feel like a kid anyhow."

She remained calm and said, "I think you've had enough excitement for one day."

"Then tomorrow we'll celebrate, right?"

"All right," she said softly.

"Meantime," he said, and his eyes twinkled, "I have to do something to express my feelings. I know! Liebowitz!" He said the name as if it were a battle cry.

He dialed the number. "Liebowitz? Horowitz!"

"Sam! Sam, it's good to hear from you!" Liebowitz said. "I called and called and you never called back, so I thought you didn't want to see me."

"Didn't want to see you? What kind of *meshugaas* is that? A man wouldn't want to see an old friend? It just so happens I was very busy. You know, when you're away for weeks, there's a lot to catch up on."

"I understand," Liebowitz said simply.

"Listen, Phil, I got to ask you a very important question." Horowitz laughed. "Do you remember how to play pinochle?"

Chapter Twelve

HE HAD slept late. The evening at Liebowitz's had been longer than he was used to. The pinochle had gone very well. He won seven hands, putting him four dollars ahead for the night.

Before he left, Liebowitz's wife, Rose, kissed him. "Don't be such a stranger, Sam. We love to have you."

Now, from his bed, he heard the usual bustle out in the living room. Mrs. Washington, good, kind, faithful Mrs. Washington. How lucky that Marvin found her. That may well have been the most outstanding thing that Marvin had ever done. Horowitz must do something to symbolize their victory. A gift, maybe. He would find some pretext to sneak downtown.

He rose, had breakfast, and told Mrs. Washington he had to see his accountant. Instead, he took a taxi to Tiffany's.

There he strolled the green-carpeted aisles, stopping from time to time to look at some costly piece of gold set with diamonds or rubies. He did that only to impress the clerks. Finally he eased himself over to the simpler solid gold ornaments. He asked to see and feel two bracelets. While he was admiring them, his eye caught a pin that was made of knotted gold rope.

"I would like to see that one," he said, pointing.

The clerk set the pin down on the black velvet board. Horowitz felt its weight, which was impressive. The fine handwork pleased him. He was sure she would love it. Anything fancier would not be Mrs. Washington.

At his most casual, he asked, "And how much is this piece?"

"Four hundred and seventy-five dollars," the clerk responded.

"Polish it up, take off the price, put it in a nice box, and wrap it like a gift. With some red ribbon around it."

Such a movie, so much shooting and flying around in space, who can keep up with the story? Horowitz thought to himself.

But when he glanced to his side and saw the rapt look on Conrad's face, Horowitz felt all the noise and confusion were worthwhile. And when in the moment of greatest dramatic tension Louise instinctively seized Horowitz's hand and held on tightly, he was deeply touched. He covered her hand with his own, thinking, There is something so special about the warmth and the softness of a child's needing hand.

When the film was over, they went to the Tavern-on-the-Green in Central Park. The maître d' showed them to a table that looked out on the courtyard. Horowitz beckoned the waiter and ordered champagne, and Shirley Temples for the children.

When the drinks arrived, he made a toast. "Conrad and Louise, a word about your grandmother. She is a fine woman. The type of human being one is privileged to meet too rarely in this life. What Lincoln did for black people, she did for me. So let's drink to her!"

He raised his glass and sipped. The children joined in with their colorful, cherry-crested ginger ale.

"And now," Horowitz said, "the surprise of the evening!" He reached for the small box. As he held it out he said, "It's for you, Mrs. Washington."

She stared at the box. "No . . . I don't think I should."

"I bought it special for you. It's a thank-you and a token of a long-lasting friendship."

"I can't, really."

Horowitz smiled understandingly. "My fault. I shouldn't have surprised you this way. I'll open it!" He took off the ribbon and paper and opened the small velvet box. "There!" He searched her face for a smile of delight and approval. When she did not react, except to betray a slight misting of her eyes, he said, "Please? At least try it? It can't hurt."

333

She reached for it and held it to her collar. The gold gleamed in elegant contrast to her simple navy dress.

"Very pretty, Grandma," Louise said.

"Gee, cool!" Conrad added, awed by the impressive pin.

Reluctantly Mrs. Washington returned the gift to its velvet bed. "Really, no, I can't."

"Why not?" Horowitz asked, distressed. "I'm at least entitled to an explanation."

"Not now," she said softly. "Tomorrow."

THE next morning, as had become their custom, Mrs. Washington brought her coffee in and sat at the other end of the dining-room table. Usually she would talk freely. Today, nothing.

Finally Horowitz said, "Mrs. Washington, after all you did for me, if a man wants to express a little appreciation with a gift, how does it look for a woman to insult him? I ask you."

"Mr. Horowitz, I had no intention of insulting you. It just wouldn't be right."

"Wouldn't be right?" he chided. "Between us, what's not right? A simple way of saying thank you. Thank you for enduring all my complaints, my moods, which I must admit have not always been exactly delightful. Thank you for making me go out in the wheel-chair. Thank you for the million times you made me do what I didn't want to do. Mainly, thank you for keeping me a free man."

After a long silence, during which tears welled up in Mrs. Washington's eyes, he asked more gently, "Mrs. Washington? What did I do wrong? Did I hurt your feelings?"

"You're making this very difficult, Mr. Horowitz."

"What's difficult? Look, if you don't want to accept it now, I'll keep the package here until you change your mind. It can be a week from now, or even a year from now. Agreed?"

"Mr. Horowitz," she said firmly, "the reason I cannot accept your very fine gift is that you expect I will be here a year from now. Or even a month from now."

He grasped the edge of the table with both hands. "Mrs. Washington, are you trying to tell me something?"

"I'm trying to say that I will be leaving soon," she said simply.

"Leaving? You can't!" he protested, rising to his feet. "Why?"

"Because I am no longer needed here," she said.

"That's an excuse!" he accused. "I know what it is! I know!"

He walked into the living room and sat at his table. Arms folded, he stared out the window at the park. A few moments later she followed him in, carrying a dustcloth. He proceeded to talk, not to her but to an imaginary third person.

"A woman should carry such a grudge all these weeks, who would believe it? Just because that very first day I said a few things. . . . Okay, so they were not nice . . . and I didn't know she was already here. Is that such a crime she has to desert me?

"Come to think of it, I don't think she has a legal right to leave me. I am going to call Marvin and ask him if a nurse has the right to abandon a patient. There must be a law!"

He glanced at her slyly, to see if he had made any impression on her. But that silent, stubborn woman was still dusting.

Suddenly he exploded. "I know New York is dirty! But there can't be this much dust in the Sahara Desert!"

"You are shouting at me," she said.

"Okay, I'm sorry," he apologized. "Now, if you can stop dusting, perhaps you can sit down and tell me why you are deserting me like this."

She sat in the chair opposite him. "Not deserting," she corrected, "leaving."

"Okay, leaving. But why? We . . . we are so used to each other. We have come to understand each other. And, I hope, respect each other. You are a fine person, Mrs. Washington. And there is some of Hannah in you too. I don't know what you would call it, but sometimes I have read in books a word: *nobility*. I think that may be the word for you."

"Mr. Horowitz," she said quietly, "I am a nurse. You don't need me anymore. But somewhere there is a patient who does."

"I don't need you? I? Samuel Horowitz, whose day begins when I hear you unlock the door? Who waits every morning to hear what you have to report about Conrad and Louise? Who looks forward to our discussions in the park?"

"Don't you understand?" Mrs. Washington said. "What you need is someone to keep house, to cook. But you do not need a nurse. Even Dr. Tannenbaum says so."

"Tannenbaum!" Horowitz disparaged with a wave of his left hand, until he realized he was proving her point, so he switched to using his right hand. "Tannenbaum is a horse doctor!"

"Mr. Horowitz, you are no longer a patient. You are almost completely well. You proved that. To Dr. Tannenbaum. To Mona. But most of all, you proved it to me."

"And this is the thanks I get? To be deserted?"

But finally he realized that he could not change her mind. "When . . . when did you plan to leave?" he asked.

"Dr. Tannenbaum spoke to your son, who spoke to your former housekeeper, Bernadine. She can be back on Monday."

"So you leave at the end of the week?" he asked sadly.

She nodded.

It was a bright, cool Sunday, the sort of late August day in New York that promises a delightful September and October. The park was crowded with baseball teams, with walkers, joggers, and lovers. The whole world seemed to be celebrating the end of a hot summer and the beginning of autumn.

Mr. Horowitz and Mrs. Washington strolled along the walk, under the green leafy trees. Horowitz used his cane but with far less effort than weeks ago.

Mrs. Washington had to admit she was proud of him. She had to admit, as well, that she had come to like this man. She even loved him, not in the way women love men, but in the way that one human being can love and respect another human being. He was a tough man, with a strange kind of pride. Like Horace.

When they came upon the ice-cream vendor, Mr. Horowitz invited, "A little ice cream, Mrs. Washington?"

She hesitated. "Yes, I think that would be nice."

"A sort of farewell party," he said pointedly.

They sat on an old green bench and ate their cones. "From tomorrow on it won't be the same," he said. "And yet it will be the same as before. There'll be Bernadine. And walks in the park. And widows. Always the widows. They'll see me sitting alone, and like vultures, they'll be circling me, waiting to strike."

"You shouldn't feel that way about widows," Mrs. Washington said softly. "We have a lifetime habit. We need someone to care for. Someone to worry about. Someone to wait home for at the end of the day."

"I'm sorry. I didn't mean to offend you. Will I see you again? I mean, am I just one more patient from the past? Or can I consider that we are friends?"

"There's no reason we can't be friends."

"You mean I could call you from time to time? Like when I am stuck with a pair of tickets. You know how it is, there's always a theater party for a worthy cause. So how would it look a man should buy one ticket? For a worthy cause, the least you can buy is a pair. You know what I mean?"

"Uh-huh," she said.

"Is that uh-huh, yes? Or uh-huh, no?"

"Uh-huh, possibly," she responded, then added, "And it wouldn't do any harm for you to call Mona, too, from time to time. She may be a little domineering, but she loves you."

"She is a little domineering like the Johnstown flood was a little damp," he scoffed.

"She's your daughter, and that gives her some rights."

"Okay, I'll call her," he finally acquiesced. "Maybe I'll even visit her for the High Holidays. Yes, ten days. I could stand ten days with Mona. But not a minute more."

His dinner was over. Mrs. Washington was about to fix her hat in place when he asked, "Mrs. Washington, for old times' sake, one last hand?" And he shuffled the pinochle cards.

She hesitated a moment. "It's Sunday. My daughter is home with the children. Yes, I think there's time for one last hand."

He dealt the cards. "Double or nothing?"

Since he had yet to pay any of his gambling losses, she sighed and agreed, "Double or nothing."

Whereupon she took the first trick and melded eighty kings. By the time the game was over, he had been routed.

"Mrs. Washington, if there was a Bible on this table, could you swear on it that you never played pinochle before you entered this house?" he asked with considerable irritation.

"Yes."

"Remarkable," he granted. "You aren't satisfied the blacks took

337

over basketball, baseball, and football. Today it's pinochle! Tomorrow the world!"

When she was ready to leave, Horowitz came out of the bedroom carrying the gift box and a small envelope. At the sight of the box, her eyes stared at him forbiddingly.

"Take it for me," he said gently. "To make an old man happy. How would it look I should go back to Tiffany and say, 'I want a refund. She didn't like it.'"

He took her hand and tried to close her fingers about the box. When she resisted, he chided jokingly, "If you can't do that, Mrs. Washington, we'll have to start you on marbles and buttons." His eyes were growing a bit moist now. She stared into them. "Pay no attention," he said. "The teary eyes of age."

She took the box. He also handed her an envelope.

"What's that?" she asked.

He put on his best pretense at irritation. "Nineteen dollars! Pinochle winnings! Blood money! You ought to be ashamed of yourself, Mrs. Washington! A cardsharp like you could make a fortune on one of those cruise ships! And a perfect front, a grandmother who is also a nurse. Well, I am a man who pays his debts."

WHEN Mrs. Washington arrived at home, her daughter asked, "How was it, Mama?"

"He was very upset, poor man." She opened her purse and took out the box. "I had to take the pin."

She brought out the envelope and smiled. "And this. Pinochle money." She ripped it open. A ten, a five, and four singles fell out. There was also a note. And a slip of paper affixed to it.

Dear Mrs. Washington: Because you are a very proud woman I have to do this my way. The enclosed check is *not* for you. It is for Conrad and Louise. Put it in a savings bank in their names. And by the time they need money for college or some other good purpose, it should amount to something. Whatever you do, you have no right to send it back. It belongs to the children. So for their sake, and mine, please do as I ask.

Your affectionate friend,
Samuel Horowitz

He had signed his name with the same flourish as appeared on the bottom of the appended check for five thousand dollars.

Mrs. Washington stared at the check, and her eyes filmed over.

"Mama?"

Mrs. Washington sniffled and said, "It's nothing. Only the teary eyes of age."

IT WAS early summer, the twenty-fifth of June, the twentieth day of Sivan on the Hebrew calendar. Samuel Horowitz, attired in a proper dark suit, emerged from his building to stand under the canopy and feel the warm sun.

"Cab, Mr. Horowitz?" Juan asked, smiling.

"No, thanks, Juan."

He started up Central Park West, using his cane more as an affectation than a necessity. He crossed at the corner and headed for the synagogue. At the door the sexton asked solicitously, "Yahrzeit, Mr. Horowitz?"

"Yahrzeit," he admitted.

Horowitz walked down the aisle and took a place in the front row of the sanctuary. He looked up at the crimson velvet and goldembroidered ark which contained the scrolls of the Torah. It was a symbol of God, to which most Jews addressed their prayers and, sometimes, also addressed those who had departed.

Samuel Horowitz stared at it and thought, Hannah, darling, last year I was late. But there was a reason. This year, you will notice, I am on time. And not only on time, but I walked here. On my own. So I want you to know that I am all right. Yesterday I talked to Mona on her 800 number and she is all right. And the grandchildren too. Bruce switched over from Harvard and is studying physics at MIT. When he graduates, he'll be able to blow up the whole world. And Candy is going into teaching braindamaged children. I saw both of them on Passover in San Diego.

The main point, Hannah, darling, everything is fine, the family is fine. And if you were here, that would really be fine. Hannah, I love you and I miss you. Not just this day, but every day.

The sexton began conducting the morning service. At the proper time Samuel Horowitz recited the *Kaddish* for his dear departed Hannah.

When the service was over, he left the temple and started down Central Park West back to his building.

On the park side of the street, on a green bench, unobtrusive in the shade of a tree, a neatly dressed black woman watched.

He had done it, she said to herself. He had observed his wife's Yahrzeit on the required day, and walked to and from the synagogue so smoothly no one would have suspected he had had a stroke a year ago.

Gratified, Mrs. Washington rose and went down to the subway, on her way to take care of yet another new patient.

Henry Denker

Henry Denker is that rarity, a born New Yorker. He has the street *nous*, the sparkle, the wry sense of humour and the rich ethnic background that so characterize a native of that city.

Like Horowitz, his parents were hardworking and self-made. Both Austrian Jews, they emigrated to America at the turn of the century, and like so many others of their generation, they worked in the Manhattan sweat-shops. Eventually they established their own fur business and had a comfortable living. They believed that education was the key to life. Three Denker daughters became teachers, and Henry attended New York University Law School.

After graduating in 1934, Henry Denker went into private practice, specializing in what he calls "show business law". "It wasn't as glamorous as I thought it would be," he says, "but I caught that fatal disease, a love for entertainment." During World War II, he moved out of law and into writing as a profession. He wrote some radio plays and in 1947 published his first novel, followed several years later by a Broadway play. He has been a prolific writer ever since.

Mr. Denker lives on Central Park West with a beautiful view of the park. To keep fit he walks a lot, and it was while strolling in Central Park that he got the idea for *Horowitz and Mrs. Washington*. "So often," he says, "I'd see an elderly white male patient being wheeled by a black female nurse. I started thinking about what a story there could be in such a relationship." The character of Horowitz is loosely based on his own father, who also played pinochle and uttered frequent ho-ho-hos.

Now and then Mr. Denker considers moving out of New York. "Tax-wise," he says, "it would be the smart thing to do. But I just can't leave." The Big Apple, for all its high state taxes, still has Henry Denker under its spell.

Bullet Train

A CONDENSATION OF THE BOOK BY

Joseph Rance AND Arei Kato

ILLUSTRATED BY SANFORD KOSSIN
PUBLISHED BY SOUVENIR PRESS

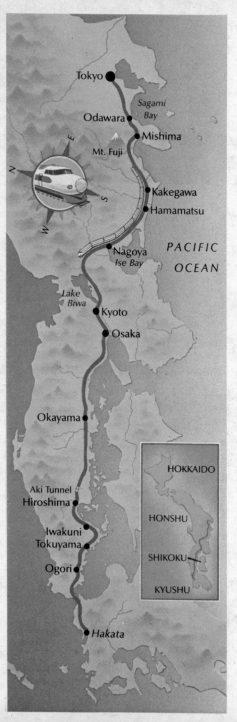

Gleaming like a silver torpedo in the hot July sun, Hikari 109 hurtles through the Tokyo suburbs bound for the coast. The fifteen hundred passengers aboard the superfast Japanese Bullet Train settle back for a safe and pleasant journey.

The nightmare begins when a telephone rings in Tokyo's railway control centre. "There's a bomb on the Hikari 109," says a wheezing voice. "If the train stays above fifty miles per hour, it's perfectly safe, but if it falls below that speed, the bomb will automatically detonate."

A frantic railway operations chief, backed by every aid known to modern technology, tries to avert disaster. But for Aoki, the train's motorman, the world narrows to the flickering needle on the speedometer dial in front of him. Somehow the bomb must be located and defused before the end of the line . . . .

Tokyo Shimbun Daily   *March 27, 1978*

Gelignite stolen

THE THEFT of twenty sticks of blasting gelignite was reported by the foreman from the Ocean Expo construction site in the Kanda district of Tokyo, earlier today.

Police believe it likely that the thief is someone who works, or has worked on the site, since he obviously had knowledge of where the explosive material was stored.

The names of possible suspects have not so far been released, and police inquiries are continuing.

Prologue: July 13, 1978

The factories and workshops on the Shimura Industrial Estate in Tokyo throbbed and clanged with mechanical life as another early-morning shift got under way; yet in the midst of all the noise and bustle one building was silent and lifeless. Its broken windows reflected the bright morning sun in winking shards of light. The perimeter fence sagged wearily, topped with rusting barbed wire, and inside the compound massive hulks of derelict machinery lay half obscured by grass and weeds. The only indication that this had once been a thriving and successful business was a metal sign, hanging by a single hinge above the gate, which bore the bleached and faded wording: Okita Precision Tool Company.

What had been the main workshop was now a shadowy, empty cavern. Dark pools of stagnant water seeped into the crumbling concrete floor, and above, a pale wash of daylight filtered through cobwebbed skylights. All was silent except for the echoing *plink-plonk* of water.

The ringing of a telephone in the office at the rear of the building drilled through the silence, and Okita, who had been lying, tense and waiting, on a camp bed, levered himself upright. It was a few minutes after eight.

This was it, Okita thought, nervous anticipation making his hand tremble as he reached for the phone on the desk. Now that things were actually happening he felt curiously buoyant. The months of planning, the meticulous preparation, the endless discussions. Nothing could go wrong, he was sure, because between the three of them they'd thought of everything. The plan was perfect.

The caller didn't identify himself, but said at once, "The egg has been laid and is ready to hatch."

"Has the bird left its nest?" Okita asked softly.

"Not yet. But I'll know when it does." The caller paused. "How are things at your end?"

Okita hesitated. Should he tell Koga now or wait till later? A fly buzzed in the stillness and he watched it with his sunken eyes as he answered quietly, "Fujio was arrested yesterday."

The caller's tone sharpened. "The cops got him? What for?"

"Take it easy," said Okita calmly. This was the reaction he'd feared. Koga was young and volatile, and his emotions ran high. "The police took him in after a brawl in a bar. He'd been drinking, that's all."

"Can he be trusted to keep his mouth shut?"

"About what?" Okita said easily. "He wasn't involved. We got the stuff and Fujio got paid, that's all that interested him. He's the least of our worries." Over the line Okita heard the muffled clink-clank of shunting goods wagons. He said, "Have you checked the time of your flight here?"

"Ten forty."

346

"Don't miss it. We'll meet as arranged."

Okita put down the phone and lit a cigarette, then eased himself back against the crumpled pillow. The small room was hot and airless, and already he was starting to sweat as the heat of the day built up. He looked down at his stomach, at the spread of flesh and sagging muscle. A couple of years ago he'd been in pretty good shape for a man nearing fifty, but too much drink had played its part in his body's steady deterioration. No drink today, he vowed. Today he had to keep sharp and alert.

Watching the blue cigarette smoke spiral lazily to the plywood ceiling, Okita lay on the camp bed, absorbed in thought. The shell of the silent factory seemed to slumber all around him.

THE YOUNG MAN was thin, almost to the point of emaciation, his body as spare and as tense as a steel spring. Coming out of the phone booth, he dropped the canvas holdall at his feet and leaned against the wooden fence, slowly peeling off his tight black leather gloves. His narrow face was pock-marked, framed by lank shoulder-length hair, and his dark eyes burned as if from fever.

Shaking out his last cigarette, Koga crumpled the packet and tossed it into the dry drainage ditch which ran adjacent to the perimeter road. Beyond the high chain-link fence were the rows of freight cars in the Hokkaido Freight Yard. Koga had smoked the cigarette two-thirds of the way down when he saw one of the huge diesel engines, the number 5293 painted in yellow on its cab, jerk and clank into motion, ponderously gathering speed as it hauled thirty heavily-laden wagons onto the mainline track. Koga watched the train lumber round the curve. His eyes didn't leave it until it finally vanished in the distance.

Part One: Ultimatum

09:40—HIKARI 109—TOKYO CENTRAL

Standing at the long curved sweep of Platform 15, the Hikari 109 Super Express gleamed like a slim silver-grey torpedo in the brilliant July sunshine. With its unmistakable streamlined nose, sleek low profile and the broad blue stripe running the length of its sixteen coaches, this was one of the fleet of Bullet Trains, the pride of Japanese National Railways, which at speeds of up to 130 miles per hour provide the fastest passenger rail service in the world. The Hikari 109 covered the 729 miles from Tokyo to Hakata in 6 hours 56 minutes.

Laura Brennan, one among hundreds of passengers waiting to board, had dressed for coolness, in a blue checked shirt and pleated skirt, with a cardigan draped across her slender shoulders. But although it was still early in the day, the air was already hot and muggy, and Laura rather envied one young Japanese girl she had seen, cool and as fresh as a flower in the traditional silk kimono. However, comfortable as it looked, Laura thought, it would hardly do for her. She smiled at the image of Dr. Laura Brennan of the US Army Hospital in Tokyo, stepping onto the dais dressed like a geisha to read her paper on Purulent Conjunctivitis to the medical conference in Osaka. No, not quite suitable. . . .

All around, people were fanning themselves with folded newspapers and railway timetables. Most were businessmen, as alike as a regiment of soldiers in their lightweight suits, white shirts and polished shoes. But there were tourists as well—some with children—and quite a few young people, students by the look of them, on summer vacation.

Glancing at her watch, Laura saw there were less than ten minutes to go before departure. Why the delay in boarding? Surely the famed efficiency of Japanese National Railways wouldn't let her down? Especially after she had persuaded Matt to go out of his way to drop her at the station before driving on to the army base at Toride where he worked.

Laura observed the people nearby, seeking someone who might know if there was a delay, and, more importantly, with whom she could communicate, for even after two years of living in the country she still hadn't mastered more than a few basic Japanese phrases. True, knowledge of the language wasn't necessary in her work, dealing as she did with American servicemen and their families: even so, she felt, this didn't excuse her laziness. Particularly when her husband, through dogged perseverance, had become fluent in Japanese. Although Matt made light of it, he was one of the few officers at the base to have made the effort, which

was typical of his painstaking approach to any task he set his mind to. It was a quality that endeared him to her very much.

Laura turned and caught the eye of a slim, narrow-shouldered business man in a neat fawn suit. He wore heavy black spectacles and carried an expensive pigskin attaché case with heavy metal clasps. The Japanese guard their business secrets as if they were the Crown Jewels, she thought wryly.

Smiling, she said in English, "Pardon me, I wonder if you could help? The Hikari is due to leave at ten, isn't it?"

The man made a formal bow. "Yes, ten o'clock precisely."

"I just wondered if there'd been some delay."

"No, no." He seemed anxious to dispel this notion. "The Hikari will depart on time, have no fear. But it is a strict railway regulation that every train must be cleaned before each journey." He gestured towards the train where, at that moment, two cleaners in grey overalls were emerging with dusters and small portable vacuum cleaners. "You see—"

Laura nodded her thanks. It was a national characteristic, she had found, this unquestioned obedience to rules and regulations, and while it amused her, it was also rather alarming. They depended so completely on the systems they had created, had such faith in technology. . . . Which mightn't be so bad, Laura reflected, until the day the machines broke down—or took over. . . .

"Are you travelling far?" the businessman asked her.

"To Osaka. I'm attending a medical conference."

"We will arrive in Osaka at ten minutes past one," he said. "I travel often on this line. It is a very efficient service."

Minami had good reason to praise the fast and reliable Hikari Super Express: it was his lifeline to the heavily-industrialized strip along the Pacific coast, two hundred miles to the west, in which was concentrated over seventy per cent of Japan's industry. As area sales manager with the Yotsuboshi Trading Company, it was his job to negotiate the major contracts in that region and to sort out any problems which might arise. Today's trip, unfortunately, was to do with the latter—the delivery and installation of some papermaking equipment had fallen behind schedule and the client was on the verge of cancelling the contract. As a.result, Minami had been up most of the night trying to arrive at a delivery schedule that would satisfy the client. Locked inside his pigskin attaché case was a sheaf of new proposals that represented his last-ditch attempt at retaining the contract.

Naturally none of his agitation showed on his bland round features. As he turned aside from the tall, dark-haired woman, he was unable to resist a sidelong glance. Probably in her mid-thirties, he judged. She had poise and grace and cool self-possession, and was very much the professional woman—all qualities he admired.

Laura Brennan, amused at his appraisal of her, adjusted the cardigan around her shoulders, then glanced round as a buzz of excited chatter swept along the crowded platform. People were craning their necks to look at a handsome young Japanese man with glossy black hair, who had stepped off the escalator leading up from the concourse below. He was wearing a green satin jacket, a shocking-pink T-shirt, high-heeled cowboy boots, and an assortment of chains looped round his neck, and was preceded by a film crew, the cameraman scurrying backwards in order to photograph his flamboyant figure. Surrounded by a dozen adoring teenage girls, the young man continued his royal progress up to Coach 12, one of the two luxury Green Cars reserved for first-class passengers. Pausing, he swivelled round dramatically and, with his best profile to camera, began signing autographs.

At nineteen years of age, and with four hits to his credit, Tee Togo was one of the hottest pop music properties around. The idea of taking the Hikari express had been suggested to Tee Togo's manager by a television company that was making a documentary film about a "typical" day in the life of a pop star. The trip wasn't strictly necessary—the television director simply wanted to show Tee Togo lounging in Green Car luxury with some hundred-mile-an-hour scenery as a spectacular backdrop. This footage would then be spliced onto existing film of a concert he had given a month earlier, and the completed documentary would have the appearance of a single, continuous day.

At a prearranged signal from the director, the young pop star smiled artfully over his shoulder at the camera and stepped into the doorway of the Green Car. The performance was over.

There must have been twelve or thirteen hundred people waiting to board the train, Laura reckoned, but there was no pushing or squabbling, just a patient queue at each door. She had already studied the plan of the Hikari Super Express on the back of the timetable. Apart from the first four second-class coaches at the front of the train, every other seat was reservable, including her own in Coach 7. Just about everything had been provided: the train was air-conditioned and, in addition to a restaurant and a buffet, there were two public telephones on board.

After standing in the queue, awaiting her turn to board, Laura stepped into the coach grateful for the cool air within. The seating was arranged in groups of three and two, divided by a carpeted aisle. There was ample leg-room, and the windows were tinted to reduce the sun's glare. Both the carpet and the seat coverings were sea-green, with cushioned headrests of pale lemon. Not sumptuous exactly, Laura decided, but comfortable, and tastefully appointed.

She hoisted her small suitcase onto the overhead rack and settled down in her seat. Now, was she going to be the dedicated doctor of ophthalmology and run through her lecture notes or would she relax with a magazine? Matt sometimes accused her—half jokingly—of being obsessed with her work to the exclusion of everything else. Very well, for once she'd take things easy. She'd sit back in comfort while the Bullet Train whisked her down the coast to Osaka, and let the scenery, like a freshly-painted water-colour, unroll before her.

PLATFORM 15 was rapidly emptying as the last of the passengers filed aboard. Outside Coach 6, Keiko reluctantly joined the queue, her dark eyes darting from the central escalator to the stairway at the far end of the platform. She had deliberately hung back, hoping that Abiko, her husband, might suddenly appear. He had begged her not to make the trip now that her pregnancy was so advanced, but she had felt confused. She wanted the best for her unborn child. Should she return to her parents' home to have her baby, or stay cramped and miserable in the tiny two-room basement flat, sweltering in the city's heat?

At first their marriage had been perfect. While Abiko studied for an engineering degree, Keiko worked as a filing clerk, and with her salary and Abiko's education grant they had managed to scrape along, wanting nothing except each other. Then she became pregnant and when she had to give up her job they found themselves in desperate straits. Bills piled up and they began to

352

bicker. Their two rooms seemed like a prison, with Abiko haggard and distraught, blaming her because he was falling behind in his studies. So she had made what seemed to her the only sensible decision. She would go to her parents in Nagoya to have her baby.

The queue moved forward. Keiko hesitated, glancing once again towards the escalator and the stairs. Abiko must have seen the note she had left him by now. Why didn't he come and stop her?

Then her resolve hardened. Carefully, one hand pressed to her belly, she entered the train.

A SHORT SQUAT woman in grimy overalls stood by the track and peered nearsightedly into the gloom under Coach 2. She could just make out the legs of her companion. He'd better get a move on, the woman thought. The train was due to leave at any minute.

"Come on, Sato," she called out irritably.

She detested this job, especially in hot weather. It was dirty and smelly and gave her a backache. There were sixteen large rubbish bins, one in each coach, and the cleaners had to get underneath the train to empty the bins down metal chutes and into a heavy rubbish cart. "What's the trouble?" she asked Sato grumpily. "It's time you were finished."

There was a hollow clang of metal followed by Sato's muffled voice. "The chute's outer hatch is a bit stiff. I can't get it to shut properly. Won't be a minute."

The woman looked nervously along the smooth tapering line of the Bullet Train. "If you don't hurry up, you'll get us run over!"

Sato emerged from beneath the train and straightened up. "Finished," he announced cheerfully, and pushed the rubbish cart along the concrete walkway towards the front of the train. He was young, of medium height, with a solid pair of shoulders and muscular arms beneath his rolled-up sleeves. His hair was spiky and close-cropped, a style he still favoured from his days in the army, and a matchstick jutted from the corner of his mouth, a habit he'd acquired from watching American movies on TV.

The fat woman shuffled after him, still complaining. "This job gets me down in the hot weather," she said.

"Doesn't bother me." Sato gave her a quick grin, then glanced back over his shoulder. For just an instant his eyes were hard and searching, but the amused manner returned almost at once. Putting his shoulder to the cart, he heaved it up a shallow ramp to the disposal bay and again looked back, as if to satisfy himself about something. From this angle, almost head on, the smooth rounded prow of the train looked like the nose of a big passenger jet. Overhead, the twenty-five kilovolt power grid threw an intricate spidery shadow across the steeply raked windows of the driving cab where the motorman was preparing for departure.

Turning away, Sato squeezed the fat woman's shoulder playfully. "Well, that's over with. We can take it easy, eh?" He opened a metal door and ushered the woman through to a landing on the public stairs leading up to the platform. A few stragglers were hurrying to catch the train, and Sato, about to close the door, caught sight of three men mounting the stairs towards him. His face went rigid.

The man in the middle, a good six inches shorter than his companions, was as broad and as solid as a tank, with the massive barrel torso of a *Sumo* wrestler. His forehead slanted outwards, overhung by a fringe of hair, and the rest of his features were flat. It was a gargoyle of a face, frightening in its ugliness.

Sato started to move back out of sight, but it was too late. The man's tiny slitted eyes met his and widened fractionally. Fujio had recognized him.

Head lowered, Sato ducked swiftly down the stairs past the three men, leaving the fat woman blinking in surprise. Then he strode across the crowded entrance hall and out through the main doors. There he paused, chewing nervously on the matchstick while he debated what to do. He couldn't go to the factory. Okita had insisted on there being no personal contact until . . . afterwards. But he had to be told. This could wreck *everything*. Sato came to a decision. There was a bar on the corner of the next street. He'd phone from there.

THE THREE MEN came out onto the platform and walked briskly towards the rear of the train. Detective-Sergeant Ozaki, the tallest of the three, kept close to his massive prisoner, for he trusted Fujio about as far as he could throw him.

This morning the detective was in a very bad humour. He was to have gone off duty at noon. Then, less than two hours ago, his captain had sprung this escort detail on him, and Ozaki had been faced with the tricky task of explaining to his wife why their planned trip to the Nikko National Park was off. Luckily, she had understood—he hoped. Only six weeks married, Ozaki was still in the first flush of romantic bliss, and eager to get home after work. He calculated that the train was scheduled to arrive in Osaka shortly after one o'clock, and from there to Police Headquarters at Kobe would take perhaps an hour. If there was no delay in handing over the prisoner, Ozaki could be back in Tokyo by eight that evening.

Reservations had been made for him and Fujio in Coach 14. They had almost drawn level with the door when the other member of the escort, Nagata, the duty policeman which every Super Express was obliged by law to carry, suddenly stepped across to lead the way into the coach, causing Ozaki to stumble into him.

The prisoner saw his chance and took it. Moving remarkably fast, he broke away and ran back towards the stairway, scattering small groups of people and yelling at the top of his voice.

Ozaki raced after him. Younger and fitter than Fujio, he caught up with him at the stairs and launched himself in a flying tackle which brought the big man crashing down, the wind knocked out of him. The detective leaped to his feet and unceremoniously hauled the prisoner to a sitting position.

"I'm in no mood to play games, Fujio," he panted, unhooking a pair of handcuffs from his belt. With Fujio staring at him sullenly, Ozaki snapped the handcuffs onto his thick hairy wrists.

Duty Policeman Nagata came puffing up, clearly out of condition, and rather sheepishly started to stutter an apology. Ozaki cut him short. "Forget it. Are you all right?"

Nagata nodded, though he looked shaken. Duty policemen, Ozaki knew, were glorified railway stewards, with no proper police training, and this specimen looked sorrier than most.

Ozaki jerked the prisoner to his feet and led him along the platform. The windows of the train were lined with people, intrigued by the spectacle. As they boarded the train the clock suspended on its silver rod from the station's domed roof ticked away the final seconds to ten o'clock. Doors were slammed and locked. The few people left on Platform 15 waved their last goodbyes, wishing friends and relatives on the 10:00 a.m. Hikari Super Express a safe and pleasant journey.

Operations Chief Hiroshi stood before the angled glass wall of his office overlooking the operations room of centralized traffic control, sipping a cup of sweet black coffee. Located in a four-storey red-brick building at the north end of Tokyo station, this was the nerve-centre of the Shinkansen, the most heavily used mass transportation system in the world. On any one day, the 729-mile line from Tokyo to Hakata carried upwards of a million people, and the split-second scheduling of 250 high-speed Bullet Trains required a clear head, steady nerves, and a calm temperament.

For Hiroshi that morning had begun like any other, with a four-mile jog in the countryside near his home, followed by a light breakfast. Afterwards he prepared a small tray and took tea up to his wife. The peaceful interlude was, as always, interrupted by the arrival of his young daughter. As it happened, today was her fifth birthday, and after planting a kiss on her father's cheek, she had solemnly inquired if it was time to get ready for her party. Not just yet, Hiroshi had replied. He had to go to work first. But he'd be home early, and he'd bring with him a wonderful surprise. Neither his daughter nor his wife knew what to expect; Hiroshi had secretly ordered a collie pup with floppy ears and a white patch over one eye, and just hoped that it would be welcomed equally by both of them.

Hiroshi drained the cup and placed it on the desk behind him. Time to get moving. Already there was a bustle of activity in the circular operations room below. A sixty-foot-long control board dominated the room, providing an animated graphic display of the entire Shinkansen network. The board was divided into seven sections and a controller, wearing a headset, was in charge of each section. Behind the controllers, on a central dais, was a back-up team of route planners, engineers and technical experts, with a computer staff at individual consoles.

Whenever he surveyed his little empire, Operations Chief Hiroshi felt a quickening of pride. In all, he had nearly fifty people under him. The Shinkansen had been the first fully-automated rail control system ever developed. Established in the early sixties, it was still among the most sophisticated of any in the world, and no railway authority could boast of a better safety record. With

356

such a fine record behind them and other exciting advances ahead, Hiroshi felt his pride was more than justified.

On the main display board, a red light winked on. The second hand on the large segmented clockface was sweeping towards ten o'clock and the Hikari 109 was requesting departure clearance. Every Bullet Train was under constant surveillance by CTC Operations and with the aid of the computer system, COMTRAC, its speed, the distance between trains, and all arrival and departure times were monitored with pinpoint accuracy.

Out in the operations room itself, Controller Mori was about to acknowledge the red light above Platform 15. He was responsible for Section 1 of the main display board—the route from Tokyo to Odawara—which alone contained 200 control points and 1300 indicator lights. The display was in the form of an illuminated grid set against a dark green background, with each train a numbered bar of orange light. As the trains moved, so did the orange bars.

Studying the board, Controller Mori saw that 109's line was cleared for traffic and that the feeder sub-stations along the route were registering optimum electric power output. He spoke quietly into the microphone attached to his headset: "Hello, Hikari 109. We acknowledge your signal."

"Hello, Control, this is Motorman Aoki. Request departure clearance from Platform 15 at 10:00 hours."

"You have it, Hikari 109. Depart according to schedule."

In the driving cab of the Super Express, Motorman Aoki opened the main throttle control. Instantly there was the subdued hum of power, and on the ATC (Automatic Train Control) display screen in front of him he saw confirmation that all electrical and mechanical systems were operating satisfactorily. Under the guidance of the ATC—an onboard computer—the train began to accelerate automatically. It would reach the maximum permitted speed of 130 miles per hour and there was little for Motorman Aoki to do except sit back and keep an eye on his instrument panel.

Gathering speed, the Bullet Train moved through the Tokyo suburbs, leaving behind the heat and fumes of the capital and heading southwest towards the coast and the first clean, cool breezes wafting in from the Pacific.

Sato went straight through the bar to the phone booth at the rear. It was stifling inside and the stink of the rubbish bins still hung about him. He'd hated that job, but it had been part of the plan to find work as a cleaner so Sato had accepted the necessity, even though his whole being rebelled at having to take orders from petty-minded officials. He loathed any kind of authority; that was why his stint in the army had been such an unqualified failure—that plus the fact that he had been caught pilfering.

His hand tightened on the receiver as the connection was made. "It's me," he said at once. "I saw Fujio at the station with a couple of cops. He's on the train!"

"Did he see you?" Okita sounded his usual calm self.

"Yes, and I'm certain he recognized me. What are we going to do?"

"Nothing. He can't tell them what he doesn't know." There was a slight wheeziness in Okita's voice, the penalty of too many cigarettes. Sato thought the habit disgusting. A fervent believer in keeping fit, he ate the right foods, exercised regularly, and took great pride in his sturdy physique. A girl had once told him that he reminded her of a young Charles Bronson, and ever since, Bronson had been his favourite film star.

"What about you?" Okita asked. "Did everything go all right?"

"Yes. We're all set. The ten o'clock Hikari." Sato caught sight of his reflection in the glass panel of the booth. He instinctively tensed the muscles of his right arm to admire the effect. Charles Bronson. The Streetfighter.

"We carry on as planned," Okita said.

"Sure," grunted the Streetfighter, changing his pose.

OKITA PUT DOWN the phone and lit a cigarette. He stood at the window and gazed unseeingly at the wilderness of grass and weeds and rusting machinery in the compound outside. The trouble with Sato was that he had no sense of responsibility, Okita realized. He wouldn't deliberately let anyone down, but at any moment he might be distracted by a stray thought or a pretty girl, and the effect would be the same. The young man tended to live in a Hollywood-style dream world, and Okita was afraid that he might confuse this make-believe with what had now become a grim reality.

But maybe he was being too hard on Sato. After all, it was Sato who had stood by him when his family and friends had deserted him—though in those days, Okita realized with brutal honesty, he could hardly blame them—his drinking would have tried the patience of a saint. Eventually even his wife and daughter had left him, and it was then that Sato had befriended him, and it was precisely Sato's easy-going qualities that had pulled him through.

No, it was wrong, a betrayal of friendship, to think that Sato might let him down. If anything, it was the other one—Koga—who deserved to be the focus of concern.

Koga was everything that Sato was not: shrewd, dedicated, highly intelligent. But he was also an extremist, liable to be carried away by a zeal that bordered on fanaticism. In both manner and temperament Koga remained the archetypal student. Indeed, Okita still thought of him as "the student", even though Koga had been expelled from Jonan University over a year ago.

And it was Koga who had first planted the seed of the idea in Okita's head. Without him, their scheme would never have seen the light of day. OK, so a good-natured wastrel and a hot-eyed fanatic weren't the ideal bedfellows for such an enterprise, but who was Okita to demand perfection in others?

How would he describe himself? Failed businessman? Failed engineer? Failed husband and father? Certainly a failure until fate had come along with another use for his talents. He had played the game according to the rules and failed, so now he had thrown away the rule book and was determined to win on his own terms. It was a gamble, of course. He realized that. The biggest gamble of his life.

10:07—HIKARI 109—YOKOHAMA

From her window seat in Coach 7, Dr. Laura Brennan looked idly out at the sprawl of low, flat-roofed suburban dwellings which extended as far as the eye could see. She and Matt often grumbled about living near the centre of the capital, with its crowding and frenzied pace, but it was infinitely preferable to this soulless wasteland. At least in the city they had American and European movies, museums and art galleries, a symphony orchestra.

Japan was, overall, a most beautiful country. What struck Laura about Japan was how neat the countryside looked; how carefully planned, as if someone had worked to create a formal garden on a national basis, scaling down the landscape to the level of the comfortably human. Even the mountains seemed to have been placed according to a master plan, to add drama and contrast.

She and her husband liked both the country and the people. After nine years of living on and around army bases in the United States, they had needed a change of scene, and had been pleased at Matt's posting to Japan. Laura had found a job at the US Army Hospital, just outside Tokyo, and been able to continue working in her speciality in the hospital's ophthalmic research unit. Along with two colleagues, one American, one Japanese, she had helped develop several new techniques of diagnosis and treatment. Her latest research had led to this invitation to read a paper at the International Medical Conference in Osaka. Half petrified, she nevertheless looked forward to discussing her work with some of the most eminent people in the field.

The train's public address speaker emitted a sudden burst of music, followed by a pleasant female voice reciting the times of the scheduled stops, first in Japanese and then in English: "Nagoya—12:03 . . . Kyoto—12:53 . . . Osaka—1:12 . . ."

No one paid it much attention. In the spacious comfort of Coach 11, Takazana, the diminutive 71-year-old president of Kyoto Electronics, was receiving a neck massage from his travelling companion and "private nurse", Michiko. The old man, barely five foot three in his hand-stitched shoes with built-up heels, was in a foul temper. No one was allowed a private compartment on the Hikari 109, no matter how influential he might be, so Takazana was having to suffer the indignity of sharing a Green Car with other first-class passengers.

Unlike the other coaches, which had one hundred seats each, the two Green Cars had only sixty-five reclining seats. There were deep pile carpets and individual reading lights, curtains, and personal call buttons to summon the attendants. Still, as founder and president of Japan's third largest electronics company, Takazana was accustomed to nothing but the best, and this was not it. Normally he would have flown to the plant at Kyoto in his Lear jet, but last-minute technical problems had necessitated a swift change of plan, which was why he and Michiko, his beautiful twenty-two-year-old mistress, found themselves speeding westward on the Hikari Super Express.

Michiko kissed the nape of his thin neck. "Do you feel better now?" she asked in a demure little voice.

"Yes, yes," he said testily. He leaned back in his seat and closed his pale eyelids, reminding the girl of a frail bird seeking to regain its strength by resting in the sunlight.

Michiko watched him for a moment, her delicate hands smoothing the silken kimono over her knees. Her long scented tresses were pinned up, her eyes and lips heavily accentuated in the manner of the geisha. Old Takazana set great store by the ancient arts and traditions, and for her part, Michiko didn't mind wearing traditional costume. Beneath the ornately-decorated garment with its voluminous sleeves was a shrewd and sophisticated young woman, known to her friends by the Westernized nickname of "Mickie". If Takazana wanted to cling to the past—fine—she would humour him. He was her gilt-edged meal ticket and Mickie liked to eat well.

Takazana opened his eyes. "I want my tablets. And get me something to drink. Tea with lemon."

The girl pressed the bell. From her sleeve she took out a small plastic vial and shook two white tablets into the palm of her hand. Prescribed for a faint heart murmur, they were supposed to be taken in moments of stress. Mickie knew that the old man was terrified by the thought of death. All his vast wealth and power would weigh as nothing when the time came. And when, she wondered, would that time be?

In the adjoining Green Car, Tee Togo was enjoying himself hugely. Sprawled in his seat, wearing headphones plugged into a cassette recorder on his lap, the pop star was miming his latest recording as the camera zoomed in for a close-up.

"Right . . . great. . . ." said the director, as he visualized the shot on film. "That's it. . . ." He was so deeply involved with the effort of artistic creation that he was completely unaware of the head guard, in his dark green uniform with the gold piping, standing directly behind him in the aisle.

"Excuse me, sir. Do you have written permission to film on this train?"

Yamada, the head guard, was polite but firm. He didn't want to offend anyone, but he knew his duty.

The director looked round, frowning. "Look, friend, give us a break. We'll be through in a minute, OK?"

Forcing himself to remain calm, Yamada said in the same patient voice, "I'm afraid I can't allow you to film on the train. It's a strict company rule that written permission must be obtained before any filming can take place in, on, or near National Railways' property."

By now Tee Togo had finished miming the song. Having got what he wanted, the director became profusely apologetic. "Sorry —I hadn't realized. Hope we didn't disturb anyone." He beamed, then winked at the sound engineer.

Biting back his anger, Yamada glowered at the film crew and went along the aisle towards the guards' compartment, situated at the end of Coach 12.

In Coach 14, Detective-Sergeant Ozaki had taken the precaution of handcuffing himself to the prisoner. This brought some uneasy looks from the other passengers, but that couldn't be helped. Ozaki wasn't going to give Fujio another chance to escape.

Something was puzzling the detective. On their way to the station Fujio had been in reasonably good spirits, as if resigned to his fate. But then, out of the blue, he had tried to make a break for it. What had brought on this abrupt change was completely beyond Ozaki's comprehension. Now, slumped in his seat next to the window, Fujio was staring morosely out the window. Ozaki couldn't figure it out. . . .

The Bullet Train was now twenty-three minutes and forty-nine miles out of Tokyo, travelling at top speed along the gentle curve of Sagami Bay. Throughout the train there was an air of relaxation. The first four coaches—the unreserved section—were crowded with people, even standing in the aisles. The buffet in Coach 9 was doing brisk business, and apart from two or three empty seats in the Green Cars, the Hikari 109 was full to capacity.

10:25—CTC Operations—Tokyo Central

Operations Chief Hiroshi and his deputy, Sunaga, were on their way down the open metal stairway which led from the catwalk in front of their adjoining offices to the operations room.

"What's the trouble?" Hiroshi asked, as they passed through a pair of double doors and walked down the corridor.

Sunaga shrugged, his creased, leathery face impassive. "Haven't a clue," he said. "You know our police chief and the flaps he gets into. Probably a cow on the line somewhere."

Hiroshi grinned, his lean, dark face lighting up so that he suddenly appeared younger than his thirty-four years. He liked Sunaga's down-to-earth manner. The deputy operations chief, twelve years his senior, was a man of wide practical experience who'd started with the railways as an apprentice fireman on the old steam locomotives. Hiroshi valued his first-hand knowledge of every aspect of rail operation.

Makoto, the chief of National Railways Police, was sitting at his desk staring mutely at the telephone when they entered his office. He looks ill, Hiroshi thought, then remembered that Makoto suffered from a gastric ulcer which the doctors had been unable to cure. Mindful of this, Hiroshi tempered his impatience and said genially, "Well, what little problem are you going to dump in our laps today? Vandals? Somebody nicked the plugs from the washbasins?"

The police chief raised his eyes and gestured towards the phone. "We've just received a bomb threat," he said.

"Not another one?" Hiroshi groaned. "Damn it all! That's—what?—the fourth or fifth this month."

"In June we had seventeen," Deputy Sunaga reminded him.

Hiroshi nodded glumly. Every such call had to be treated seriously, even though in the past they had all turned out to be hoaxes. He sighed. "Which train is it? I'll have to instruct them to stop and make a thorough search."

Police Chief Makoto wet his lips. "This time we can't stop the train," he said weakly, and pressed the playback switch on the cassette recorder attached to the telephone. "Listen."

The crackle of a telephone line filled the room and a voice, wheezing slightly, began to speak. "I'm not going to repeat this, so listen carefully. There's a bomb on the Hikari 109 which left Tokyo for Hakata at ten o'clock this morning. The device—"

The caller was interrupted by Police Chief Makoto's voice. "What are you talking about? Who's that speaking?"

"I told you to listen carefully." The voice went on, calm,

expressionless. "The bomb is activated by a trigger mechanism which comes into operation at fifty miles per hour. Providing the train keeps above that speed it's perfectly safe, but if it falls below fifty miles per hour the bomb will automatically detonate."

There followed a brief silence, then the police chief saying, "How do I know you're serious? This could be a hoax."

"I am serious and I can prove it. I planted a similar device on a diesel locomotive which left the Hokkaido Freight Yard at ten minutes past eight this morning. Number 5293. It isn't due to stop until it reaches Oiwake, but if you want to find out how genuine this threat is, slow the train down to less than twelve miles per hour. Then you'll see."

There was a sharp click, then Makoto calling, "Hello . . . hello. . . ?"

The police chief switched off the recorder and the silence crowded in, making the room seem claustrophobic. Finally, Sunaga said, quietly, "He doesn't sound like a crank."

"What about tracing the call?" Hiroshi demanded.

Police Chief Makoto avoided his gaze. "There wasn't time," he said gruffly. He grimaced as a sharp pain stabbed his insides— his old malignant friend reacting on cue to the panic that swept over him.

Hiroshi turned to his deputy. "What about the freight train?"

Sunaga shook his head. "I've heard no report of an explosion and it would have come through to me first." He stared at Hiroshi gravely. Hiroshi had been appointed operations chief eighteen months before, the youngest man ever to have held the post, and in the highly-complex day-to-day operation, he had shown a keen intelligence and presence of mind. But now, thought Sunaga, comes the real test. "I'll contact Hokkaido and have them check on the freight train." He turned to go.

"Wait a minute, Sunaga, let's think this through." The operations chief studied his watch. "It's now 10:32, which means the Hikari 109 is less than seven miles from Odawara. From there to Nagoya is 105.8 miles, a travelling time of one hour and twenty-four minutes."

Nagoya was the first scheduled stop for the Bullet Train, which meant they had one-and-a-half hours in which to make the crucial decision whether to allow the train to stop or to instruct

364

the driver to carry on. The latter course would result in the disruption of the entire Shinkansen route and the mammoth task of rescheduling every one of the 250 Bullet Trains in operation—not a decision to be taken lightly.

"For the moment," Hiroshi said, "we'll keep strictly to the schedule. I'll contact the Hikari 109 and have them carry out a security check while the train is moving. You get in touch with the Hokkaido authorities and find out the situation with the freight train." He knew he could rely on Sunaga in a crisis, a trust he wasn't prepared to allow Police Chief Makoto.

"I'll get on to it right away." Sunaga went to the door and paused, his grizzled face thoughtful. "He didn't make any demand, so what's he after? What's the motive?"

The police chief nervously wadded his handkerchief into a ball and wiped his forehead. "Maybe it is a hoax after all. Surely if he's serious he'd have demanded money, or the release of political prisoners—something."

"But if he's telling the truth . . ." There was no need for Hiroshi to spell out the implications. If there really was a bomb on the train, set to explode should its speed fall below fifty miles per hour, nearly fifteen hundred people were captive on a Bullet Train that couldn't stop.

But sooner or later the train *had* to stop. At the end of the line, at Hakata, there was no loop to bring it back in the opposite direction. Designed with a driving cab at either end, for the return journey it simply reversed its running order.

"Come on, let's get moving," Hiroshi said to his deputy, and they went out. Left behind, the police chief prayed that it was all a stupid joke. He knew he didn't have the stamina to endure such an ordeal, and pressed his hands to his stomach, trying to ease the gnawing pain.

10:35—HIKARI 109—ODAWARA

It seemed to Motorman Aoki that he could smell the bracing sea air as the Bullet Train sped like a silver-grey arrow through the seaside resort of Odawara on the curve of Sagami Bay. Purely his imagination of course, because the train was sealed and he was breathing air cycled through the train's air conditioning system. Still, it was a pleasant enough illusion.

Seated on either side of the cab in their high-backed padded chairs, Aoki and his assistant, Uchida, watched over the banks of instruments and controls. The main panel, in front of the motorman, contained the throttle and braking levers, while in the centre was the display screen of the Automatic Train Control system. The ATC fed a constant stream of updated information on any obstacles ahead, wind velocity, and the distance between them and other trains. In fact, there was little enough for them to do. Supervised by Centralized Traffic Control in Tokyo, the Bullet Train ran automatically and at an electronically controlled speed.

Some of the drivers on the Shinkansen route got bored, but not Aoki. It had been his childhood ambition to drive a Bullet Train, and at twenty-four, he loved the job with a passion that his assistant, Uchida, found hard to comprehend. He had assembled a large collection of books and magazines on the railways of the world. He knew all the crack express trains: the Italian Super-rapido operating between Rome and Milan, the Spanish Le Catalan linking Barcelona with France and Switzerland, the French Mistral on the Paris–Marseilles run, and he was proud that the Bullet Trains of Japan were among them.

Glancing down at the speedometer, Aoki saw that the red needle was nudging 128.4 miles per hour. Through the steeply-angled windows of the cab, trees, fields and houses, bridges—all merged into a streaky blur of colours on either side.

"Section 2 clear to Nagoya," Uchida informed him.

Aoki nodded and leaned across to punch up a route map on the ATC display. Soon they would reach one of the spectacular viaducts on the Shinkansen route—this one—1,320 yards long—supported on pneumatic caissons sunk fifty feet into solid rock. This bridge alone had taken engineers two-and-a-half years to build. There were tunnels as well, two of them nearly five miles long.

"Attention please!"

Uchida raised one eyebrow as a girl's voice issued from the public-address speaker on the rear bulkhead. "Sounds like Miss Imperial Hotel," he declared, using his pet name for Yoko, the prettiest stewardess on the line. "Asked her for a date yet?"

Aoki flushed slightly. He was quiet, soft-spoken, handsome, but rather shy with girls, and Uchida, the jovial extrovert, liked to rag him about romantic attachments. In truth there was none, even though several of the stewardesses—Yoko among them—had made it clear that if he so chose, Aoki could have his pick of them. This irked Uchida because he had been trying to date "Miss Imperial Hotel" for months, with a singular lack of success.

The girl went on to announce to the passengers the facilities available on the train. She was just finishing when the radio-telephone buzzed. Unhooking the handset from the cab wall, Aoki said crisply, "Hikari 109."

"Hello, Hikari 109. This is Operations Chief Hiroshi."

Aoki and Uchida exchanged looks. It wasn't usual for the chief to call in person; normally one of the controllers relayed instructions.

"We have a problem, Aoki." Hiroshi paused. "We've received a warning about a bomb on the train."

The motorman stared down at his hand, pleased to see that it was perfectly steady. Hoax bomb threats were rather common, but this was Aoki's first. He knew the procedure by heart. "OK, Chief, where do we stop?"

"You don't," Hiroshi said. "You don't stop. I want you to carry out a security check *while the train is moving.*"

Aoki frowned. "That won't be easy, Chief."

"I'm aware of that," Hiroshi said evenly. "But this device is linked in some way to the speed of the train. If the speed drops below fifty miles per hour, the bomb will detonate."

It took a moment for this to sink in. "You mean if we stop—"

"The train will explode. . . ."

Aoki felt the blood drain from his face.

"Our technical people here," Hiroshi went on, "will try to work out how such a device would operate and where it could have been planted. Meanwhile, I want you to reduce your speed—"

"*Reduce* it?" Aoki was confused.

"Yes—to gain time," Hiroshi explained. "At your present speed, it's five hours fourteen minutes to Hakata. I've processed the figures through COMTRAC and the computer has come up with an average speed of sixty-three miles per hour for you to maintain—this will give us a safety margin over the fifty miles an hour limit, *plus* an extra five-and-a-half hours running time. Have you got that?"

Of course. They had to gain every minute they could, delay their arrival in Hakata to the last possible moment. Because there the line ended . . . *the line ended.* . . .

"Aoki?" Hiroshi was saying. "Have you got that?"

The motorman cleared his throat. "Yes . . . sixty-three miles per hour." Something else had occurred to him. "What about the ATC? It's programmed to stop at Nagoya."

"We'll override the ATC from here," Hiroshi said. "You'll go straight through. Just concentrate on keeping your speed at sixty-three miles per hour and carrying out a security check. I want every inch of that train searched."

"OK, Chief. I'll arrange that with the head guard." Aoki was staring out at the shining rails. "This must be just another hoax, mustn't it?"

"We don't know," the operations chief told him frankly. "Apparently there's a similar device on a freight train that left Hokkaido early this morning. We're checking on that now. I'll let you know as soon as we have any news." He hesitated. "I needn't tell you how important it is not to alarm the passengers unnecessarily. We're relying on you, Aoki."

The motorman hung up and looked at Uchida. "Get back there," he said, "and explain the situation to Yamada yourself. And make sure there's no one within earshot."

Without a word, Uchida left the driving cab. Aoki reached for the braking control. He pushed the lever forward and watched the red needle creep back round the dial and stop at sixty-three miles per hour.

10:42—FREIGHT TRAIN 5293—ABIRA

The heavy diesel locomotive with the yellow number on its cab laboured across the featureless plain south of Abira on the island of Hokkaido. Being the least developed of Japan's four main islands, Hokkaido was regarded as a cultural and economic backwater. But backwater or not, the railway authorities had acted swiftly when news of the bomb threat came from CTC Operations in Tokyo. Within minutes, the station master at Abira was preparing a note to be thrown in a leather satchel into the cab of the freight train as it passed through his station.

The driver and his mate reacted with amazement. Was this

368

some sort of practical joke? But the message was brutally to the point: there was a bomb on board which would detonate when the train's speed fell below twelve miles per hour. They were to get well clear of Abira station, and, when they saw a signal flare, set the brake and jump out. If the threat was real, there would be no damage to life or property out there in the open fields.

It was the driver's mate who spotted the three police patrol cars beside a level-crossing about half a mile ahead. As the locomotive lumbered on the two men saw a figure in railway uniform raise his arm. The next moment a flare burst like a huge orange flower over the track.

The locomotive's driver yanked the brake lever full on. The wheels locked with a screech and the huge locomotive shuddered and slowed.

"Now—Jump!" the driver shouted to his mate and, poised in the cab doorway, knees bent, he flung himself out, hit the grass verge and tumbled over in a flurry of arms and legs. His mate followed, landing nearby, shaken but unhurt. At once the police and railway officials scattered, diving for cover.

The driver watched from under his crooked elbow, his chin pressed into the earth. He saw a blinding flash, felt the shockwave, as the massive bulk of the locomotive reared up for a moment before falling across the track with a crash like thunder. Carried on by their own momentum, the heavily-laden freight cars piled into it, the entire train writhing in on itself and building a mountain of sheared metal and splintered timber.

In the silence that followed, Freight Train 5293 lay on the track, distorted beyond recognition, a pall of oily black smoke rising slowly in the warm air like an ominous question mark.

10:47—HIKARI 109—MISHIMA

Head Guard Yamada assembled his staff of four in the guards' compartment in Coach 12, and briefed them on the situation. He was a tall, spare man with ramrod bearing, whose fifteen years' service with the National Railways had taught him the value of discipline and company policy. "We shall follow standard procedure for this security check," he stressed, pointing with a bony forefinger to the plan of the Hikari 109 on the wall. He turned to Ando, the youngest guard. "You'll take coaches one to four."

At twenty-one, Ando was excited that there was actually a bomb alert, a real-life drama, in his first month on the Bullet Train.

Yamada's finger moved along. "Yoko, coaches five, six and seven."

The stewardess nodded, her hands clasped tightly so as not to betray her nervousness.

"Nagata, you check the restaurant and buffet cars," Yamada instructed the duty policeman. "And make sure the kitchen is searched *without* telling the staff about the threat."

"How do I manage that?" asked Nagata, ill at ease.

"Use your initiative," the head guard said dryly. He knew that Nagata had a nagging wife, which probably explained his apprehension—the poor man would have to explain why he was late getting home, and a bomb on the train wasn't a good enough excuse unless he happened to get blown up by it.

Yamada went on briskly, "I'll take Coach 10 and the Green Cars, which leaves coaches thirteen to sixteen to you, Kenichi. Now, as far as the passengers are concerned this is a routine baggage check. I'll make an announcement to that effect. Any questions?"

"What about restricted access areas, sir?" asked Kenichi. "The control circuits and the maintenance entry points?"

"The assistant motorman will cover those," Yamada said, pleased that Kenichi had thought to raise the point. Perhaps the young man was learning after all, he reflected. Kenichi tended to be so slapdash in his ways. Just recently, when checking the fire extinguishers, he had accidentally set one of them off and sprayed foam ankle-deep in the corridor of Coach 10. "At least we know it works," he had observed brightly.

Dismissing his staff, Yamada took the microphone from its wall bracket and cleared his throat. "Attention please! This is the head guard speaking. We are about to carry out a routine baggage check throughout the train. Please identify your baggage when asked to do so . . . ."

That was suitably low-key he felt as he moved out into the Green Car. Indeed, none of the passengers there showed the slightest interest. They probably haven't even noticed that we've slowed down, Yamada thought, though he estimated that their speed had dropped to less than seventy miles per hour. Moving

370

slowly down the coach he began to make careful sweeps of the luggage racks, his experienced eye noting each item and identifying its owner, missing nothing.

DETECTIVE-SERGEANT OZAKI watched uninterestedly as Kenichi, the guard, came along the aisle of Coach 14, pausing every few moments to lean across and read a luggage label and then ask which of the passengers claimed it. Ozaki was struck, though, by the expression on his prisoner's face—an odd mixture of fear and cunning. "What's the matter, Fujio?" the detective asked.

The big man shrugged. "You'd think there was a bomb on the train the way they're searching everything."

His hoarse voice carried and several passengers turned to look in his direction.

"Shut up,". Ozaki ground out.

But Fujio, leering, seemed to find the speculation amusing. "You don't believe all that about a routine baggage check, do you?"

"That's enough, Fujio. You're just out to cause trouble."

The prisoner slumped back into the corner, the ghost of a smile lingering. Causing trouble was the one thing he was good at and, in between spells as a labourer, he'd dabbled in petty crime. Both activities had conspired to get him into the mess he was in today.

Four months earlier, while working on the Ocean Expo construction site in Tokyo, Fujio had stolen twenty sticks of blasting gelignite, intending to sell them to one of his underworld contacts. The deal didn't work out, which left him broke as usual, and with a quantity of high explosives stashed away that nobody seemed anxious to buy.

He was having a drink in a bar in a slum area of the city, when he happened to meet a student, a young political extremist named Koga. Fujio mentioned the gelignite, and Koga said he knew someone who might be interested. The next night he showed up with two other men, a middle-aged man called Okita who seemed to be the leader, and a younger man who spent most of his time chatting with the barmaid. Soon the money and the gelignite changed hands, much to Fujio's relief. He didn't ask or want to know why the three needed high explosives. The less he knew about it, the better.

In the months that followed Fujio had heard stray rumours on the grapevine, mainly to do with forged travel documents, but he hadn't been able to piece them together. He hadn't been all that interested until this morning at the station, when he'd seen one of the men—the fellow with short spiky hair who'd fancied his chances with the barmaid—disguised in the overalls of a cleaner. It was then that Fujio began to understand. The pieces slotted into place, finally making sense. A chilling and horrific kind of sense.

ALONE IN THE CAB of the Hikari 109, Motorman Aoki listened tensely to the operations chief over the radio-telephone. "We've just received word from the authorities in Hokkaido. The freight train exploded as the caller said it would. Whoever this man is, he's proved his ability to construct and plant such a device."

"But how? Linked to the running gear?"

"We don't know yet," Hiroshi admitted.

Sweat trickled down Aoki's back. This one was for real. Their only hope had exploded with the freight train.

"Has your train been searched?" Hiroshi asked.

"The head guard and his staff are still at it. They haven't found anything so far."

"I've set up a special team to handle this," Hiroshi said. "My deputy, Sunaga, is in charge. Whoever this man is, whatever the group he belongs to, he's got to come back with a demand of some kind—then we'll know how to deal with it and with the threat."

The motorman let go a breath he hadn't realized he'd been holding. "I understand, sir."

Part Two: *Ransom*

11:00—FREIGHT YARD—HOKKAIDO

Less than twenty minutes had elapsed since the explosion of the freight train, and already the police and railway authorities had mounted two priority investigations. A team of forensic experts was on its way to the scene of devastation, hoping to find remnants of the bomb and its triggering mechanism in the scattered wreckage. Meanwhile, a squad of detectives and technical experts was combing the Hokkaido Freight Yard where the train had been berthed overnight. In groups of two and three they raked over every inch of ground, especially along the road outside the perimeter fence, the likeliest point of entry. It would have been fairly easy for someone to scale the fence at night and install the device, hidden by the massed ranks of freight cars. On impulse, one of the detectives crossed the road and looked inside a telephone booth. It failed to yield any clues. Then he noticed a dried-up drainage ditch adjacent to the road, and reluctantly began picking through the scraps of paper and bits of broken glass. Something caught his eye.

"Come and take a look at this," he called out to one of his colleagues working along the fence.

The man crossed the road to join him. Taking a pair of tweezers from the leather bag on his shoulder he plucked the crumpled cigarette packet from the ditch and held it up. "Looks pretty recent," he said.

"Any chance of prints?" the detective asked.

"Could be." The man shook open a small plastic bag and dropped the cigarette packet inside. "I'll take it back to the car and run a preliminary test."

"You never know," the detective said, "might be something," though he didn't sound too hopeful. "If you do get anything positive, have headquarters run it through the computer. The prints might just match some in Central Records."

11:15—CTC OPERATIONS—TOKYO CENTRAL

It was a fine irony, Hiroshi thought, to command the most advanced communications and data processing hardware in the world, and yet for all that be powerless to act.

"Why doesn't he call? It's nearly an hour. What's he waiting for?" he said to his deputy, Sunaga, who stood next to him.

"Perhaps he wants to be sure about the freight train explosion. There's no point in making his demand until we're convinced the threat is real."

"I'm convinced," Hiroshi said with a gesture of impatience. "Has Takada figured out how the bomb was planted on the express?" Takada was the chief engineer of the Bullet Trains.

"No, and I don't think he will," the deputy said frankly. "Let's face it, he's an engineer, not an expert in high explosives."

"You're right," Hiroshi said. "We need a bomb disposal expert. Call the Ministry of Defence and ask for their assistance, but for God's sake don't say why we need it."

The telephone rang and the operations chief snatched it up. The set of his shoulders relaxed as he spoke with somebody in the meteorology department. Earthquakes were always a menace in Japan, and seismographs monitored each section of the line. If a tremor above a certain strength was detected, the power supply cut off automatically, bringing the trains in that section to a halt. Luckily no tremors were predicted for the next twenty-four hours.

When he had finished the call, Hiroshi turned and gazed down at the main display board. He calculated that Hikari 109 had 626 miles of track left, which at 63 miles per hour meant that there were almost exactly ten hours remaining.

11:25—HIKARI 109—KAKEGAWA

Having drawn a blank on the first search, the head guard instructed his staff to carry out a second. Meanwhile Uchida, the assistant motorman, was investigating areas of restricted access. In Coach 7 he was peering into a circuit box when a passenger emerged from the lavatory and glanced inquisitively over his shoulder.

"What's wrong, some kind of technical trouble?" Minami asked. Even now he held tightly to his pigskin attaché case.

"No, nothing to worry about," Uchida said shortly.

But Minami persisted. "Is it anything to do with the fact that we've slowed down?" He held out his gold Seiko watch. "We're running twenty minutes late."

Uchida quickly closed the circuit box and said, "There's been a slight delay, but it's nothing to worry about." Then he set off back to the driving cab.

Minami, annoyed, watched him go and then moved to the window. They weren't doing above seventy, he estimated. At this rate he would be an hour late for his appointment. Why did this have to happen today of all days?

In Coach 10, other passengers were expressing their annoyance, and Kenichi, the guard, was struggling to preserve a measure of authority as a woman acidly demanded to be told why the luggage was being checked again. "Well, you see—" Kenichi began, and then ran out of inspiration.

"Yes, what's going on, anyway?" asked a man across the aisle.

Everyone was looking at Kenichi, who gazed hesitantly from one to the other through his rimless spectacles. "Yes, well, you see, it's to make sure—" he floundered unhappily on "—that no one is carrying anything dangerous."

"Dangerous?" somebody echoed. "Like what?"

Before he could reply the man across the aisle said to his companion, "We had baggage checks like this when I travelled on the Hikari last November. Some crank had phoned in a bomb threat and they had to stop the train and search everything."

"Is that it?" the woman asked. "A bomb threat?"

Her voice acted like a spark, igniting a dozen others, questioning, demanding: "If there's been a bomb threat, you should stop the train at once!" "Are your damn schedules more important than passengers' lives?"

Kenichi retreated ineffectually, utterly at a loss.

In Coach 2 of the unreserved section at the front of the train, Yoko, the stewardess, was putting on a brave face, laughing and joking with a party of schoolchildren on their way to Lake Biwa for a camping holiday. She felt deceitful, pretending that everything was fine, yet it would have been irresponsible not to maintain the subterfuge. Besides, she had faith in the operations centre in Tokyo. The engineers and technical experts there were the finest in the world, so of course they would resolve the situation.

She had already checked Coaches 4 and 3, and now, waving goodbye to the children, Yoko moved into the leading coach, which accommodated the driving cab. She knew from the duty roster that Aoki was the motorman on this trip. With him rested the responsibility for everyone on board. How was he taking this? she wondered, feeling the desire to offer him a word of support. She liked Aoki and wished she could show him that he hadn't been forgotten by the rest of the crew. But she resisted the impulse to go into the cab. It was strictly against company regulations, so, with a slight, regretful shake of her head, she started down the aisle.

The controller in charge of Section 2 swivelled round in his chair and called out, "The head guard of Hikari 109 is calling, sir."

The murmur of voices in the operations room died away as Operations Chief Hiroshi, his face taut and pale, stepped up onto the central dais. An operator put the relay on public address and all eyes were raised to the speaker grille as Hiroshi said, "Go ahead, Yamada."

"I've no idea how it happened, sir, but some of the passengers seem to know we've received a bomb threat," Yamada reported. "They're demanding that the train be stopped and searched. Naturally I've done my best to reassure them, but . . ." he paused. "Perhaps it would be better to tell them the truth."

Hiroshi looked towards his deputy, who slowly shook his head. Sunaga was right, Hiroshi decided, they couldn't make an announcement just yet. Not until they'd located the bomb and had deactivated it. "No, Yamada," he said. "We can't risk a panic. You'll have to do everything you can to contain the situation."

"For how long? Can you give me some idea?"

Suddenly the controller in Section 2 rose to his feet, both hands pressed to his headphones. "Chief, urgent message from Hamamatsu! There's a breakdown on the main Hakata line!"

On the illuminated grid the red light flashed on below the Hamamatsu station marker, indicating a stalled train . . . and Hikari 109 was only seven miles away. Hiroshi rapped out, "Yamada, there's a breakdown ahead of you. I'm clearing this channel." He stabbed a button on the communications console and said, "Get me the motorman on Hikari 109," and called out, "Engineering section, give me everything you have on the breakdown. Sunaga, stand by with readings from COMTRAC."

The operator said, "Motorman on the line, sir."

"Aoki, this is Hiroshi. There's a breakdown at Hamamatsu on the main line. Reduce speed to fifty-eight miles per hour."

"Understood. Reducing speed to fifty-eight." He sounded calm, and Hiroshi prayed that the motorman's nerves were as steady as his voice. "Chief, the ATC computes we have less than seven minutes to Hamamatsu. Can the track be cleared in time?"

"We're in touch with Hamamatsu now." Hiroshi signalled

impatiently to the engineer, who was speaking on the telephone. Come on, come on, Hiroshi thought, fretting away the seconds.

At last the engineer said, "The problem's in the heavy voltage transformer. It's going to take at least an hour to repair."

"Can they shunt the train off the main line quickly?"

The engineer shook his head. "It's a Kodama express. Fourteen coaches. Take them fifteen, twenty minutes."

Hiroshi fixed his eyes on the display board, swiftly reviewing alternative plans of action. "All right, everybody, stand by. We're switching the Hikari 109 to the up line at the Hamamatsu cross-over and then back again, bypassing the breakdown. Status report on the up line west of Hamamatsu."

The controller said, "Bullet Train Hikari 228 is on the up line, sir, travelling east."

Damn it! Hiroshi thought, and looked towards Sunaga, hunched over the display screen. "Give me the computer update on both trains. Distances and times of arrival at the cross-over."

"Hikari 109, travelling west, is five-point-six miles from Hamamatsu and will arrive in five minutes twenty-two seconds. Hikari 228 is eleven miles away and will arrive in precisely five minutes."

The deputy's face was bleak. There was no time to clear the up line of the oncoming train. And it would reach the Hamamatsu cross-over just twenty-two seconds ahead of the Hikari 109. If they switched the Hikari 109 to the up line and the other train hadn't cleared the points, there would be a collision. Yet if they didn't make the switch, Sunaga thought grimly, the Bullet Train would remain on the down line and run into the rear of the breakdown.

Hiroshi was again studying the display board. Two trains, travelling in opposite directions at a combined speed of nearly 200 miles per hour, crossing each other with only seconds to spare. Was it possible? It had to be. He came to a decision. "Tell the junction controller at Hamamatsu that we'll coordinate the switch-over from here and that he's to wait for the instruction."

Then he spoke into the microphone. "Aoki, listen carefully. We can't clear the breakdown off the main line in time so we're transferring you briefly onto the up line at Hamamatsu. But there's an express on that line, due to arrive there at almost the same moment. To give the express time to get past first, you must reduce your speed still further."

"We're running at fifty-eight miles per hour now, Chief. That's a fine margin if we're going to stay above fifty."

"I know, Aoki, I know," Hiroshi said. "But bring it down as low as you can. We need to gain every second before you reach the junction." Reducing the speed of a 432-ton Bullet Train by an exact amount was by no means easy, he knew. It was nearly impossible for the motorman accurately to gauge how much braking pressure to apply to achieve a certain speed: normally an odd mile-per-hour didn't matter; now it was crucial.

"I'll do my best, Chief," Aoki said, and for the first time his voice betrayed a slight tremor. "Commencing to brake."

Everyone in the operations room watched the main display board as the two orange bars drew steadily closer to the flashing red light at Hamamatsu. They waited, hardly daring to breathe.

For the motorman the world had narrowed to the speedometer dial on the panel in front of him, with its slender red needle. Gripping the brake lever, Aoki eased it forward, his whole being focused on this one simple task. The red needle flickered and began to fall. That's right, nice and easy, Aoki encouraged it, watching the needle dip past 57 . . . 56 . . . 55. . . .

Better ease off. Hold it at 54. Can't risk anything lower. But then he saw that the needle was still falling. He couldn't stop it. Despite his efforts it was creeping lower . . . 53 . . . 52. . . .

Tightening his grip, he closed his eyes and counted to five. When he looked again, the needle was dead against fifty-two miles per hour and it was steady. He wiped the sweat from his forehead before reporting, "Fifty-two miles per hour and holding."

Hiroshi's voice, calm as ever, came over the handset. "Maintain that speed for two minutes fifteen seconds. Then take it up to seventy-five. When we switch you to the up line you're going to have to disconnect the ATC system. Otherwise it will register the cross-over and cut out all your electrical circuits. Are you with me?"

Aoki looked across at his assistant, Uchida. Disconnecting the ATC would automatically bring in the emergency braking, a fail-safe device in case the ATC malfunctioned. The motorman said, "What happens when the emergency braking comes on?"

"That's why you will have to bring your speed up to seventy-five," Hiroshi explained. "You'll need the momentum to overcome the emergency braking and get you through the junction. Once you're on the up line you'll reconnect the ATC and the braking will be automatically switched off. Is that clear?"

"Yes, understood," Aoki said. He reviewed the coming sequence of events. Something shrilled like an alarm bell in his mind. "Chief, the speed limit for the Hamamatsu cross-over junction is sixty-four miles per hour. If we go through at seventy-five we'll derail!"

"There's no other way. We've got to take that chance."

On the main display board in the operations room Hiroshi saw that the Hikari 228 was one and a half miles from the junction, the Hikari 109 just over two miles away. The two bars of orange light were closing rapidly. Everything now depended on pin-point coordination. . . . Hiroshi raised the microphone to his lips. "Aoki, take her up to seventy-five—now!"

Over the speaker came a report from Hamamatsu signal box: "We have a sighting. The Hikari 228 is approaching the junction. The Hikari 109 is 950 yards away."

"Prepare to disconnect the ATC," Hiroshi instructed Aoki. "Ten seconds and counting—nine—eight—seven . . ."

In the cab Uchida's hand hovered over the bar switch.

". . . three—two—one—*cut out!*"

Uchida slammed the switch into the off position. Immediately the fail-safe circuits came into operation, and there was the high-pitched metallic screech of brakes. The train's speed dropped. Would they clear the junction and have time to re-connect the ATC before it fell below fifty?

Aoki and Uchida could see the Hikari 228 on the other track racing towards them at top speed. It reached the cross-over when they were still two hundred yards away and Aoki snatched a look at the speedometer. Sixty-eight miles per hour and falling rapidly. . . .

On the main display board the two orange bars converged. Hiroshi's face was like stone as he waited for the Hamamatsu signal box to confirm that the up line was clear. At last the message came—"Hikari 228 has passed the junction"—and at once he rapped out, "Change the points!"

An audible gasp went round the operations room as the orange bar marked 109 suddenly reappeared on the up line. Hiroshi closed his eyes in thankful prayer. They were through. They'd made it.

"Aoki, now reconnect the ATC," Hiroshi said urgently.

The red needle was still falling . . . 55 . . . 54 . . . 53 . . . Leaning over the ATC panel in the driving cab, the motorman hit the bar switch. At once he felt the train surge forward as the emergency brakes were released; then they were picking up speed and leaving Hamamatsu behind for the open countryside.

Aoki leaned back in his padded chair, his hands trembling, and spoke into the handset. "We're on the up line, Chief. Speed fifty-nine and increasing. Shall I hold it at sixty-three?"

"Yes," Hiroshi said. "We'll switch you back onto the down line at Toyohashi. And well done, both of you."

12:05—EXPRESSWAY NO. 7—TOKYO

Sirens blaring and blue lights flashing, a police motorcycle escort cleared the fast lane of the westbound expressway for the grey Chevrolet with the US army plates. Minutes later they were in the centre of the city. Ignoring stop lights, they turned into the approach to Tokyo Central and swept up to a red-brick building north of the station.

In the back seat of the Chevrolet, Major Matthew Brennan, bomb disposal specialist of the US Army 14th Ordnance Group based at Toride, was wondering how a peaceful Thursday morning had happened to self-destruct in his face. It was breaking every statute in the State Department's book for the 14th Group to get embroiled in matters of Japan's internal security. Yet, not twenty minutes ago, his commanding officer had said amiably, "We're not really getting involved, Matt. National Railways want somebody to advise them, that's all. Sorry to lay this on you, but do what you can."

Which naturally he would, Matt thought, hanging onto the strap as his driver brought the car to an abrupt halt. But he still didn't like this sort of back-door consultation.

As he stepped out of the car two uniformed railway policemen saluted smartly and led the way into the building. Once in the lift, Matt was uncomfortably aware that his six-foot-three, fourteen-stone frame seemed to take up all the available space. Self-consciously he stared straight ahead until the door slid open.

The two policemen set off briskly along a corridor and held open a pair of double doors. Matt found himself in a large circular control room, permeated by an air of tension that he instantly detected, like an old familiar scent.

"Major Brennan?"

Matt shook the leathery hand of a short, thick-set man with a lined, weatherbeaten face. "I'm Sunaga, Deputy Operations Chief." The man hesitated, then asked, "You do speak Japanese?"

At his nod Sunaga's stern expression softened and he smiled briefly. "Thank you for coming. What have you been told?"

"That you need technical advice, nothing more."

"I see." Sunaga met the big American's look squarely. "We've received a bomb threat on one of our Super Express Bullet Trains. The criminals haven't made their demands known, but they soon will. We need you to advise us on where the device might be located and how to deactivate it."

"I'll do whatever I can," Matt said. He was thinking uneasily about Laura on the ten o'clock Hikari express. Resolutely he pushed the thought to the back of his mind. "Will you brief me on the situation?"

Turning to a pair of double doors, Sunaga ushered Matt through. "We've had to call a press conference," he said, "which the operations chief is now holding downstairs. Rumours have begun to circulate, Major, and we'd rather give an official version than have ill-founded speculation. It'll save time if you sit in on it."

On the floor below, crammed into what was normally an open-plan office, were reporters from every national newspaper and magazine, and all the major news bureaus, plus television and radio people. Sunaga found a quiet corner, from where he and Major Brennan could observe without attracting attention.

At the far end of the room, in the glare of television arc lights, Hiroshi stood facing a battery of microphones and cameras. The official statement prepared by the railway's public relations department was now concluded, and he looked up guardedly, steeling himself for a tough grilling session. And something else was bothering him. Once the news was broadcast, passengers on the train would be sure to pick it up on their transistor radios. Could he reasonably ask for a temporary news blackout? It wasn't asking a lot, in view of the panic it might avert, but perhaps, knowing the media as he did, it was a vain and rather naïve hope.

Questions were now coming from all parts of the room and Hiroshi nodded to a young TV reporter at the front of the throng.

"Can you give us details of the Hikari's revised schedule? What time will it arrive in Hakata?"

"It was due to arrive at 5:00 p.m., but as the train is now running at sixty-three miles per hour it will reach Hakata at about 9:30."

"How many people are there on the train?"

"There are 1,473 passengers and 19 crew—motormen, guards, a stewardess, catering staff—a total of 1,492 people altogether."

A man from *Time* magazine raised his hand. "Are there any Americans on the train? Europeans?"

"Almost certainly, yes," Hiroshi replied. "But as there isn't a passenger list on the Bullet Trains I can't be more specific."

"Do the passengers know about the bomb threat?" asked one of the senior reporters with the *Tokyo Shimbun Daily*.

Hiroshi shook his head. "In view of the distress it might cause we've decided not to tell them. For that reason I am appealing to the radio people here not to broadcast the news for the time being."

There were groans of dismay. "You mean getting blown up in ignorance is preferable to being forewarned?" a radio reporter suggested sarcastically. "You can't expect us to keep quiet when the story will be broadcast over television!"

Hiroshi bit back his anger, saying nothing, as a woman reporter from the back of the crowd asked, "Why can't the train be stopped and searched? That's the usual procedure, isn't it?"

Hiroshi nodded. "Yes, it is, but according to our information this particular device is linked to the running gear—and we don't want to halt the train until we're absolutely sure how the device operates. Our engineers are working on that problem now."

"And what happens if they haven't solved it by the time the train gets to Hakata and has to stop?"

This was the question Hiroshi had been dreading, but he answered levelly, "By then the bomb will have been disarmed and there will be no danger, none at all."

"How can you be so sure?"

"The bomb will have been disarmed," Hiroshi repeated stolidly, but it was an assurance that clearly didn't satisfy them, for there was a flurry of questions.

He held up his hand for silence. "As operations chief the responsibility for the safety of the Hikari 109 and everyone on board lies solely with me," he stated quietly. "Here and now I am prepared to stake my career on the Bullet Train's safe arrival in Hakata without a single passenger being killed." The room was hushed, all eyes riveted on the figure in the concentrated glare of light. "That is my pledge to you, to the people on the train and to their friends and relatives."

Above the heads of the reporters Hiroshi caught a glimpse of a tall American officer standing discreetly to one side with his deputy, Sunaga. Impatient now to get away, he nodded to the PR man and said, "That's it, ladies and gentlemen."

As reporters and TV crews began to stream out, Hiroshi headed for Sunaga. His deputy introduced him to the major, and Hiroshi said, "We appreciate your help, Major Brennan. God knows we need it." He led the way upstairs, saying over his shoulder, "I take it you heard enough to know what all this is about?"

The American said: "The Hikari 109. It left Tokyo Central at ten o'clock this morning. Is that correct?"

There was a hoarse edge to his voice, that made both Hiroshi and his deputy stop and stare at him. Finally Hiroshi said, "Yes, the Hikari 109. . . . And we're going to save that train and its passengers—every last one of them."

"I hope to God you're right," Matt said, his throat working. "Because one of them is my wife."

POLICE CHIEF MAKOTO pressed the record tab on the cassette recorder, and nodded sharply to his aide, Senda, who sat before a red telephone across the room.

The aide, a young officer of Railway Police, spoke softly into his receiver. "Our man is on line three. Trace the call."

Makoto now answered his own telephone. "Shinkansen operations centre. Police Chief Makoto speaking."

"Listen and don't interrupt," the caller said tonelessly. "You're taping this, so I won't waste time repeating it. By now the freight train will have exploded and you know my threat is real. In exchange for information about defusing the bomb on the

Hikari 109 I want five—repeat *five*—million American dollars. I want it in one-hundred-dollar bills. I will tell you how and when—"

"Five million!" Makoto protested. "Impossible . . ."

"You have no choice," the man said remorselessly. "Either you pay or every man, woman and child on the Bullet Train is finished. One hour from now I will give you instructions on how, when and where the money is to be delivered. By then I expect you to have the money ready. Wait for my call."

"All right, yes," Makoto said hurriedly, wondering frantically how to keep the caller on the line while the trace was made. "Now wait, listen . . . what about the bomb?"

"Don't take me for a fool, Makoto. You're trying to gain time. You'll hear from me in one hour."

The line went dead. Makoto hung up and stared across at Senda without really seeing him.

The aide put down the red phone and shook his head. "No good. He rang off before they could finish the trace."

12:30—CTC Operations—Tokyo Central

As deputy operations chief it was Sunaga's task to coordinate the activities of the engineers, technical experts, and investigation teams which were being brought in to help avert the threatened disaster. What now compounded his anxiety was the fact that the Tokyo Police Special Investigation Squad had been called in to spearhead the hunt for the criminals. Its head was Superintendent Hanamura, a balding man with a reputation for ruthlessness. Without question he would take a hard line, which was why Hiroshi had asked his deputy to sit in on the preliminary briefing session with their own incompetent but harmless police chief. Hiroshi's priority was the safety of the passengers on the train. Hanamura's would almost certainly be the capture of the terrorists.

An office opening off the central area had been hastily transformed into an investigation centre for Superintendent Hanamura and his squad. It was equipped with a hotline to Tokyo police headquarters, a row of telephones manned by two specialist operators, and a television monitor showing the progress of the Hikari 109 on the main display board. Now an acrimonious debate was in progress between Superintendent Hanamura and the railway police chief, Makoto. At issue was whether the criminals intended to leave the country.

Superintendent Hanamura remained offensively bland, his dead-fish stare seeming to go right through the railway police chief without seeing him. "Five million American dollars is not much use to them in Japan. Not unless they intend to go into the paper reclamation business," he added dryly.

At that moment another member of the police squad, Lieutenant Tashiro, burst into the office.

"Central Records have identified the man involved in the freight train explosion," he announced elatedly, brandishing a torn-off teleprinter slip to which was attached a small photograph. "They traced the prints from a cigarette packet found near the Hokkaido Freight Yard. Luckily the man has a record."

"Let me see." There was no trace of excitement in Hanamura's voice as he began to read aloud: "'Masaru Koga. Born 22 October 1958, Sapporo, Hokkaido. Ex-leader of left-wing student movement at Jonan University. Arrested May 1977 for attacking a police officer during a riot. Two-year suspended sentence. Expelled from university in June 1977. No record of criminal or political activity since that time. Last recorded address (September 1977): Apartment 12a, Akane-so, Toshima District, Tokyo.'"

Hanamura displayed the photograph, a police mug shot of a sneering youth with wild staring eyes in a pock-marked face, and lank, greasy hair. "Tell Central Records we need twenty glossy prints of this," Hanamura said to one of his operators, who immediately picked up a phone. Then he addressed a young policeman, Sergeant Goto. "Put out an all-points alert for the arrest of Koga. I want him brought in for questioning."

"One moment, Superintendent," Deputy Sunaga said quietly. "If Koga is our man and we arrest him, suppose he refuses to tell us anything? Isn't our first priority to get information on the bomb —and then make an arrest?"

"Has it occurred to you," Hanamura said acidly, "that there is nothing whatever to stop Koga and his associates from collecting the ransom and then refusing to say where the bomb is located?"

Sunaga nodded. Both he and Hiroshi had considered the possibility. But above everything they feared precipitate action from Hanamura's Special Investigation Squad.

"I agree, Superintendent," Sunaga said, "there's a risk either way." His eyes locked onto Hanamura's flat stare. "But the safety of the passengers comes first, and if we antagonize Koga or any of his associates they might decide not to give us the information we need. And that is one risk we are not prepared to take."

Hanamura clicked his tongue, as if debating something, then nodded reluctantly. "Very well, we'll postpone any arrests for now. But," he warned, "our investigations will continue."

When Sunaga had gone, the superintendent turned to Sergeant Goto. "What are you waiting for? I told you to put out an all-points alert for Masaru Koga." He gestured brusquely to Lieutenant Tashiro. "Contact the Sapporo Police Department. Koga was born in that city and he might have relations or friends there who are sheltering him. Get to it."

"Very good, sir."

Superintendent Hanamura turned to the television monitor, which showed the orange blip of the Hikari 109 approaching its first scheduled stop at Nagoya, and studied the screen. He totally ignored Railway Police Chief Makoto, who was gazing at him, appalled.

13:07—HANEDA AIRPORT—TOKYO

Carrying a scuffed canvas holdall, Koga stepped off JAL Flight 504 from Sapporo, and joined the line of passengers heading for the Tokyo reception area. To the casual observer the thin, long-haired youth wearing a creased leather jacket was in no way remarkable. But behind the wrap-around dark glasses which completely hid his eyes he was keenly surveying the crowds of people. Koga felt a pitying scorn for them, and for all humanity. They were as indistinguishable from each other as so many ants on a dung hill. He alone was unique, separate, an individual with the willpower and intelligence to forge his own destiny.

Koga spotted the man from halfway across the arrivals lounge. He was standing nonchalantly by the barrier, studying the faces of the passengers as they filed through. Although dressed in a dark business suit, he plainly had Police stamped all over him.

As Koga moved closer to the barrier, he speculated. Was this a routine check or were the police investigating all arrivals from Hokkaido following the freight train explosion? He couldn't risk being picked out, not with his record. He had just ten seconds to think of something.

The family in front of him was about to pass through—the father and mother, and a little girl of about eight holding a large teddy bear. A long blue ribbon was tied round its neck trailing to the ground. As they moved forward Koga put out his foot and trapped the ribbon under his shoe. The girl, tightly clutching the toy, was jerked backwards and lost her balance. She fell down and burst into tears. The policeman, himself a family man, bent down to hoist the little girl to her feet, and in three paces Koga was past him and through the barrier, heading for the exit.

Then the automatic doors sighed open and he was through.

13:13—HIKARI 109—NAGOYA

The Bullet Train was now leaving the lush countryside and approaching the first scheduled stop at Nagoya, a port city at the apex of Ise Bay. Already the train was running an hour late—it should have reached Nagoya at 12:15—and passengers were grumbling at this delay on a line famous for its punctuality. Many of them wondered why there hadn't been the usual announcement advising them to get their belongings together.

Keiko began to get ready anyway. She was relieved to be almost home, but she felt a deep pang of shame at having deserted her husband. At the thought of Abiko alone in their tiny flat, she had to fight back her tears. She picked up her small suitcase and made her way carefully to the platform at the end of the coach.

The Bullet Train was rounding the final curve on its approach to the station. Normally the train would have slowed here, but today it kept on going. What on earth was happening? Suddenly the head guard announced over the speaker that the Hikari 109 would not be stopping at Nagoya.

Just that, nothing more. Not a word of explanation.

For a moment the people near Keiko simply stared at one another, dumbfounded. Then there was a chorus of dismay, mingled with angry shouts and muttered oaths. The noise seemed to swell inside Keiko's head until it blotted out everything else, and a spasm of pain shot through her belly like the twist of a knife. She swayed backwards, feeling the world slide away.

A soldier caught her just in time. Supporting her dead weight, he looked round for help. Another man sprang forward and the two of them manoeuvred the semi-conscious girl back along the aisle to a seat which a woman had hurriedly vacated. Keiko lay back, moaning, beads of sweat standing out on her forehead. Then she gasped with relief as the pain subsided, leaving her weak and shaking, holding her stomach with both hands.

The woman leaned over her. "My God. She's started. She's in labour." She looked at the soldier. "What can we do?"

He stood indecisively for a moment. "We'll get her to the guards' compartment," he said. "Will somebody give me a hand?"

The man came to his aid again and with difficulty they carried the girl down the aisle. She was barely conscious, adrift in a sea of pain, lost, alone.

IN COACH 12 the guards' compartment was under seige. Irate passengers were at the narrow doorway demanding to know why the train wasn't stopping as scheduled. Holding up both hands placatingly, Yamada, the head guard, tried to explain that it was due to a technical fault which would soon be rectified. His explanation didn't have the desired effect, and one man in particular became openly belligerent.

"I *have* to get off here," he shouted. "That's the emergency brake," he went on, pointing past the head guard's shoulder. "You can stop the train from here. Go on, man, operate it!"

Yamada backed away, shielding the emergency brake lever, a red stirrup handle in a chrome casing. It was secured in the OFF position by a brass pin which could be easily removed.

"If you won't, I damn well will!" the man said, pushing the head guard aside and fumbling with the brass pin.

Yamada blanched. A single downward jerk of the handle would bring every brake on the sixteen coaches into operation. He hardly had time to yell, "Don't!" before there was a wail of frustration from the corridor.

"It's too late! We're going through the station . . . ."

FROM HER SEAT in Coach 7 Laura had watched the passengers standing in the aisle, still holding their suitcases, as the express moved on through Nagoya Station. Some were angry, others obviously at a loss as to what to do next. But what amazed her was the extraordinary behaviour of some of the businessmen. The normally polite, deferential executives made a mad scramble for the coach's public telephone. In the melee that developed, Laura glimpsed Minami clutching his precious pigskin attaché case and shouting at the man who was on the phone.

Even now Minami could hardly believe that Nagoya was behind them. The next stop, Kyoto, was almost a hundred miles away. He would be late for his appointment. He must get in touch with his client and somehow convince him that the delay was unavoidable. But how could he do that with this oaf hogging the phone?

It was too much. Lunging for the receiver, Minami attempted to wrest it from the man's grasp. But all at once he found himself in the middle of a heaving, struggling mass of bodies. A fist hit him in the back, another blow dislodged his spectacles. He fell to his knees, searching desperately for his glasses, which were somewhere on the floor among the shuffling feet.

Watching from the far end of the coach, Duty Policeman Nagata swallowed nervously. Beside him, Yoko, the stewardess, was frowning. "Shouldn't you do something? Somebody's going to get hurt."

Nagata shrank away. "Too late," he mumbled abjectly. "Never stop them now. Only thing is to tell them the truth."

"Tell them!" Yoko said, alarmed. "Don't be a fool."

But Nagata was edging backwards towards the door of the coach. He mouthed at her, "Leave it to me. I'll sort it out," and before Yoko could object he had scurried away.

Moving swiftly along, Nagata comforted himself that this was the only sensible course of action. After all, didn't the passengers have a right to know? He hurried on through the next coach, too preoccupied to notice the pop star, Tee Togo, slumped in his customary position, listening on earphones to his transistor radio.

To Tee Togo's annoyance a new Neil Diamond chart entry had been interrupted by a newsflash. But now he was listening raptly, as he heard words that his brain had trouble in understanding.

"Bullet train . . . bomb threat . . . left Tokyo at ten o'clock this morning . . . not been able to locate . . . ."

Togo shut his eyes, blocking out reality. This wasn't really happening, not to him.

Moments later a voice came over the speakers throughout the train.

"Attention everybody! This is the duty policeman speaking. We weren't able to stop at Nagoya because a bomb has been planted on the train which will detonate if our speed falls below fifty miles per hour. The bombers have demanded a ransom and once this has been paid we shall receive instructions on how to disarm the bomb. In the meantime would everyone please return to their seats and stay there. There is no cause for alarm. Everything is under control. I repeat—everything is under control."

Most of the passengers in Coach 14 reacted to the announcement with stunned shock; indeed there was almost total silence until a middle-aged woman two seats behind Detective-Sergeant Ozaki started screaming. Ozaki could not stand it. Unlocking the handcuff from his own wrist, he fastened it instead to the central seat support. He went to the woman and shook her roughly, stopping her in mid-scream. When he returned to his seat, he noticed his prisoner was sweating heavily.

"What's the matter, Fujio? Scared?" Ozaki's tone was lightly mocking. It amused him to see Fujio's brutal, bullying façade begin to crumble at the first sign of pressure.

Fujio stared out at the passing countryside. If he could only get free . . . then maybe he would have a chance. He tried to shift his position but his movement was restricted by the handcuff holding him to the seat support. Then the dim light of inspiration flickered in his eyes. Maybe there was a way after all.

". . . . AN EMERGENCY CASE—if there's a doctor on board would he please come to the guards' compartment in Coach 12—This is extremely urgent. Thank you."

Listening to the speaker announcement, Mickie wondered whether to offer her assistance. Her present "occupation" had come about as a direct result of her nursing career. Having answered an advertisement for a private nurse to look after the aging president of the Kyoto Electronics Corporation, she had quickly found that Takazana's needs were not medical at all. Within a month he'd made her a business proposition impossible to refuse. He'd had legal documents drawn up to guarantee her a rosy financial future providing she remained with him till his death.

Thus the present circumstances struck her as being rather ironic. It was conceivable that neither she nor Takazana would live to see the end of the day.

The old man hadn't so far uttered a word. He was gazing into space, the prominent bones of his small head clearly outlined under the covering of dry, flaking skin.

Now he stirred. "We're all going to die," he said, speaking rapidly. "I must get off. There must be a way. I know the president of the Railway Board personally. Get a message to him right away. He'll arrange something. Something. A helicopter. Yes, that's it. They can fly a helicopter above the train and take me off. I must get off. I must—"

The words slurred together as the thoughts whirled faster and faster inside his head. He had wealth and power and influence. He would use it all to be released from this doomed train.

Under the pale mask of make-up, Mickie's face was still and watchful. "What about me?"

"Must get off," the old man repeated mindlessly. "Must—"

"Don't you care what happens to me?" Mickie said, stridently.

Takazana hadn't heard. He was staring into space again.

INSIDE THE guards' compartment, the young guard, Ando, knelt at the trestle bed gazing helplessly at the young woman. He had been instructed to look after Keiko and to see that she was comfortable, but other than offering her a glass of water, he was without inspiration. As he wondered despairingly just what he was supposed to do, there was a tap at the door and a slim, dark-haired woman entered the small compartment.

"Doctor—you need doctor?" Laura's Japanese was bad but the young guard understood. He nodded vigorously, his eyes showing heartfelt relief.

Laura leaned over the girl. Obstetrics wasn't even remotely in her line of work and it had been twelve—thirteen?—years since she'd assisted with a delivery. However, it didn't require an expert to see that the girl was in the first stage of labour. Pulse rate 97. Temperature slightly above normal. Contractions every two-and-a-half to three minutes. Delivery might take place at any time within the next two to eight hours.

Laura turned to the young guard.

"Do you speak English?" she enunciated very slowly.

Ando smiled at her, moon-faced, and raised his eyebrows. Laura looked around the compartment with its single narrow window. This was going to be difficult. With nothing but the most basic amenities, they were going to have to deliver this woman's child. She considered for a moment, and then delved into her handbag for a small loose-leaf notebook. On separate pages she sketched the items she required: Scissors. Napkins or tablecloths. Length of string. Soap and hot water. Towels. Bucket.

She needed disinfectant too but couldn't think how to communicate this with a sketch. Of course—a First Aid box—there was sure to be one on the train. She drew a box with a cross on it, and Ando pointed eagerly to a small cabinet on the wall behind the door. Thank God for that. At least it was a start.

The young guard took the sketches and went to the door, happy now to have something to do. But Laura held up her hand. "One more thing." She tipped her head back and drank from an imaginary bottle. "Brandy. Cognac. Yes?"

He repeated, "Brandy," nodded several times, and went out.

Laura took a deep, steadying breath. Clearing her mind of all distractions, she turned her attention to the woman on the bed.

13:28—CTC OPERATIONS—TOKYO CENTRAL

Hiroshi poured coffee into three plastic cups and handed them around. Matt Brennan was leaning over the desk to study the blueprints and technical specifications that Chief Engineer Takada had laid before him. They included every detail of Hikari 109's electrical systems and running gear. Matt had been staring at them for over half an hour, trying to concentrate while stray thoughts of his wife badgered him. Laura's face hovered in his mind, and he could even smell her perfume.

He straightened up, and with an effort of will shut away the image of his wife. He turned to the chief engineer. "Tell me again about the power units. Are the motors all linked to the same electrical system?"

"That is correct."

Takada was helpful but Matt sensed a certain reserve. Did he feel his territory was being encroached upon by outsiders? No matter. There wasn't time to fret about such things.

"And they can only be operated from the driving cab?"

"Yes."

"The motorman checked all systems and could find no malfunction?" Matt asked the operations chief. It was ground already covered, but he had to be sure. When Hiroshi nodded he said, "What about all the circuits that control the running gear?"

"The assistant motorman checked those and found nothing."

"So we *have* to assume that the link with the bomb was made somewhere here—" with his finger Matt traced the running gear beneath the coach. "Does that make sense?" he asked Takada.

The chief engineer shrugged. "I'm not a bomb disposal expert. I wouldn't know."

"We're not discussing bombs at the moment," Matt said with a flash of irritation. "The main problem is to find out how the device is triggered by the train's speed, and where. Once we know that, it can be disarmed, by breaking that connection. The bomb itself is secondary." He stabbed his finger at the blueprint. "That's the area to concentrate on."

"So," Hiroshi interjected, "it *has* to be connected to the wheels in some way, is that right?"

"Yes," said Matt. "And the equipment they used must be pretty sophisticated. We're not dealing with amateurs." He sipped his coffee pensively, looking down into the operations room, at the lights on the display board. The Hikari 109 was midway between Nagoya and Kyoto, the next scheduled stop.

Takada said guardedly, "Now that the government has come up with the ransom money maybe all this is unnecessary. They get the money, we get the information."

"Providing they keep their word," Hiroshi said shortly.

"They will. They have to." But even as Takada said it Matt realized that it was by no means inevitable. They could take the five million dollars and vanish. Or it was even conceivable that there was no way of getting at the bomb to disarm it. That it had been planted without any provision for its deactivation.

There came a clatter of footsteps on the metal stairway and Senda, Police Chief Makoto's aide, entered with the preliminary report on the freight train explosion. He handed it to Hiroshi, who read it out. "'Minimum of four sticks of gelignite used. Attached to rear axle of the diesel locomotive and activated by an electromagnetic speedometer. The movement of the wheels produced a current which was fed to a detonator, set to respond at a given reading. In this case twelve miles per hour.' " He looked at Matt. "Any good?"

"Does it specify the type of speedometer?"

Hiroshi scanned the list of fragments itemized on the sheets. "It just says, 'Standard equipment, as fitted to Bullet Trains.'"

"Standard Bullet Train equipment?" Matt's eyes narrowed. He looked at Takada. "Who manufactures your speedometers?"

"We have different suppliers, but most of the existing ones were made here in Tokyo by the Okita Precision Tool Company— until they went out of business a couple of years ago."

"Could the criminals have got hold of a couple of them?"

After a moment's reflection Takada nodded. "I imagine there's surplus stock around. But don't ask me where."

"I suppose you realize what this means," Matt said gravely. "If the rear axle of the locomotive was used on the Hikari 109 also, we can't reach the device from inside the train. . . ."

Senda looked shocked. "But if we can't reach it . . ." His voice faded as he became aware of the terrible implications.

In the silence that followed Matt's eyes were thoughtful. He glanced at the operations chief. "Can you instruct the motorman to slow the train as much as possible—to, say, fifty-seven miles per hour?"

"Yes," Hiroshi answered at once. "What do you have in mind?"

"I'd like photographs, or better still movie film, of the underside of the train, taken from between the rails. It might be that we can spot something—loose wires, perhaps, a bulky object—attached to the running gear."

It was a chance in a million and they all knew it. But any action was preferable to the endless waiting. "I'll arrange it," Hiroshi said.

The phone rang and the room went very quiet as the husky voice of Police Chief Makoto came over the desk speaker. "It's on. We just had a call. He wants one man to take the money and drive west on Expressway No. 4. I've spoken with Superintendent Hanamura and we've decided to send Lieutenant Tashiro."

"Where's the rendezvous?"

"He didn't say. Just that the officer should drive west on

Expressway No. 4 and stop at the Esso petrol station opposite the Meiji Shrine Garden."

"What about the bomb?"

"He said we'll receive full instructions about how to handle it when he's collected the money and is sure nobody's tailing him."

Hiroshi put the phone down and looked at Matt across the desk. "Let's pray he's telling the truth."

"We've no choice, have we?" Matt said stonily.

Part Three: Double-Cross

13:55—OMIYA PARK—TOKYO

Lieutenant Tashiro held the aluminium attaché case on his knees with one hand while with the other he steered the small motorboat close to the left bank of the river. Dense vegetation grew down to the water's edge here, but up ahead the stream was hemmed in by sheer sandstone cliffs.

Tashiro had followed instructions to the letter. Taking Expressway No. 4, he had pulled in at the Esso station opposite the Meiji Shrine Garden. The attendant had informed him that a man had phoned not five minutes before to say that Tashiro should stop at road marker 419 about a quarter of a mile along the highway. There he would find a package. The detective did so and found a shortwave radio receiver, its tuner taped to a particular frequency. Switching it on he heard a man's voice tell him to drive to Omiya Park. There he was to hire a pleasure boat on the river and take it upstream, keeping close to the left bank.

Omiya Park, one of the largest in the Tokyo area, covered over seventy acres, most of which had been left in a natural state. Even in summer, it was possible to spend an entire day here and not meet more than half a dozen people.

The criminals had chosen the spot well, Tashiro thought as he steered the boat along the bank of the stream.

He had been instructed to take the radio receiver with him, and leave it switched on. Now, suddenly, it emitted a burst of static.

Then a voice—this time a different one, he was sure—said distinctly, "Twenty yards away on your left."

Tashiro could see nothing ahead but the sandstone cliffs rising to a height of sixty feet or so. Then, as the boat entered a shadowy gorge, he spotted a rope hanging down the cliff face almost to the water.

"Fasten the rope to the case," said the voice on the radio.

Tashiro grabbed for the rope. Struggling to keep the boat steady, he tied the rope securely through the handle. Almost immediately, as if everything he did was being observed, the case was hauled upwards.

In seconds it had vanished.

SATO SPAT his matchstick into the gorge and grinned as, with a final triumphant heave, he pulled the aluminium case up to the clifftop. His muscular body was bathed in perspiration, as much from nervous excitement as from physical exertion. All along he had been thinking how Charles Bronson would do it, and in his mind's eye had seen the whole thing framed in a camera lens. But hell, Bronson was only an actor—this was for real.

Unfastening the rope, Sato dropped the small radio transmitter into his pocket, hefted the case and turned away from the cliff to make his way down the hillside. He felt it was a stroke of genius on Okita's part to have chosen this location for the pick-up. Everything had clicked into place with the satisfying precision of a well-oiled piece of machinery. But then that was Okita's special talent—faultless planning and impeccable engineering.

His grin froze as he saw a dozen figures in white jerseys and shorts jogging up the hill towards him. A keep-fit group. Well, so what? He looked innocent enough, he told himself, even with the case.

Suddenly the tranquil park was assaulted by the whirling clatter of helicopter blades. Sato looked skywards in amazement as a police helicopter swooped low enough over the clifftop for him to make out the figure of a balding man, leaning out with a loud-hailer to his lips. "This is Superintendent Hanamura of the Special Investigation Squad. The man on the cliff is wanted by the police. Detain him until my officers can get there. He mustn't be allowed to escape!"

Sato looked around in desperation. The joggers were less than twenty yards away, blocking his retreat. There were too many of them to fight. Backing towards the cliff's edge, he risked a glance over his shoulder. The gorge was steep and the water had flurries of white, indicating submerged rocks.

Baring his teeth in a snarl and flinging the case to the ground, Sato did what Bronson would have done. For a moment he stood poised on the edge of the cliff and then he jumped.

He hit the water feet-first and disappeared. From the helicopter circling above, Superintendent Hanamura scanned the stream for any sign of the dark crew-cut head. Suppose he'd been knocked unconscious and drowned? Well, that would be too bad, but the aluminium case was still there on the clifftop. He'd prevented the bastard from getting away with the money. Anybody foolish enough to tangle with the squad got exactly what was coming to them.

Sato let himself be carried downstream by the swift current until his lungs were bursting. Then he rose to the surface near the water's edge and, sheltered by the dense foliage, crawled onto the bank and lay there, chest heaving, listening to the clatter of the helicopter as it circled overhead.

Minutes later, Sato was wheeling his Suzuki from the gully where he'd hidden it under some brush. The motorcycle started on the first kick and he rode off along a dirt track which looped north towards the park exit.

He approached the exit with caution, considering what he should do next. Even though he didn't have the money, if he could get clear of the park without being seen, there was no reason not to make the rendezvous with Okita at the Poporo roadhouse as arranged. He'd dump the machine and they'd use Okita's car.

He tensed as he went through the gate, but all was quiet. Easy now, he warned himself. You're just a young guy taking a ride on a sunny afternoon. Keep the speed down to about forty-five. No sweat. The cops would never expect him to head for the city.

He was congratulating himself on his strategy when he spied a police car, its siren wailing, coming towards him. It went on by, and Sato grinned into the wind. Then he heard the squeal of tyres and over his shoulder saw the car rocking on its springs as it U-turned and came after him.

Crouching low over the handlebars, Sato gave the engine full throttle. The machine leaped forward, the road blurring in front of him. Damn, they worked fast, he thought. OK, so this was for real. But however good they were, they'd never lay a finger on the Streetfighter.

He was entering a built-up area now and the traffic was getting heavier. Doing ninety, Sato weaved in and out, causing cars and trucks to swerve. But try as he might, he couldn't shake off the pursuing police car. Forty yards ahead he saw traffic lights changing from green to red, and gritting his teeth, stomach flat down on the tank, he went through, barely avoiding a bus that lumbered into his path.

Behind him, Sato heard the grinding screech of brakes and a crescendo of car horns. The siren was still braying but fainter now, sounding mournful.

Should he head directly for the Poporo roadhouse? It was less than a mile away. Sato came to a decision. Choosing a side street on the opposite side of the road, he steered the Suzuki directly across the oncoming traffic, barely avoiding a collision with a laundry van. Bronson himself couldn't have done it better.

Jinking left and right down a labyrinth of quiet back streets that he knew well, he worked his way back onto the Kofu Highway, approaching the roadhouse from the east. Already he could see the neon arrow of the Poporo sign about a quarter of a mile ahead.

Nearly there—he'd done it! He eased back on the throttle, and glanced casually behind as he prepared to pull off the highway. A police car, no light, no siren, was less than twenty yards behind. Where the hell had that come from? Sato's thoughts scurried like snowflakes in a storm. He'd have to outrun them again, then double back and hope that Okita would still be waiting.

Bending low over the machine, Sato sped past the roadhouse. He glimpsed Okita's stocky figure in the car park, and then concentrated on the highway once more, sweat running into his eyes and the sun dead ahead, blinding him.

They'd been so clever—or so they thought—with the helicopter stunt. But to Sato it proved just one thing: the police were more interested in making an arrest and holding onto the money than in saving the lives of the people on the train.

Sato was now doing ninety in the fast lane, his eyes screwed up against the wind, when he saw a slip road coming up. He decided to go for it. The police car would never make the turn.

Without slackening his speed, he slammed on the brakes and screwed the machine round in a sliding arc, fighting to maintain traction on the tarmac surface. He felt the tyres slither and his muscles strained to pull the machine round. Then he confidently regained control. The cops wouldn't forget the Streetfighter in a hurry! He was picturing the headlines in the newspapers when the front wheel of the Suzuki hit the kerbside, throwing him head-first into the crash barrier which broke his neck.

Fifty yards down the highway the police car slithered to a halt and reversed with a shrieking whine to the side road. Traffic slowed, and from one of the cars that passed, Okita stared out, his face completely expressionless, the horror yet to show on it.

14:25—CTC OPERATIONS—TOKYO CENTRAL

The details, relayed via Police Headquarters, came over the desk speaker in the hushed investigation room adjoining the operations area: Unknown suspect. Aged about twenty-three. Killed in accident. No identification. No information on bomb or its location. No leads on accomplices. . . .

The room was silent, the atmosphere dangerous, as if a spark would ignite it. Hiroshi, his breathing audible, was staring rigidly at Police Chief Makoto, who reached shakily for a cigarette. Matt's fists were clenched. This was madness, he thought. Were the police deliberately trying to kill everyone on the train? Surely Superintendent Hanamura realized that what mattered—the only thing that mattered—was to locate and disarm the bomb? For the first time the possibility of failure took shape in his mind. *Laura*, he thought despairingly, *why did I let you go?*

With menacing softness Hiroshi spoke to Police Chief Makoto. "Did Hanamura tell you he was going to tail Lieutenant Tashiro to the pick-up point?"

Makoto squirmed under Hiroshi's gaze. "No—well, not the precise details. The superintendent felt that if they got away with the ransom we'd never hear from them again. He wanted to catch them red-handed with the money and then force them to give us the information we need."

Deputy Sunaga said flatly, "So what happens now? Now that you've managed to kill one of them and shown we can't be trusted, do you think the others are going to cooperate?"

The police chief pressed a hand to his stomach. "We'll hear from them again—we're sure to. They want the money."

"The money," Hiroshi said in a low voice. "Understand this, Makoto. I don't give a damn about the money. We are responsible for that train and the lives of everyone on it." He placed both fists on the desk and leaned forward until his face was inches away from Makoto's. "Don't you understand? We have no alternative, *none*, but to follow their instructions to the letter. When we have found the bomb and disposed of it, *then and only then* can you and Hanamura play your cops-and-robbers games. Afterwards, not before!"

Hiroshi turned away in disgust and left for the adjoining operations room with his deputy and Major Brennan. There were fewer lights now on the main display board, as other trains were cleared from the path of the Hikari 109. Hiroshi looked at Matt, unable to conceive of what the big American must be going through. Yet, in spite of his personal involvement, nothing showed. Maybe the discipline comes from the kind of job he does, Hiroshi thought.

A messenger came up and handed a slip of paper to the operations chief. He glanced at it and stepped up to the communications console. "Get me the motorman on Hikari 109," he told the operator.

"On the line, sir."

Hiroshi picked up the microphone. "Hello, Aoki. I want you to take your speed down to fifty-seven miles per hour."

"Is anything wrong?"

"No, everything's all right. We've set up cameras at the Nishiki Viaduct to film the underside of the train. Hopefully something is visible and we'll be able to locate the bomb."

"Very good, Chief." The motorman sounded relieved. "What's happening there? Have the criminals been in touch again? I thought we'd have heard something by now."

Hiroshi hesitated, then said carefully, "The police are handling negotiations but it's taking longer than we anticipated."

"That means we won't be stopping at Kyoto."

"I'm afraid not. But it won't be long now till we'll have some good news for you. I promise." He set down the microphone, wondering how much his promise was worth.

14:35—SAPPORO—HOKKAIDO

The detective from the Sapporo Police Department held up the photograph. "Is this your brother?"

The man gave a disgruntled sigh and glanced across the living room at his wife, who was sitting forward in the armchair, her hands kneading together anxiously. "What's he done this time?"

"His full name is Masaru Koga?"

Koga's elder brother nodded impatiently. "Yes. Yes. What's he been up to? Demonstrating again?"

"I've no idea," the detective replied, obeying orders not to give anything away. "We've been asked by the Tokyo police to make routine inquiries. Nothing to be alarmed about." Then he said casually, "Do you know his present whereabouts?"

"We haven't heard from him for ages. Must be over a year now." The man shrugged. "No idea where he might be." He didn't sound as if it concerned him one way or another.

"What about old letters, diaries, address books?"

"He took all his stuff with him when he cleared out." The man's tone became caustic. "His room used to be stacked with all kinds of left-wing rubbish—pamphlets, posters—"

"What about the bill that came?" his wife ventured timidly.

The man nodded slowly, remembering. "It came about six months ago—from a bar, I think. We didn't pay it," he added dourly, and then said to his wife, "See if it's still around."

When she returned, she handed the bill to the detective. It was from the Twilight Bar in the Toshima District of Tokyo. There was nothing more. The detective thanked the couple and departed.

14:40—HIKARI 109—KYOTO

Minami watched morosely as Kyoto Station slid past the window, his view of the scene fragmented by the crack in the left lens of his spectacles. He'd been lucky to retrieve his glasses at all, after that stupid ruckus over the telephone.

Sighing, he looked down at the pigskin attaché case. All that work—wasted. And what would the sales director have to say?

They were now more than eighty miles down the line, and every second that passed took him farther and farther away from Nagoya. Surely the railway authorities couldn't be right in thinking the train would explode if it was stopped? It was preposterous. In any case, how could they possibly find the bomb if the train wasn't stopped and properly searched?

Seized by a sudden impulse, Minami picked up his attaché case, made his way to the guards' compartment and rapped on the door.

"Yes, sir, can I help you?" The head guard could see his agitation. From inside the door Minami heard harsh rapid breathing —it sounded like a woman—cut short by a sharp cry of pain.

"Are we stopping at Osaka?"

Yamada shook his head slowly. "I'm afraid I can't say, sir. We must await instructions from Tokyo."

"Listen," Minami said tersely. "I have to get in touch with my company. You have a telephone in here, don't you? At least let me use it."

"I'm afraid I can't allow that, sir. This telephone is for official use only, and in any case it's a direct line to the operations centre. I suggest you use the public telephones."

"I can't get near the damn things." Minami shot a glance over his shoulder, reached into his pocket and pulled out a wad of banknotes. "Look, all this is yours," he hissed conspiratorially. "Just let me use the phone for a minute."

Yamada stiffened at the insult to his honour. Not deigning to dignify Minami's suggestion with a reply, he slammed the door shut in his face and fastened it. Then he moved to the side of the young woman's bed and looked down. The facilities were pitifully inadequate. Unless the birth went smoothly, both mother and child would be in danger, though having a doctor on the train was at least one small mercy, he thought.

Laura looked up from wiping Keiko's brow with a towel. "The pains are every two minutes now. The baby is near."

Yamada nodded. "Everything here. You want?"

Laura gave a strained smile. "Yes. Thank you."

Yamada smiled briefly and went out, leaving Laura anxiously watching over the woman in labour. Keiko was doing her best to endure the pain but without drugs or oxygen she was being driven to the limit of her tolerance. Kneeling by the side of the

404

bed, Laura talked to her in a gentle, soothing voice, and every few minutes she pressed her ear to Keiko's abdomen, listening for the foetal heartbeat. It sounded fast and regular, a light pit-*t*-pat-*t*-pit-*t*-pat that told her everything was proceeding normally. Delivery would probably take place within the next two hours.

14:47—SHIMURA INDUSTRIAL ESTATE—TOKYO

Back at his derelict factory Okita stood by the window, looking out at the rusting machinery among the weeds and waist-high grass. In his left hand he held a whisky glass, while in his right a cigarette burned unheeded.

Sato, Okita thought. Sato dead? He had seen his broken body with his own eyes, but still he couldn't grasp the fact that the young man who had befriended him in his darkest hour was now lying torn and mangled on a mortuary slab.

Okita remembered the time when he had been in need of a friend. His world, the thriving engineering company he'd built up, had collapsed around him. His firm had supplied electronic control equipment to large manufacturers and, through a supplier, to the National Railways. With the Japanese economy booming, the Okita Precision Tool Company had looked forward to a prosperous future.

Then, in late 1975, the worldwide oil crisis shook the economy. The giant corporations began to cut back on production and first to feel the effects were the hundreds of small and medium-sized sub-contractors which relied on them for long-term work. Scores of firms went bankrupt. By 1977 it had become inevitable that Okita's company, deeply in debt, would also fail.

It was then that Okita's serious drinking began. Everyone—even his wife and daughter—seemed to have lost faith in him, and Okita desperately needed someone to whom he could pour out his troubles. Sato proved to be such a person. They spent every night in some bar or other. Sato had been recently discharged from the army—dishonourably, as he used to make plain with a broad grin.

Into their twilight world of down-and-outs stepped the sinister presence of the student, Koga. A born misfit, Koga frequented the bars in search of drugs to sell on the campus of Jonan University where he had a reputation as a political agitator. His talk was filled with hatred and Okita thought him a dangerous fanatic and wanted nothing to do with him.

Indeed, but for Sato's accident the alliance between these three disparate personalities would never have come into being.

At the warehouse where Sato worked, a stack of heavy crates had collapsed, trapping him and badly bruising his ribs. It was clearly an industrial accident, but the company had refused to pay for hospital treatment or for the earnings lost during the six weeks Sato lay at home, strapped up and in great pain. Okita had cared for him, visiting him every day with food and pain-relieving drugs. Afterwards, embittered and angry, Sato had poured out his story to Koga in a bar one night, and Okita could still recall the shock he had felt when the student leaned across the table and said softly, "Why don't you blow the bastards out of existence? Get them with a bomb."

The thought of breaking the law had never before entered Okita's head. Yet Koga's suggestion generated within him a strange nervous excitement that was fuelled by the loss of self-respect he had suffered when his company had collapsed. Two weeks later Okita unrolled his plans before Sato and the student. "We're not going to waste our time bombing a warehouse," he told them. "We're going to try for something bigger. Much bigger. And it's going to make us rich!"

Okita was to construct the control equipment, including an electromagnetic speedometer of the type his company used to make. The student, using his contacts on the fringes of the under-world, was to obtain the explosives. Working with Okita's blue-prints they were able to figure out how the speedometer with a dynamo and explosive charge could be attached to the underside of a train. Using a dummy rig, Sato got the fixing time down to six and a half minutes.

Already trained in the use of high explosives, Sato would be the one to attach the device to the running gear of the Bullet Train. Without too much difficulty he got a job as a cleaner at Tokyo Central Station, and found that the large metal rubbish cart he used each day might have been purposely built for the job of getting the control device and the ten sticks of gelignite to the train without anyone becoming suspicious. . . .

Okita sagged wearily. Everything had gone sweetly—each phase of the operation a triumph of organization—and yet it had ended in failure and the death of his last and only friend. . . .

The phone rang like an alarm bell in the small sweltering office. It was the student. Okita told him in three sentences what had happened. After a long pause Koga said, "What do we do now?"

It was a struggle to speak, let alone to think. "You'd better come to the factory. We'll have to talk about it."

Okita put the phone down and pressed both hands to his face, his shoulders shaking.

14:52—HIKARI 109—OSAKA

Lying on an earthquake belt which stretches from New Zealand to Alaska, the four main islands of Japan are constantly trembling. Most of the tremors are slight, but seismographs record an average of twenty a day. Osaka, the second largest city in Japan, lies in one of the most susceptible zones.

Osaka was Hikari 109's next scheduled stop, and was only five minutes away. Passing from Coach 13 into the Green Car, Duty Policeman Nagata encountered the head guard, followed by half a dozen arguing and gesticulating passengers. "I don't believe all this nonsense about a bomb," one of them was saying.

"Why don't you tell us what's happening?" someone else demanded.

Then everyone joined in. Yamada did what he could to pacify them but many of the passengers were on a knife-edge, and it wouldn't be long before nerves snapped under the strain. How could he and his few staff possibly cope with mass hysteria?

Further along the Green Car, Tee Togo crouched forward in his seat, fiddling with the dial of his transistor radio. Suddenly he turned up the volume and the words of the announcer sliced through the babble of voices. ". . . we have just heard that one of the suspects believed to be involved with the Bullet Train bomb threat was killed while attempting to escape from the police. An unconfirmed report suggests that the man, in his early twenties, died before he could give any information. . . ."

Lurching to his feet, Tee Togo staggered wild-eyed along the aisle towards Yamada. His voice came out at screaming pitch. "*He's dead!* We'll never find the bomb now. . . . He's dead and the secret's died with him. . . ."

Realizing he could no longer hope to calm the passengers, Yamada sidled back to the door of the guards' compartment. He raised a placatory hand. "All right. Please! I'll get in touch with the operations centre at once and get the latest information." Then he hurried into the guards' compartment and bolted the door behind him.

In the operations room Hiroshi answered Yamada's call at once. Briefly the head guard told him of the growing unrest. The passengers were hungry for facts and they wanted them now.

Hiroshi gave them, filling in the details about the death of the man sent to collect the ransom, and about police efforts to trace another man thought to be involved. "This is the situation to date. I leave it up to you how much you think they ought to know. We've taken high-speed film of the underside of the train and our technical people are waiting to examine it. As soon as we have anything new I'll get back to you."

"And that's it. Everything." Yamada said dully.

"Yes," Hiroshi said, sensing Yamada's disappointment and feeling of betrayal. "We still have six hours, Yamada. Don't give up hope. We'll beat this thing. One way or another we'll come through." He rang off.

15:00—SHIMURA DISTRICT—TOKYO

At the wheel of an unmarked police Toyota, Sergeant Goto drove through the mean, drab streets of Shimura on his way to check out the Twilight Bar in the Toshima District of the city. A member of the squad for only six months, he still regarded the superintendent with a cautious respect, though at times Hanamura's rough and ready tactics scared him. Like that caper with the helicopter, shadowing Lieutenant Tashiro's car to the pick-up in Omiya Park. And look how it had ended—one dead suspect and no leads.

He touched the slips of paper in his pocket, the details of the unpaid drinks bill telexed from the Sapporo police, and a mug shot of Masaru Koga. He doubted that the inquiry would yield anything; the bombers were too smart to be tripped up by unpaid bills.

Passing an open air market, Goto idly looked at the bright canvas stalls and the crowds of shoppers. His glance passed over the hurrying figure of a man in a leather jacket just as he happened to look furtively over his shoulder. In the next second the detective was swinging the Toyota into the kerb and grabbing the radio-mike from the dashboard. There was no mistaking the long hair, the pitted face, the thin insolent mouth. It was their man. *Koga.*

"Suspect sighted in Shimura District—advise Superintendent Hanamura."

Half out of the car, he saw the student turn the corner near a cast-iron railway bridge which carried the local train line. Goto set off, dodging through the mid-afternoon shoppers. Around the corner he caught a quick glimpse of Koga disappearing into an alleyway. Goto ran after him. Then it flashed through his mind that the student could be armed and hiding, just waiting for him to show himself in the alleyway to pick him off. The sergeant skidded to a halt, flattening himself against the brickwork before peering cautiously into the alleyway. No sign of him, yet from here it looked to be a dead-end.

Goto drew his Walther PP automatic and stepped out. He kept close to the wall, moving slowly, alert for the tiniest movement or sound. After thirty paces, he came to an archway which led into a deserted side street, ripe for demolition. Opposite a row of derelict shops stood a wooden fence surrounding a scrapyard.

Goto cursed and holstered his weapon. It would need thirty men at least to search the area thoroughly.

A few minutes later, back on the main street, he wondered how he was going to explain his failure to the super. He felt sick. Damn it, he'd been within yards of the student and allowed him to get away!

Directly across the street a concrete ramp led up to the platform of the district railway station, and the detective came to a dead stop as there, ascending the ramp, was Koga! Unheeding of traffic, Goto ran across the street and leaped up the dozen steps to the ramp. This time there'd be no failure. A train rattled over the bridge and into the station. Koga had almost reached the platform; in a single reflex action Goto was down on one knee holding the Walther in both hands as he sighted along the barrel.

The thin figure was perfectly silhouetted against the sky. Goto fired. There wasn't even time to give the obligatory caution. Koga

409

lurched forward, clutching his left shoulder, and staggered out of view.

Goto raced eagerly to the top of the ramp as the train pulled out. The platform was empty. He looked wildly around, then down at a few spots of blood on the green tiles. Koga had given him the slip again. . . .

15:17—CTC OPERATIONS—TOKYO CENTRAL

"You mean to say you lost him *twice?*" Superintendent Hanamura's voice had risen fractionally above its usual clipped monotone. Without waiting for an answer from Goto, he said, "I'll put out a priority alert for the Shimura and Toshima Districts. Report directly to me as soon as you have anything." He slammed the receiver down and turned to Lieutenant Tashiro. "Get that organized with headquarters. We'll cordon off the area. Koga won't get far."

Hiroshi swung on his heels, white with anger, and left the investigations room. He had heard enough. It astounded him that even now, after what had taken place, Hanamura could be so callous as to risk hundreds of lives by going all out to make an arrest.

In his office Hiroshi found Matt Brennan with a powerful magnifying glass, examining glossy blown-up photographic stills from the film shot at Nishiki Viaduct. An edgy silence filled the office like a bad smell. What little detail the cameras had been able to pick up was murky and ill-defined, and it was impossible to tell whether anything out of the ordinary was attached to the running gear.

Matt fumbled in the pocket of his army tunic for his tobacco pouch. He watched Hiroshi leafing through the stills. "Are they making any progress downstairs?" Matt asked, thumbing tobacco into his pipe.

Hiroshi told him about Sergeant Goto's report, that the student had been seen and hit in the shoulder. He didn't discuss Hanamura's indefensible obstinacy; some things were better not mentioned to a man in Brennan's position.

He tossed one of the stills aside and said savagely, "These are useless! Is this the best you can do?"

The photographic expert, a small, meek-looking man, jumped.

"I'm sorry, sir. There simply wasn't enough light to get a decent image. If we had proper arc lighting—"

"How long will it take to arrange?"

"An hour, maybe longer, it's hard to say—"

"Do it."

15:30—SHIMURA INDUSTRIAL ESTATE—TOKYO

Okita lumbered to his feet, his heart pounding in his chest. Somebody or something had crashed against the rear door of the building. He moved to the window and squinted out. A moment later he was unbolting the iron door and hauling Koga inside, grimacing at the dark red stain which covered the front of the young man's shirt.

As Okita lowered him onto the camp bed Koga winced, his thin, wasted face deathly pale. "There was this cop," he said through parched lips. "Thought I'd lost him . . . ." He groaned as Okita eased the leather jacket off his shoulders. "Took a shot at me . . . ."

"Don't talk. Save your strength."

The wound was bad. The bullet had shattered Koga's left shoulder blade and made a shredded hole in the left side of his chest muscle. There wasn't much Okita could do. He had bandages and adhesive tape in the cupboard, but what Koga really needed was immediate hospital treatment.

"Leave it, doesn't matter about me," Koga protested feebly. "We have to get . . . the money . . ."

"If I don't stop this bleeding you'll die," Okita told him forcibly, and he cleansed and bound the wound as best he could, wondering bleakly if this was the end. Sato dead and Koga wounded—why go on with a plan that had become such a dismal failure?

Finally he said. "We're beaten."

Koga's eyes focused on him. "What the hell are you talking about? What's the matter with you? Are you scared?"

"No. . . . It's just that . . ." Okita shook his head hopelessly. "It was to be the perfect crime. Nothing could go wrong. Nobody would get hurt. And now look at us."

"OK, so tell me what good giving up will do," Koga said, his dark eyes glittering with the old fanaticism. "That's crazy talk. We can still win—" His face went rigid with pain. "Our fall-back

412

plan—the Kanda flyover—" His head fell back, his eyes shrouded with pain.

Okita gazed at him, then said quietly. "All right. We'll try again." He rose heavily, and placed the telephone within reach of the bed. "I'll be back in one hour."

15:45—EXPRESSWAY NO. 5—TOKYO

The cream-coloured Samba pick-up truck kept to the slow lane of the southbound expressway heading towards the centre of the city. Then, following the loop around to the northeast, it passed over the busy downtown streets, taking a six-lane elevated highway which snaked fifty feet above the quiet avenues surrounding Ueno Park.

At the third lay-by, a mile and a half beyond the city centre, Okita pulled off and stopped alongside the guard rail. Only the 22-storey Takora Hotel, a slender column of aluminium and glass, overlooked it. Most of the buildings here were below the level of the flyover, which was why he'd chosen the spot.

After putting out a red warning triangle to indicate a breakdown, Okita took his helmet from the cab, dragged the Kawasaki KH100 motorcycle from the rear of the truck to the ground, and rode off. He took the first exit road, crossed underneath the flyover, and re-entered it on the opposite side, heading back towards the city. After a mile and a half he repeated the manoeuvre, which brought him onto the access road, roughly half a mile before the lay-by where he'd left the truck. From here he had an uninterrupted view of the traffic streaming out of the city.

Setting the motorcycle on its stand, Okita removed his helmet and paused for a moment before entering a phone booth. He couldn't help remembering how he and Sato together had planned this as a fall-back to the location in Omiya Park. Okita could still hear his voice: *Nobody will get hurt. Nobody will get killed. . . .* He felt a choking anger as he picked up the receiver and started to dial.

16:04—CTC OPERATIONS—TOKYO CENTRAL

Police Chief Makoto took the call in the investigation room. The familiar voice grated over the desk-speaker. "You don't care what happens to the people on the train, do you? You want us behind bars and you want to save the money, and that's all."

"If those people die it will be your doing," Makoto blurted out rashly.

"You shut up and listen. This is your last chance. Do *exactly* as I tell you or you'll never hear from me again."

"All right—I guarantee it," Makoto promised, dry mouthed.

"I want one man in a National Railways Police car to take the northeast route on the Kanda flyover. At the third lay-by he'll see a pick-up truck with an emergency triangle. He's to put the money on the driver's seat and leave the area. If he's not there in ten minutes, the whole thing is off. Got that?"

"What about the bomb?"

"You'll hear from me as soon as I've got the money—and when I'm sure there's no one tailing me."

He rang off.

Senda, Makoto's young aide, stepped forward. "I'll go, sir."

Makoto nodded as he lit a cigarette. "Get started. It's going to take you almost ten minutes to get there."

Senda hurried out. Superintendent Hanamura was already on the hotline to Police Headquarters, requesting the positions of all patrol cars in the vicinity of the Kanda flyover. Makoto watched him, feeling his stomach turn to water.

16:15—Kanda Flyover—Tokyo

Okita watched the blue and white National Railways Police car go by. To be absolutely certain that the car wasn't being tailed he decided to wait one minute and then follow. He climbed into the saddle, adjusted his helmet, kicked the Kawasaki into life, and studied his watch. Fifteen. Thirty. Forty-five. Sixty. . . .

After passing the second lay-by, Senda slowed the car and peered through the windscreen, holding the radio mike close to his mouth.

"I can see the truck. It's a 1975 cream Samba pick-up, license 19BT-4337. There doesn't appear to be anyone around."

Makoto's voice crackled over the speaker. "Make the drop as instructed and leave the area."

Pulling up into the lay-by behind the truck, Senda grabbed the aluminium case, went up to the driver's window, tossed it inside the cab, returned to his car and drove off.

414

SUPERINTENDENT HANAMURA had ordered roadblocks set up on the flyover for the Samba pick-up truck. Now, he flicked a switch on the panel. "Patch me through to Car 9."

There was a frizzle of static and a voice answered, "Car 9 here. We're at the Takora Hotel. Maintaining surveillance from the roof as instructed." There was a pause, then, "We have a sighting on the Samba pick-up. Nobody in the immediate area as yet."

"Report as soon as you have something."

THROTTLING BACK, Okita coasted in alongside the pick-up. Hefting the aluminium case out of the cab, he strapped it to the rack of the motorcycle, and rode off. The operation had taken less than fifteen seconds.

He carried on to the next lay-by, half a mile along the flyover and stopped. Setting the machine on its stand, he stripped off helmet and jacket, took a pair of grey overalls from one of the side panniers and put them on. From the other he pulled out a nylon rope-ladder, secured it to the guard rail and dropped it over. Then he strapped on a leather belt with a spring-release hook, clipped the case to it, heaved himself over the barrier and began to climb down. Three minutes later he was sliding in behind the wheel of a dark-blue Honda Civic in a side road next to Ueno Park. He wound down the window to get air, put the car in gear and drove off. As far as he knew nobody had seen a thing.

SUPERINTENDENT HANAMURA listened to the report from Car 9.

"The suspect was seen collecting the money from the truck on a motorcycle. We couldn't identify the make or see the colour from this distance. Suspect then rode off."

Hanamura switched over, calling on all cars to be on the look-out for the motorcycle. "At all costs he must be apprehended. Repeat: he *must* be apprehended!"

Makoto observed the superintendent through a cloud of cigarette smoke. The minutes went by. Hanamura waited, his face imperturbable. He was confident. There was no escape. They had him.

At last a message came through from a patrol car on the flyover. "Sir, we've located the motorcycle." Hanamura leaned forward in anticipation, his thin lips tightly compressed. "It has been abandoned on the flyover and the suspect apparently has escaped down a rope-ladder strung over the parapet. There's no sign of him now."

Hanamura's grey eyebrows came together. A tiny muscle twitched in his hollow cheek. "Are you telling me he got away?"

"Yes, sir." Silence. "Sir?"

Makoto cleared his throat as if to offer a few words of regret, sympathy even, but they died on his lips under the terrible baleful glare that Hanamura turned upon him.

THE DEPUTY put his head around the door of Hiroshi's office. "It's done. He's got the money." Sunaga's weathered face bore an expression of almost puckish amusement. "He gave them the slip. The police set up roadblocks, but he got clean away."

"So, if he keeps his word, we should hear from him in the next ten minutes," Matt put in quietly.

The operations chief nodded. "Sunaga, contact the train and let them know. They could use some good news for a change."

Sunaga left the office and Hiroshi produced a bottle of sake from the bottom drawer of his desk. He poured out two stiff measures and raised his glass. "Not long to go now, my friend."

Matt hesitated before he drank, staring into his glass. Unaccountably he felt a shiver of apprehension prickle his spine. He wanted to share in Hiroshi's confidence, but couldn't.

16:30—HIKARI 109—OKAYAMA

Sprawled once more in his seat, Tee Togo was almost his old self. The head guard had announced that the ransom was paid and the news had worked like a miracle. The star's earlier panic was gone now. Soon the authorities would receive instructions for dismantling the bomb. He winked at the beautiful young stewardess making her way towards him along the aisle.

Yoko gave him her professional smile. The change in everyone she encountered was dramatic. It was as if, having been granted a reprieve, they were seeing the world with fresh eyes.

Yoko was on her way to the guards' compartment to help the American doctor with the woman in labour when the train entered a tunnel. All at once the lights flickered and then went out. Immediately the red emergency lighting came on. But the train's speed had slackened and in the next instant Yoko was jolted forward as the background whine of electric power units died away and the sound of terrified screams filled the coach.

MOTORMAN AOKI snatched up the handset, his face bathed in the dim red glow of the emergency lights in the driving cab. "Control! Control! We've lost all power and the ATC has brought in auxiliary units. Our speed is dropping fast. What's happening?"

Called from his office, Hiroshi leaped down the metal stairway to the operations room, rapping out orders. "Everybody full alert. Status report on Section 5." On the main display board the orange bar marked 109 was shown to be within a tunnel.

Reports began to come from controllers and engineers: "Complete auto-transformer shutdown on Section 5." "Both 275 and 220 kilovolt power lines non-operational."

The chief engineer ripped a teleprint from the machine and read it aloud. "Meteorology reports earthquake eighty kilometres south of the train, Richter scale 7." He stared at Hiroshi. "That must be it—the seismographs in Section 5 registered the tremor and automatically shut down the power."

Hiroshi spoke into the microphone. "Aoki, what's your speed?"

"Sixty-three miles per hour and falling. . . . Chief, you have to do something—we'll be down to fifty in less than a minute!"

Hiroshi didn't waste time in answering. He called out to the power engineer, "What's the situation on Section 4?"

"Feeder lines operational. It's outside the tremor area."

"Can you cover Section 5 from there—from the Okayama booster station?"

"I—I'm not sure," the engineer stammered. "If I override the master circuit control—"

"I don't want a lecture, just do it!" Hiroshi returned to Aoki. "We're trying to cover the shutdown from the Okayama booster station in Section 4. What's your speed now?"

"Fifty-six and falling . . ." Aoki's voice broke. "It's no good, Chief, there's only thirty seconds left. . . ."

YOKO FOUGHT her way through a frenzied mob of passengers. They knew. They had all felt the slowdown and realized that the bomb was about to explode. The spectre of mass carnage had gripped their minds in all its terrifying reality. Some were clawing at the windows, some were screaming, an elderly couple were on their knees, praying. Yoko could do nothing.

In the driving cab, strangely resigned to whatever would happen next, Aoki watched the red needle drift around the central dial. It touched fifty-three and dipped lower.

Ten seconds to oblivion.

Across the cab, Uchida was sitting bolt upright in his high-backed padded chair, looking straight ahead into the blackness. What would it be like? A lightning flash of searing heat, erupting flames? Why didn't he feel scared? he wondered.

Aoki saw the needle nudge down to fifty-one miles per hour and he started to count silently to himself. The red glow in the cab faded. He caught his breath. Then bright lights came on, dazzling him. Unbelievably the train surged forward.

He looked at Uchida, and together they listened to the mounting hum of power with expressions of mingled disbelief and joy.

"They did it," Aoki whispered. And then he was shouting, "They did it!" and he reached out to wring Uchida's hand, his face breaking into a great beaming smile.

For some the new lease of life had come almost too late.

Takazana, the 71-year-old president of Kyoto Electronics, lay back against the seat, his breath fluttering, his heart labouring, and he raised one frail hand in a gesture of urgent need.

Mickie knew that he wanted the vial of tablets inside her kimono sleeve. Without them he would die.

The clawlike hand faltered as his rheumy eyes sought hers. How easy it would be, she thought, to do nothing—just let him die. She would be a rich woman, could live the kind of life she had always dreamed about. . . .

Takazana was still gazing at her. He reminded her of a tiny baby, weak and helpless, yet possessing that indomitable spark which refuses to let go of life. She thought, too, of the woman in the guards' compartment struggling to give birth. A new life coming into the world . . . an old life leaving it.

Mickie felt emotion well up inside her, a mingled sense of awe and compassion, and she took the vial from her sleeve. Cradling Takazana's head against her shoulder, she slipped two tablets into the dry gasping mouth and reached for the glass of water.

At the rear of the coach, not many feet away, another battle between life and death was taking place.

To Laura's heartfelt relief the first moments of delivery had gone well. The stewardess, who spoke English, had arrived in time to translate her instructions for the girl. Everything had happened so fast that she'd hardly had time to wonder if Matt knew about the bomb threat. She told the stewardess, "When she feels the contraction tell her to breathe quickly and push hard."

Yoko spoke briefly to Keiko, who gripped the sides of the bed, her face pale and damp. She was thinking of Abiko. He would want her to be brave. For him—and for their child—she would overcome her fear. A spasm came and she closed her eyes and pushed, gritting her teeth to stifle a cry.

"That's fine," Laura encouraged. "Now tell her to relax. Tell her everything is all right. The baby is almost here."

Keiko lay back and Laura smiled warmly. So young and so alone. The poor girl must be terrified. Whatever had induced her to travel so near her time? Why wasn't her husband with her? The contractions grew stronger and the baby's head appeared.

"Push! *Push!*" Laura exhorted, her own body tense with the desire to see the girl through this, the most difficult moment. Reaching forward, Laura found and supported the baby's head, now fully emerged. Its nose and mouth had to be cleared to allow that first life-sustaining breath of air into its lungs.

Laura leaned closer. Her throat contracted in a wave of panic. The baby's face had a bluish tinge, its tiny mouth was open, gasping. What could be wrong? Think, woman, think! Every second was vital. Her hands explored the baby's neck and found that the umbilical cord was wrapped tightly around it. The baby was being choked to death.

Instantly Laura became the cool, objective professional, summoning all her skill and experience. The throttling cord had to be cut, but first it must be tied off in two places. Otherwise both mother and child would bleed to death. Careful not to communicate any anxiety to the mother, Laura said briskly, "Yoko, bring me those two lengths of nylon twine and the scissors."

"Is anything wrong?"

"We have to work fast. The baby isn't breathing. We have two minutes, three at the most. Hand me the twine."

419

"Oh no . . ."

It was a difficult procedure. Working as swiftly as she could, Laura tied the twine around the tight slippery cord. The baby's face was turning a dark suffused purple. The infant needed oxygen and soon. I won't let you die, Laura was thinking.

The ligatures completed, she took the scissors and cut the cord between them. Finally the child was free, and under Laura's guiding hands the birth was completed. But there was no sign of breathing. Was it too late? No, dammit, there was still hope. Never give up . . . never. . . .

While Yoko comforted the exhausted mother, Laura tried every thing she knew to restore the baby's breathing and circulation, working feverishly to clear the air passages and give mouth-to-mouth resuscitation. Then she tried gentle heart massage with the pads of her fingers, more resuscitation, more massage. For fifteen minutes she refused to accept what was now the harsh yet unavoidable truth.

Keiko's baby was dead.

Numbly, Laura wrapped the child in a cloth and placed it at the foot of the bed. Her only thought now was for the mother.

The afterbirth had ejected, but there was more bleeding than was normal. Laura could do little but staunch the flow with towels. If it continued, Keiko would surely need a transfusion. Already, she estimated, the girl had lost two pints of blood and was losing more every second.

Part Four: Explosion

16:40—TAITO DISTRICT—TOKYO

Okita drove the little Honda Civic into the petrol station and said to the young attendant who ambled out, "Fill her up and check the oil, would you?"

The aluminium case was safely locked away in the boot. The money was all there, in neat bundles fastened with rubber bands. Okita felt light-headed and euphoric. He had just pulled off one of the most sensational crimes ever committed, and perversely all he wanted to do was to giggle. It was so funny. He glanced at his watch and said, "All right if I use your phone?"

The attendant nodded indifferently. Okita strolled into the garage and stepped inside the phone booth. He had three calls to make. The first was to the Sun-Plaza coffee shop.

"Sorry to bother you. I was in your place earlier this afternoon and I think I left something behind. It's a large buff envelope which contains some important documents. I seem to remember putting it down in the window recess near the entrance."

The waitress was only away for a few seconds. She sounded harassed. "Yes, it's here. What do you want me to do with it?"

"Thank goodness. If you'll hang onto it I'll come over and pick it up. My name is Kaneda. I'll ask for it at the cash desk."

The second call was to the factory. Koga answered, and Okita said without preamble, "I've made the pick-up."

"You've got the money?" Koga's voice was weak but even so his elation broke through.

"Just as we specified. One-hundred-dollar bills. I wasn't followed." Through the open door Okita saw that the attendant was now checking the oil. He went on rapidly. "I'm at a garage in the Taito District. I should be back at the factory in twenty minutes. Be ready to leave."

The third call was to CTC Operations at Tokyo Central. When he was put through to the chief of Railway Police, he said, "Listen, Makoto. I'm only going to say it once." The attendant had closed the bonnet and was wiping his hands on an oily rag. "Send a man to the Sun-Plaza coffee shop in the Shimbashi District. Tell him to ask one of the waitresses for an envelope left there by Kaneda. It contains everything you need—a diagram of the bomb's location and instructions on how to disarm it. Have you got that?"

"Yes." Makoto sounded scared. "But how do we know—"

The attendant came through the door. Okita hung up and reached for his wallet to pay the man.

16:50—CTC OPERATIONS—TOKYO CENTRAL

There was sudden animation in the crowded investigation room, as Hiroshi said, "What the hell are we waiting for? Let's get somebody over there right away."

421

Superintendent Hanamura said, "I'll send one of my men." He nodded to Lieutenant Tashiro.

Tashiro was on his way to the door when Matt joined him. "I'm going too. It'll save time if I can study the instructions in the car." This was his time at last to do something positive to save the train. And save Laura.

He left with Tashiro just as a uniformed officer entered and handed a yellow flimsy to the superintendent. "From Central Records, sir, on the man who was killed. They had his fingerprints and the license number of the motorcycle. They were able to trace him through the Traffic Offences section."

Hanamura read aloud, "'Sinji Sato. Age twenty-four. Convicted September 1977 of minor traffic violation involving a Suzuki motorcycle, registered in the Toshima District. Fined 12,500 yen. No criminal record.'" He scowled. "That's no use to anybody—"

Hiroshi plucked the sheet from his fingers. "Wait a minute. What about this? Sato wasn't insured and had to give the name of a guarantor. . . . A man called Tetsuo Okita."

Hanamura regarded him flatly. "So what?"

"The control equipment used in the freight train explosion was manufactured by the Okita Precision Tool Company. So are the speedometers fitted to the Bullet Trains."

Hanamura picked up the phone. "What's the company's address?"

"It used to have premises on the Shimura Industrial Estate—" Hiroshi stopped abruptly. "That's in the same district where the other one—Koga—was seen. That must be the hideout."

Hanamura's eyes gleamed as the connection clicked in his mind. The Okita Precision Tool Company. Tetsuo Okita.

Hiroshi left the superintendent to his triumph. He wanted no part of it. All that mattered was getting hold of the instructions for disarming the bomb. On the main display board he saw that the Hikari 109 was 3 hours 47 minutes from the end of the line at Hakata. Enough time? It *had* to be.

The operator at the communications desk held up the microphone. "For you, sir. The head guard on Hikari 109."

"We couldn't save the baby," Yamada informed him sadly. "The doctor did all she could—"

"What about the mother?"

"She's lost some blood. She may need a transfusion."

"Let's be thankful there was a doctor on board." Hiroshi paused. Finally he said, "I've got some good news for a change, Yamada. We've had a call saying where to pick up the instructions about the bomb. Two men are on their way there now."

Yamada couldn't believe it. "You're sure? It's genuine?"

"Yes, I think it is," Hiroshi said. "Listen, Yamada, let the passengers know right away. Tell them it won't be long now."

"Yes, Chief. Yes, right now!"

17:05—SHIMBASHI DISTRICT—TOKYO

At the wheel of the police car Lieutenant Tashiro cursed in a low monotone. They were in heavy downtown traffic, weaving, switching lanes and squirming through gaps with only inches to spare. Matt was leaning forward, willing the car to go faster, adrenalin pumping through him in wild anticipation.

Two blocks away from the Sun-Plaza, a sixty-foot fire tender, siren blaring, cut in front of them. Tashiro had to stamp on the brake. At the next intersection it turned left. They followed it. The street of shops and small restaurants was obscured by a pall of dense black smoke.

A knife twisted in Matt's bowels. The street was a shambles. Two fire tenders were already deployed in front of the Sun-Plaza coffee shop; firemen were unreeling hoses, and policemen were clearing the area of spectators. Matt saw several waitresses huddled next to a patrol car, staring up at the billowing smoke.

"What happened?" Matt demanded of the nearest policeman.

The officer jerked his thumb towards the girls. "According to one of them it started in the kitchen of the coffee shop."

Matt pushed past him and said tersely to the waitresses, "Which of you was expecting someone named Kaneda to pick up an envelope from the Sun-Plaza?"

A tall thin woman piped up, "I took the call. He said he'd be round to collect it right away."

"Where did you put the envelope?"

"On the counter next to the register . . ."

Without hesitation Matt grabbed a hose from one of the firemen and advanced towards the coffee shop entrance, directing a jet of water ahead of him through the curtain of black smoke.

423

"What the hell are you doing?" But Tashiro was seconds too late. Matt had disappeared into the thick choking fumes.

One arm shielding his head, Matt fought his way into the coffee shop. Floor, walls and ceiling were alight with orange flame, but he was able to make out the square shape of the cash register, its paint blistered and bubbling. Tashiro materialized at his side, yelling in his ear, but Matt ignored him and plunged ahead, spraying water in an arc to clear a path. He could see the counter now; flames were dancing along its surface. Shimmering patterns of heat distorted his vision so that he couldn't be sure if the envelope was there. Every step was agonizing. He could smell his hair scorching, feel his eyes stinging, but nothing mattered—nothing existed but the counter, four paces away, and the envelope.

He could see it now, a pale brown rectangle curling at the corners. His hand was inches from it when the world caved in. Burning timbers fell on him in a shower of sparks. His last despairing thought was that he had failed... the train would explode....

Tashiro was of a light build, and the American must have weighed fourteen stone. Yet the lieutenant, locking his arms across Matt's chest and heaving with all his strength, managed to pull Matt free and drag him backwards through the flaming wreckage into the lobby. Then two firemen appeared, and between the three of them they carried the unconscious man clear of the building just as the entire ceiling fell with a crackling roar.

Minutes later Matt opened his eyes and looked into Tashiro's smoke-blackened face. For an instant it felt wonderful to be alive. And then he remembered.

17:10—SHIMURA INDUSTRIAL ESTATE—TOKYO

It was the end of another working day. Cars, buses and motor-cycles clogged the roads radiating from the industrial estate, but Okita, driving against the flow of traffic, was relatively unhindered. He had to get Koga away from the factory, and somehow find a doctor who would attend to his wound. Originally arrangements had been worked out to leave the country on separate flights: reservations, forged passports, visas, everything. Now that plan would have to be abandoned.

Okita turned into the inner ring road. A quarter of a mile ahead he could see the concrete shell of the factory. The old place had

been the perfect cover, he was reflecting, when suddenly he heard the sound of sirens and two patrol cars screamed past him and shuddered to a halt outside the factory gate.

Okita stopped at the kerbside, staring through his windscreen as armed and uniformed men spilled from the cars. He thought of Koga lying helpless in the factory. The student was trapped, while he himself could only sit and watch, hands gripping the wheel until the knuckles showed bone-white.

Inside the factory, Koga heard the distant wail of sirens, and lurched to his feet, his pock-marked face dead-white and running with sweat. His bandaged shoulder throbbed like a giant pulse. Staggering the few steps to a metal cabinet, he threw it open. There on the second shelf was the stuff he needed: two sticks of gelignite, a box of percussion caps, and several rolls of heavy adhesive tape. He knew what he was going to do. They would never take him—never! With a tremendous effort, Koga crossed the dim cavern of the main workshop and climbed the metal stairway which led to a gantry high above. He could hear cars outside, and shouted orders and running feet. He made it to the gantry and fell down, retching. He forced himself to stand upright and pushed open the iron door to the flat concrete roof.

Beyond the low roof parapet he could see the police, guns drawn, advancing warily into the compound. One of them glanced up and spotted him. He yelled a warning to the others. Koga sank to his knees, hidden from view, and set to work.

First the tape, wrapped round his body. Yes, he could manage it with only one hand. Now bind the gelignite against his stomach. Next the percussion caps, just as Sato had taught him. He felt proud that he possessed the expertise to prime high explosives and thereby arrange for his own destruction.

He raised himself up and looked over the parapet. Traffic had crept to a halt on the inner ring road. He had his audience: hundreds of people waited silently, enthralled. For the first and only time in his short life, Masaru Koga was the star attraction.

In the compound below the police had taken cover. The sergeant in charge, keeping out of sight, shouted through cupped hands. "The building is surrounded! Give yourself up!"

Koga stood up, in full view. It struck him as a monstrous black joke that these so-called guardians of society thought he was

426

beaten. It wasn't their victory—it was his. He was master of his own fate and would die as he had lived. An individual, deciding his own destiny.

Teetering on the edge of the parapet, Koga grinned insanely. The sergeant, staring up at him, could see the red-stained bandage. Then he made out what Koga had strapped to his waist. "God in Heaven," he whispered hoarsely. "He's wired himself with dynamite . . . he's a human bomb!"

At his command his men fell back beyond the fence. Dropping down behind a patrol car, the sergeant wondered what the hell to do. Raising himself cautiously, he bellowed, "Listen to me, Koga! Don't be a damn fool! There's no need to—"

But Koga was lost in his own mad dreams. He lifted his right fist high in a salute of mocking defiance.

Then his fist came down, swift and sure, onto the heads of the percussion caps at his waist.

As Okita watched, Koga vanished in a bright orange blast that shattered the roof of the building.

17:25—CTC Operations—Tokyo Central

Everyone in the operations room was bereft of hope since the police report on the Sun-Plaza fire had come in. It was the lowest point of the seven-hour ordeal.

Suddenly Hiroshi remembered his daughter, her birthday party, his promise to be home early. But first he had a job to finish. She wouldn't understand until she was much older, but this was his present to her. He took a deep breath and asked the operator to contact the motorman. Aoki's voice came cheerfully over the speaker. "Hello, Chief, what's the situation? Can we go ahead?"

Conflicting emotions passed like shadows across Hiroshi's face. He wet his lips. "We couldn't get the information, Aoki. The instructions were destroyed in a fire."

Silence. "What now?" Aoki said finally, his voice hard.

"We still have over three hours." Hiroshi hoped his voice didn't betray his own lack of conviction.

His deputy stepped up to the curved desk and took the microphone. "Aoki, this is Sunaga. We're having another try at filming the train. We've set up cameras on the other side of the Aki Tunnel, near Hiroshima, this time with a full battery of lights.

427

Hiroshima TV will process the film in their labs and transmit it to us on a closed-circuit channel. We want you to reduce speed to fifty-five miles per hour as you reach the tunnel. Is that clear?"

"Yes, understood. Do you really think there's a chance?"

"Yes I do," Sunaga asserted positively. "You don't think the National Railways are prepared to let you get away after they've invested all that time and money in training you, do you? They'll want another thirty years service out of you yet, Aoki. Look at me—way over the hill and they still won't let me go."

"You're not as ancient as all that," Aoki responded, a shade more brightly.

"Maybe not. I can still drink you youngsters under the table."

"I don't drink much, but I'll accept the challenge."

"You're on. When you get back, we'll head for the nearest bar. First round's on me."

He switched off the transmit button and Hiroshi gripped his shoulder gratefully. "Thanks, Sunaga."

Senda, Makoto's aide, appeared with a file. "Here is some information we've dug up on Okita. After he went bankrupt in 1977, his wife and daughter left him. He apparently started hitting the bottle, and since then he's been living in the factory on the Shimura Industrial Estate. Everything points to Okita's being the one who planned and organized the operation. Now it seems there's been an explosion at the factory. The other one, Koga, blew himself up."

"Koga—dead." Hiroshi leaned forward, pinching the bridge of his nose between thumb and forefinger. "That means that Okita is probably the only person alive who knows about the bomb." He turned decisively to Sunaga. "Are the TV cameras still set up downstairs?"

The deputy nodded. "What's on your mind?"

"There's one thing we haven't tried. A direct appeal." As he strode towards the door, he came face to face with Matt and Lieutenant Tashiro, their eyes red-rimmed, their hair and clothing scorched. The American's left hand was bandaged.

"I thought they'd taken you to the hospital?"

"They tried," Matt retorted, "but we had other ideas. What's happening here? Are we any nearer to locating the bomb?"

"Sunaga will bring you up to date." Hiroshi smiled wanly.

"Glad to see that you're all right," he said, and was gone.

"Then we still don't know," Matt said grimly.

Sunaga could only shake his head.

17:40—Meguro District—Tokyo

Yasuko Okita was preparing dinner in her parents' kitchen when her mother appeared in the doorway. The old woman's hands were pressed to her face and her mouth worked uselessly.

"What's wrong?" Yasuko cried, rushing towards her.

The old woman pointed feebly to the TV set in the living room where a grave-faced announcer was saying, ". . . but the police have no knowledge of the whereabouts of Tetsuo Okita. Due to the urgency of the situation, the head of Centralized Traffic Control of the National Railways will make a direct appeal . . ."

Yasuko stared at the screen as the announcer droned on. What had all this to do with her husband? Another man appeared, his dark eyes clouded with worry. "If you're watching this broadcast, Tetsuo, please believe that every word I say is the truth. It isn't a trick. The instructions and plans you left for us at the Sun-Plaza were destroyed in a fire. You are the only person left who can help us, so you must contact us with the information on where the bomb is located and how to defuse it." The head of Traffic Control paused, a sheen of perspiration on his pale forehead. "One phone call, that's all, and you'll have saved the lives of hundreds of people. Even five million dollars, Tetsuo, won't buy you a clear conscience if you allow those people to die."

Yasuko turned blindly to her mother. "Can it be true?" she whispered. "Is Tetsuo really responsible for that . . . act of madness? He never harmed anyone in his life."

"Except you and his daughter," her mother said coldly.

Remembering those final horrible months of her husband's drunkenness, Yasuko couldn't hold back the tears. She wept openly while her mother tried to comfort her.

Neither woman heard the doorbell until it had shrilled several times. The old lady answered it, and the tall figure of a police superintendent entered the room, followed by his sergeant.

Hanamura wasted no time. He fired question after question, ignoring Yasuko's distressed condition. She was the wife of Tetsuo Okita, correct? When and where had she last seen her husband?

Did she know any of his friends? Where might be he hiding out?

Again and again Yasuko told him tearfully that she'd had nothing to do with Okita for more than a year.

"Not a single letter or phone call?"

"No, nothing."

"I see. . . . What about a photograph of your husband?"

"I destroyed them—burned them all when I left him."

"Do you expect us to believe that?"

"But it's the truth. I wanted nothing that would remind me of him!" she protested, becoming more and more upset by the relentless barrage of questions.

Her seventeen-year-old daughter, Kimi, who had been at a friend's house down the street, suddenly rushed in, cheeks flushed, her long hair swirling over her shoulders. "Mother—they're talking about Daddy on television! He's wanted by the police—" Then she saw the two men, and stood stock still.

18:00—TOKYO BAY—CHIBA

In a motel room in Chiba, not far from Narita International Airport, Okita was crouched over a small writing table, pen in hand, a half-filled tumbler of neat Scotch at his elbow, gazing at a blank TV screen. He took a single deep swallow, grimaced, then set the glass down.

Even five million dollars, Tetsuo, won't buy you a clear conscience if you allow those people to die. . . . Okita choked down his rage. What did they know of dying? With his own eyes he'd seen two people die in the past few hours. Was it so recently he'd seen Sato and Koga killed? He couldn't believe it.

Okita's hand shook as he wrote out two labels. Two brown paper packages lay on the bed, each containing the amount as agreed. He addressed one to Sato's parents, the other to Koga's brother. The remaining two million dollars, Okita's share of the ransom, was strewn in bundles over the faded green bedcover. He was a fabulously rich man. Friendless. Alone. Hunted.

18:07—HIKARI 109—HIROSHIMA

When the train slowed and the passengers saw the bright arc lights flashing by, speculation rippled through the coaches. Why were they still photographing the train? Didn't they have the information they needed? Fear, feeding upon itself, rose to a pitch of barely controlled panic.

In Coach 14, Detective-Sergeant Ozaki was called on to help calm an hysterical woman a few seats back. He left his prisoner, Fujio, still handcuffed to the seat support. With the detective preoccupied, Fujio decided his moment had come, and went down on his knees between the seats. He allowed the bracelet of the handcuffs to slide down the metal seat support to the floor, then, bracing himself, shoulders hunched, he gripped the handcuffs' chain with both hands and began to heave. Nothing budged. Fujio took an enormous breath and tried again, his neck bulging from the strain. Suddenly, there was a splintering crunch and the screws were wrenched from the floor. Fujio slipped the bracelet free of the support and was on his feet, charging along the aisle and into the next coach before Ozaki realized what was happening. The detective went after him, gun drawn, but Fujio had a head start.

In Coach 10, Duty Policeman Nagata was rooted to the spot by the sight of the huge man charging towards him. The next thing he knew he'd been sent sprawling by a solid forearm. Ozaki ran past. "Come on! We've got to get him before he kills somebody!"

With insane fury Fujio smashed his way through the buffet car, the restaurant car, then into the narrow kitchen. There, with the snarl of a cornered beast, Fujio snatched up a long carving knife, grabbed a young waitress, and held the knife at her throat.

Ozaki skidded to a halt in the doorway, his gun levelled. Nagata was close behind.

"One move from either of you and she gets it!" Fujio rasped, holding the terrified girl tight against him. "You!"—to one of the cooks—"Open the service door."

The cook sidled across to the outer door. Nagata said tremulously, "Please don't. If you open that door, the train will stop automatically. The bomb will explode. . . ."

"So what. Do you think I care, cop? By then I'll have jumped."

Fujio jerked his head at the cook, who slid back the bolt. Nagata panicked. He leaped forward and grabbed the cook's arm. Thrusting the girl out of the way, Fujio lunged at the duty policeman trying to stop him, but Ozaki moved fast. With a vicious chop he brought the muzzle of the gun down on the back of Fujio's neck. The knife skittered away as Fujio fell.

"I must get off," he mumbled brokenly. "I don't want to die. There's dynamite on the train."

Ozaki stood over him. "What do you know about dynamite?" The detective raised his gun. "If you want to save your skin, Fujio, you'd better tell me everything you know. Everything!"

Fujio shrank away. "I . . . I supplied the dynamite, that's all. I don't know where they planted it, I swear."

"But you know who did it."

Fujio nodded. "Three of them. I sold the dynamite to a student called Koga, but an older man—Okita—he planned it. I heard later they were going to collect a ransom and leave the country."

"This man Okita. Where's he hiding out?"

Fujio shook his head wildly. "I don't know. He had a—yes, I remember now—a forged passport." Fujio licked his lips. "The name on it was . . . yes, Numata. That was it."

The detective turned and snapped at Nagata. "Get through to Tokyo. Tell them one of the men they're after is leaving the country. Forged passport in the name of Numata. Get to it."

18:25—CTC OPERATIONS—TOKYO CENTRAL

In the darkened room adjoining the operations centre, three men were sitting forward tensely in their chairs, eyes fixed on a large television monitor. The photographic expert was talking them through the film transmitted by Hiroshima TV. "We're looking at the undercarriage of Coach 4 . . . This is Coach 5 . . ."

"I don't see anything," Matt said, straining his eyes.

When the sequence ended, Sunaga sighed. "These are better than the first lot but it's still impossible to pick out anything. What about you, Takada?" he asked the chief engineer.

"Nothing," Takada shrugged, clearly unhappy with the result.

"Let's see it again," Matt ordered. "Tell them to run it very slowly." Fists clenched, he ground out savagely, "There has to be something. There has to be!"

18:30—PRESIDENT'S OFFICE—TOKYO CENTRAL

The president of the Railway Board was a slight, soft-spoken man with delicate hands and snow-white hair. Sitting in his office on the second floor, he gazed sombrely at Hiroshi, who found it impossible to conceal his impatience at being called away from the operations room. Come on, he thought, get on with it.

"You must understand that this isn't my decision," the president stated quietly. "It's what the government has decided . . . ."

Hiroshi repressed a sigh. The president went on. "The government feels that time is running out and it now seems unlikely that the bomb will be defused. Under the circumstances—well, an explosion in the countryside is preferable to one in a heavily built-up area like the terminus at Hakata."

Hiroshi couldn't believe what he was hearing. "Do you mean deliberately stop the train? You can't be serious."

"I'm afraid I am."

Aghast, Hiroshi said, "No, it's madness!"

"The decision has been made. The area selected is rural and sparsely populated."

"Supposing the motorman refuses to obey the instruction?" Hiroshi said, seeking loopholes.

"The motorman will not be consulted," the president said. "When the train is five miles past Ogori we shall shut down all power on the Shinkansen."

Ogori, the place of execution, was one hour away. Hiroshi's anger erupted. "I won't agree to it! We'd be killing those people in cold blood when there's still a chance, when there's still *time*."

"How much time?"

Hiroshi looked at his watch. "Two hours and twenty-five minutes to the terminus."

The president said in his gentle voice, "I understand what this means to you, believe me. But can't you see what will happen if we allow the train to reach Hakata? The terminus is in the heart of the city. Many more people—thousands perhaps—might die in the explosion."

Hiroshi turned away, his face haggard with strain.

"The decision isn't ours," the president said softly. "We have to do as we're ordered. The government has decided."

Hiroshi left the president's office without a word and returned to the operations room with a sense of defeat and a sick heart. Just then a door at the rear of the room opened and Matt, followed by Sunaga, strode in. Hiroshi hardly registered their presence until the American said: "There's a device of some kind attached to the leading axle of Coach 2."

Hiroshi slowly turned his head. "You've found it?" he said.

Matt nodded and glanced at Sunaga. "We think so. It's a small device linked by wires to what could be a dynamo."

Hiroshi swung round and gripped his shoulder. "How long will it take to defuse it? Less than an hour?"

"It all depends on how complex it is and how easily it can be reached from inside the train. We'll have to find a point of access, a maintenance hatch or something."

"I'll check the plans of the coach layout," Sunaga proposed.

"Right, do that." Hiroshi then asked the American, "What now? What do you need?"

"First thing—a radio-telephone extension into Coach 2. Have the motorman standing by with a toolkit. When he's located the bomb I'll talk him through each stage." He saw the glimmering of a smile on the face of the operations chief and added stonily, "Don't think it's going to be easy. We've a long way to go yet."

"But we're making progress at last. Now they won't dare cut the power . . ."

Matt stared at him. "What are you talking about?"

"Never mind." The faint smile was still on Hiroshi's face as he reached for the microphone.

18:45—HIKARI 109—IWAKUNI

The three men stood on the small platform at the front of the second coach. The head guard, Yamada, and the young guard, Ando, were watching Aoki anxiously, as with both hands pressed to his headset, he strained to hear Matt's voice above the clatter of wheels.

"The device is fixed to the leading axle of the coach."

"Yes, the leading axle. Which side?" Aoki asked.

"The lefthand side. There must be some way of reaching it from inside the train. Locate the means of access and I'll tell you what to do next."

Aoki and the guards began a close search of the bulkhead and the flooring. There were no inspection hatches, no removable panels. Aoki reported this, and after a pause Matt said, "Try the rubbish bin. Sunaga says that it's connected by a disposal chute to the underside of the train."

"Yes. The rubbish bin." Aoki pointed and Yamada lifted the

metal lid, set into the wall. The bin had been searched before. But now Ando emptied it of refuse, and Aoki was able to shine his torch down into the slanting steel shaft, nearly five feet deep. At the very bottom the beam picked out something.

"I see them! Two wires—looped out through the lower hatch."

"Well done," Matt congratulated him. "Now listen carefully. One of those wires will connect the speedometer to a relay on the dynamo. The other will connect the dynamo to the charge. What you must do, Aoki, is cut the *second* of those—the wire from the dynamo to the charge. Whatever you do, *don't cut the first wire!*"

Bent double as he leaned into the steel shaft, Aoki was seized by a paroxysm of fear. If he cut the wrong one the bomb would detonate. He said hoarsely into the tiny microphone: "How do I know which wire is which?"

"One of the wires—the one connecting the speedometer to the dynamo relay—should have extra insulation. Can you spot that?"

Aoki held the torch at arm's length and peered closer. "One of them seems to be slightly thicker and has small grooves—"

"That's the one," Matt said tersely. "Now what you have to do is cut the *other* wire. The thin one. Got that?"

"Yes." Aoki moistened his lips. "The thin one."

He squirmed out of the chute, discarded the headset, and took the pliers that Yamada offered. A look passed between them, then Aoki inhaled a steadying breath and once more leaned inside the chute. This was it. One snip and it would all be over. One way or the other. He reached down with the pliers, but even at full stretch he was several inches short of the wires.

He straightened up again. "It's no good. I'll have to get inside. Give me a hand."

Yamada and Ando helped the motorman climb into the chute. His feet scrabbled for a foothold against the smooth metal sides and found none. Held by the two guards, he lowered himself until his feet were touching the lower hatch through which the rubbish was emptied. Then bending at the knees he groped for the wires. The train lurched, the lower hatch flew open with a resounding clang and he slid downwards.

For a frozen moment Aoki was suspended half in and half out of the chute, his legs dangling above the rushing tracks. Then a hand clamped itself round his upper arm and another grabbed him by the collar. Together the two guards hauled him out. Aoki was shaking, unable to utter a sound. He closed his eyes and leaned back against the wall.

"Those wires," Yamada said, chest heaving from his exertions, "must have prevented the hatch from closing properly."

"Let's take a look," Aoki said, but when they did so, they could see nothing except the hatch swinging to and fro above the blur of the tracks. The wires were gone.

SURROUNDED BY a tense circle of engineers and technical staff, Matt was seated at the communications desk, holding the microphone in his bandaged left hand. He was trying to visualize what had happened. The wires had disappeared—then they must be hanging free, underneath the train. So near, he thought. Aoki had almost had the wires in his hand. . . .

He thumbed the transmit button. "You say the hatch is open?"

"Yes."

"The wires must be still connected. Can't you get to them through the open hatch?"

"How?" It was less a question than a plaintive cry.

"Can you break away the sides of the chute? Get to them that way?"

"Break it? What with? It's steel plate, welded. We'd need an oxyacetylene torch."

Hiroshi leaned towards the chief engineer. There was still a way. But they had to move fast. He said, "Arrange for oxyacetylene equipment and a gas cylinder to be put on a maintenance wagon at Tokuyama." He called out to the controller on Section 7. "Is the up line clear?"

"All the way to Hakata."

"Then we'll bring the maintenance wagon alongside the Hikari 109 and pass the equipment across. Tell them to clear Coach 16 and smash one of the windows facing the up line." He looked at the clock. "They'll be approaching the maintenance depot at Tokuyama in about fifteen and a half minutes. Tell the crew to stand by to receive the equipment."

Matt sat back in the chair, his shirt clinging damply to his back. It was seven o'clock. Normally he and Laura had dinner at this hour. Fighting down emotion, his face remained inscrutable.

19:15—HIKARI 109—TOKUYAMA

The driver of the diesel locomotive stood at the cab window with his hand on the throttle as the nose of the Bullet Train drew level and gradually overtook him. He glimpsed the assistant motorman inside, staring across at him without expression. The poor wretch, thought the driver. It was like observing someone in a condemned cell.

He estimated that the Bullet Train was maintaining a steady sixty miles per hour. His own speed was fifty-seven miles per hour. Now came the tricky part—aligning the maintenance wagon with the last coach and matching their speeds exactly while the equipment was ferried across.

In Coach 16 all was ready. The head guard had enlisted the aid of guards Ando and Kenichi, and kneeling on the seat next to the broken window, his eyes watering in the wind, he watched the large open door of the wagon edging into line. A four-man crew was standing by with a plank, ready to bridge the five foot gap.

The crew foreman signalled, and Yamada's team prepared to receive one end of the plank and make it secure. This was easy. Moving the cumbersome gas cylinder across in what was effectively a sixty-mile-an-hour gale would be the real test.

The cutting equipment was attached to ropes which were tossed from the maintenance wagon through the window of Coach 16, and eagerly grasped by Yamada's team. They hauled away, and when the equipment was safely on board, they prepared to receive the heavy gas cylinder. Again ropes were thrown and the guards set to work, pulling the cylinder along the narrow plank. "Nearly there!" Yamada shouted encouragingly. "Come on now, heave!"

In the maintenance wagon, the intercom buzzed. The foreman picked up the handset and heard the driver say: "There's an obstruction four hundred yards ahead! A signal gantry between the tracks!"

The foreman yelled to his crew to stand clear and gestured frantically to the head guard to indicate the obstruction ahead. Yamada leaned out and grabbed hold of the cylinder head and began to heave with all his strength. His team responded on the ropes, staggering back as the long torpedo-like cylinder slid through the window into the coach. In the next instant there was an explosive crack as the plank smashed against the signal gantry and was swept away in a tangle of sheared timber.

AOKI APPLIED the hissing white flame of the oxyacetylene torch to the outer steel casing of the rubbish bin and watched through his dark goggles as the blobs of molten metal ran down. He knew he had to make a hole large enough to give him access to the running gear. Down there—somewhere—hung the two wires connecting all their lives to eternity.

"How much more?" Yamada asked, leaning forward.

"Nearly there, I think. If I cut along the base it should come loose. Be ready to grab it."

Aoki moved the cutting head the last few inches and the plate came free. The two guards lifted it aside, and as the running gear was revealed, the noise of the wheels swelled deafeningly.

"Can you see the wires?" Yamada shouted above the racket.

Aoki flung away the goggles and peered down. There the wires were, swaying gently to and fro. Yamada held his feet, Ando his waist, and he reached down at full stretch through the jagged gap and lifted the two wires towards him. One was thick and ribbed, the other shiny and thin.

He held the wires in his left hand, the pliers in his right. Such a simple thing to do. He held his breath and snipped.

Nothing happened.

After the longest moment of his life, Aoki breathed again.

19:35—HIKARI 109—OGORI

Everywhere on the train a hush had settled. In every coach people sat silently, locked in their own thoughts. The only sound on the Hikari 109 was that of the train itself, the bass hum of the power units, the staccato rhythm of the wheels.

For nine hours the motorman had been under intolerable physical and mental stress. Now the ordeal was almost over. Three miles beyond Ogori, where a road slanted in from the left, Aoki saw a line of parked vehicles—fire tenders, ambulances and three dark-green army ordnance trucks. Over the speaker he heard Hiroshi's voice, very controlled. "Begin to slow down."

Aoki looked at Uchida. He smiled, and then—as he'd done a

438

thousand times before—he took hold of the brake control lever and unhesitatingly pushed it forward.

The long silver-grey train slowly crept to a halt, standing motionless on the track three miles outside Ogori. The Hikari 109 Super Express had stopped at 19:42 precisely. Smoothing the lapels of his crumpled uniform and summoning up his best official manner, Aoki squared his shoulders and spoke into the handset. "Motorman Aoki reporting, sir. The Hikari 109 has stopped safely three miles east of Ogori. Awaiting further instructions."

Yoko, sitting now with the children in Coach 2, found that tears were streaming down her face. She hugged the children to her. Many of the adult passengers, too, were weeping openly. There was no wild elation at finding themselves alive. Just a mood of quiet reverence, as if a precious possession, thought to be lost for ever, had been restored to them.

Laura stood at the narrow window of the guards' compartment, looking anxiously towards the waiting fleet of ambulances. There was a good chance that Keiko would be all right now. But they'd have to get her to a hospital quickly.

Despite her genuine concern for the girl, Laura found her thoughts turning to Matt. The desire to feel his arms around her stabbed through her heart like a physical pain, and the landscape fragmented and blurred as her eyes filled with tears.

In the Coach 11 Green Car, Mickie was unable to contain her bubbling delight. As Duty Policeman Nagata came along the aisle she rose and impulsively kissed his cheek. Nagata blushed, swallowed, then hurried on his way. Goodness, whatever would his wife say? Kissed by a geisha! Still giggling at his confusion, Mickie turned gaily towards Takazana and the smile froze on her lips. The old man lay propped in his seat, his head to one side, his eyes glazed. There was no need to check his pulse. At the very moment that the train had stopped, Takazana had relinquished his feeble grip on life. His hands lay open on his lap, palms uppermost, like the claws of a small dead bird.

19:50—CTC OPERATIONS—TOKYO CENTRAL

After congratulations all around, the happy circle of technical staff and engineers had left the operations room. Now the place was quiet; Shinkansen operations wouldn't resume until the morrow. Hiroshi stood with Matt contemplating Section 7 of the main display board on which the bar of orange light had stopped.

"One hour and sixteen minutes to Hakata," Matt said.

"It was close," Hiroshi said softly. "Too close."

Matt looked at the operations chief's drawn face. "You ought to get some rest. You look awful."

Hiroshi grinned faintly and touched the scorched sleeve of Matt's uniform. "You're giving me advice?"

Matt felt weary, but it was a pleasant languor. Laura was alive, he'd see her in the morning. His life stretched ahead once more. He said, "Come on, I'll buy you a drink."

Hiroshi restrained him. "I know how difficult it must have been for you, with your wife aboard that train. I want to say thank you."

Matt shrugged. "It wasn't easy for any of us," he said awkwardly. "What matters is that we did it. Come on, let's have that drink."

They walked towards the exit and passed the open door of the investigation room. Hiroshi paused, frowning. Superintendent Hanamura and the police chief were sitting in front of the television monitor watching a repeat of the appeal Hiroshi had broadcast earlier.

"Why are you still running that film?" Hiroshi asked curiously.

"There's still a chance," Makoto said brightly, "that Okita might see it and get in touch. He might accidentally reveal—"

Incredulous, Hiroshi stormed into the room. "You mean you haven't made an announcement yet? What about all those people waiting to hear if their families and friends are safe?"

"We intend to make an official announcement five minutes before the train is due to arrive at Hakata," Hanamura informed him blandly. "I'm sure no one would begrudge us the chance to apprehend the man responsible." He added smugly, "I would remind you that we're only doing our duty."

Hiroshi lunged forward, but Matt grabbed his arm. "It's too late," he said. "Leave it."

Speechless, the operations chief turned away and almost collided in the doorway with the president of the Railway Board, who had come down to congratulate him.

Hiroshi found his voice. It was low-pitched, almost threatening.

440

"I wish to hand in my resignation, effective now. I'll confirm it in writing by nine o'clock tomorrow morning."

The president was taken aback. "In heaven's name, why?"

It was Superintendent Hanamura who said in his scathing drawl, "It would seem that he doesn't approve of our methods."

"*Your methods.*" Hiroshi rounded on him, spitting out the words. "Your methods consist of treating people as though they were just another expendable commodity. It's only thanks to Major Brennan here that these people are still alive. All you cared about was making an arrest." His voice sank to a whisper. "Your squad has to come out of this looking good, its reputation intact. In that prison cell mind of yours, that's all that matters."

There was a long silence. Hiroshi and Matt left.

20:00—NEW INTERNATIONAL AIRPORT—NARITA

Sergeant Goto was stationed near the TWA desk, pretending to browse through a travel brochure. Police inquiries to the airlines had confirmed that someone named Numata was booked on Flight 073 to San Francisco, departing at 20:30 hours. If that should be Okita, they would have him cold, Goto thought. Thirty plainclothesmen and three squads of uniformed police were deployed in and around the airport. It was sealed tighter than a drum.

Goto glanced up as a middle-aged man hurried up to the desk carrying a large suitcase and a new leather briefcase. The man had a pouchy face and sunken eyes and his hair was thick and black.

Goto stiffened. Right age group. Late forties, early fifties. He watched covertly as the man approached the counter.

"I'm booked on Flight 073." He had a wheezing smoker's voice.

"Yes, sir. What name?"

Goto's heart skipped a beat.

The man coughed and said gruffly, "Sakuma."

"Here we are, sir. Goro Sakuma. Flight 073, San Francisco. Have a good trip, sir."

The clerk handed over the ticket and the man bustled off.

Under the thick black wig Okita was perspiring as he went across to the check-in counter. There was not the slightest doubt that the man with the neat moustache near the TWA desk was a policeman. Yet he hadn't been challenged. He congratulated himself on his foresight in having switched his forged documents for Koga's. Fujio had been on the train and there was always the remote chance that he might have known something of Okita's plans. But Koga, the outsider, would never have breathed a word of his own arrangements.

He headed for the departure lounge, which was only moderately full, found an armchair, and settled back. A moment later he heard his name, Okita, quite distinctly, and jerked his head round. On a TV set in the far corner of the lounge, they were showing a repeat of the appeal by the operations chief. Okita caught the words: "One phone call, that's all it needs, and you'll have saved the lives of hundreds of people. . . ."

Okita glanced at his watch. Ten minutes past eight. There was just time before boarding the plane. He picked up his briefcase and went to the row of telephones and dialled Tokyo Central.

"Yes, can I help you?"

"I have information you need about the bomb on the Hikari 109. Listen carefully. . . ."

When he was finished he returned to his seat. He felt calm now, glad to have cleared his conscience. It had never been his intention to harm a living soul.

"Would passengers for Flight 073 to San Francisco please proceed at once to Gate 9. Flight 073 is now boarding. . . ."

Okita tucked the precious briefcase under his arm—it contained his share of the money—and moved with the flow of passengers towards the departure door. Not long to go now, he thought. Through Gate 9 and into the darkness beyond. Onto the aircraft—and freedom!

A thin-faced man in a neat dark jacket, obviously a policeman, was standing with two people by the gate, studying the faces of the passengers. Okita was perhaps five yards away when his spine went rigid with the shock of recognition. The two people were his wife and daughter.

What now—run? He still had a chance. Or take a gamble that they wouldn't give him away? Yasuka, don't betray me.

As he came up to the gate his wife looked straight at him. Even in his disguise it was clear that she had recognized him instantly, but her eyes didn't flicker.

Then he heard his daughter, Kimi, release an involuntary gasp.

The detective, alerted, scanned the faces in the queue. "You've spotted him, haven't you?" he said, gripping the girl's elbow.

"No," Kimi protested. "I made a mistake."

Okita edged to the far side of the queue, then turned and ran for the escalator. He hadn't gone ten paces when the detective saw him and raised a pocket transmitter to his mouth. Okita ran on.

"Daddy!"

From the top of the escalator he heard his daughter's piercing cry. "Daddy, please . . . please don't die!"

Looking back he saw her running forward, arms outstretched, and caught a last fleeting glimpse of her face, streaked with tears, before he turned and plunged headlong into the crowd.

HE WAS LOST. Lost in a world of shadows.

Okita had managed to work his way round to the maintenance area at the far end of the airport. Enormous black buildings merged with the night here, and in the distance he could hear the wail of sirens and see the flash of blue lights. Where was he? He had no idea.

Without warning a searchlight stabbed down from a tower, pinning him in its brilliant cone, and he scuttled into the surrounding darkness like a beetle seeking refuge.

"Okita!" A voice echoed over a loudhailer. "We've got the airport covered, there's no escape. Give yourself up!"

He had to keep going. . . . If he could reach the fence he might make it—but where was the fence? He ran blindly, his lungs on fire, the briefcase banging painfully against his leg. More cars, lights flashing, sirens blaring. They were closing in, pushing him onward into the wall of darkness.

Suddenly his legs gave way and he went down on his knees, gasping and coughing. But sounds behind forced him to his feet again and he stumbled on, immeasurably weary. It seemed to Okita that he had been running for ever, lost in a cruel, endless nightmare.

"Stop! Stop or I fire!"

It was a police sergeant, not twenty yards away.

Okita ignored him and kept on, lugging the briefcase across the scorched concrete as the roar of a Boeing 747 drowned everything in an ocean of noise. The jet came on, picking up speed, huge and relentless, lights winking hypnotically. Okita cowered back, shielding his head instinctively.

Distantly he heard the detective shout something and then felt a searing pain in his neck. Yet strangely it was his heart that hurt. The briefcase slipped from his fingers and as he stooped to pick it up all the strength drained out of him. He fell, face down, arms and legs splayed.

The case sprang open and two million dollars swirled up like confetti in the slipstream of the Jumbo as it lifted off directly overhead.

Flight 073 to San Francisco.

Still kneeling, holding his automatic in both hands, Goto watched the money drifting lazily towards the earth as the aircraft vanished into the night.

The Making of an International Success

Publishing novels is usually a fairly simple matter. The author submits his book, the publisher accepts it. He then edits it, has it printed, distributes it to the bookshops, and arranges, where possible, for its appearance in paperback, with the book clubs, and—if it has very special appeal—in Reader's Digest Condensed Books. The publishing of *Bullet Train*, however, was a lot more complicated. It was not submitted to the publisher. Instead, he went out and found it.

Very few Japanese books are ever seen in Europe. On the other hand, Japanese films are seen here quite often. And so it was that *Bullet Train*, as a film, came to be shown in Paris. Ernest Hecht of Souvenir Press saw it there, immediately recognized its exciting qualities, and found that it had been based on a novel by the Japanese author, Arei Kato. Eagerly he had this novel translated, and then looked for a British writer capable of adding the further touches essential for a western readership.

The author he chose was skilful and experienced—a man with sixteen books already to his credit, along with innumerable short stories, travel articles, and television scripts. For his work on *Bullet Train* this author chose to write under the name of Joseph Rance, a nom-de-plume, deliberately assumed to mark what is, he says, "a new departure for me and totally different from my previous books."

The work is certainly a fascinating achievement both for him and for his enterprising publisher. Between them they have brought to Britain, from the far side of the world, a fine and unusual story. Could it, we hope, be the first of many?

"*The last enemy that shall be destroyed is death*"

I CORINTHIANS XV. 26

The Last Enemy

A CONDENSATION OF THE BOOK BY
RICHARD HILLARY

PUBLISHED BY MACMILLAN

*"Never in the field of human conflict was so
much owed by so many to so few."*

Richard Hillary was one of those few. This is
his story, told in his own poignant words . . . .
Published first in 1942, it achieved an
immediate triumph, both popular and literary,
for it spoke straight from its author's
heart to the heart of this proud nation.
It speaks still.

Prologue

September 3, 1940 dawned dark and overcast, with a slight breeze ruffling the waters of the Estuary. Hornchurch aerodrome, twelve miles east of London, wore its usual pallor of yellow morning fog, which lent an added air of grimness to the dimly silhouetted Spitfires around the boundary. From time to time a barrage balloon would poke its head grotesquely through the mist as though looking for possible victims.

We came out onto the tarmac at about eight o'clock. I was worried. We had been bombed a short time before, and my plane had had to be fitted with a new cockpit hood, which as yet would not slide open smoothly along its groove. I feared it never would, and I shouldn't be able to bale out in a hurry if I had to. The corporal fitter and I set upon the hood in a fury of haste, filing and oiling, oiling and filing, until at last it began to loosen. But agonizingly slowly: by ten o'clock, when the mist had cleared and the sun was blazing down out of a clear sky, it was still sticking halfway along the groove.

Then down the loudspeaker came the emotionless voice of the controller: "603 Squadron take off and patrol base; you will receive further orders in the air." As I pressed the starter and the engine roared into life, the corporal stepped back and crossed his fingers significantly. I felt the usual sick feeling, and then I was too busy getting into position to feel anything.

"Uncle George" Denholm and the leading section of three took

449

off in a cloud of dust; Brian Carbury looked across and put up his thumbs. I nodded and opened up. I was flying in Brian's section, with Stap-me Stapleton on the right. The third section consisted of only two machines. Our squadron strength was eight.

We headed southeast. At about 12,000 feet we came up through the clouds which spread out below like layers of whipped cream. The sun was brilliant, which made it difficult to see. I peered anxiously ahead, for the controller had given us warning of at least fifty enemy fighters approaching very high.

We all saw them at the same moment: 500 to 1,000 feet above us and coming straight on like a swarm of locusts. As soon as they saw us they dived, and the next ten minutes was a blur of twisting machines and tracer bullets. One Messerschmitt went down in flames on my right, and a Spitfire hurtled past in a half-roll; I was weaving and turning in a desperate attempt to gain height, with the machine practically hanging on the airscrew.

Then, just below me and to my left, I saw a Messerschmitt climbing and away from the sun. I closed in to 200 yards and gave him a two-second burst: fabric ripped off the wing and black smoke poured from the engine. Like a fool, I did not break away, but put in another three-second burst. Red flames shot upwards and he spiralled out of sight. At that moment, I felt a terrific explosion, and my whole machine quivered like a stricken animal.

In a second, the cockpit was a mass of flames: instinctively, I reached up to open the hood. It would not move. I tore off my straps and managed to force it back; but this took time, and when I reached for the stick in an effort to turn the plane on its back, the heat was so intense that I could feel myself going under. I remember a second of sharp agony, thinking "So this is it!" and putting both hands to my eyes. Then I passed out.

When I regained consciousness I discovered that I was free of the machine and falling rapidly. I pulled the ripcord of my parachute and checked my descent with a jerk. Looking down, I saw that my left trouser leg was burned off, that I was going to fall into the sea, and that the English coast was deplorably far away. About twenty feet above the water, I attempted to undo my parachute, failed and flopped into the sea with it billowing round me.

The water was not unwarm and my life jacket kept me afloat. I looked at my watch; it was not there. Then, for the first time, I noticed how burned my hands were: down to the wrist, the skin was dead white and hung in shreds. I felt faintly sick from the smell of burned flesh. By closing one eye I could see my lips jutting out like motor tyres. I made a further attempt to undo the harness, but owing to the pain of my hands, soon desisted. Instead I lay back and reviewed my position.

I was a long way from land; my hands were burned, and so, judging from the pain, was my face; it was unlikely that anyone on shore had seen me come down and even more unlikely that a ship would come by; I could float for possibly four hours more in my Mae West life jacket.

I had perhaps been premature in considering myself lucky to have escaped from the machine. The water now seemed much colder, and my teeth had started chattering. To quiet them I kept up a tuneless chant, varying it from time to time with futile calls for help. I noticed with surprise that the sun had gone in. I looked down at my hands, and not seeing them, realized I had gone blind. So I was going to die. Surprisingly I was not afraid, only profoundly curious that within a few minutes or a few hours I was to learn the great answer.

I decided that it should be in a few minutes. Reaching up, I unscrewed the valve of my Mae West. The air escaped in a rush and my head went under. It is said by people who have all but died in the sea that drowning is a pleasant death. I did not find it so. I swallowed a large quantity of water. Then my head came up. I tried again, to find that I was so enmeshed in my parachute that I could not move. For the next ten minutes I tore my hands to ribbons on the catch. It was stuck fast. I lay back exhausted, and then I started to laugh: there was something irresistibly comic in my grand gesture of suicide being so simply thwarted.

It is often said that a dying man relives his whole life in one rapid kaleidoscope. I merely thought gloomily of the squadron returning to base, of my mother, and of the few people who would miss me. Outside my family, I could count them on the fingers of one hand.

I began to feel a terrible loneliness. My mind wandered aimlessly, and I remember, as in a dream, hearing somebody shout. It seemed far away and quite unconnected with me. . . .

Then arms were dragging me; my parachute was taken off (and

451

with such ease!); a brandy flask was pushed between my swollen lips; a voice said, "OK, Joe, it's one of ours and still kicking;" and I was safe, in a boat. I was neither relieved nor angry: I was past caring.

The Pilot

The foundations of an experience of which my crash was, if not the climax, at least the turning point, were laid in Oxford before the war.

Oxford has been called many names, from "the city of beautiful nonsense" to "an organized waste of time." The harsher names have usually been the inventions of Oxford's own undergraduates.

By the summer of 1939 I had been there two years and was not yet twenty-one. I had spent those two years at Trinity College rowing a great deal, flying a little—I was a member of the University Air Squadron—and reading somewhat.

We were a small college of less than two hundred, but a successful one, with Club presidents, numerous Blues, and a small but select band of scholars. Trinity was, in fact, a typical incubator of the English ruling classes before the war. We were most of us comfortably enough off, held together by a common taste in sport, literature and idle amusement, by a deep-rooted distrust of standardized patriotism, and by a somewhat self-conscious satisfaction in our ability to succeed without apparent effort.

Now, war was imminent. We were depressed by a sense of its inevitability. While lacking any political training, we were convinced that we had been needlessly led into the present crisis by a crowd of incompetent old fools. We hoped merely that when war came it might be fought with a maximum of individuality and a minimum of discipline.

Though we were still outwardly complacent and successful, there was a very definite undercurrent of dissatisfaction and frustration amongst nearly everyone I knew during my last year. Even more evident was a seed of self-destruction among the more intellectual members of the university. Despising the middle-class society to which they owed their education, they affected a dilettante political leaning to the left. Of this leaning was a friend of mine in another college, David Rutter. He was also a pacifist.

"Patriotism," he would say, "is a false emotion. When this war comes, which, thanks to the muddling of our government, come it must, whose war is it going to be? You can't tell me that it will be the same war for the unemployed labourer as for the Duke of Westminster. What are the people to gain from it? Nothing!"

But though his arguments against patriotism were intellectual, his pacifism was emotional. He had a completely sincere hatred of violence and killing, and the spectacle of army chaplains wearing field boots under the surplice revolted him.

Secretly I admired David, but I was already in the University Air Squadron and I should, of course, join the air force. "In a fighter plane," I said, "we have found a way to return to war as it ought to be, war which is individual combat, in which one either kills or is killed. It's exciting, it's individual, and it's disinterested. I shan't get maimed: either I shall be killed or I shall get a few pleasant putty medals and enjoy being stared at in a night club. Your unfortunate convictions, worthy as they are, will get you at best a few white feathers and at worst locked up."

The press referred to us as the Lost Generation and we were not displeased. Superficially we were selfish, but the war gave us the opportunity to prove to ourselves and to the world that our effete veneer was not as deep as our dislike of interference.

For myself, the war solved all problems of a career. I wished to be a writer, and the war promised a chance of self-realization that would normally take years to achieve. As a fighter pilot I hoped for a concentration of amusement, fear, and exaltation which would be impossible to experience in any other form of existence.

I was not disappointed.

SEPTEMBER 3, 1939 fell during the long vacation, and all of us in the University Air Squadron reported that day to the Volunteer Reserve Centre at Oxford. We were told to stand by. Then we were drafted to an Initial Training Wing where we never saw an aeroplane and seldom attended a lecture. I was commissioned on the score of my proficiency certificate in the University Air Squadron, and moved to another wing. Here I found myself with an old friend, Noel Agazarian.

Noel had been sent down from Oxford over a slight matter of breaking up his college; he intended reading for the Bar. With an Armenian father and a French mother he was by nature cosmopolitan, intelligent, and a brilliant linguist, but an English education had discovered that he was an athlete, and so his university triumphs were of brawn rather than brain. With his pleasantly ugly face, he was an amusing companion and a very good friend.

Although we were officers, route marches were nevertheless obligatory; and by some odd chance Noel and I always seemed to be in the last section on the march. Prominent and eager at the start, we were somehow never to be seen by the end. Through a certain low cunning we also managed to skip entirely quite a number of parades and lectures.

That such behaviour was uncooperative did not occur to us. We had joined the air force to fly, and not to parade around like Boy Scouts. We didn't bother to consider that elementary training might be essential, or that a certain confusion of organization was inevitable at the beginning of the war. There admittedly can be no excuse for our behaviour but I think an explanation is to be found in the fact that Dunkirk had not come: the war was still one of tin soldiers and not yet of reality.

Then one day it was announced that we were to move. Our period of inactivity was over.

Noel, Peter Howes and I were to report for flying training at a small village in the northeast of Scotland. As we were likely to be together for some months, I was relieved to be going with people whom I knew and liked.

Peter Howes had been reading for a science degree. Lanky and of cadaverous good looks, he was never so happy as when, lying back smoking his pipe, he could expound on sex (of which he knew very little), on literature (of which he knew more), and on mathematics (of which he knew a great deal).

After a fortnight's pep course to which we submitted with no very good grace, Peter, Noel, and I drove up to Scotland together. We arrived in the late afternoon of a raw, cold November day. When we had reported to the adjutant, Peter drove us down to the little greystone house in the neighbouring village that was to be our home for many months.

Our landlady, a somewhat bewildered old body, showed us with pride the room in which we were to sleep. It was without heating. The iron bedsteads stood austerely in its middle with an enamelled washbasin in one corner. A bewhiskered ancestor looked stonily at us from over the washstand. The room was scrupulously clean. We assured her that we should be most comfortable, and returned, a little chastened, to the camp.

At the beginning of the war there was a definite prejudice in the air force against volunteer reserve officers. We were known as weekend pilots, as the long-haired boys. We were to have the nonsense knocked out of us by the chief ground instructor who took to his task with enthusiasm. Nevertheless, thanks to the fact that we got on well with our fellow pilots, and to Noel's infectious good humour and lack of affectation, we gradually settled down and our lives became a regular routine of flying and lectures. We three flew Harvards, American fighter trainers.

My recollection of our Scottish training is a confusion of, in the main, pleasant memories. Of our flying instructors: Noel and I were very lucky—Noel was handed over to Sergeant Robinson, I to Sergeant White. They were great friends, and rivalry began between them to see who could first make a pilot out of such un-promising material. White was a taciturn little Scot with a dry sense of humour. I liked him at once and, thanks to him, I developed into a quite moderate pilot. For weeks he sat behind me in the rear cockpit muttering, just loud enough for me to hear, about the bad luck of getting such a bum for a pupil. Then one day he called down the intercom, "Man, you can fly at last. Now I want you to show our friend Sergeant Robinson that he's not the only one with a pupil that's not a half-wit."

Of my first solo cross-country flight: a little red light inside the cockpit started winking at me, and then the engine cut. The red light continued to shine like a brothel invitation while I racked my brain to think what was wrong. I was down to 500 feet, and more frightened of making a fool of myself than of crashing, when I remembered. It was the warning signal for no petrol. I quickly changed tanks, and flew back, determined to learn my cockpit drill thoroughly before taking to the air again.

Of cotton wool clouds: I shall never forget the first time I flew really high and, looking down, saw wave after wave of white undulating cloud that stretched for miles in every direction like some fairy city. I dived along a great canyon; the sun threw the reddish shadow of the plane onto the white cliffs that towered on either side. It was intoxicating. I did a slow roll. I could see nothing. I could not tell whether I was on my back or right way up. I lost about 2000 feet and came out of the cloud in a screaming spiral, but still fortunately a long way above the earth. I straightened up and flew home with another lesson learned the hard way.

Of formation flying: the most popular and exciting part of our training. At first I was very erratic, perilously close to the leader one minute and a quarter of a mile away the next. But gradually I improved. We had a flight commander who bravely insisted on us flying in a very tight formation, the wing-tip of the outside machine in line with the roundel on the leader's fuselage. It certainly gave us confidence. Then one day the CO of advanced training watched us. I think he nearly had a stroke, and from then on we confined our tight formations to less public parts of the sky.

Of my first night flying: it was a dark night, but cloudless. I pulled on my gloves and slipped my feet into my fur-lined boots. Then Sergeant White and I crunched our way across a slight carpet of snow towards the machine, a squat dark patch against the grey of the horizon. I climbed into the front cockpit, settled myself comfortably, and plugged in my ear-phones. "All set."

"Right, Hillary. Run her up."

The rigger disappeared. I pulled the stick back into my stomach and gradually opened the throttle. The engine burst from a stutter to a great even roar of sound. I throttled back, waved away the chocks and let the machine roll gently forward.

About a hundred yards from us lay the flare path, a line of dimly glowing light. I flashed out my letter on the Morse key, had it returned in green, and swung the machine into the wind. As we gathered speed and the flickering lights of the flare path tore past, I knew I was too tense, my hand clenched on the control stick. I felt White give a slight push on the rudder. The tail came up and with one slight bump we were off the ground.

Reassuringly came White's voice: "Climb up to a thousand feet and do a normal circuit. Watch your speed."

Automatically as we climbed I hauled up the undercarriage, and nudged the pitch lever into coarse. I straightened out at a thousand feet, and pushed rudder and stick together to do a gentle turn on the left. Then I looked around me. Below lay the flare path, a thin snake of light, while ahead the sky was studded with jewels.

I relaxed, lifted my head, and took a lighter hold of the stick. Behind me I could hear White humming softly. I tapped out my letter and a flash of green answered from the ground. I banked again and flying downwind, released the undercarriage: another turn and I changed into fine pitch. Turning into the flare path, I saw the lights rushing up to meet us and could feel myself tensing up again. We were up to the first flare and I started to ease the stick back.

"Not yet, you're too high." I felt the pressure on the stick as White held it forward. We were up to the second flare and still not down. I had a moment of panic. I was going to stall, we were going too fast, I was making a fool of myself. Then a slight bump, the wheels rumbling along the runway, and White's voice, "Hold her straight, man." We were down.

Twice more we went round before White poked his head into the front cockpit: "Think you can take her round yourself now?"

"Sure."

"Well, off you go then, and for God's sake don't make a mess of it. I want some sleep tonight."

For the first few minutes I flew automatically, but with a subdued feeling of excitement. Then I lifted my eyes from the instrument panel and looked for the horizon. I could not see it. Heavy clouds obscured the stars, and outside the dimly lit cockpit lay pitch darkness. I looked for the flare path and for a moment could not pick it up. I glanced back at the instruments. I was gaining speed rapidly. That meant I was diving. Jerkily I hauled back on the stick. My speed fell off alarmingly. For a moment I was paralysed. Enclosed in that small space and faced with a thousand bewildering instruments, I had a moment of complete claustrophobia. I must get out. I was going to crash. I did not know in which direction I was going. Was I even the right way up? I half stood up in my seat. Then I saw the flare path. I was not lost: I was in a perfectly normal position. I dropped back into my seat feeling ashamed.

The feeling of being shut in was gone, and I began to enjoy myself. I had to make a couple more circuits before I got the signal to land. Then the wheels were skimming the ground and I was down. Slowly, I taxied and climbed out. White met me as I walked into the hangar. "OK," he said, "you'll do."

We sat down and he handed me a cigarette. Outside someone was coming in to land. He was given a green on the Aldis lamp and throttled back. He was past the first flare, past the second, past the third and still not touching down when the engine roared into life and he was off again.

"Oh, God," said White, "he's in coarse pitch."

We could just hear the hum of the engine headed towards the sea. Ten minutes went by; twenty minutes. Nobody spoke. Then the officer in charge of night flying walked into the hangar. "All spread out and look. Move out to the sea."

We found him on the shore, the machine half in and half out of the sea. Sergeant White peered into the cockpit.

"In coarse pitch," he said, "as I thought." Then after a slight pause, "Poor devil."

I remembered again my moment of blind panic and knew what he must have felt. In his breast pocket was £10, drawn to go on leave the next day. He was twenty years old.

Of people: the other pilots on our course were a diverse lot, ranging from schoolboys of eighteen to men of twenty-six. They had taken on their short service commissions because they were bored with their jobs and sensed the imminence of war, or, amongst the youngest, simply for the joy of flying. After the day's work we would gather in the mess to pass the evening. There, as the months went by, one could watch the gradual assimilation of these men, so diverse in their lives, into something bigger than themselves, into the composite figure that is the air force pilot.

Much that is misleading has been written on the pilot. He has become the nation's hero, and the attempt to live up to this false conception bores him. For, as he would be the first to admit, on the ground he is a very ordinary fellow.

It is only in the air that the pilot can grasp that feeling, that flash of insight, that matures him beyond his years. On the ground he asks only to be allowed to relax, to get out of uniform, to drink a little, play a little. On leave he wants to get home to his wife or to have an occasional carouse in London. Yet he is really only happy when he is back with his squadron, back in his plane where, isolated, he plays his part in man's struggle against the elements.

458

The change in Peter Howes was perhaps the most interesting. From an almost morbid introspectiveness, his personality blossomed, like some plant long untouched by the sun, into an open acceptance of the ideas of the others.

I remember one night early on we were discussing air force slang and its origins. "You must understand," he said, "that in our service we have a number of uneducated louts from all over the world, none of whom can speak his own language properly. It thus becomes necessary to invent a small vocabulary of phrases, equipped with which they can carry on together an intelligible conversation." At that time he was a very bad pilot, and his English was meticulous. Three months later he was an excellent pilot but his vocabulary was pure RAF. I don't know if there is a connection, but I wonder.

From time to time a squadron of long-range bombers would come dropping out of the sky. For a week or so they would make our station their headquarters for raids on Norway, the heavy drone of their engines announcing their return as night began to fall. One day nine set out and four returned. I watched the pilots in the mess that night but their faces were expressionless: they played bridge as usual and discussed the next day's raid.

Then one day a Spitfire squadron dropped in. It was our first glimpse of the machine which Peter, Noel, and I hoped eventually to fly. The deceptive frailty of their lines fascinated us and we spent our spare time climbing onto their wings and inspecting the controls. We "long-haired boys" continued to refuse to consider the war in the light of a crusade for humanity. We concerned ourselves merely with what there was in it for us, and for that reason were most anxious to fly single-seater fighters.

The course drew to a close. We had done a good many hours flying, taken our wings examination and somehow managed to pass. We waited our final postings with impatience.

Their arrival was a bitter disappointment. At this early stage there had been few casualties in Fighter Command and there was little demand for replacements. Noel, Peter and I were all slated for Army Cooperation. This entailed six weeks' further training at Old Sarum before we should finally be operational—on Lysanders, machines which Peter gloomily termed "flying coffins".

And so we said goodbye to Scotland and headed south.

459

DURING THE DRIVE we talked ourselves into a belated enthusiasm for Army Cooperation, and as we came onto the road skirting the Old Sarum aerodrome we saw the field slanting downhill from the hangars with Lysanders picketed around the edge. We gazed at them with interest. Squat, high-winged monoplanes, they looked as though they could take quite a beating.

The countryside lay quiet in the warm glow of the summer evening. A few minutes' flying to the south was the sea, and then France. Within a few weeks Britain's army was to be struggling desperately to get back across that narrow stretch of water.

The course was run with great efficiency. We spent from nine o'clock in the morning to seven in the evening alternating between lectures and flying. To our delight, on the course we discovered two old friends, Peter Pease and Colin Pinckney. They had both been in the Cambridge Air Squadron before the war.

Peter was, I think, the best-looking man I have ever seen. He stood six-foot-three and his slightness was deceptive for he weighed close on thirteen stone. He had profound integrity of character and an outward reserve which masked a deep shyness. He was soft-spoken, with an innate habit of understatement. I never knew him to lose his temper.

Colin was the same height but of broader build. He openly admitted that he derived most of his pleasure in life from a good grouse-shoot and a well-proportioned salmon. He was somewhat more forthcoming than Peter but of fundamentally the same instincts. They had been together since the beginning of the war. I was to become the third corner of a triangle of friendship, the record of which will form an important part of this book.

The work at Old Sarum was interesting. We studied map reading, aerial photography, Morse, artillery shoots, and long-distance reconnaissance. The Lysander proved to be a ponderous, old gentleman's plane, heavy on the controls but easy to handle.

Of flying incidents there were few, though once I did my best to kill my observer. We were on our way back from a photography sortie when I decided to do some aerobatics. I started off by doing a couple of stall turns. Behind me I could hear him shouting in what I took to be enthusiastic approval. After the second stall turn I put the machine into a loop. When we were up and over I straightened it out and looked back. There was no sign of him. I shouted. Still he did not appear. I had a sudden feeling of apprehension. That shouting—could it mean. . . ? I peered anxiously down over the side.

At that moment a white face emerged slowly from the back cockpit, a hand grabbed my shoulder and a voice shouted in my ear: "For God's sake, I'm not strapped in!"

I headed back for the aerodrome and, after making a quick circuit, deposited him gingerly on the field. His cries had been not of joy but of fear, and when we had started down on our loop he had dived to the bottom of the cockpit, clutching feverishly at the fixed camera on the floor for support and convinced that his last hour had come.

Every night at nine o'clock the mess was crowded with officers parked round the radio, hearing of the overrunning of France and the desperate retreat of the British Expeditionary Force.

Then came Dunkirk: tired, ragged men, who once had been an army, returning now without even their equipment. For us the evacuation was still a newspaper story, until Noel, Peter Howes, and I got the day off, motored to Brighton, and saw the reality for ourselves.

The beaches, streets, and pubs were a crawling mass of soldiers, British, French and Belgian. They had no money, but were being royally welcomed by the locals. We collected two French soldiers and a Belgian dispatch rider, and took them off for a drink. The bar we chose was a seething mass of sweating, turbulent khaki. Before we could even get a drink we were involved in half a dozen bitter arguments over the lack of British aircraft over Dunkirk. Knowing personally several pilots who had been killed, and with some knowledge of the true facts—that had we not for once managed to gain air superiority behind them, over Flanders, the men would never have left Dunkirk alive—we found it hard to keep our tempers.

We sat on till well into the night, talking, arguing, singing, getting tight, they tired and relaxed, their troubles for the moment over, we taut and expectant, braced by our first real contact with the war, eager to get started. Finally, through an alcoholic haze, we made our farewells and staggered out into the street. Somehow we located the car and set off back for Old Sarum. We were late and Howes drove fast. Coming out of a bend he took the bank with his nearside front wheel, skidded, touched the brake, and hit the bank again. For a moment we hung on two of the wheels, and then we turned over, once, twice. There was a crash of splintering glass, a tearing noise as two of the doors were torn off, and then, but for the sound of escaping petrol, silence.

That week I had bought myself a new service cap and I could see it wedged under Noel's left knee. "Get off my cap, blast you!" I shouted, destroying the silence and bringing down on my head a storm of invective, from which I gathered that none of us was seriously hurt. "It looks," said Howes, "as though Fate doesn't want us to go out this way. Maybe we have a more exciting death in store for us." Looking back, unpleasantly prophetic words.

A day or so later all leave was cancelled, no one was allowed farther than half an hour's call from the aerodrome, and the invasion scare was on. An order came that all officers were to carry sidearms, and at the station armoury I was issued with an antiquated, short-nosed .45 and six soft lead bullets. With only six there was little temptation to waste any of them practising, but one day, by low cunning, I managed to get myself another twelve and loosed off. The first round fired but the second jammed. I had .455 bullets for a .45 revolver.

We had completed our six weeks and were ready for drafting to our squadrons, when a miracle happened. Owing to the sudden collapse of France, it had been decided we were to go not to Army Cooperation but to fighter squadrons.

Of all of us, I think Noel was the most elated. His face wore a permanent fixed grin which nothing could wipe off. "Spitfires at last," he kept repeating. We were to leave at once for training at an Operational Training Unit in Gloucestershire, close to the Welsh border.

To our delight our instructors were No. 1 Squadron—about the best-known squadron in the RAF for the part they had played at Maastricht Bridge. We regarded them with considerable awe. They were friendly and casual, but they expected cooperation and they got it. Time was short and we had much to learn.

We learned many things then new to fighter tactics. We learned for the first time the German habit of using their fighter escorts in stepped-up layers all around their bombers, of their willingness to fight with height and odds in their favour and their disinclination to mix it on less favourable terms; of the vulnerability of the Messerschmitt 109 when attacked from the rear and its almost standardized method of evasion when so attacked—a half roll, followed by a vertical dive right down to the ground.

We learned that we should never follow a plane down after hitting it, for it weakened the effectiveness of the squadron; and further was likely to result in an attack from the rear. If we were so outnumbered that we were forced to break formation, we should attempt to keep in pairs, and never fly on a straight course for more than two seconds. We should straighten up only when about to attack, closing in to 200 yards, and letting go with all eight guns in short snap bursts of from two to four seconds.

We learned the importance of getting to know our ground crews and to appreciate their part in a successful day's fighting. And we learned, finally, to fly the Spitfire.

I faced the prospect with some trepidation. Here for the first time was a single seater, a machine in which I must solo right off; and it was the fastest machine in the world.

I was put through half an hour's instrument flying under the hood of a Harvard, and then I was ready. At least I hoped I was ready. Kilmartin, a slight dark-haired Irishman in charge of our flight said: "Get your parachute and climb in. I'll just show you the cockpit before you go off."

He sauntered over to the machine, and I found myself memorizing every detail of his appearance with the clearness of a condemned man on his way to the scaffold—the chin sunk into the folds of a polo sweater, the leather pads on the elbows, and the string-darned hole in the seat of the pants.

The dull grey-brown of the Spitfire's camouflage could not conceal its clear cut beauty. As I climbed awkwardly into the low cockpit, I noticed how small was my field of vision. Kilmartin swung himself onto a wing and started to run through the instruments. I heard nothing. I was to fly a Spitfire, I was about to achieve my ambition, and I felt nothing. I was numb, neither exhilarated nor scared. I noticed the white enamel undercarriage handle. "Like a lavatory plug," I thought.

"What did you say?" Kilmartin was looking at me and I realized I had spoken aloud. "Have you got all that?" he asked.

I pulled myself together. "Yes, sir."

"Well, off you go then. About four circuits. Good luck!"

I ran quickly through my cockpit drill, swung the nose into the wind, and took off. I had been flying automatically for several minutes before it dawned on me that I was actually in the air, and halfway round the circuit. I turned into the wind and came in low, cut the engine just over the boundary hedge, and floated down on all three points. I took off again. Three more times I came round for a perfect landing. It was too easy. I watched with satisfaction several machines bounce badly as they came in. Then I taxied rapidly back to the hangars and climbed out nonchalantly. Noel, who had not yet gone solo, met me.

"How was it?" he said.

"Money for old rope," I said.

I didn't make another good landing for a week.

The flight immediately following our first solo was an hour's aerobatics. We also had to put in an oxygen climb to 28,000 feet, an air-firing exercise, formation attacks, and numerous dogfights.

The oxygen climb was uneventful but lengthy. Helmet, goggles, and oxygen mask gave me a feeling of restriction, and from then on I always flew with my goggles up, except when landing. The results of this were to be far-reaching.

When we were sent up for a dogfight, two of us would go off together for forty minutes and endeavour in every way possible to "shoot" each other down. On one occasion I went up with Kilmartin, my flight leader. We climbed to 10,000 feet, and he intimated that he would attempt to get on my tail. He succeeded. In frenzied eagerness I hurled my machine about the sky. Never, I felt, had such things been done to a plane. They must inevitably dislodge him. But a quick glance in my mirror showed me that he was quietly behind me like a patient nursemaid following too boisterous a charge.

I landed considerably mortified and prepared for some withering comments. Kilmartin climbed out of his machine with a sly grin. "Do you feel as dead as you should?" he asked.

I nodded.

"That's all right," he said. "I meant you to. Now I'll give you a few tips for the next time."

He told me then of the uselessness of most aerobatics in actual combat. Their only value was to give a pilot a feeling of mastery

WAR IN THE AIR

over his machine. To do a loop was to present a slow-moving sitting target to your opponent. A slow roll was little better. For complete evasion, the two most effective methods were a half roll and a controlled spin—especially if you had been hit, for it gave an impression of being out of control. For the rest it was a question of turning inside your opponent (sometimes pulling up and above him, the more effectively to dive down again), of thinking quickly and clearly, of seizing every opportunity and firing at once, and of a quick break away.

All this and more he impressed upon me, and I did my best to carry it out on my subsequent flights. But my clearest memory of the course was the bridge. It was across the Severn and linked England to Wales. It was a narrow bridge with close-set arches and it was the occasion of a long-brewing quarrel for Noel and me.

Noel, Peter Howes, and I were beginning to get on one another's nerves. With Howes it took the form of withdrawing into himself, saying little and avoiding our company. For Noel and me, fundamentally closer and considerably quicker-tempered, there had to be a showdown: the bridge provided it.

Noel, low-flying down the Severn, came to the bridge and flew under it. He came back and told me. From then on the bridge fascinated and frightened me. I had to fly under it. I said as much to Peter Pease. He gave me a long quizzical stare.

"From a flying point of view," he said, "to fly under that bridge proves nothing: it's extremely stupid. But from a personal point of view it can be of value, *if* you don't tell anybody about it."

He was right of course. To fly under the bridge simply to come back and say that I had done so would be sheer exhibitionism. Yet I knew I would fly under it. I had to for my own satisfaction.

There was a strongish wind blowing, and as I came down to a few feet above the river I had on quite an amount of drift. The span of the arch looked depressingly narrow; I had to force myself to hold the stick steady. For a moment I thought I was going to hit with the port wing, and then I was through.

It was later in the mess and we were playing billiards when Noel asked me if I had done it. By now we could not even play billiards without the game developing into a bitter struggle for supremacy. As Noel nearly always won, he could not have chosen a worse moment to speak.

"Well, did you?" he asked.

I played a deliberate shot and didn't answer. He laughed. "Surely our little winged wonder isn't getting soft?"

I put down my cue. "Listen, Noel," I said. "For months you've been smugly satisfied that you're a better pilot than I am. So just because I went solo before you, you had to go off and make a bloody fool of yourself under some bridge just to prove you're still a hell of a pilot. You make me sick."

He looked at me bitterly. "Well, Little Lord Fauntleroy, this *is* a new angle. All right. Stick around the hangars crawling to the instructors. Maybe they'll give you a good assessment yet." And with that he pounded red into a corner pocket to win the game. I stalked out of the room and slammed the door.

Next day squadron vacancies were announced. I walked down to the adjutant's office with Peter Pease and Colin Pinckney. 603 Squadron (City of Edinburgh) had three vacancies. It was out of the battle area (the first battle over Dover had already been fought), but it was a Spitfire squadron and we could all three go together. We put our names down.

Noel decided to go to Northolt to 609 Squadron to fly Hurricanes, and Peter Howes to Hornchurch to 54 Squadron.

The following day I was to drive up with Peter Pease, and we made an early start. I piled my luggage into his car and prepared to climb in after it. Then I hesitated and turned back. I found Noel in his room, packing. We were both embarrassed. I held out my hand. "Goodbye and good luck," I said.

"Goodbye Dick," he said. "We've drifted rather a long way apart lately. I'm sorry. Don't let's either of us drift up to Heaven."

While he was speaking Peter Howes had come in to say goodbye. "You two needn't worry," he said. "You both have the luck of the devil. If the long-haired boys are broken up, I have a hunch I'll be the first to go."

We told him not to be a fool and agreed to meet, all three of us, in three months' time in London. They came with me to the car.

"Take care of yourself," they said.

WE HAD TWO DAYS in which to get to Edinburgh and we spent one night in Yorkshire, where we broke our journey at the comfortable house of Peter's parents. I was a little depressed. To kick

470

our heels in Scotland with the war at last about to break in the south was not my idea of design for living. Peter, however, was unruffled and satisfied that we should be in the thick of it before very long.

In Edinburgh it was cold and the damp mist lay heavy on the streets. We drove straight out to the aerodrome and reported to our CO, Squadron Leader "Uncle George" Denholm. From him we learned that the squadron was operating farther north, "A" flight from Dyce and "B" flight from Montrose. There was one Spitfire replacement to be flown up to Dyce; Colin had arrived by then and got the job, so Peter and I drove up together to join "B" flight at Montrose instead.

The aerodrome lay just beyond the town and stretched parallel to the sea, one edge of the landing field merging into the dunes. For a few miles around the country was flat, but mountain peaks reared abruptly into the sky, forming a purple backdrop for the aerodrome. Montrose was primarily a Fighter Training School where future pilots crowded the air in Miles Masters. As the only possible enemy raids must come from Norway, half a squadron was considered sufficient for its protection.

At our dispersal point at the northwest corner of the aerodrome there were three wooden huts. One was the flight commander's office; another was reserved for the wireless equipment and technicians; the third was for the pilots and ground crew.

From its ceiling hung models of German aircraft, on the back wall by the stove were pasted seductive young ladies drawn by Petty, and on a table in the middle of the room a gramophone was playing, propped at a drunken angle on a pile of old books and magazines. In a corner there was another table on which were a couple of telephones operated by a corporal. Two beds against the walls, and several old chairs, completed the furniture.

As we came in, half a dozen heads were turned towards the door and Rushmer, the flight commander, came forward to greet us. Like the others, he wore a Mae West and no tunic. Known by everyone as Rusty on account of his dull-red hair, he had a shy manner, a friendly smile and an ability tacitly to ignore anything he did not wish to hear, which protected him alike from outside interference from his superiors and from too frequent suggestions from his junior officers on how to run the flight. Rusty had been

471

with the squadron since before the war: in action he always led the Red Section. Blue Section Leader Larry Cunningham had also been with the squadron for some time. He was a Scotsman, tall and thin, without Rusty's charm, but with plenty of experience.

Then there was Brian Carbury, a six-foot-four New Zealander, with crinkly hair and a roving eye. A shoe salesman before the war, he had come to England and taken a short service commission. He was to prove the squadron's greatest asset. Another from overseas was Hugh Stapleton, a thick-set South African, with a mass of blond hair which he never brushed, and a pair of patched trousers which the squadron swore he slept in. He was known as "Stap-me" because of his predilection for Captain Reilly-Ffoull in the *Daily Mirror*, his favourite literature.

Pilot Officer Berry, commonly known as Raspberry, came from Hull. Short and stocky, with a heavy black moustache above a mouth that was always grinning, even on the blackest days, he radiated an infectious good humour. "Bubble" Waterston was twenty-four, but looked eighteen, with his short-cropped hair and open face. His acceptance of everyone and his unconscious charm made him the most popular member of the squadron.

Then there was Boulter, with the face of an intelligent ferret; "Broody" Benson, nineteen years old, a fine pilot and possessed of only one idea, to shoot down Huns; Don MacDonald who had been in the Cambridge Squadron and had an elder brother in "A" flight at Dyce; and finally Pip Cardell, a recent addition to the squadron still bewildered, excited, and a little lost.

Out before the huts crouched our Spitfires, the boldly painted names on their noses standing out in the gathering dusk, names as divergent as Boomerang, Valkyrie, and Angel Face. Mine I called Sredni Vashtar, from the immortal short story by Saki.

Sredni Vashtar was a ferret, worshipped and kept in the toolshed by a little boy called Conradin: it finally made a meal of Conradin's most disagreeable guardian, Mrs. De Ropp. Conradin in his worship would chant this hymn:

Sredni Vashtar went forth,
His thoughts were red thoughts and his teeth were white,
His enemies called for peace, but he brought them death. . . .

I thought it appropriate.

472

For the first week or so, Peter and I were not to be operational. Indeed, all we had on duty at a time was one Readiness Section of three machines. The Germans were occasionally sending over single raiders from Norway, but there was little difficulty in shooting them down. Operations would ring through, the corporal at the telephone in the pilots' room would call out, "Red Section scramble base," one of us would fire a red Very light to clear the air of training aircraft, and within a couple of minutes three machines would be in the air climbing rapidly to intercept the enemy.

So good was the ground control that it was not infrequent to make an interception forty miles out to sea. The section would carry out a copybook attack; the bomber would come down in the sea, and her crew, if still alive, would push off in a rubber boat, waving frantically. The section would radio back the derelicts' position, turn for home, and that would be that.

On one occasion, when I was still not operational, I was flying up the coast when I heard Operations order our Blue Section into the air and start radioing the bomber's position—about four miles south of me. Without reporting my intention, I set off after it, delighted at the prospect of returning and nonchalantly announcing the German's destruction singlehanded.

It was a cloudy day, and I began a series of slow climbs and dives in and out of the clouds in search of my quarry. Finding nothing, I turned back and landed. It was not until Brian Carbury landed with his section and inquired sweetly whether I'd had fun that I learned how nearly I had been killed. Having received no notice of any other friendly aircraft, and seeing a machine popping in and out of the clouds, he had been just about to open fire when he recognized me as a Spitfire.

Next day Rusty made both Peter and me operational. "I think it will be safer for the others," he explained.

For the most part, life at Montrose was very agreeable, especially once Stap-me and Bubble had let me in on their secret. We three flew together and therefore had the same time off. As typical a pair of easy-going pilots as one could expect to meet anywhere, they might have been expected to spend their spare time with blondes in fast cars or with the chaps in the local. In point of fact they played hide-and-seek with children.

Tarfside was a tiny hamlet a few miles down the road from

Invermark, and to it this summer had come a dozen or so Scots children evacuees. They were under the care of Mrs. Davie, the admirable and unexacting mother of two of them. Their ages ranged from six to sixteen.

How Stap-me and Bubble had first come upon them I never discovered but from the moment I saw those children I too was under their spell. Kilted and tanned by the sun, completely natural and unselfconscious, they were essentially *right* against the background of heather, burns, and pine. In the general confusion of introductions, one little fellow, the smallest, was left out. He approached me slowly and gravely.

"I'm Rat Face," he said.

"How are you, Rat Face?" I asked.

"Quite well thank you. You can pick me up if you like."

I gave him a pick-a-back, and all day we played rounders, hide-and-seek, or picnicked, and as evening drew on we climbed up into the old hayloft and told stories, Stap-me, Bubble and I striving to outdo one another.

News of the children at Tarfside soon spread through the squadron, and no three machines would return from a practice flight without first sweeping in tight formation low along the valley where the children, often grouped on a patch of grass by the road, would wave and shout and dance in ecstasy.

Although our leaves did not coincide, I saw a fair amount of Peter Pease but I still found him exasperatingly elusive. I knew only that he was more than comfortably off; his father owned property which in due course, as the eldest son, he would inherit; he had been brought up in the orthodox Tory tradition, the belief that this was as it should be. I had an urge to get behind his reserve and, by drawing him into argument, discover how his mind worked. But whenever I thought I had him cornered, he would smilingly excuse himself and retire to his rooms to write letters. What I did not know was that he was in love.

I wanted particularly to make him talk about the war, to hear his arguments. I had an idea that the issue for him was an apprehension of something related to faith and not to any intellectual concept.

My chance came when we were sent down from Montrose to Edinburgh by train to fly up a couple of new Spitfires. We had the compartment to ourselves. I asked him straight out his reasons for fighting the war. He gave me a slow smile.

"Well, Richard, you've got me at last, haven't you?" He sat back in his corner and thought for a moment. Words didn't come easily to him.

"I don't know if I can answer you to your satisfaction," he said, "but I'll try. I would say that I was fighting the war to rid the world of fear—of the fear of fear is perhaps what I mean. If the Germans win this war, England will be run as a concentration camp, or at best a factory. The courage to love, to create, to take risks, whether physical or intellectual or moral, will die, and mankind will wither. Does that satisfy you?"

"That's all big words," I said. "It's all negative. Isn't there something positive you want?"

Peter flushed slightly. "Something positive? But of course. I want to see a better world come out of this war."

"What do you mean by *better?* Christian, I suppose."

"Yes, Christian, of course. I don't know any other way of life worth fighting for. Christianity means to me, on the social plane, freedom, man's humanity to man. I believe we should all make our contribution, even though it's a mere drop in the ocean, to the betterment of humanity. I know that sounds sentimental, and of course you don't agree."

I nodded. "You're quite right. I don't. I think your Christianity clouds the issue. To be perfectly brutal about it, I am fighting because after the war I shall be a writer, and I believe that, in war, especially in the air force, one can swiftly develop all one's faculties to a degree it would normally take half a lifetime to achieve. In a Spitfire we're back to war as it ought to be—if you can talk about war as it ought to be. Back to individual combat, to self-reliance, total responsibility for one's own fate. One either kills or is killed; and it's damned exciting."

"Richard, I don't understand you," Peter said. "You proclaim yourself a realist, and yet you are so fuzzy-minded as to assume you'll be allowed to write in a German-dominated world. You'll be able to think, perhaps, in a concentration camp, but not to impart what you think."

"Of course I won't. Don't take me for a bloody fool. We're agreed about the necessity for smashing the Germans. It's the purpose that we're arguing about. I want to smash them in order to be free to grow; you in order to be free to worship your God and lead your villagers in prayer. I am a selfish swine and am in the war only to get what I can out of it. But what about you? You're a landowner—a sort of dodo, a species nearly extinct. . . . Do you expect to make the world a better place for your dependents to live in solely through Christianity; and if so, how?"

Peter opened the carriage window and sat staring out at the passing countryside. He was struggling to find words; and what he said came out slowly and was nothing new. It came to this. He would be as decent to those in a less fortunate position as he possibly could, more especially to those dependent on him. He hoped that his role would consist in helping them, protecting them, keeping alive that ancient sturdy self-reliance of the true-born Englishman that had made England what she was.

The day was darkening, and in the half-light Peter's bony face had taken on a decidedly ascetic look. "I can see," he said, "that neither of us is going to convince the other. But I am sure you will change your tune. It won't be long either. Something bigger than you and me is coming out of this, and as it grows you'll grow with it. You are not entirely unfeeling, Richard. It needs only some psychological shock, some affront to your sensibility, to arouse your pity or your anger sufficiently to make you forget yourself."

"I doubt it," I said; and at that we left it.

We spent the night at Edinburgh, collected the two Spitfires and flew back to Montrose. Before I had switched off, Bubble was climbing up onto the wing. "Get your things packed and hand them over to Sergeant Ross. We're on our way."

It had come at last. The whole squadron was moving south. It could mean only one thing. With the German offensive already in full swing, we too should now be "in it".

Broody Benson was hopping up and down like a madman. "Now we'll show the bastards!" Stap-me was capering about shaking everyone by the hand, and Raspberry's moustache looked as though it would fall off with excitement. "Eh, now they'll cop it and no mistake," he chortled.

Rusty quickly allocated us to sections, and "B" flight roared across the aerodrome, and headed south.

For a moment I thought Rusty had forgotten Tarfside, but then I

476

heard his voice in the headphones, "Once more, boys," and in four sections of three we were banking to starboard and headed for the mountains.

They had heard the news, and as we went into line astern and dived one by one in salute over the valley, none of the children moved or shouted. With white boulders they had spelt out on the road the two words: "Good luck".

We rejoined formation and once again headed south. I looked back. The children stood close together on the grass, their hands raised in silent farewell.

Twenty-four of 603 Squadron flew south that day; of those twenty-four just eight were to fly back.

AT SEVEN O'CLOCK on that tenth day of August 1940, we landed at Hornchurch. Part of 603 Squadron was immediately in action. They came back with smoke stains along the leading edges of the wings showing that all the guns had been fired. They had acquitted themselves well, although caught at a disadvantage of height.

"You don't have to look for them," said Brian Carbury. "You have to look for a way out."

From this flight Don MacDonald did not return.

At this time the Germans were sending over comparatively few bombers. They were making a determined attempt to wipe out our entire fighter force, and from dawn till dusk the sky was filled with Messerschmitt 109s and 110s.

Half a dozen pilots always slept over at the dispersal hut to be ready for a surprise enemy attack at dawn. This entailed being up by four thirty and by five o'clock having the machines warmed up and the oxygen, sights, and ammunition tested. From then until eight o'clock at night, planes were almost continuously in the air. Pilots ate when they could, baked beans and bacon and eggs being sent over from the mess.

On the morning after our arrival I walked over with Peter Howes and Broody. Howes was with another squadron and worried because he had as yet shot nothing down. Every evening when we came into the mess he was to ask us how many we had got and then go miserably to his room. His squadron had had a number of losses and was due for relief. If ever a man needed it, it was Howes.

We left him at his dispersal hut and walked over to where our machines were being warmed up. The voice of the controller came unhurried over the loudspeaker, telling us to take off. We ran for our machines.

I climbed into the cockpit. Time seemed to stand still. I knew that that morning I might kill for the first time. That I myself might be killed or injured did not occur to me. Later, I did consider it in an abstract way when on the ground; but once in the air, never. I "knew" it could not happen to me. I suppose every pilot "knows" that—even when he is in fact taking off for the last time.

We ran into them at 18,000 feet, twenty yellow-nosed Messer-schmitt 109s, about 500 feet above us. Our squadron strength was eight, and as they came down on us we went into line astern and turned head on to them. Brian Carbury, who was leading the section, dropped the nose of his machine, and I could almost feel the leading Nazi pilot push forward on his stick to bring his guns to bear. At the same moment Brian hauled hard back on his own control stick and led us over them in a steep climbing turn to the left. In two vital seconds, they lost their advantage.

I saw Brian let go a burst of fire at the leading plane, saw the pilot put his machine into a half roll, and knew that he was mine. Automatically, I kicked the rudder to the left to get him at right angles, turned the gun-button to "Fire" and let go in a four-second burst with full deflection. He came right through my sights and I saw the tracer from all eight guns thud home. For a second he seemed to hang motionless; then a jet of red flame shot upwards and he spun out of sight.

For the next few minutes I was too busy looking after myself to think of anything, but when they turned and made off, and we were ordered to our base, my mind began to work again.

It had happened.

My first emotion was one of satisfaction, satisfaction at a job adequately done, at the final logical conclusion of months of specialized training. I had a feeling of the essential rightness of it all. He was dead, and I was alive, and it could so easily have been the other way round.

I realized in that moment just how lucky a fighter pilot is. He has none of the personalized emotion of the soldier, handed a rifle and bayonet and told to charge. The fighter pilot's emotions are those of the duelist—cool, precise, impersonal. He is privileged to kill well and with dignity.

From this flight Broody Benson did not return.

After the hard lesson of the first two days, we became more canny and determined not to let ourselves be caught from above. We would fly on the reciprocal of the course given us by the controller until we got to 15,000 feet, and then fly back again, climbing all the time. By this means we usually saw the Huns coming in below us, and were in a perfect position to attack. If caught at a disadvantage, they would never stay to fight, but always turned straight back for the Channel.

I remember that once I was stupid enough actually to fly alone as far as France. I had been trying to catch a returning Messerschmitt for about ten minutes and, inland from Calais, was just about to open fire when I saw a squadron of twelve Messerschmitts coming in on my right. I was extremely frightened, but turned in towards them and opened fire at the leader. I could see his tracer going past underneath me, and then I saw his hood fly off, and the next moment they were past. I didn't wait to see any more, but made off for home, pursued for half the distance by eleven very determined Germans. I landed a good hour after everyone else.

From this flight Larry Cunningham did not return.

During this period we were always so outnumbered that it was practically impossible, unless we were lucky enough to have the advantage of height, to deliver more than one squadron attack. After a few seconds we always broke up, and the sky was a smoke trail of individual dogfights. The result was that the machines would come home individually.

After an hour, "Uncle George" would make a check-up on who was missing. Often there would be a telephone call from some pilot who had made a forced landing at another aerodrome, or in a field. Or it would be a rescue squad announcing the number of a crashed machine; then "Uncle George" would cross another name off the list. At that time, the losing of pilots was somehow impersonal; nobody, I think, felt any great emotion—there wasn't time for it. "Uncle George" himself was shot down several times but always turned up unhurt; once we thought Rusty was gone for good, but he was back leading his flight the next day; one sergeant pilot in "A" flight was shot down four times, but he seemed to bear a charmed life.

My own most amusing though painful experience was when I was shot down myself acting as Arse-end Charlie to a squadron of Hurricanes. Arse-end Charlie is the man who weaves backwards and forwards above and behind the squadron to protect them from attack from the rear. There had been the usual dogfights over the south coast, and the squadron had broken up. Having only fired one snap burst, I climbed up in search of friendly Spitfires, but found instead a squadron of Hurricanes flying in sections of stepped-up threes, but with no rear-guard. So I joined on.

I learned within a few seconds the truth of the old warning, "Beware of the Hun in the Sun." I was making little sweeps from side to side, and peering earnestly into my mirror when, from out of the sun and dead astern, bullet holes started appearing along my port wing. There is an appalling tendency to sit and watch this happen without taking any action, as though mesmerized. I managed to pull myself together and go into a spin, at the same time attempting to call up the Hurricanes and warn them. But my radio had been shot away, and black smoke began pouring out of the engine, so I thought I had better get home. But as the windscreen was soon covered with oil I realized that I couldn't make it and decided instead to put down in the nearest field before I stalled and spun in.

I chose a cornfield and put the machine down on its belly. Fortunately nothing caught fire, and I had just climbed out and switched off the petrol, when to my amazement I saw an ambulance coming through the gate. This, I thought, was real service, until the corporal and two orderlies who climbed out started cantering away in the opposite direction, their necks craned up to the heavens. I looked up and saw about fifty yards away a parachute, and suspended on the end, his legs dangling vaguely, Colin. He was a little burned about his face and hands but quite cheerful.

We were at once surrounded by a bevy of army officers and discovered that we had landed practically in the back garden of a Brigade cocktail party. A salvage crew took charge of my machine, a doctor took charge of Colin, and the rest took charge of me, handing me double whiskies for the nerves at a laudable rate. I

480

was put up that night by the brigadier, who thought I was suffering from shock, largely because by dinner time I was so pie-eyed that I answered all his questions with a glassy stare.

The next day I went up to London by train, a somewhat incongruous figure, carrying a helmet and parachute. The prospect of a long and tedious journey by tube to Hornchurch did not appeal to me, so I called up the Air Ministry and demanded a car. A WAAF sergeant protested that she must have the authorization of a wing commander. I told her forcibly that at this moment I was considerably more important than any wing commander, painted a vivid picture of the complete disorganization of Fighter Command in the event of my not being back at Hornchurch within an hour, and clinched the argument by telling her that my parachute was a military secret which must on no account be seen in a train.

By the afternoon I was flying again.

One morning I woke late to the noise of machines running up on the aerodrome. It irritated me: I had a headache.

Having been on every flight the previous day, the morning was mine to do with as I pleased, and it must have been getting on for twelve o'clock when I came out onto the aerodrome to find the usual August heat haze forming. I started to walk across to the dispersal point on the far side. There were only two machines on the ground, so I concluded that the squadron was already up.

Then I heard a shout, and our ground crew drew up in a lorry beside me. Sergeant Ross leaned out: "Want a lift, sir?"

"No thanks, Sergeant. I'm going to cut across."

"OK, sir. See you round there."

The lorry trundled off down the road in a cloud of dust. I walked on across the landing ground. At that moment I heard the emotionless voice of the controller.

"Large enemy bombing formation approaching Hornchurch. All personnel not engaged in active duty take cover immediately."

I looked up. They were still not visible. At the dispersal point I saw Bubble and Pip Cardell make a dash for the shelter. Three Spitfires, just landed, turned about and came past me with a roar to take off downwind. Our lorry was still trundling along the road, maybe halfway round, and seemed suddenly an awfully long way from the dispersal point.

I looked up again, and this time I saw them—about a dozen, shining in the bright sun and coming straight on. At the rising scream of the first bomb I instinctively ducked. Out of the corner of my eye I saw the three Spitfires, now about twenty feet up, catapulted apart as though on elastic. The leader went over on his back and ploughed along the runway with a rending crash; No. 2 put a wing in and spun over on his airscrew, while the plane on the left was blasted wingless into the next field.

I remember thinking stupidly, "That's the shortest flight he's ever taken," and then my feet were nearly knocked from under me, my mouth was full of dirt, and Bubble, gesticulating like a madman from the shelter entrance, was yelling, "Run, you bloody fool, run!" I ran. I covered the distance to that shelter as if impelled by a rocket and shot through the entrance while once again the ground rose up and hit me, and my head smashed hard against one of the pillars. I subsided on a heap of rubble.

"Who's there?" I asked, peering through the gloom.

"Cardell and I and three of our ground crew," said Bubble, "and, by the Grace of God, you!" A sudden concentration of the scream and crump of falling bombs made it impossible to hear more. For about three minutes the bedlam continued, and suddenly ceased. In the utter silence which followed nobody moved. Then Bubble spoke. "Praise God I'm not a civilian! Of all the bloody frightening things I've ever done, sitting in this shelter was the worst."

It broke the tension and we scrambled out. The runways were certainly in a mess. Gaping holes and great gobbets of earth were everywhere. Right in front of us a bomb had landed by my Spitfire, covering it with grit and rubble.

I turned to the aircraftsman standing beside me. "Will you tell Sergeant Ross to have a crew give her an inspection?"

He jerked his head towards one corner of the aerodrome: "I think I'd better collect the crew myself, sir. Sergeant Ross won't be doing any more inspections."

I followed his glance and saw the lorry, its roof about twenty yards away, lying grotesquely on its side.

We walked over to find that the three Spitfire pilots were quite unharmed but for a few superficial scratches, in spite of being machine-gunned by the bombers. Operations was undamaged;

no hangar had been touched; the mess had two windows broken.

The station commander ordered every available man and woman onto the job of repairing the aerodrome surface, and by four o'clock there was not a hole to be seen. Thus, apart from four men killed in the lorry, there was nothing to show for ten minutes' really accurate bombing from 12,000 feet. It was a striking proof of the inefficiency of the Germans' attempts to wipe out our advance fighter aerodromes.

One evening there was another terrific attack on Hornchurch. This time there were twelve Dornier 215s flying in close formation. As they headed back for France I was on my way back to the aerodrome. I sighted them about 5,000 feet below me, and dived straight down in a quarter head-on attack. It seemed impossible to miss, and I pressed the button. Nothing happened: I had already fired all my ammunition. I could not turn back, so I went straight through the formation, to land on the aerodrome with the machine quite serviceable, but a little draughty.

From this flight Bubble Waterston did not return.

August thus drew to a close with no slackening in the enemy offensive. Yet I personally was content. This was what I had waited for for nearly a year, and I was not disappointed. We had little time to think of the future. At night one switched off one's mind like an electric light. Sufficient unto the day was the emotion thereof.

It was one week after Bubble went that I crashed into the sea.

The Patient

I was falling. Falling slowly through a dark pit. Terror, moving with me, touched my cheek with hers and I felt the flesh wince. Faster, faster. . . . I was hot now, on fire and screaming soundlessly. Dear God, no! No! Not that, not again. The sickly smell of death was in my nostrils and a confused roar of sound.

Someone was holding my arms. "Quiet now, there's a good boy. You're going to be all right." I tried to reach up my hand but could not. "They've put something on your face and hands to stop them hurting and you won't be able to see for a little while. But you mustn't talk: you're not strong enough yet."

Gradually I learned what had happened. I was in Margate Hospital. My face and hands had been sprayed with tannic acid, which had formed into a hard black cement. My eyes were coated with a thick layer of gentian violet. My arms were propped up in front of me, the fingers extended like witches' claws, and my body hung loosely on straps just clear of the bed.

In my four days in that hospital I can recollect no moments of acute agony; only a great sea of pain in which I floated almost with comfort. Two days without eating, and then periodic doses of liquid food taken through a tube. An appalling thirst, and hundreds of bottles of ginger beer. Being blind, and not really feeling strong enough to care.

My parents came down to see me. On the morning of the crash my mother had been on her way to her Red Cross work, when she felt a premonition. She turned back and arrived home to hear the telephone ringing. It was our squadron adjutant. Embarrassed, he started on a glamorized history of my exploits in the air. My mother cut him short to ask where I was. He managed after about five minutes of incoherent stuttering to get over his news.

They arrived in the afternoon. Outside my ward a twittery nurse explained that they must not expect to find me looking quite normal, and they were ushered in. The room was in darkness. Then the blinds were shot up, all the lights switched on, and there I was. As my mother remarked later, the performance lacked only the rolling of drums. For the sake of decorum my face had been covered with white gauze.

We spoke little, my only coherent remark being that I had no wish to go on living if I were to look like Alice. Alice, who had once been our maid, had as a child been burned and disfigured by a Primus stove. I was now unable to get her out of my mind. They sat quietly and listened to me rambling for an hour. Then it was time for my dressings and they left.

The smell of ether. Matron once doing my dressings with three orderlies holding my arms; and a nurse weeping quietly at the head of the bed. A visit from the lifeboat crew that had picked me up, and their inarticulate sympathy. Their discovery that an ancestor of mine had founded the lifeboats, and my pompous and unsolicited promise of a subscription. Sweat, pain, smells, cheering messages from the squadron, and an overriding apathy.

Finally, I was sent to the Masonic Hospital in London (for Margate was used only as a clearing station). Two nervous ATS women were to drive me. With my nurse in attendance, and wrapped in an old shawl, I was carried aboard the ambulance and we were off. For the first few miles I felt quite well, dictated letters to my nurse, drank bottle after bottle of ginger beer, and gossiped with the drivers. We were all very matey.

But after about half an hour my arms began to throb, I stopped dictating, drank no more ginger beer, and the drivers lost their way. Wasn't it awful and shouldn't they stop and ask? No, they certainly shouldn't: they could call out the names of the streets and I would tell them where to go. By the time we arrived at Ravenscourt Park, I was pretty much all-in.

I was put in a private ward and had the impression of a hundred excited ants buzzing around me. My nurse said goodbye and started to sob. I too found myself in tears; I suppose I was in a fairly exhausted state. So there we were, snivelling about the place and getting nowhere. Then the charge nurse came up and took my arm and asked me what my name was.

"Dick," I said.

"Ah," she said brightly. "Richard the Lion Heart."

I attempted a polite laugh but all that came out was a groan, and I fainted. The house surgeon took the opportunity to give me an anaesthetic and remove the tannic acid from my left hand.

At this time the theory was that in forming a hard cement tannic acid protected the burned skin from the air, and encouraged it to heal. As it started to crack, it was chipped off with a scalpel, but after a few months' experience it was discovered that nearly all pilots with third-degree burns so treated developed secondary infection and septicaemia, and its use was discontinued.

Both my hands were suppurating, and the fingers were already contracting under the tannic and curling down into the palms, but the risk of shock was considered too great for them to do both hands.

I must have been under the anaesthetic for about fifteen minutes and in that time I saw Peter Pease killed.

He was after another machine, a tall figure leaning slightly forward with a smile at the corner of his mouth. Suddenly from nowhere a Messerschmitt was on his tail about 150 yards away.

For seconds nothing happened. I had a terrible feeling of futility. Then I shouted, "Peter, look out behind!"

I saw the Messerschmitt open up. A burst of fire hit Peter's plane. For a moment it hung motionless, then it turned slowly on its back and dived to the ground. I came to, screaming his name, with two nurses and the doctor holding me down on the bed.

Two days later I had a letter from Colin. My nurse read it to me. It was very short, hoping that I was getting better and telling me that Peter was dead.

I was told later that for my first three weeks I did little but curse and blaspheme, but I remember nothing of it. Though two VADs fainted while helping with my dressings, the nurses were wonderfully patient and never complained. Then one day I found that I could see. My nurse was bending over me doing my dressings. I watched her for a long time, grateful that my first glimpse of the world should be of anything so beautiful. Finally I said: "Sue, you never told me your eyes were so blue."

For a moment she stared at me. Then, "Oh, Dick, how wonderful," she said, and dashed out to bring in all the nurses on the block. I felt absurdly elated and studied their faces eagerly, gradually connecting them with the voices I knew. "This is Anne," said Sue. "She is your special VAD and helps me with your dressings. She was the only one of us you'd allow near you for about a week. You said you liked her voice."

Anne's smile was as enchanting as her voice. I began to feel that hospital had its compensations. The nurses called me Dick and I knew them all by their Christian names. Quite how irregular this was I did not discover until later. At first my dressings had to be changed every two hours in the daytime. As this took over an hour to do, it meant that Sue and Anne had practically no time off. But they seemed not to care. It was largely due to them that both my hands were not amputated. I think I was a little in love with both of them.

All the nursing staff of the Masonic were very carefully chosen, and during the blitzing of the district, which took place every night, they were magnificent. The Germans were presumably attempting to hit Hammersmith Bridge, and we were treated night after night to the scream and crump of falling bombs. They always seemed to choose a moment when my eyes were being irrigated, my poor nurse poised above me with a glass undine in her hand. At night we were moved into the corridor, away from the outside wall, but such was the snoring of my fellow sufferers that I persuaded Bertha to allow me back in my own room after Matron had made her rounds.

Bertha was my night nurse. She was large and gaunt with an Eton crop and a heart of gold. She made it quite clear that she had no intention of letting me get round her as I did the day staff, and ended by spoiling me even more. One night the Germans were particularly persistent, and I heard a stick of bombs gradually approaching the hospital, the first some way off, the next closer, and the third shaking the building. Bertha threw herself across my bed; but the fourth bomb never fell.

She got up quickly, and arranged her cap. "Nice fool I'd look if you got hit in your own room when you're supposed to be out in the corridor," she said, and stumped out of the room.

One day my doctor said I could get up. I was able to totter about the passages and could be given a proper bath. I was still unable to use my hands and everything had to be done for me. One evening during a blitz, my nurse placed a prodigiously long cigarette-holder in my mouth and lighted the cigarette in the end of it. Then she went off to get some coffee. I was puffing away contentedly when the cigarette fell into my pyjama trousers and started smouldering. I shouted "Oi!" Nobody heard me. "Help!" I shouted somewhat louder. Still nothing happened, so I delivered my imitation of Tarzan's elephant call of which I was quite proud. It happened that in the ward opposite there was an old gentleman who had been operated on for a hernia. The combination of falling bombs and my animal cries made him dive over the side of the bed, to his considerable discomfort. Convinced of the ruin of his operation and the imminence of death, he added his cries to mine. From then on I was never left alone for a minute.

For the first few weeks, only my parents were allowed to visit me and they came every day. My mother would sit and read to me. Quite how much she suffered I could only guess, for she gave no sign. One remark of hers I shall never forget. She said: "You should be glad this has happened to you. Too many people told you how attractive you were and you believed them. Now you'll find out who your real friends are." I did.

When I was allowed to see people, I had an unexpected visitor. I knew at once who she was. She was in mourning and was the most beautiful person I had ever seen, with a grace of movement strikingly reminiscent of Peter Pease.

"I hope you'll excuse me coming to see you like this," she said; "I am Denise. I was going to be married to Peter. He often spoke of you, and wanted so much to see you. So I hope you won't mind me coming instead."

There were so many things for us to talk over, but the room seemed of a sudden full of hurrying jolly nurses. Her shyness was painful, the time came for her to leave, and I had said nothing I wanted to say. As soon as she was gone I dictated a note, begging her to come again. She did.

From then until I was able to get out, her visits did more to help my recovery than all the expert medical attention, for she was the very spirit of courage. She and Peter were two halves of the same person. She believed passionately in the cause for which he had given his life, in freedom, in freedom from fear and oppression, not only for herself but for the whole world.

"For the whole world." Did I believe that? I still wasn't sure. There was a time—only the other day—when it hadn't mattered to me if it was true or not that a man could want freedom for others than himself. She made me feel that this might be no mere catch-phrase of politicians, since it was something to which the two finest people I had ever known had willingly dedicated themselves. I was impressed. I saw there a spirit far purer than mine. But was such selflessness for me? I didn't know. I just didn't know.

I lay and watched summer turn to winter. Through my window I watched the leaves of my solitary tree turn brown, and then fall. I watched the sun change from a ball of fire to a watery glimmer, watched the rain beating on the glass and small clouds drifting above. Colin came down whenever he had leave from Hornchurch and brought me news of the squadron.

Ken MacDonald, Don's brother who had been with "A" flight, had been killed. He had been seen about to bale out of his blazing machine at 1,000 feet; but as he was over a thickly populated area he had climbed back in again and crashed in the Thames.

Pip Cardell had been killed. Returning from a chase over the Channel he appeared to be in trouble just before reaching the

English coast. He jumped; but his parachute failed to open and he came down in the sea. When the boat got to him he was dead.

Peter Howes had been killed. He had been transferred to our squadron, still worried because he had failed to bring anything down, and from his second flight with us he failed to return.

As a counter to this depressing news Colin told me that Brian Carbury and Raspberry had the DFC, and the squadron's confirmed score was nearing the hundred mark.

Thinking of these men that I had known, of the living and the dead, I wondered that it was the Carburys and the Berrys of this war, tough practical men who had come up the hard way, who were blasting the Luftwaffe out of the sky while their more intellectual comrades were in the main being killed. Yet they too were fighting for the things that Peter had died to preserve.

Was there perhaps a new race of Englishmen arising out of this war, a race of men bred by the war, a harmonious synthesis of the governing class and the great rest of England; that synthesis of disparate backgrounds to be seen at its best in the RAF? And would representatives of this new England unite, after the war, to settle problems which six thousand years had failed to solve?

The day came when I was allowed out of hospital for a few hours. Sue got me dressed, and with a pair of dark glasses, cotton-wool under my eyes, and my right arm in a sling, I looked fairly presentable. I walked out through the swing-doors and took a deep breath. London in the morning was still the best place in the world. The smell of wet streets, of sawdust in the butchers' shops, of tar, was exhilarating.

I walked slowly through Ravenscourt Park and looked into many faces. Life was good, but if I hoped to find some reflection of my feeling I was disappointed. One or two looked at me with pity, and for a moment I was angry; but when I gazed again at their faces, closed in as on some dread secret, their owners hurrying along, unaware of the life within them, I was sorry for them. I felt a desire to stop and shake them and say: "You fools, it's you who should be pitied and not I, for this day I am alive and you are dead."

After this I was allowed out every day, usually until nine o'clock, when I returned through the blitz and the blackout.

"London can take it" was already becoming a truism; but I had been put out of action before the real fury of the night attacks. I had seen nothing of the damage, and from newspapers and visitors had gained only a somewhat hazy idea of what was going on. I set out to see for myself.

London nightlife did exist. Restaurants and cocktail bars remained full every night of the week, but the diners-out were no longer the clientele of café society. Instead they were the soldiers, sailors, and airmen on forty-eight hours' leave; or members of the women's services, and civil servants and government workers seeking a few hours' relaxation after a hard day's work. And while half London was enjoying itself, the other half—anti-aircraft crews, the Auxiliary Fire Service, air-raid wardens—guarded their areas watchfully until with the break of day, London shook herself and went back to work.

Now and then I lunched at home with my mother, who was working all day in the Prisoners-of-War Organization, or my father would leave his desk long enough to give me lunch at his club. Most evenings I spent with Denise at her family's house in Eaton Place. From teatime until eight o'clock, when I had to go back to the Masonic, we would sit and talk—mostly of Peter, but also of the war, of life, and death, and many lesser things.

Two years before the war she had joined the ATS but she had left to marry Peter. Now she wished to see nobody but Colin and me, Peter's friends. It was as if she considered that as a person she was dead. There seemed nothing I could do to rouse her; I tried pity, I tried understanding, and finally I tried brutality.

It was one evening before dinner, and Denise was leaning against the mantelpiece. "When are you coming out of mourning?" I asked.

She looked at me. "I don't know," she said. "Maybe never."

"Oh, come, Denise," I said. "You know life better than that. I loved Peter, too, but there's no creeping away into a dream world. You ought to be grateful to the gods for having enriched you. Instead, you mope."

I dared not look at her as I went doggedly on. "To go back and back to places where you were happy with Peter, to touch his clothes, dress in black for him, say his name, is pure self-deception. Reality cannot be shut out for long."

I took a quick look at her. This was far worse than badgering

Peter in the train. Her face was tense, slightly flushed with what I hoped was anger, not pain.

"Death is love's crucifixion," I said brutally. "You go out with Colin and me because we were his friends. We are a link. But we will go away. What are you going to do then?"

She went over to a sofa opposite me and sat looking out of the window, her face still tense. When she spoke, her voice was so gentle that I had trouble hearing her.

"You're wrong, Richard," she said. "You like to think of yourself as a man who sees things too clearly, too realistically, to have any respect for the emotions. But I *know* that everything is not over for Peter and me. I know it with all the faith that you are so contemptuous of. We *shall* be together again." She looked straight at me with a kind of triumph in her face. "I suppose you're trying to hurt me to give me strength, Richard, but you're only hurting yourself. I have the strength. And let me explain where it comes from. I believe that in this life we live as in a room with the blinds down and the lights on. Once or twice, perhaps, it is granted us to switch off the lights and raise the blinds. Then for a moment we have a glimpse of what lies beyond this life."

Her voice was now strong. "Peter and I are eternally bound up together. And you, with your unawakened heart, are in some curious way bound up with us. Oh yes, you are! You lay in hospital and saw Peter die as clearly as if you had been with him. Ever since his death you have been different. You are conferring value on life by feeling Peter's death as deeply as you do."

Much of what she said struck home. It was true that Peter was much in my thoughts, that I felt him somewhere near me. It was true that the mystical experience of his death was something outside my understanding, and yet, and yet. . . . I could not help but feel that with the passage of time this sense of closeness must fade, that its very intensity was in part false, occasioned by being ill. Right or wrong, Denise's way and her ideals were not mine and I should be mistaken in attempting to make them so.

I HAD NOW been in hospital over two months and it was thought that I was sufficiently recovered for operation.

Shortly after my arrival at the Masonic the air force plastic surgeon, A. H. McIndoe, had come to see me. I was made ready a good hour before, bathed and shaved, my dressings elaborately correct. The charge nurse ushered him in fussily. Of medium height, he was thickset and square-jawed. Behind hornrimmed spectacles a pair of tired friendly eyes regarded me speculatively.

"Well," he said, "you certainly made a job of it, didn't you?"

He started to undo the dressings on my hands and I noticed his fingers—blunt and capable. By now all the tannic had been removed. He took a scalpel and tapped lightly on something white showing through the granulations of my right forefinger.

"Bone," he remarked. He looked at the contracted eyelids, and pursed his lips.

He had got up to go when I asked him how long it would be before I should fly again. "Next war for you," he said, "those hands are going to be something of a problem." I felt no emotion at all. I suppose I had known it for some time.

Two days later I was driven down to Sussex.

At the Masonic I had been the only action casualty, very ill and outrageously spoiled. Having little experience of hospitals, I had taken it all as a matter of course. As a result the East Grinstead hospital was something of a shock.

It was one of several hundred Emergency Medical Service hospitals. Taken over by the Ministry of Health at the beginning of the war, these were nearly all country-town hospitals and were not geared for a wartime emergency; they were too small. To overcome this difficulty the Ministry of Health had supplied them with "blisters"—huts to accommodate the anticipated flow of troops.

There were two main wards: one for women residents of the district; the other for local men, with eight beds for action casualties. Then there were the blisters.

It was to the main building that I went for my new eyelids. I came in late, with another pilot, Tony Tollemache. Tony had crashed in March. Coming in to land, his Blenheim had turned over and caught fire, throwing him free. His passenger was also thrown free; but under the impression that he was still inside, Tony had climbed in again and wandered up and down the flaming machine, looking for him. He had been badly burned on his face, hands, and, above all, legs. For this action he got the Empire Gallantry Medal and nearly a year in hospital. He had already had several operations, and was now due for a graft on his left hand.

WAR ON THE GROUND

Tony and I had a fair measure of whisky inside us, and started noisily to get undressed. Our beds were next to each other: opposite us was a Hurricane pilot, with a six-weeks' growth of beard and a surgical bandage over his eyes.

"Is he blind?" I whispered to Tony.

"Blind?" he roared. "Not half as blind as we are. No, me boy. That's what you're going to look like when McIndoe's through with you."

"Mr. Tollemache, are you daft, coming in late and making all that noise? And tell your fine friend to take his shoes off the bed."

This was my first introduction to the ward charge nurse. There she stood majestically, feet apart and hands on hips . . . only to spoil the effect by a shrill cackle of laughter when she caught sight of the red pyjamas I was unpacking.

"It's the wrong address you're at with those passion pants," she said. "This is a hospital, not a country house weekend."

Shortly afterwards Sister Hall came into the ward, and stopped at the foot of my bed. She was short, with grey hair, and the permanent struggle between her tight-lipped mouth and smiling eyes was at the moment being definitely won by the mouth.

"Good evening, Mr. Hillary," she said. "You and Mr. Tollemache are to be operated on tomorrow morning. I hope you will settle in here quickly; but I want it understood that in my ward I will tolerate no bad language and no rudeness to the nurses." She gave me a hard look and walked through the ward.

Tony waited until she was out of earshot. Then: "A tough nut," he said, "but she's the best nurse in the hospital."

Shortly before the lights were put out McIndoe made a round of the ward followed by half a dozen assistants. "By the looks of you both," he said, "we'll need to use a stomach pump before we can give you any anaesthetic." He passed on and we settled down to sleep.

In the morning we were wakened early and "prepped" by Taffy, the Welsh orderly. My eyelids were to be a "Thiersch" graft (a layer of skin thin as cigarette paper) taken from the inside of my left arm. Taffy shaved the arm and armpit, then sterilized the arm and bound it up in a loose bandage. He did the same to Tony's leg, from where the skin was to be taken for his hand.

The charge nurse trundled in a stretcher on wheels, parked it beside Tony's bed, pushed his feet into an enormous pair of bed socks, and stuck a hypodermic needle in his arm. This contained an injection to make one drowsy before being wheeled into the operating theatre. Tony then climbed onto the trolley, which was screened off, and after about half an hour he was wheeled away, to be back later, very white on the unburned patches of his face and breathing ether all over the room.

It was my turn for the trolley. The injection did not make me very drowsy. Feeling bored I asked for a cigarette from one of the others and puffed away contentedly behind the screen. But I had not counted on the eyes of Sister Hall. For a second she must have stared unbelievingly at the thin spiral of smoke; then she was inside the screen, the confiscated cigarette in her hand and herself looking down on me with disapproval. Pulling the screen to with a jerk, she walked on, her measured tread the very voice of outraged authority.

It was time for me to go. Tony's stertorous breathing followed me down the ward. I was welcomed by the anaesthetist, vast and genial, with an apparatus that resembled a petrol station on wheels. Then McIndoe came in wearing a skull-cap and multi-coloured gown, for all the world like some Bedouin chieftain. The anaesthetist took my arm and pushed the needle in gently. "Well, goodbye," he said, and I lost consciousness.

When I came round I was comfortable, but I could not see.

Five days without reading had distinct disadvantages. As I could not read, I talked, and groused and swore, especially at any arbitrary rule. In particular, I considered the hospital visiting hours nothing short of monstrous. Denise, who was now back in the ATS with an important job, could get off only at odd moments to come and see me. I asked Matron if she might come in the morning if she could get down from London, and the Matron very reasonably agreed. Denise arrived, but due to a misunderstanding she was told that visiting hours were from two till four, and she had therefore to kick her heels for several hours in the town.

By this time I was so enjoying my sense of persecution that, when, on the stroke of four, Sister Hall entered and said, "All visitors must leave now," I would gladly have committed murder, but Denise laid a warning hand on mine and I held my peace.

The next day McIndoe took down the dressing and I saw again.

"A couple of horse blinkers you've got there," he said; and indeed, for a day or so, to see in front of me I had to turn my face up to the ceiling. The new eyelids moulded in very rapidly, however, and soon I could raise and lower them at will. It was a remarkable piece of surgery, and an operation in which McIndoe had yet to score a failure.

Within a few days Tony and I were allowed out for a fortnight's convalescence before coming in again for further operations.

As I was getting ready to go, Sister took me on one side and slipped a small package into my hand.

"You'll be wanting to look your best for the girls, Mr. Hillary, and I've put in some brown make-up powder that should help."

I started to protest but she cut me short. "You'll be in again in a couple of weeks," she said. "Time for quarrelling then."

We returned after a short but pleasant convalescence—Tony for his last operation, one top lid, and I for two lower ones.

When the dressings were taken down I looked exactly like an orang-utang. McIndoe had pinched out two semicircular ledges of skin under my eyes to allow for contraction of the new lids. What was not absorbed was to be sliced off when I came in for my next operation, a new upper lip. The relief, however, was enormous, for I could close my eyes almost completely and did not sleep with them rolled up, the whites showing like a frightened animal.

Once again we returned home to convalesce, living from day to day, sometimes a little bored, a little depressed and restless, but analysing this restlessness no farther than as being the inevitable result of months in bed.

In January of 1941 I returned to the hospital for the removal of the ledges under my eyes and the grafting of my new upper lip. I was in no way cheered by the discovery that the only available bed was in Ward 3.

Ward 3, housing some of the worst cases, stood about fifty yards away from the hospital. It was a long, low hut, with twenty beds down each side, the beds separated from each other only by lockers. Towards the far end the lockers degenerated into soap-boxes. Windows were let into the walls at regular intervals on each side: they were never open. Down the middle there was a table with a wireless on it, a stove, and a piano.

Immediately on the left of the entrance passage was the saline bath, a complicated arrangement that McIndoe had been using with great success for the rapid healing of extensive burns. Next to this, in a curtained-off bed, was a girl of fifteen, Joan, terribly burned by boiling sugar her first day in a factory. Joan was in this ward because there was no other saline bath in the hospital (there were only three in England), and she could not be moved any distance. She screamed fairly regularly, and always before being lifted into the bath; her voice was thin, like that of a child of seven. As the time for her bath approached there was a certain tension throughout the hut; everyone would start talking rather loudly, and the wireless was turned up.

For the rest, there was a blind man learning Braille with the assistance of his wife, several RAF pilots, a Czech, and sundry troops, unlikely to forget Dunkirk as quickly as most.

The morning after I arrived, Sister gave me an injection at nine o'clock, and an hour later, wearing my red pyjamas for luck, I was wheeled across the fifty yards of open space to the hospital theatre feeling rather like a businessman arriving at his office. The anaesthetist gave me an injection and I lost consciousness.

On coming round, I realized that I was bandaged from forehead to lip and unable to breathe through my nose. After that the day was a blur; a thin wailing scream, the radio playing "Each Day is One Day Nearer", injections, a little singing, much laughter. After this, oblivion, thank God.

The next morning I awoke in a cold sweat after a nightmare in which my eyelids were sewn together and I was leading the squadron in an Avro trainer. In the evening one of the doctors took the bandages off my eyes. I was left with a thick dressing across my upper lip which pressed against my nose, and two sets of semi-circular stitches under my eyes. Later McIndoe made a round and peered anxiously at the scar under my right eye, which was blue and swollen. He moved on. There was comparatively little noise, but the ward smelt and I was depressed.

The next few days remain in my memory as an unpleasant dream. Some of us were to be isolated, owing to suspicion of a bug. We climbed onto trolleys and were pushed across the yard to one of the main wards, from which a bunch of protesting women had been evacuated. As we were pushed up the steps to our new quarters we were greeted by four nurses wearing masks, white aprons, and rubber gloves.

Opposite me was Squadron Leader Gleave with a flap graft on his nose and an exposed nerve on his forehead: in Ward 3 he had been unable to sleep, nor could the night nurse drug him enough to stop the pain. Next to him was Eric Lock, a tough little Shropshireman who had collected twenty-three planes, a DSO, a DFC, a bar, and cannonshell wounds in the arms and legs. Beyond him was Joseph, the Czech sergeant pilot, also with a nose graft; and Yorkey Law, a bombardier, blown up twice and burned at Dunkirk, with a complete new face taken in bacon strips from his legs, and no hands.

We were allowed no visitors and could write no letters.

On the second day a small colony of streptococci settled on the squadron leader's nose. The rest of us waited grimly.

On the third day our heads were shorn and our scalps anointed with M&B powder. We submitted to this with varying amounts of protestation: the squadron leader was too ill to complain, but Eric Lock was vociferous and the rest of us sullen.

After the huts our new ward was luxurious, and the nurses were efficient and not unfriendly, though the enforced wearing of masks made them a little impersonal. Our language was always rough and sometimes offensive, but they seldom complained. Tony Tollemache came once to say goodbye through the window: he was returning to Hornchurch. Otherwise we saw nobody.

On February 14, I developed earache. Never having had earache before, I found the experience disagreeable to a degree: it was as though someone with a sharp needle was driving it at regular intervals into the side of my head. That night I was put onto Prontosil and knew beyond any doubt that I had the streptococcus.

I slept fitfully, aided in my wakefulness by the pain in my ear, Eric's snores, and the groans of the squadron leader.

In the morning the pain in my ear was considerable and I felt sick from the Prontosil. But it was now eight days since my operation, and the dressing on my lip was due to be taken down. At lunchtime one of the doctors took off the bandages, to the accompaniment of appreciative purrs from his satellites. I asked for a mirror and gazed at the result. It was a blow to my vanity: the new lip was dead white, and thinner than its predecessor.

In fact it was a surgical masterpiece, but I was not in the mood to appreciate it. I fear I was not very gracious. The lip was duly painted with mercurochrome, and the doctors departed. The relief at having the bandages removed was enormous, but I dared not blow my nose for fear that I should blow the graft away.

That night I slept not at all: the pain in my ear was a continuous throbbing and I felt violently sick from the Prontosil. At about two o'clock I got up and started pacing the ward. A night nurse ordered me back to bed. I invited her to go to hell with considerable vigour, but felt no better. She called me a wicked ungrateful boy and I fear that I called her a cow. Finally I returned to bed and attempted to read until morning.

On February 17, an ear, nose and throat specialist visited me. His manner was reassuring. He felt behind the ear and inquired if it pained me. I replied that it did. That being so he regretted the necessity, but he must operate within half an hour for what appeared to be a most unpleasant mastoid. I asked if I might be moved to Sister Hall's ward, and the doctors very decently agreed.

I went back, changed into my red pyjamas and was wheeled along to the emergency theatre. With a feeling of relief I felt the hypodermic needle pushed into my arm, and within five seconds I was unconscious.

For the next week I was very ill, though quite how seriously I could only judge by the alacrity with which all my requests were granted. Sister Hall nursed me all day and most of the night. I had regular morphia injections and for long periods at a time I was delirious. The bug had got into my lip and was biting deep into the skin at three places. I was in worse pain than at any time since my crash. After the plastic operations I had felt no discomfort, but now with the continuous throbbing in my head I thought I must soon go mad. I would listen with dread for the footsteps of doctors, knowing that the time was come for the piercing of the hole behind my ear to keep it open for draining, a sensation that made me contract within myself at the mere touch of the probe.

It was during my second night in Sister Hall's ward that a 2,500 lb. bomb landed a hundred yards away but did not explode. I heard it coming down with a curious whirring rustle, and I prayed that it would explode and take me with it. For a moment I thought it had, so great was the force of impact, but as I realized slowly that it had not, I found that tears were pouring down my face: I was sobbing with mingled pain, rage, and frustration. Sister immediately gave me another morphia injection.

It was decided that while the excavation squad was digging the bomb out, everybody possible must be evacuated to the far side of the hospital. I imagined I would go along with the others, but McIndoe decided it would be too dangerous a move.

Sister looked at me: "I'm afraid that means Ward 3," she said. At that something exploded inside me. McIndoe's chief assistant came into the ward to arrange for me to be moved and I let fly.

I had not spoken since my operation and I saw the surprise in his face as I hauled myself up in bed and opened my mouth. Wild horses, I said, would not drag me to that garbage-can of human refuse. I had come into hospital with two scars on my upper lip: now I had a lip that was pox-ridden and an ear with enough infection in it to kill a regiment. There was only one thing to be said for the British medical profession: it started where the Luftwaffe left off. An outburst to which I now confess with shame, but which at the time relieved my feelings considerably.

"You're not making this very easy," he answered mildly.

"You're damn right, I'm not," I said, and then felt very sick and lay down.

Sister Hall was magnificent. "I think perhaps he should stay here in his present state, sir," she said. "I'll fix something."

The doctor looked grateful, and left. I saw that she was smiling. "Well, Mr. Hillary," she said, "quite like old times."

Somehow she obtained permission to convert one of the consulting rooms farther down the hospital into a ward for me. That night McIndoe came in, still wearing his operating robes, and sat down on the end of the bed. He talked to me of the inevitable difficulties of running the unit. He knew, he said, that I had had a tough break, but I must not let it get me down. He looked dead tired, for he had been operating all day. I felt a little ashamed.

The next day my mother and Denise motored down to see me. I was grey in the face from the Prontosil, and they both thought I was on the way out, though of this they gave no sign. Poor mother. The crash, the hospital, the operations—she had weathered them all magnificently. But this last shock was almost too much.

During the last five months I had gradually built up to my

usual weight of twelve stone. In the next week I sweated my weight down to nine stone. Yet I also began to feel more human. As the bomb had been removed and the evacuated ones brought back, I returned to the main ward and the regular hospital routine.

It was shortly after this that Edmonds was placed in the bed next to mine. Edmonds was the worst burned pilot in the air force to live. Taking off for his first solo at night, he had swung a little at the end of his run. The machine had turned over and burst into flames. He had been trapped inside and fried for several minutes before they dragged him out. When he had first been brought in McIndoe had performed two emergency operations and then left it to time and careful dressings to heal him enough for more.

Never once had Edmonds complained. It would take years to build him a new face. He was cheerful, and such was his charm that after two minutes one never noticed his disfigurement.

He was now first on the list for operation. Both his top lids and his lower lip were done together and he was brought back to the ward, even-tempered as ever. Three days went by and I noticed an ominous dribble down his right cheek from under the dressing across his eyes. It was the streptococcus at work again, and it was bitterly ironical that McIndoe's first eyelid failure should be on Edmonds. He was immediately put on to Prontosil and by the next morning was a greeny blue. After lunch some idiotic woman came in and exclaimed how marvellously well he looked. Instead of turning his face to the wall or damning her soul, he managed to smile and said: "Yes, and I'm feeling much better too."

I remembered my own recent outbursts and felt rather small.

The following day my ear surgeon told me that I might go back home in a week to convalesce. McIndoe told me that he would not operate on me again for three months, and my mother came down from town and told me that Noel Agazarian had been killed.

At first I did not believe it. Not Noel. It couldn't happen to him. That left only me—the last of the long-haired boys. I was horrified to find that I felt no emotion at all.

I WAS convalescing when the letter came.

At the time I was very comfortable, but I had a flat, let-down feeling. It was natural enough after the mastoid; but I knew it went deeper than that.

504

The letter was from David Rutter: he had read about Noel in the paper and asked if I could come to see him. David Rutter, the pacifist, a man with, in a different way, as great an integrity as Peter's, whom I had not seen for more than a year. He was working now on the land. Eager to see him I caught a train to Norfolk.

David met me at the station, wearing an old tweed jacket and corduroy trousers: he looked very fit. He seemed glad to see me, and as we climbed into his small car he told me shyly that he was married. We soon drew up outside a square brick bungalow.

His wife greeted me politely but defensively. She was a large good-looking girl, blonde hair hanging over her shoulders. She began at once to talk—about birds—in an aggressive monologue.

David cut in. "It's all right Mary," he said in a tired voice. "Richard's not belligerent." He turned to me apologetically: "I'm afraid I don't see many of my old friends any more and when I do there's usually a scene, so Mary's a bit on the defensive."

We talked for a while of safe subjects—his work, the district, and his evening visits to the local pub. David was restless, pacing up and down the room, rubbing a nervous hand over his hair. His wife followed his every movement. I realized that she was an unhappy woman. It was not that she had no faith in David; it was that he no longer had any faith in himself. I asked him what the CO boards had been like.

"Oh, moronic but well-meaning," he said. Then he sat down and stared moodily into the fire. "Yes, they were certainly moronic; but they were right. That's the hell of it."

For a moment he sat in silence, then he began to talk. From time to time he would glance at my face, and as he talked I realized that while I might carry my scars a few years, the scars of his action would be with him always. David was a broken man.

In the last year he had watched his theories shattered, one by one. As country after country had fallen to Hitler his carefully reasoned arguments had been split wide open: it *was* as much the war of the unemployed labourer as of the Duke of Westminster. Never in the course of history had there been a struggle in which the issues were so clearly classless. It had become a crusade.

"I've finally decided that I have now no right to refuse to fight. It is no longer a question for personal conscience but for the conscience of civilization." He gave me a wry smile. "It has taken me more than a year to see this. Do you think I should join up?"

The question caught me unawares. Sitting there smugly with the "honourable scars" of a battle that still was not mine, I felt all of a sudden very small. "I don't know, David," I said. "That's a question only you can decide."

When I rose to leave it was already dark. David drove me to my train. As we got out of the car the searchlights were making a crisscross pattern of light in the sky: all around us was the roar of anti-aircraft fire.

David held out his hand. "Goodbye, Richard," he said. "You always were the lucky bastard."

There was a heavy raid on and the train crawled interminably. I thought of Noel, of the two Peters, of the others in the squadron, all dead; and how the David that I had known was dead too. They had all, in their different ways, given so much: it was ironical that I who had given least should alone have survived.

Liverpool Street Station was a dull, grey blur. I managed to get a taxi and make a start across London.

"I'm afraid we'll be stopped soon, sir," said the taxi driver. At that moment there was a heavy crump unpleasantly close and glass flew across the street.

"See if you can find a pub and we'll stop there," I shouted.

A few yards farther on he drew in to the kerb and we got out and ran to a door under the sign of "The George and Dragon". Inside there was a welcoming aura of bright lights and beery breaths, and we soon had our faces deep in mugs of mild and bitter. Outside the German night offensive intensified.

In one corner sat a private in battledress and a girl drinking scotch. She was talking very loudly and laughing immoderately. The barmaid gave me a conspiratorial wink. But she was wrong: the girl was not drunk, she was very, very frightened, and with good reason. I had never before heard anything like this. The volume of noise shut out all thought; it was an orchestra of madmen playing in a cupboard. I thought, "God! what a stupid waste if I were to die now." I took a long pull at my beer.

I was pushing the glass across the counter for a refill when we heard the bomb coming. The girl in the corner was still laughing and for the first time I heard her soldier speak. "Shut up!" he said. Then everyone was diving for the floor.